RED ARROWS
THE INSIDE STORY

First edition, published in 2001 by

WOODFIELD PUBLISHING
Woodfield House, Babsham Lane, Bognor Regis
West Sussex PO21 5EL, England.

ISBN 1-903953-13-8

Red Arrows

THE INSIDE STORY

*A personal account of a decade with the
world's most famous aerobatic display team*

Tony Cunnane

Woodfield Publishing
~ WEST SUSSEX · ENGLAND ~

The Author – Bridgnorth, 1953.

Contents

About the author

TONY CUNNANE, A RETIRED SQUADRON LEADER RAF pilot, became the first full-time Public Relations Officer for the Red Arrows in 1989. Since then he has written hundreds of articles for aviation magazines and other forms of media about the Red Arrows. He started the official Red Arrows' Internet site in 1996 (hosted by Deltaweb Publishing) and by the time he retired in March 2001 he had contributed over 150,000 words to its many news pages. The number of 'surfers' increased dramatically as the site become known around the world and it now forms part of the official

Tony Cunnane – The Voice of the Red Arrows 1989-2000

Ministry of Defence RAF web site. In 1997 he wrote a book, *Reds Arrows – A Year in the Life of*, published by André Deutsch. The Lincolnshire media described him as 'the voice of the Red Arrows' when he retired.

In the last 11 years, Tony has travelled with the Red Arrows to South and East Africa and the Middle and Far East, as well as on the historic visit to the Soviet Union and Hungary in 1990. He has collected a huge database of facts, figures and anecdotes about the Team. He has hosted many thousands of visitors and answered countless letters, faxes, telephone calls and emails. When he was about to retire in September 2000 at age 65, Tony was asked to stay on for another 6 months to cover the Team's deployment back to their former base at RAF Scampton.

This book, illustrated with previously unpublished pictures taken by the author himself, tells the real inside story of the world's premier aerobatic display team.

The Voice of the Red Arrows... The Lowest Form of Life?

Let me set my stall out straight away. The Red Arrows are the world's premier aerobatic display team.

I have never heard a member of the Team make that claim. As a matter of fact I have never used that expression myself – until now, that is. Had I done so people would have declared, 'Well he would say that wouldn't he – he's their PRO.' It is, however, the sort of statement that regularly appears in magazine articles, newspaper features, and air show brochures, and is heard in radio and television interviews whenever and wherever the subject of air shows crops up. It must really get up the noses of the only two other European teams that might have a claim to be awarded that appellation, to say nothing of the two excellent US military teams that are less frequently seen in Europe and who are constrained by much more restrictive flying regulations which make their highly professional displays seem rather boring by comparison.

Members of the public usually assume that there must be intense rivalry between the major aerobatic teams, especially those in Europe. Not so, in my experience. The pilots and ground crew are on excellent terms with their counterparts; they regularly meet each other at international air shows and socialise afterwards whenever possible. Like all pilots they spend a lot of time discussing flying techniques. Certainly they pinch each other's ideas for new manoeuvres but they have never made any secret of that fact and in any case someone called Charles Colton once said that imitation is the sincerest form of flattery – and he was British.

In October 1989, at the very end of the European flying display season, five internationally renowned air force aerobatic teams, the French, Italian, Portuguese, Spanish and Swiss, travelled to RAF Scampton in Lincolnshire to celebrate the end of the Red Arrow's 25th season. Thus, for the first time we think, six jet aerobatic teams appeared on the same programme. At the time of that show I had been the Red Arrows' public relations officer for barely five weeks so I cannot claim to have had much to do with the organisation of it, but I did host the media. I stood by as a young and pretty lady television reporter interviewed the Leader of the *Frecce Tricolori*, the Italian team.

'Tell me Captain,' she asked cunningly, 'which is the best team, the Red Arrows, the *Patrouille de France*, or the *Frecce Tricolori?*'

Without a moment's thought the wise captain replied, 'The *Patrouille* are the best with eight aircraft, the Red Arrows are the best with nine,' a wicked pause then, with a proud glint in his eyes, 'but we are the best with ten aircraft.'

I thought then what a diplomatic answer that was and I have quoted the story many times since when I have been asked a similar question. Nevertheless, professional aviation experts and ordinary members of the public in many countries do believe that the Red Arrows are the best of all and they think that for a number of reasons.

The Red Arrows aim to have something going on directly in front of the crowd from the moment the Team Commentator announces their arrival over the public address system until the final manoeuvre is completed. That might seem an obvious thing to do but not all the other teams achieve it. Certain manoeuvres flown by some teams take up so much sky that individual aircraft occasionally disappear from sight beyond the horizon – and not only in murky visibility. Some teams have lengthy gaps within their programme to give the various aircraft time to re-group or re-position after a diverging manoeuvre, while with other teams you are never quite sure whether their show has ended or not.

The Red Arrows pride themselves on their tight show – and I mean tight in the sense that the aircraft are always as close as practicable to the spectators. Successive leaders have always maintained that there is no point in going outside the sight of the main block of spectators. That is easy to achieve in conditions of excellent visibility and cloudless skies but it is quite a different matter to achieve it when there is cloud below the maximum height of a loop, about 6,000 feet, or when the horizontal visibility is restricted by haze, drizzle, or pouring rain.

A special feature of any Red Arrows' display is that there are three variants of it: the full, rolling and flat options. The rolling show is flown when the base of the clouds is so low that the aircraft would disappear into them at the top of a loop; the flat show is flown when the cloud base is less than 4,500 feet so that aircraft would disappear at the apex of a barrel roll or when visibility is so poor that the aircraft need to stay even closer to the centre of the display line than they would normally do. The Red Arrows' Team Leader choreographs these three variants in such a way that he can instantly change between them, in any order, in mid-display to take account of rapidly changing weather conditions. The changes are generally transparent to all but the most knowledgeable fans of the Red Arrows. None of the other teams is able to do this.

I would venture to suggest that everyone in the United Kingdom has heard of the Red Arrows. The Falcons, the RAF's parachute display team, are sometimes mistakenly referred to as the Red Devils, who are actually the British Army parachute display team. The Falcons, understandably, get very upset about such mistakes – and I suppose the Red Devils are not best pleased either. I can recall just one occasion in all my time working for the Red Arrows when they were referred to as the Red Devils. The culprit was a reporter on a national red top newspaper, presumably young and inexperienced, who was either the subject of a set-up in her news room or who had not done her research properly.

'Will you tell me please where the Red Devils will be performing this weekend?' she asked.

'I'm sorry but I don't have that information,' I replied evenly with metaphorically raised eyebrows and ready to make a small joke at her expense.

'I would have expected the PRO to know where his team was performing,' she interrupted in high dudgeon before I could explain.

'I do!' I said and, after a short pause, I explained the difference between arrows and devils. 'So, do you want to know where the Red Arrows will be this weekend or where the Red Devils will be?'

'I don't know,' she replied miserably. 'I'll have to check back with the office.'

I told her where the Red Arrows would be that weekend, at home because they were on Easter leave, and gave her the contact number for the Red Devils.

The Red Arrows turn up unexpectedly all the time and sometimes in unlikely places, even in the close season. Two high speed locomotives have been named after them, one on what used to be called British Rail's East Coast Main Line and the other on Virgin's inter-city Cross Country line. For most of 2001 there was a large photograph of a Red Arrows' Hawk in the bar of the Woolpack Inn in Yorkshire Television's long-running soap opera 'Emmerdale' and one of the 2001 Team and his wife made a brief appearance as an extra in one episode. At least one lady I know of commissioned her own coffin in the shape and colour of a Red Arrows' Hawk – her final resting place as she calls it. The casket is complete with retractable wings so that it will fit conveniently into a standard hole in the graveyard when required. Several national and local newspapers got hold of this story and one Sunday paper used the headline 'The Dead Arrows!'. Not the sort of publicity I would have wished but at least it was publicity.

There is hardly a country in the world that has not heard of the British Red Arrows – that is how the Team is usually known overseas. It niggles some senior officers that the Team is better known as the British Red Arrows rather than the Royal Air Force Red Arrows. One year the Team Manager was instructed by a very senior officer to use the words Royal Air Force prominently on the front cover of the annual glossy brochure to ensure that there was no doubt in anyone's mind to which organisation we belonged. The Team had given displays in 52 countries by the end of the 2001 Season. Whenever the Red Arrows transit through a foreign country en route to displays elsewhere, there are almost always official requests for the Team to give a display at the transit airfield, or an airfield nearby, and those requests usually come from the highest level, and I do mean highest level, through the British Embassies and High Commissions. We try to oblige whenever possible. Such impromptu displays are not usually part of a full-blown air show but thousands of people will turn out just to see the famous Red Arrows.

I regularly received emails, letters, faxes and telephone calls from enthusiasts in all parts of the world asking when we would be appearing in one of their air shows or how they should go about arranging a one-off display by the Red Arrows. I once had an email from a group of Australian ex-pats working on a commercial project in a jungle clearing in Balikpapan in the wilds of Borneo asking when we would be visiting them because they had heard that the Red Arrows are the greatest. They promised us a plentiful supply of ice-cold 'tinnies' after the show but, sadly, no suitable opportunity presented itself during my time. Many requests crossed my desk from individuals in the UK asking for the Red Arrows to give private displays but those requests were far, far outnumbered by the number of people requesting flights with the Red Arrows. More of that later but the quick answer is that you cannot fly with the Red Arrows.

There are, of course, some people who do not like the Team and part of my job was to deal with complaints. I always, I hope, dealt with complaints sympathetically but some complainers do not want sympathy. 'After all,' I used to say, 'the Red Arrows are in the business of giving pleasure to millions so even a single complaint is one too many.' One woman who called to complain really annoyed me and almost caused me to lose my temper. The Red Arrows had noisily and unexpectedly flown close to her home in the west country. Knowing where the Red Arrows were based, she chose to use Directory Enquiries to get the telephone number for RAF Cranwell so that she could lodge her complaint direct. Unfortunately there is no telephone operator at Cranwell these days so the number she was given was that of a remotely-based call centre operator who was unable to connect her with anyone despite trying several extension numbers. We have all done battle with digital telephone exchanges and call centres so on that score I could certainly sympathise with the lady. In frustration she had then dialled a number at the Ministry of Defence in London and she gave the unfortunate official who answered that telephone a hard time. He explained that he had no personal knowledge of Red Arrows' activities and helpfully gave the lady my direct line number. Shortly afterwards I spoke to her – or rather she spoke to me. She ranted on, using abusive and very unladylike language, for 22 minutes about not being able to contact 'anyone important'; I know how long the call lasted because I always logged calls dealing with complaints. I could barely get a word in edgeways and so I had no opportunity to explain that when the Red Arrows had flown close to her home they were quite legally in low level transit from Exeter Airport to a public display at Weymouth. Had I been able to do so, I would have apologised for the annoyance the Team had caused her.

'I come from a Navy family but my son is a senior aircraftman in Germany,' she volunteered, as though that was relevant to her complaint. A senior aircraftman is actually the second lowest rank in the RAF. 'I know all about squadron leaders. My son has told me that you're the lowest form of life. My husband has written letters to the newspapers you know!'

With that, thankfully, she hung up on me and I made a suitable note in my log. Later that same day she subjected the PA to the Station Commander to a verbal barrage that completely bemused him because he had no idea what she was talking about. Later still she harangued a wing commander who had no connection at all with the Red Arrows. As was the way of things, both the Station Commander and the wing commander called me to find out what was going on.

The lady's family surname was unusual so I could easily have traced her son. I was tempted to telephone the man's squadron commander but in the end I did not do so because her son in Germany would probably have been humiliated and deeply embarrassed by her behaviour. Instead I wrote a polite letter to this lady, making no mention of her inappropriate language, explaining what the Red Arrows had been doing on that afternoon and apologising for disturbing her. She then complained in writing to the Ministry of Defence stating that my explanation was totally unacceptable and that my letter was snooty. Well, what did she expect from the lowest form of life? Neither the MoD nor I heard anything more from this lady.

Curiously, some of the Team's most vociferous 'knockers' are within the ranks of the Royal Air Force itself. The pilots sometimes have to endure sniping from fellow pilots and taunts about being merely 'posers'. There is a large element of jealousy in this as well as a lack of understanding. The plain fact is that most RAF pilots could not do what the Red Arrows pilots do in the air, let alone cope with the demands on the ground. To give but one example, it is rarely a pleasure going to cocktail parties at overseas Embassies and five star international hotels after a long and tiring flying day. The pilots are expected to hold a cocktail glass in one hand, a finger bite in the other, remain polite while trying to juggle both in order to sign autographs in a flimsy book or on a photograph, and at the same time smiling at television cameras and carrying on several different conversations without showing any sign of irritation. Try it for yourself sometime and see how you get on! As a matter of fact I have always thought that official cocktail parties are hugely over-rated but they do, I suppose, serve a business purpose. With any luck, having now retired, I need never again go to a cocktail party.

In my decade as the Red Arrows' PRO there were several half-hearted attempts, allegedly emanating from high level sources within the RAF, to disband the Team. Those attempts were usually leaked in advance, whether accidentally or deliberately I never discovered. It was almost as though the instigators were testing the water to see what reaction there would be. They all came to nothing. As the 1990s drew to a close, when private finance initiative became a buzz phrase, the RAF belatedly came to recognise that the Red Arrows could be a potential source of income through sponsorship deals. We who have been privileged to work for the Red Arrows had known this for years but there was, apparently, neither a mechanism for the RAF to earn money instead of spending it, nor a will to create such a mechanism.

Throughout 2001 it seemed as though everyone was talking about public relations, mainly as a consequence of several very high profile stories and scandals in the national media. The phrase itself, public relations, had become so well understood that it was usually truncated to just the initial letters and nowadays PR is often used to describe not just the activity but the person who does it. Indeed, the PR person is now frequently the subject of the PR output, something that never used to happen – and now I am doing it myself.

I knew it was time for me to hang up my flying helmet when the title of my post, and all other public relations posts in the Ministry of Defence, was changed to Corporate Communication Officer, which does not slip off the tongue quite so readily as Public Relations Officer.

To me at least, the word communication still suggests something to do with wirelesses, teleprinters, and chattering Creed relays, all of which featured in the early part of my RAF career. As a matter of fact, when I did finally retire in March 2001 there still seemed to be some disagreement in official circles about whether the new in-word was communication, singular, or communications, plural. Both were used as though they were synonymous, which they are not, and that betrayed a singular lack of communication if nothing else.

The last edition to come my way of the PROs' reference book was boldly labelled on its front cover:

'MINISTRY OF DEFENCE
DIRECTORATE GENERAL CORPORATE COMMUNICATION
PUBLIC RELATIONS DIRECTORY'

- the compilers obviously hedging their bets. In that document, RAF Strike Command was listed as having a Corporate Communication Branch while Personnel and Training Command, the Red Arrows' own superior formation, had a Corporate Communications Branch. The Royal Navy, who never did like the other Services' acronyms, still had listings for PROs together with lots of SPROs, DSPROs – and even an ASPRO at Plymouth. Quite a headache! The Royal Navy Reserve had a Public Affairs Branch, while the Army was sticking to Information Services – which, on reflection, is probably the best title of all for what we publicity seekers do.

Over the years, most people have become used to this phrase 'public relations' and know roughly what it means, even if it does not, and never did, accurately describe what most PROs do. According to the vast Encarta World English Dictionary, my favourite tome for idle browsing but not the one I use on the rare occasions when I need help with The Times' crossword, public relations is 'the practice or profession of establishing, maintaining or improving a favourable relationship between an institution, or person, and the public' – and it takes a singular verb. Sadly the 2001 edition of Encarta did not get around to defining Corporate Communication so there is no help there as to whether it should be singular or plural.

One of the most satisfying elements of my work was dealing with ordinary members of the public, maintaining and I hope improving relationships by answering their questions, organising their visits, and sending them brochures, pictures, stories and autographs of the pilots. As far as the media were concerned, I often used to say that my job was the easiest PR job around because whilst most PROs have to work long and hard to make their contacts and get their stories published, I could sit back, wait for the media folk to contact me and then select the ones I wanted to deal with. Of course, I did not do that.

There is a world of difference between what Sir Robert Armstrong famously referred to as being 'economical with the truth' and the telling of downright lies – and I am sure Sir Robert would agree with that! I have never, as far as I am aware, told a lie to any reporter. When I have been economical with the truth, and I have been several times in the course of my duties with the Red Arrows, as I will reveal from time to time in this book, it was because the reporters did not ask the right questions and that was their fault not mine.

Sometimes, for a variety of reasons, a PRO needs to suppress stories or dodge an issue but I have always maintained that PROs should never say 'no comment' to a reporter. A simple example explains my reasoning. If a reporter were to ask me, 'Has the Station Commander stopped beating his wife?' and I replied 'No comment' the reporter could quite truthfully write either, 'the press spokesman would not say if the Station Commander had stopped beating his wife' or 'the press spokesman did not deny that the Station Commander had been beating his wife.' Anyway, quite apart from not achieving the desired result, I think that saying 'no comment' is rather rude.

In the 11 complete seasons I worked for the Red Arrows they gave 1,096 public displays in 44 countries and many times that number of practice displays, fly pasts and other appearances. I hosted, or helped to host, over 10,000 visitors to the Team's headquarters, first at Scampton, then Cranwell and finally Scampton again. My last day of work was 14 March 2001. There was no ceremony then to mark my final departure because I had been officially dined-out of the Squadron some months earlier on one of several earlier planned retirement dates. I have never liked farewells and I have never been to any squadron reunions throughout my 47 years in uniform. I always told everyone on the Team that I would leave my office when my work was done and not go back. That was how I wanted it. Accordingly, on my last day I was at the Red Arrows' Headquarters just long enough to make sure my successor was happily settled in. She was neither settled in nor happy, but I did my best anyway! The Red Arrows were away from base that day so, after a couple of hours, I was able to slip quietly out of the squadron buildings without saying goodbye and without anyone noticing. I drove the six miles to my home and took off my uniform for the final time.

From time to time during my final few months in post, I casually hinted in the squadron coffee bar that my next book, to be published after my retirement, would tell the real inside story of the Team. Whenever I mentioned that, I noticed worried looks which caused me to wonder if there was some important thing, or some particularly newsworthy events, that I had missed. I do not think I missed much! This is that book. It is the story of the Red Arrows seen from within rather than from a journalist's or historian's point of view. In spite of many requests from former Red Arrows and others, this book is not a definitive history of the team; rather I have picked out some of the events that I think significant, particularly interesting, or amusing. It is also my personal story of how I came to spend more than a decade as the Public Relations Officer for the Royal Air Force Aerobatic Team, 'the Voice of the Red Arrows' as the Lincolnshire Echo daily newspaper rather flatteringly put it in a feature article about my retirement.

I am grateful to the Editors of the local, regional and national newspapers mentioned in the book for permission to quote extracts from their publications. I also wish to thank EJ, that superb photographer, film-maker and long-time friend of the Red Arrows for permission to reproduce some of his superb pictures. In my opinion, no book about the Red Arrows is complete without including examples of his work.

1

An Introduction to Train Spotting

I WAS DESTINED TO BE INVOLVED WITH AVIATION and to be a storyteller long before the Red Arrows were ever thought of. The intrepid pilots of Sir Alan Cobham's world famous Flying Circus were performing over Woodhouse Moor barely five miles away, when I was born on 17 September 1935 in a council house in Middleton, then a brand new estate in the southern outskirts of Leeds, while a thunder-storm was raging overhead. I have often wondered if the Red Arrows' Circus, the blue-suited technicians who fly in the back cockpit of the Red Arrows' aircraft on transit flights, are named after Cobham's Flying Circus but no-one seems to know. To be honest, hardly anyone I met in my time working with the Red Arrows had heard of either Sir Alan Cobham or his flying circus so there is probably another explanation.

In 1937 my father gave up his job as a travelling collector for the Prudential Insurance Company and joined His Majesty's Prison Service. After completing his initial training in Love Lane, adjacent to Wakefield Prison, he was posted to Strangeways Prison on the boundary between Manchester and Salford, to serve his probationary period. In expectation of a permanent posting to Strangeways at the end of the probation period, we moved from 3 Acre Mount in Middleton to a dingy prison house in Salford, a house not unlike like those depicted in Granada Television's Coronation Street. In June 1938 my sister Kathleen was born in that house and my very earliest memory is of running up and down our street shouting triumphantly at the top of my voice to anyone who happened to be listening, 'Our Kathleen's come!'

Another of my early memories is of an incident that occurred in late-1939. One balmy, sunny day a Spitfire flew low over our house and then zoomed skywards into the wide, blue yonder performing a Victory Roll. I was mightily impressed with what I saw. Of course I did not know it was a Spitfire or a Victory Roll but that is what my father told me.

Soon after that Dad was posted back to Wakefield Prison, now a fully qualified prison officer, and we moved, 'flitted' as it was known in those days, back to Yorkshire again. Two days after moving into 29 Cotton Street, a smart new pebble-dashed semi at the end of a cul-de-sac off Denby Dale Road, Wakefield, our former house in Salford was completely demolished by a stray German bomb probably intended for Manchester docks. That unexpected posting turned out to be a life saver.

Cotton Street today seems so much shorter and narrower than I had remembered it, but it has not changed much. A teenager who owned a powerful motor cycle and occasionally took me for rides on the pillion, lived with his parents and sister in a house two doors from ours in 1939 and he still lives in the same house in 2001. These days there are always cars parked along the verges; no-one in the Street owned a car when I lived there. The dead end of Cotton Street was ideal for train spotting. The embankment carrying the LMS main line from Manchester to Wakefield Kirkgate via Horbury Junction went right past our house at bedroom window level. Immediately beyond the end of Cotton Street, the line passed underneath the main LNER London to Leeds line into Wakefield's other station, Westgate. Both lines are still there and busy, although most of the trains now belong to GNER, Arriva or Virgin. Mallard, Sir Nigel Gresley, Flying Scotsman, Union of South Africa, Dominion of Canada, Sansovino, and other famous locomotives, steamed dirtily past my bedroom window daily throughout the war years. 'Ar 'ouse' was a train spotter's paradise and to this day I retain a fascination with railways – much to the amusement of my friends on the Red Arrows.

I first learned about the need for precision in speech and writing, and the problems that dialects can cause, shortly after I started my formal education at what everyone called the 'little school', Christ Church Infants' School just off Thornes Lane. The school buildings are still there but the church after which the school was named was demolished many years ago. I can clearly remember my very first day at school, 12 August 1940. That date has always been synonymous in my mind not only with the start of my formal education, but with Granddad Winter's birthday and the start of the grouse shooting season, even though as a city child I had no idea what grouse were nor why they had to be shot on that particular day. For a five-year old it was a fascinating ten-minute walk from home through the long, low, and ever-muddy pedestrian tunnel underneath the LMS railway, past the 'big school', St James, to which I would graduate when I reached the age of seven, and then left onto Thornes Lane.

There I would cross over the road by the Co-op, where we were registered for rations. The Co-op was a fascinating shop, always lit inside by spluttering gas lights because the blackout blinds on the windows seemed to be permanently drawn. There were liberal quantities of sawdust strewn on the wooden floor and all manner of exciting tins, packets and bottles piled up on shelves which stretched from floor to ceiling. Even at the age of five I could read all the labels. For some reason one side of the label on the HP brown sauce bottles was always in French and I can still remember some of that: 'Cette sauce de haute qualité est un mélange de fruits orientaux' – or something like that. I used to enjoy reciting the whole label in French from memory.

I remember particularly a bacon slicing machine which stood on one counter. Every time I went into the Co-op I carefully studied the mechanism to see how it was that the platen holding the bacon moved smoothly backwards and forwards when the shop assistant rotated the large red wheel at the front with his left hand. I can still hear the strange swishing noise as the circular blade sliced through the bacon. How deftly the assistant's right hand used to receive each slice of streaky as it dropped out of the machine and how carefully he laid it on the grease-proof paper standing on the adjacent weighing machine.

Next to the bacon slicer was a cheese board on which pieces of standard Cheddar cheese were carved using a length of wire which had a T-shaped wooden handle on the end. Somewhere secreted under the counter were the eggs; in the darkest days of the war we were lucky to get one egg per person per week. To me and my sister there never seemed to be any shortage of food in the shops but we had never known anything different and I know my parents struggled to keep us fed and nourished.

Immediately next to where the Co-op used to stand is bridge number 58 of the so-called 99 Arches, the magnificent line of high railway bridges carrying the LNER tracks from the south right into the heart of Wakefield. According to the experts there have never been exactly 99 arches. Some people say there are 93, others say there are as many as 114; the exact count apparently depends on which arch is considered to be the last in the line. On the left, in the shadow of bridge 58 was, still is, the Admiral Duncan public house, never allowed to be mentioned in our Methodist home. I often paused to peer through the grimy pub windows trying to discern what was going on inside. I could read the signs, colourfully engraved on the windows rather like the stained glass I had seen in our church, but I could not imagine why that establishment needed a 'tap room' and a 'smoke room' and my parents would not tell me.

Next door to the Admiral Duncan was a fish and chip shop where I was regularly sent to buy our dinner or supper. Dinner for most 'ordinary' people in wartime Wakefield was eaten at midday, tea at 4pm and supper at some later time if the money and the rations ran to it. Pieces of succulent, battered cod, deep fried in dripping of course not oil, were 4d and a huge pile of golden-brown chips 2d. The 'posh' people bought plaice and occasionally haddock instead of cod. If I was really lucky I would be given a free scoopful of 'scraps' – the bits of scrumptious, crispy, deep fried batter that had broken off the fish in the frying process. Modern nutritionists eat your hearts out! There were always queues long before the shop opened its doors for business but if it was very cold or very wet, the proprietor would usually let us in early while the first batch of food was still frying. I assume the queues diminished late in the evening, long after I had gone to bed. I still smile at the old Yorkshire joke:

Customer to Fish and Chip Shop Proprietor, entering the shop in a rush just before closing time: 'Have you got any chips left?'

Fish Shop Proprietor to Customer: 'Certainly, sir, plenty.'

Customer to Fish Shop Proprietor: 'It serves you right then for cooking so many!'

A large notice in the fish shop window exhorted customers to 'Bring Your Own Paper'. Out of sheer necessity we were all far more diligent at recycling things during the war than we are these days. I used to read the latest news from the pages of the Daily Mirror, the Wakefield Express, or the Yorkshire Evening Post whilst standing in the queue. Wrapping fish and chips was just one of the many uses to which newspapers could be put. When the food had been transferred to plates, nicely warmed on the hearth in front of the fire, the greasy newspaper was then put aside for fire-lighting purposes. At a very early age I learned the technique of plaiting rolled up newspaper pages to form slow burning fuses which could be used as kindling in lieu of firewood. The Express and the Evening Post, being broadsheets, were better for this purpose than the Mirror but the Mirror had the best strip cartoons – including Garth, the intrepid adventurer who could easily have been James Bond's grandfather, and the voluptuous Jane!

At the end of each day small rectangles of clean newspaper were impaled on a nail in the toilet for a less dignified purpose but they still made fascinating reading even though it was often difficult to find the end of a particular story.

'Hurry up, our Tony,' Mam used to shout through the toilet door, 'your Dad wants to come in!'

I clearly remember crying when Mum left me outside the little school on that first morning – and I believe Mum was also in tears. I also remember how reluctant I was to leave the school when she came to take me home for dinner three hours later after I had made many new friends and had a thoroughly enjoyable time. Thereafter, like all the other infant children, whatever the weather, however dark the winter mornings and evenings or the summer mornings when Double British Time two hours ahead of GMT was in force, I made my way to and from school unescorted, something no caring parent would now dream of doing.

Although born in Yorkshire, I had spent three of my first five years living in Lancashire, that distant enemy state across the Pennines hidden safely from view behind those mysterious 'mountains' just beyond Denby Dale, now known to millions as 'Last of the Summer Wine' territory. Sometimes the seemingly permanent thick and cloying industrial West Riding smog lifted temporarily and it was then possible for an hour or two to see the hills from certain vantage points in

Wakefield. Such occasions were so rare that they invariably became the main subject of the day's conversation in schools and shops and on street corners. 'What a lovely day; Albert, you can see the Pennines quite clearly from the top of Market Street.' At a very early stage in our education we were taught that hills rising more than 1,000 feet above sea level, as some of the Pennine peaks do, were entitled to be called mountains but that no longer seems to be part of the definition.

Not that we children knew much about the sea. We knew from elementary geography lessons that India and Africa were countries 'over the sea' and we knew that they were British because they were coloured red on maps in books and on the large globe of the world which stood on a table in one of the classrooms. We knew that the people who lived there were different from us: one of our favourite hymns sung at Morning Assembly started off, 'Over the sea there are little brown children', but we were told, and believed, that they were all God's children just like we were. The 'seaside' was something different; our parents spoke nostalgically about Bridlington, Filey and Scarborough, places that no-one visited during the war. I longed to go to such places but I never saw the sea until I was 11 years old and the war was over. I do not remember ever learning much about Europe at infants school although, naturally, we knew that Herr Hitler lived in Germany. In the evenings we could pick up on our three-valve wireless set, radio programmes, mostly in strange languages but sometimes in English, coming from Hilversum, Berlin, Paris, Athlone and even further afield. We children just accepted that they were there without wondering where they were.

I was something of an oddity at Christ Church School because I spoke in a strange alien tongue, a curious mixture of the Lancashire and Yorkshire dialects, which the other infants found rather confusing and the teachers found frustrating. The different meanings ascribed to certain words and phrases had an unfortunate result one cold and dark morning when school started during a torrential rain storm. The harassed teachers helped us children out of our sodden clothes. There was a wonderful roaring fire in the open grate in the main assembly hall. A latticed metal screen, designed to prevent clumsy children falling into the fire, stood in front of it. There were clouds of steam everywhere.

'Tony, put these socks on the fire, please,' said one of the stressed teachers as she handed me a pair of soggy socks she had just pulled off another pupil.

So I did! Fascinated, I watched the wool bubbling and shrivelling as the flames consumed the socks. Having seen what I had just done, but too late to stop me, the teacher in vain tried to rescue the socks from the fire with a poker but her well-intentioned actions merely hastened the socks' final disintegration. It was one of those many Yorkshire dialectal idiosyncrasies that 'put the socks on the fire, Tony' actually meant draping them to dry on the fire-screen in front of the fire. I remember bursting into tears of humiliation.

'If you wanted me to put the socks on the fire guard, why did you tell me to put them on the fire?' I asked with some asperity and received a slap on the face for my trouble. That teacher would doubtless have ended up in court these days for assaulting me. As it was the unfortunate lady presumably had the difficult job of explaining to the child's parents what had happened to his socks. All clothing in those wartime years was 'on the ration' so the boy probably went sockless for weeks after the incident until his parents had saved up sufficient rationing points for a new pair. My parents were duly informed of my stupidity.

'How was I supposed to know what she meant?' I asked sulkily. How indeed.

When the German bombers regularly started passing over the Wakefield area on their way to targets in industrial Lancashire, I used to listen intently night after night from our sanctuary inside the Anderson shelter at the bottom of our back garden. Harry Houtby, a near neighbour, occasionally joined us in our shelter when he was not on shift 'dahn t'pit' and while Dad was on night duty at the prison or on fire-watching duties elsewhere in the neighbourhood. Nora Batty's hen-pecked husband Wally in the early series of 'Last of the Summer Wine' still reminds me of Mr Houtby; they looked uncannily alike and they both had the same variant of the Yorkshire accent, so broad that I often had difficulty understanding what Mr Houtby was saying. He was, however, a mine of information about aircraft and it was he who taught me how to recognise the difference between the steady drone of 'wun of 'arz' and the desynchronised heterodynes of 'wun o' thee-ers' as unseen heavy bombers passed high overhead.

I can remember only two enemy bombs falling on Wakefield: one completely demolished the home of the Toppin family in Thornes Road about a mile from where we lived. If you know where to look, you can still see the gap where that house once stood. The other was a time-bomb that failed to go off and caused superficial damage to the splendid park gates along Denby Dale Road less than a quarter of a mile from our house. The failed time-bomb was eventually dug out of the ground, emptied of its lethal contents and placed adjacent to Queen Victoria's splendid monument in the Bull Ring, right in Wakefield city centre, where for a while it was used as a receptacle for money being collected 'to help the war effort.'

Soon after those incidents the German bombers stopped coming over and my parents, and most of our neighbours, obviously decided that there was no longer any need to subject ourselves to the inconvenience of sleeping in the Anderson shelters. Ours became, for the rest of the war, a repository for household goods no longer in daily use, a sort of underground garden shed and a jolly good play area to boot.

At the age of seven I duly graduated to 'the big school'. As I have intimated, I had been keen on reading for as long as I can remember but at St James' we were encouraged not only to read but also to write stories of our own invention. One day, when I was 9 or 10 years old, we were told to write what school teachers used to call a 'composition' about anything to do with home life. Most of my fellow pupils wrote about such things as 'My Pet' and 'My Favourite Dinner' but I have a special reason for remembering that one of the girls in my class wrote a piece called 'Down Our Air Raid Shelter'. I wish I could remember more than the title because, at about that time, her much older sister somehow enticed me into their dark and dank air raid shelter in the middle of the day when all the adults were out. She taught me a few things that I was not supposed to know about until I was 12 or 13 years old, but I always was a quick learner. However, my school composition was not about that and I hope hers was not! I called my piece 'A Fall of Soot' and for good measure I gave it a sub-title as well: 'Old Folks at Home'. It must have been quite good, the story that is, because I was called upon to read it out aloud to the whole school at Assembly a few days later. I was awarded a much-prized 'star' for that effort and my pride more than compensated for my embarrassment.

In the main assembly hall at the Big School hung a large framed print of W F Yeames' famous painting 'When did you last see your father?' The title was engraved on a plaque underneath the painting. The picture used to fascinate me and I often stood on my own in front of it wondering what the answer to the question was. None of the teachers ever volunteered an explanation and I always assumed that it was in some way connected to the on-going world war when so many fathers were away from home fighting for their country. It vaguely worried me that my father was still at home and not away at the war and so I always shrank from asking questions about the painting. The concept of reserved occupations was beyond me.

In my later years at St James', I became a dedicated fan of Lord Peter Wimsey. One of Dorothy L Sayers' detective stories featuring that nobleman had been serialised on the BBC Home Service and I enjoyed it so much that I borrowed Wimsey books from the adult library on Drury Lane near Westgate railway station at the rate of one per week until I had read them all. They were not an easy read, not for an 11-year old anyway, and the settings were worlds different from my home life. I was fascinated by the wealth of detail in the stories. I used to re-read some paragraphs slowly, over and over again, savouring the facts and admiring the writer's skill.

During my Wimsey period, when asked to write another composition for homework on a fictional subject of our choice, I filled an entire school exercise book with a story set in Wakefield called 'Murder in the Cathedral'– a title suggested by a book that I had just read. I wrote my story straight off at one sitting without any planning whatsoever. I remember deciding, even before I put pen to paper, that I would fill all 64 pages of the new exercise book with my story. What I cannot remember, however, is why I wanted to fill the entire book at one go. My use of phrases such as 'rigor mortis had not yet set in' and 'powder burns on the body suggest that he was shot at point-blank range', remembered from the book I had just read, clearly startled the teachers at school.

The next day my parents were summoned to explain to the Head Master, nice portly Mr Ronnie Paterson who walked with a limp, why I apparently had a morbid interest in murders and post mortems. Perhaps Dad had been telling me lurid stories about goings-on in Wakefield prison? Not so; Dad never talked about his work at home – not in my hearing anyway. 'I've had to sign the Official Secrets Act,' Dad used to tell us, mysteriously. Mum and Dad were able to convince Mr Paterson that I was just a normal child who read a lot and had a vivid imagination. The Head Master then turned to me and sternly told me that the exercise book was meant to last the whole term because of the severe paper shortage. 'There is a war on, you know,' he added, a much-used phrase in the war years used to explain deficiencies of all kinds. How could anyone not know there was a war on, I often wondered, being unable to imagine what life would be like when there was not a war on. The only compensation as far as I could tell was that sweets would not be on the ration. And what would the BBC put on the 9pm news on the Home Service if there were no war stories?

Mr Paterson gave me a new exercise book but retained the one containing my story. I do wish I had been allowed to keep it.

2

The Secret Diaries
of Tony Cunnane

FROM THE TENDER AGE OF 12 right up until the present day, I have maintained diaries in one form or another. The earliest ones were written in Letts Schoolboys Diaries. I got one as a Christmas present each year. They were beautifully bound leatherette-covered pocket books which contained all manner of facts and figures deemed to be useful for schoolboys. The 1948 edition, my very first, provided several pages of tiny print giving careers advice and I see that for careers in aviation, both civil and Royal Air Force, one had to contact the Air Ministry, London, WC2. At that tender age I had no intention of doing any such thing. There were nine pages of Latin irregular verbs, eight pages for French verbs, and two for German strong verbs. The world maps at the end of the diary had great swathes of red indicating British colonies and possessions.

I made an entry every single day, usually written in bed in the evenings. Many are quite embarrassing to read now and are really only of interest to me – and some are not even that interesting. My very first diary entry, for example, records that on 1 January 1948 I listened to Max Bruch's Kol Nidrei in Concert Hour on the BBC Home Service and that I later cycled 5.2 miles on my bicycle. Riveting stuff! Later on my jottings became longer and more adventurous. In the interests of adolescent secrecy, and to frustrate parental snooping, many of the entries were annotated with hieroglyphics, which were very meaningful at the time no doubt but which mean nothing to me now more than 50 years later. However, I can guess what the five stars alongside a date in late 1949, when I was barely 14 years old, mean.

Throughout my early RAF career the diaries included, inevitably, some details of my work. However, in the 1980s I found myself in the shady world of intelligence and then it was too difficult to maintain private, let alone work, diaries. Once I started working for the Red Arrows I resumed keeping detailed diaries.

Each year from 1965, one of the Red Arrows' pilots had been given the job of maintaining a photographic record of the year and each year the Manager had produced an official report about the Team's activities. The photographic annuals contain few words whilst the official end of season reports were mostly written in stilted service language and were probably never read by anybody. The official reports suffer from a fault that afflicts many historical records written by amateurs, and I include my own diaries in that category: they presumably meant a lot at the time they were written but because the writers did not bother to explain much of the background information that was obvious at the time, they become less useful in later years when the background has been forgotten. Young diary writers reading this, take note! When I retired from the Red Arrows I left behind for posterity large quantities of statistical information about the Team, much of it gleaned from my personal diaries. It remains to be seen if posterity is interested.

At about the age of 10 my parents, having recognised an early talent for classical music, wanted me to take the entrance examination for the Wakefield Cathedral School. That would have meant going for a sing-ing audition but, for some reason I have never been able to understand, I refused point blank to do it in spite of having quite a nice treble voice, which I used to exercise when I thought no-one was listening. I believe Mr Paterson, Headmaster of St James' School, sided with me.

In 1947, when it was time to leave the Big School, I got my young heart's desire: I won a Storie Scholarship for having the highest marks in the 11-plus examinations, the only one granted to St James' that year, and it gave me a coveted place at the Queen Elizabeth Grammar School in Wakefield, which seemed to me to be so much more desirable than the Thornes House Grammar School. QEGS was steeped in tradition and had a high proportion of boarding pupils. I was immensely proud to be a pupil there. Imagine my dismay when, having completed only two terms at QEGS, Dad was transferred to Armley Jail in Leeds. To use 1990s terminology, I was devastated by this move.

We sold the house in Cotton Street for £560 and moved to Harehills, into a grotty terraced house with cellars and attics which cost the princely sum of £750 to buy. My bedroom was the larger of two attics, uncarpeted and unfurnished apart from my single bed, cold in winter, stifling in summer, and reached via a steep flight of bare stairs with no safety rail. There was a small uncurtained skylight in the sloping roof and a bare electric light bulb dangling from the ceiling rose. The bulb was controlled by two switches, one at the bottom of the stairs and one at the top – out of my reach when in bed. In the middle of one night I awoke after sleepwalking a few steps in total darkness. Some instinct alerted me to danger and by gingerly moving one foot forward a few inches I found myself literally teetering on the edge of the sheer drop to the floor below. I backed off and got back into bed. I never walked in my sleep again from that day to this – as far as I know – and I never told anyone about that incident until now.

I was allocated a place at Roundhay School, a huge sprawling boys grammar school segregated from the equivalent girls high school by the shared indoor swimming pool, a long avenue of tall trees, and what seemed then like a vast acreage of playing fields. This was something new for me. There had been no girls anywhere near QEGS in Wakefield but at Roundhay we could see girls on the playing fields at every break time although we were forbidden to mix with them. We were also ordered to keep well clear of the swimming pool changing rooms until the girls had left. Sometimes they lingered provocatively, giggling profusely, until we arrived. In the following term, when the timetable changed and the situation was reversed, we found that if we took a little extra time to get dressed after our swimming period had ended, the girls would sometimes come rushing in and catch us apparently unawares. Either the swimming teachers trusted us or, more likely, they considered this to be part of our education. It was all very revealing!

I quickly learned, in the interests of what today we would call street cred, to drop the refined version of the Yorkshire accent I had started to learn at the Grammar School in Wakefield and adopt the rather more down-market form of speech which was the accepted norm at

Roundhay. At first I was laughed at when I pronounced my aitches and said that I lived in Harehills and went to Roundhay School. My school mates used to mimic me, albeit in a friendly, bantering fashion. At Roundhay aitches were there to be dropped and ungrammatical glottal stops were in. I soon learned to say that we lived in 'Are'ills and that I went to 'Roun-di' school and then I was accepted as one of the crowd. Latin and Greek were off the syllabus; handicrafts and chemistry were in; rugby and the school orchestra were out; soccer and girls were in. Gone too were prefects with their distinctive tasselled caps and the blind obedience to tradition they engendered. This is not a criticism of either of the schools or their staff, more a recognition of the differences between the styles of the old and new grammar schools in the late 1940s and I quickly adapted. There was one other definite improvement in my life style: instead of walking two miles to school as I had done in Wakefield, I had to travel to and from Roundhay by tram and that was almost as good as travelling by train.

Two years later there was yet another family upheaval. We returned to Salford when Dad was posted once more to Strangeways. Now it was back to an all-boys grammar school education again. In the fifth form at Salford Grammar School I shared a two-seater desk with Albert Finney for some lessons. Even then he was an accomplished actor but he probably will not thank me for remembering that his major triumph at school was in drag playing Ma Gargery, Pip's ill-tempered Aunt, in the all-male school production of Great Expectations. He was brilliant. On the final night he was quite ill – a severe dose of 'flu I seem to recall. He performed like the true star that he later became and was allowed to take his final bow in front of the curtains all on his own at the end of the first act, the only act in which Ma Gargery appeared, so that he could go home early and take to his bed.

During my time at Salford Grammar School I was completely undecided what I wanted to do for a career, hardly surprising I suppose after my regular change of schools. For a while my sights were set on becoming a professional musician of some sort. Although I say it myself, I had steadily been acquiring an encyclopaedic knowledge of classical music. I was also quite a good violinist and I had expensive lessons from Mr Cunliffe, one of the viola players in the BBC Northern Orchestra, as the BBC Philharmonic was then called, lessons that my parents could ill afford. Mr Cunliffe arranged for me an open invitation to attend radio concerts being given in the BBC's first-floor studios in Deansgate, Manchester. Frequently I was an audience of one and I used to sit on a hard straight-backed chair immediately behind the announcer. These were not public concerts and, because they were almost always broadcast live, I had to remain absolutely silent with no coughs, no squeaking chair and certainly no applause until after the red light had gone out. It amazed me that many of the concerts were broadcast live on the BBC General Overseas Service and I used to imagine that listeners in far-flung parts of the globe could hear my breathing in the quieter passages of music. The doormen, members of the orchestra and the announcers soon got used to me. A young and clean-shaven Charles Groves was at that time the resident conductor of the orchestra. He was always rather aloof and never spoke to me – I found that rather fitting for such a well-known maestro. Reginald Stead, the Leader of the orchestra, almost always had a few words to say to me after the studio had gone off the air. I felt very privileged and I enjoyed those free concerts immensely.

In spite of great encouragement from the school Music Teacher, Dr Llifon Hughes-Jones a war-time Lancaster pilot, I knew in my heart that I would never reach professional standard as a violinist. I well remember how disappointed Dr Jones was for me, and how jealous I was, when he discovered one day that one of the other students in my class, Eddie Foulkes, had perfect pitch and I did not. For days afterwards I tried in vain to memorise the exact sound of 440 hertz, the tuning of the violin open A string. To the intense irritation of everyone around me, I spent hours quietly humming what I thought was the correct frequency and constantly checking it against the tuning fork which I carried in my trouser pocket. Eventually I had to accept that you cannot learn perfect pitch: you either have it or you don't and I didn't.

My diaries of that period are a testament to my indecision about a future career. Just after sitting the exams for the General Certificate of Education in 1952, and when I should have been moving up into the 6th Form, the family moved back to Wakefield yet again. I was in total despair about the future. Once again we had a house right alongside a railway line but this time it was in Wrenthorpe, three miles north of

Wakefield, and I was no longer interested in train spotting. My parents could not afford to send me to university so there seemed little point in staying on in the Sixth Form. In any case there was no 6th Form music tuition at QEGS that year and there was no room for me at Thornes House – probably I did not appeal to them as a former QEGS pupil. Sadly, I had lost touch with most of my friends from my earlier years in Wakefield although one, Ruth Gilderdale, was to enter my life again 48 years later as a result of a TV interview I gave about the Red Arrows. More of that later. I got a temporary job in the West Riding County Council motor licensing department on St John's North to keep me occupied until it was time to register for National Service. I have never been so bored in all my life. I could, and did, hear the Town Hall clock strike every hour and very long hours they seemed.

One day in a fit of indecision, I visited the Royal Air Force Recruiting Office in Cookridge Street, Leeds to see what they had to offer a 17-year old with 6 GCE O Levels. To my surprise, the recruiting officer seemed convinced that I was pilot material, an opening that had never occurred to me. I did not tell my parents that I had been to the recruiting office therefore it came as a great surprise to them when a letter arrived a few days later inviting me to attend the Aircrew Selection Centre at RAF Hornchurch in Essex. I went, with my parents' rather bemused blessing, and it was an absolute disaster.

It was only the second time in my life that I had spent nights away from home and I was totally unprepared for the entire selection procedure. The interviews and group activities were a nightmare, partly because of my total ignorance of the RAF and anything to do with aviation and partly because of my strange speech which must have sounded very common to the selecting officers and to my fellow applicants, mainly public school boys who spoke with what I now know to be Received Pronunciation. A northern accent was simply not acceptable in the 1950s for commissioned service in the RAF. The individual intelligence and aptitude tests and the extensive medical examinations caused no problems but the teamwork exercises were humiliating. Why had not the recruiting officer in Leeds warned me what to expect? I have always suspected that he had a quota to fill and I was the best prospect he had that week or that month. On the other hand I did eventually become not only a pilot, but a flying instructor and examiner, so perhaps he recognised some latent talent.

I slunk back to Yorkshire vowing that I would never again attend a job interview without extensive research and preparation – but I did, as I will reveal shortly! The inevitable rejection letter from Hornchurch arrived a few days later. 'Do not be disheartened that we have rejected you,' it said soothingly. 'You did very well but the standard now required is extremely high.' I still have the letter and I still think it very condescending. What was the point in telling me that I was nearly good enough when I knew that it was not true. A follow up letter came from the recruiters a few days later inviting me for a further interview at the Leeds office. I went, fully intending to give the officer a piece of my mind for deceiving me about my prospects, but instead I signed on for four years as a wireless mechanic; he seemed quite relieved about that.

I knew as little about wireless and radar theory as I knew about flying aeroplanes but I was determined to prove the RAF wrong. 18 months later, after graduating top of my class from a long, extremely fascinating and highly enjoyable course at the RAF's No 1 Radio School at Locking, now buried somewhere under the M5 motorway near Weston-super-Mare, I found myself posted to Ceylon. I joined a small but strategically important radio station at a place called Gangodawila, located in a jungle clearing about 10 miles south of Colombo. Within a few months of arriving on that beautiful island I was promoted to corporal, well ahead of my time.

With my new-found wealth I signed up with the Regent Institute in London for a writing and journalism correspondence course. I never earned enough to repay my fees, an advertising promise, but that was more my fault than the Institute's. The tutor-assessed exercises took up to four months to travel to England and back by sea mail by which time I had lost interest in them and my tutor had probably lost interest in me. One of the pieces I was particularly proud of described the 6 minute 52 second total eclipse of the sun that had been perfectly visible over most of the island in cloudless skies. It certainly made the miserable two minute total eclipse that occurred on a cloudy day in August 1999 in Cornwall look pretty insignificant. Whilst my student article might have interested a publisher had I been able to get it to UK within hours of the event, three or four months later it simply was not news any more.

Halfway through my tour of duty in Ceylon, the Signals Officer, Flight Lieutenant Gibb, persuaded me to apply once again for aircrew training, quite why I never discovered. I went for a series of preliminary interviews at the Far East Air Force Headquarters at Changi in Singapore, now forever hidden beneath the magnificent Singapore International Airport. This was the first of my many visits to the island, and this time I was properly prepared. I apparently convinced the interview board that I was a good prospect and so my overseas tour in Ceylon was cut short and I was sent back to England to await another appointment at Hornchurch.

I was stationed temporarily at Hemswell, then a very busy operational airfield and home for several squadrons of Lincoln bombers. For a few weeks I was detached from Hemswell to a small out-station at Normanby, just north of Scampton, where I was in sole charge of ten high-powered short wave transmitters and a group of a dozen airmen. It was during this period that I went down the A15 to Lincoln several times and saw the extensive road works caused by the work to lengthen Scampton's main runway ready for the arrival of the V Bombers.

I did better at Hornchurch the second time around because I knew what to expect and how to play the system. Many years later, 35 years later to be precise, when I was working at Scampton with the Red Arrows, I had sneaky access to the confidential reports written on me following my two visits to Hornchurch and learned from them that on each occasion the recruiters had noted my unacceptable accent and considered me unlikely ever to become suitable for a commission. On this second visit, however, the RAF did offer me training as an air signaller which carried with it promotion to sergeant on graduation. With some reluctance I accepted what I knew to be second best. A year later I came top of the air signallers' course at RAF Swanton Morley, stitched onto my uniform the first of the three different flying brevets for which I would eventually qualify, and was posted to RAF Luqa in Malta where I spent 2½ happy years flying in Shackletons of 38 Squadron.

In January 1960, after an interview at Air Headquarters Malta, I was selected for a commission as an Air Electronics Officer to join the rapidly-growing V Force. The Squadron Commander himself met me to give me the unexpected news on Luqa airfield as I stepped out of a Shackleton having just landed back from a week in Gibraltar. I had just four days to pack up and get myself to the Officer Cadet Training Unit at RAF Jurby on the Isle of Man. I was never given any reason for the unseemly haste.

My fellow cadets at Jurby, all male apart from one middle-aged lady joining the Princess Mary's Royal Air Force Nursing Service as a Matron, ranged from teenagers to fifty-year old Master Aircrew. The course was cunningly designed so that none of us could feel at all confident of graduating, least of all the Matron who found the military training particularly irksome and totally irrelevant for the hospital work for which she was destined. I had already started to worry seriously about my chances of success when the language barrier reared its ugly head again. The Senior Education Officer told me he was worried about my speech even though the RAF was by this time a little more relaxed about regional accents. I had to undergo elocution tuition with him to rid me of my Northern accent and to persuade me to pronounce the final 'g' on -ing words, the latter an omission that no-one had previously pointed out to me. The other cadets thought it hilarious that I was having to spend time in the evenings with the 'schoolie' learning how to speak 'proper'. They were, however, less surprised than I when I was appointed Senior Cadet for the final phase of the course. A few days before our graduation it was announced that I was to be awarded the Sword of Merit for coming out top of the entry.

It was, I had been informed, customary for the Sword of Merit cadet to pay for the Guinness and Champagne, equal parts of which make up the exotic drink known as 'Black Velvet' that formed the basis of the traditional pre-graduation parties. On the morning after our party, one of the staff squadron leaders was discovered in bed with our youngest male cadet. The cadet in question had, apparently, gone to bed very early after drinking too much of the fizzy black stuff. The youngster was, understandably, somewhat put out to be woken by his fellow cadets in this compromising situation. I imagine the squadron leader was at least equally put out having fallen asleep and thereby stayed longer than he had intended, but since I was not there I can only surmise.

By the time I was informed of the incident at breakfast, the squadron leader had long gone, presumably to the Officers Mess to worry and to pack his belongings! As Course Leader it was my responsibility to report the incident to the Wing Commander or even the Station Commander but everyone, including the entirely innocent youth whose bed had been violated, begged me not to do so and I regret to record that I acquiesced with their wishes. I think we were all just keen to graduate and get away from the island as quickly as possible and not get involved in what would undoubtedly have been a protracted and very embarrassing inquiry. That incident never found its way into my diaries, with or without hieroglyphics!

We never saw the offending squadron leader again; we were told that he had gone off to the mainland on urgent compassionate leave. As far as I know, the rest of the staff at Jurby never got to hear about the incident but I may be wrong about that because I heard some years later that shortly afterwards the squadron leader had been 'outed' and forced to resign his commission. In those days it was unthinkable that a senior RAF officer should be court-martialled for homosexuality. The RAF would have been the laughing stock of the Royal Navy and Army. These days, of course, you would commit an offence merely by referring to another person's sexuality.

Winning 'the sword' gave me the honour of being Parade Commander on the Graduation Parade. The Reviewing Officer, Sir Edward Chilton, was the same Air Marshal who had recommended me for a commission in Malta. Off from my uniforms came the air signaller's 'S' brevet and on went the 'AE' one: I was now an Air Electronics Officer. In my first six years in the RAF I had held every rank up to and including sergeant and come out top in the order of merit on all the courses the RAF had given me. I point that out, not as a boast but as an indication of my determination to prove my worth to the RAF.

3

The Great White Detergent or The Farce Was With You

FOR MANY YEARS AFTER I WAS COMMISSIONED I had to make a conscious effort to revert to my northern accent when I went back on leave to family and friends in Wakefield otherwise I would have been accused of being 'posh'. Curiously, even nowadays, when regional accents are rarely commented upon, I still occasionally lapse without thinking into a mixture of Lancashire and Yorkshire expressions and intonation but I am damned if I now know which is which. What an admission for a Yorkshire man!

Shortly after arriving on 18 Squadron at RAF Finningley near Doncaster in the rank of Pilot Officer, I was appointed Press Liaison Officer for the station. There are always dozens of miscellaneous jobs that need to be done on stations and squadrons; these are allocated mostly to junior officers and are known as secondary duties. Station and squadron commanders frequently handed out secondary duties without any regard for the individuals' particular interests or skills. It was deemed good for your career to be given a job that had no appeal and for which you had no aptitude. One's performance in carrying out secondary duties was always assessed on annual confidential reports and so those officers who wished to get on in the Service usually tried their best. It is still like that today. Even the Red Arrows pilots have secondary duties to perform and they can take up a considerable amount of time. In the good old days the really keen officers, who were considered by their colleagues to be sucking-up to the Boss, would volunteer for up to half a dozen secondary duties and this left us ordinary mortals wondering how they found time to carry out their primary duties. When I arrived at Finningley I was still far too junior to think of volunteering for any secondary duty but I was delighted to be made Press Liaison Officer. I never did find out whether I was given the job because my Station Commander thought I had a talent for media work or simply because mine was the first name that came to his mind.

'Your main job, Cunnane, is to keep me and my station out of the press unless I tell you otherwise,' said the Station Commander sternly. 'I don't want you bringing any reporters onto my station – is that clear?'

It was, crystal clear, and a great disappointment to me because I had already thought of several exciting media events I wanted to offer for his approval.

Those were the days when the Cold War was at its most icy and station commanders at their most xenophobic. Finningley, with its 9,000 feet long runway straddling the boundary between south Yorkshire and north Nottinghamshire, was one of about a dozen V Force stations. It was home for the Vulcans of 101 Squadron and the Valiants of 18 Squadron. The entire V Bomber force of Valiants, Victors and Vulcans, Britain's nuclear deterrent, painted white all over for very high altitude operations, was inevitably and irreverently known by its detractors as the 'great white detergent' after a contemporary television advertisement for a soap powder. Less dedicated aircrew were often heard to refer to Britain's finest as the V Farce.

The force was kept on permanent states of readiness requiring crews to get airborne in times ranging from a fairly relaxed four hours, known variously as 'normal readiness' and 'peacetime preparedness', down to a frenetic four minutes depending on the politicians' perception of the threat at any given time. There used to be a joke that the best time for the Soviets to spring a surprise attack would be either on Christmas Day, when there was hardly anyone left on RAF stations, or any Friday evening from about 5pm when most aircrew would be at Happy Hour in the bars of the various Officers' Messes. When the Red Arrows met some visiting Russian officers at Scampton in 1991 this subject came up in general conversation and it seems that the Soviet bomber force crews used to make a joke about Friday evenings being a good time for them to start World War 3. I am not sure whether we should all be reassured by that or not! Just as boys will be boys, so aircrew will be aircrew, whichever side they are on.

Secrecy was, quite rightly, all important within the V Force. Operational knowledge was imparted on the strict 'need-to-know' basis: if you did not need to know, you had no right to know. Station commanders tended to think that any mention of their station or personnel in the newspapers was a serious breach of security and so I was rarely called upon to write any press releases. There were some interesting exceptions. The need-to-know principle did not, for example, discourage station commanders from occasionally inviting visiting cicilian VIPs to give the signal to simulate the so-called four-minute warning and then watch four mighty Vulcans roar into the skies. These semi-public practice scrambles were presumably designed to reassure the British public that they were safe from the Red hoards and at the same time warn the enemy that the RAF was ready and waiting for them. Curiously, a press photograph of the station commander encouraging a VIP to push a button supposedly giving the order to launch the aircraft was acceptable, even desirable, but a close up photograph of the aircraft themselves was not. It seemed to me a bit like publishing photographs of a celebrity switching on the Blackpool Illuminations without also publishing pictures of the illuminations.

Vulcans were used in preference to Valiants for these demonstrations at Finningley because they were so much more powerful and, therefore, more impressive. Furthermore the Vulcans had a system that enabled all four engines to be started simultaneously whereas the Valiant engines had to be started one after the other. For those simulated scrambles the aircraft were always positioned on the Operational Readiness Platform at the beginning of the runway, a large concrete area where four Vulcans could park as close as possible to the runway without impeding other aircraft wishing to take off or land. The display aircraft had light fuel loads and no weapons in the bomb bay so the take offs were always awe-inspiring however often you saw them. Usually the Vulcans climbed steeply away, often quickly disappearing into the overcast. One such scramble I watched with a press party was different from all the others. The first two aircraft turned sharply to the left and right as soon as they were airborne, the third aircraft stayed very low and accelerated away at tree-top height towards nearby Bawtry, while the final aircraft pulled up into a half loop and rolled off the top at about 5,000 feet above the ground. That manoeuvre, had it been viewed from the Bawtry end of the runway, would have looked something similar to, but much more dramatic than, one of my favourite Red Arrows manoeuvres, the Vixen Break.

Being the press officer clearly did not tax me too greatly and so I was given two more secondary duties. For six months I was the squadron's Winter Sports Officer. I knew absolutely nothing about winter sports and had no interest in them so I kept a very low profile during the long hot summer of 1960. I was also appointed Deputy Standard Bearer in preparation for the presentation of the Squadron Standard by HRH The Princess Margaret. The presentation was then delayed for a year when Princess Margaret fell pregnant so in the meantime I was given the onerous task of safeguarding the Standard in a locked room adjacent to mine in the Officers' mess.

Obviously the efficiency with which I carried out my secondary duties must have pleased both my Squadron Commander and the Station Commander because early in 1961 I was appointed to one of the few highly prestigious and much sought after General List Permanent Commissions. I was now guaranteed a career to at least age 43 as a flight lieutenant, or to 47 if I gained promotion to squadron leader and beyond. I was thereafter considered far too useful an officer to be given trivial secondary duties so I was replaced as Winter Sports Officer and made Squadron Adjutant instead with my own small but private office immediately next to the Squadron Commander's.

It was much more fun being the Adjutant because it meant I had unrestricted access to all the squadron files and correspondence. That was when I first discovered that individuals' personal files, kept in distinctive blue folders stamped top and bottom, front and back, 'Staff in Confidence', were far more interesting than the dark red, top secret files. I also soon learned that there is little real satisfaction in having access to all manner of confidential and often titillating personal information about your work colleagues if you cannot tell anyone what you know.

Wing Commander Denys Sutton was my squadron commander. He was always known as 'Clutcher' because whenever he saw you going towards the squadron coffee bar the shortest way, via the path outside his window, he was likely to call you into his office and give you a job. To avoid being 'clutched' most of the squadron personnel used to take the long route to the coffee bar, around the four outside walls of the huge aircraft hangar that housed our squadron. It could be quite lonely in the Adjutant's office!

Clutcher was a very conscientious and well-meaning officer and he gave me good advice from time to time.

'Tony, when you're a squadron commander you can do things your way,' he told me solemnly on one occasion when I had been trying to persuade him to do something he did not want to do. 'Right now I'm the squadron commander and so you'll do things my way.'

He was, of course, absolutely right and I used that very phrase myself several times later in my career when I was a squadron commander. It was Clutcher Sutton who one day got me to type a letter for his signature from the Officer Commanding Number 18 Squadron to the President of the Officers' Mess asking for permission to use the Mess facilities for a Squadron function.

'But you are President of the Officers' Mess,' I said, rather impertinently. 'Why do you need to write to yourself?'

'Because we must have decisions recorded on the files in the proper way,' he replied patiently and without a hint of reproach. Thinking it over afterwards, I felt sure that he had been hoping I would ask that question.

A couple of days later I passed through to Wing Commander Sutton, on file of course, a handwritten memo from himself as President of the Mess to himself as Squadron Commander in which he regretted that permission could not be granted for the squadron function because the Mess staff were fully committed with other duties on the date in question.

'I guessed what the answer would be,' he told me sadly. He initialled his own letter, closed the file, and placed it in the out tray.

I cannot recall that I was able to do anything really productive as PRO until the date of the very first RAF Finningley Battle of Britain

Open Day loomed. Once again I was summoned to the Station Commander.

'I want you to go, in person, to every newspaper office within 40 miles of Finningley and get the editors to print stories about our At Home Day,' said the group captain. 'I want it to be the biggest and best air show of all time.'

This was a complete change of attitude towards PR but who was I to question the ways of a group captain – after all, it was his station. Most towns and villages had a newspaper office where advertisers could hand in their small ads and where readers could order copies of pictures from recent editions. I cannot remember the exact number but I must have lobbied the staff of a couple of dozen newspapers. I did not get to see many editors, or even news editors, but I was able to hand over my carefully crafted press release, which I had typed onto a stencil and duplicated, messily, on the Roneo machine myself.

Most, if not all, of the newspapers printed the story but that was not because my release was riveting but because any news at all about the RAF was news. Incidentally, in these enlightened days of spin doctors and corporate communication, we PROs are required to refer to press releases as news releases because, in the words of one Director of Corporate Communication in the Ministry of Defence, 'we do not release the press; we release news!' Since I am renowned for my pedantry, I suppose I should approve.

When 18 Squadron disbanded in 1963, its specialist electronic warfare role having been taken over by the new Mark 2 Vulcans, I was posted from Finningley to Gaydon near Leamington Spa as an instructor on the Valiant ground school and not long after arriving there I was appointed editor of the station newspaper, 'The Gaydon Gazette'. I found a new openness in the official attitude towards the media. Gaydon was a V Bomber training unit not a front-line bomber station and so security was rather less of an issue. My métier was obviously known to my new station commander when he gave me the job. As often happens with station and in-house magazines even today, I had to write most of the stories myself.

The Gaydon Gazette was handsomely printed on glossy paper by a small firm located close to the nearby village of Kineton, the village that achieved notoriety when the local pub was revealed as the weekend hideaway of the Right Honourable John Profumo MP and Miss Christine Keeler. Mr Profumo was Secretary of State for War and an Honorary Member of the Officers' Mess at Gaydon until his story became public knowledge, but his fall from grace did not feature in any of the articles I wrote. I do recall reading a defensive statement in the national press by another Government Minister which said, 'As far as I can recall, I have never met Miss Keeler.' A good PRO, I thought at the time, would have advised him to word that statement rather more felicitously.

I learned everything I know about the printing process, proof-reading, galleys, gutters, typefaces and leading – and how to pronounce leading properly – from the enthusiastic and ever patient people who worked at the Kineton Press and that knowledge has stood me in good stead ever since.

My career then took a remarkable turn: I went for my second visit to Singapore. This time I was sent unexpectedly, but certainly not reluctantly, on a very secret six-month detachment to a staff appointment in the Far East Air Force HQ. I am not permitted to reveal details of the task that took me to Changi 37 years ago but I can reveal that I was accommodated in the Fairy Point Officers' Mess – I doubt if the RAF would call one of its messes that these days!

While I was in Singapore, I see from my diaries that on 6 May 1965, a significant date as I will shortly reveal, I missed a very important appointment – my annual aircrew medical at Gaydon. Mind you, I did have a good excuse for missing the appointment. On that very day instead of undergoing my medical examination I was enjoying a few post-prandial drinks on the veranda of the Fairy Point Mess in the company of a rather special BOAC air hostess who might easily have become Mrs Cunnane. I had met the lady in question about 10 days earlier whilst en route from Singapore to Darwin as part of the very secret duty I have already mentioned. I was travelling first class. I had a locked briefcase manacled to my right wrist but I did not have the keys for either the manacles or the briefcase. I did, however, know what was in the case because I had helped to pack the documents – indeed, I had written several of them. I was one of only two first class passengers on the flight and so the hostess and the Chief Steward both paid particular attention to my creature comforts.

High overhead the island of Bali, at about midnight local time, the hostess sat down alongside me, at my request I hasten to add. By that time I had savoured several aperitifs, consumed an excellent dinner washed down by a selection of fine wines, and knocked back a couple of Grand Marniers. I had declined the offer of a cigarette being a life-long non-smoker. After a pleasant conversation in which we swapped stories about the progress of our respective careers, I invited the lady to have dinner with me when we were both next in Singapore. To my delight, she readily agreed and returned forthwith to the galley, presumably to continue with her other duties. I then promptly fell into an alcohol-induced sleep thereby missing the only opportunity I have ever had to join the exclusive 40,000 Foot Club. I put my tiredness down to the rarefied atmosphere in the Boeing 707's pressurised cabin.

I was wakened rather abruptly by the Chief Steward leaning over me.

'Sorry to disturb you, Mr Cunnane' he said deferentially, but with a suggestion of a smirk on his face. 'The Captain requests your immediate presence on the flight deck.' He made it sound more like an order than an invitation.

I hurriedly struggled somewhat unsteadily to my feet and followed him, rehearsing in my mind the security briefing I had been given about what to do with the briefcase attached to my wrist in the event of a serious emergency occurring in flight. With some trepidation I allowed myself to be pushed through the narrow door which led into the darkened pilots' office. The 707 cockpit was small compared with the spaciousness of the modern Boeing 747's flight deck. There were seats for the two pilots, the flight engineer and little else.

'Captain, this is Mr Cunnane,' announced the Chief Steward. He then silently withdrew, closing the interconnecting door behind him.

My eyes quickly grew accustomed to the dim cockpit lighting. There seemed to be complete calm on the flight deck – no obvious signs of any emergency. Automatically scanning the skyline and the flight instruments, something an experienced pilot can do in a couple of seconds, I could see that it was a clear starlit night, that we were in straight and level flight at 41,000 feet, and that all four engines were operating normally.

'Ah, Mr Cunnane,' the Captain said grimly. 'I hope your briefcase is quite secure?'

He was a large moustachioed gentleman, perhaps 50 years of age. His safety harness was loosely fastened and so he was able, although with some difficulty because of his bulk, to turn and face me. He motioned me to sit on the occasional seat that the Flight Engineer had just folded down behind me.

'Yes, Captain,' I said meekly, sitting down and patting the briefcase reassuringly. 'Is there a problem?'

'I'm afraid there is,' replied the Captain. 'A serious problem.'

There was a pause before the three aircrew broke out laughing. I was nonplussed and then the Captain continued.

'What d'you mean by inviting my girl friend out to dinner in Singapore without first asking my permission? You Air Force types are all the same. In the airlines the Captain always has the first choice of the hostesses.'

It turned out that the two pilots and the engineer were all ex-RAF themselves. Having had a no doubt highly exaggerated account from the Chief Steward about the 'goings-on' in First Class, they thought it would be a jolly good wheeze to wind me up. Long haul civil flying always was boring for the air crews! Whether the Chief Steward fancied me himself and was jealous of my interest in the air hostess, or whether he was simply looking after the Captain's interests, I never found out. I was invited to remain on the flight deck for the rest of the trip to Darwin.

On that very day, 6 May 1965, and allowing for the time difference at almost exactly the same time as I was entertaining that air hostess to dinner in Fairy Point Officers' Mess instead of undergoing my annual aircrew medical, the newly-formed Royal Air Force Aerobatic Team was proudly giving its very first performance to a group of media gathered for the purpose at the Headquarters of the RAF's Central Flying School at Little Rissington, overlooking the beautiful Cotswold hills.

Only seven pilots performed with the Red Arrows that day, led by Flight Lieutenant Leo Jones, who was, and still is, known as Lee throughout the RAF. The occasion was first delayed and then spoilt by low cloud and rain but there was a lot of what we would today call media hype. A scratchy black and white film of the day's activities still exists and it is obvious that the whole event was all very gentlemanly. The reporters had been flown in from London in an RAF Argosy transport aircraft especially to see this new aerobatic team. They were frightfully polite, even obsequious, to the pilots they were interviewing and they and the pilots spoke English so beautifully! The reporters sat through a lengthy briefing session without a murmur and asked a number of anodyne questions – probably scripted in advance for the benefit of the film.

If only those present at Little Rissington had known what that first display by the RAF Aerobatic Team would lead to, it would undoubtedly have been better documented for posterity. The flying, however, was wonderful to watch. Such precision, such skill, such very low flying!

At this stage I need to make it clear that the air hostess has something in common with the grand opening theme in Tchaikovsky's first piano concerto. Just as Peter Ilyich's famous tune is never heard again in the rest of the concerto, that air hostess sadly plays no further part in my story, so there is no point in skipping ahead to the final chapter looking for a fairy tale ending. On the other hand, there have been so many odd coincidences in my life, especially since I have retired from the Red Arrows, that anything is possible by the time I have finished writing this book.

4

Rank, Power and Privilege

WHILST I WAS STILL IN SINGAPORE, staying at the Fairy Point Officers' Mess, the entire force of Valiant bombers was permanently grounded after a main spar failure in one particular airframe. Several hundred Valiant aircrew and ground crew were suddenly out of a job and had to be re-trained for other duties. Although I could have continued with the duties that had taken me to Singapore, I was still basically a Valiant AEO and so I was sent back to England and replaced in Singapore by a Vulcan-qualified officer. My job as an instructor at Gaydon had also disappeared with the demise of the Valiant. The powers-that-be had obviously heard about my writing abilities so they decided I was due for a desk job. I was posted to the Headquarters of No 3 Group at RAF Mildenhall as what is known as the P2 Officer, the Personnel Officer responsible for the careers of almost 700 junior officers – and I do mean 700. That number included many Air Electronics Officers like me, all of whom were either currently employed on Victor bombers or had been employed on the Valiants before they were taken out of service.

Some of the former Valiant AEOs took advantage of this unexpected break in their careers to apply for re-training as pilots. This may seem an odd thing to do but in fact many AEOs, myself included, had long thought that the writing was on the wall for our careers. Apart from a few odd jobs here and there, the only openings for AEOs were on the V Force and in Coastal Command. In spite of oft-repeated official promises that we had the same promotion prospects as pilots had, only one AEO had at that time reached the rank of wing commander and there seemed little likelihood of any of the rest of us ever reaching that or any higher rank. In fact one of my AEO friends did, many years later, retire in the rank of air commodore but there were by then only a few dozen AEOs still serving. It was widely believed in 1966 that a mandatory redundancy scheme for AEOs was on the cards.

It was almost unheard of for any aircrew officer to be permitted to re-train for another aircrew speciality, partly because by the time they applied they were usually above the age limit but mainly on cost grounds. The RAF took the not unreasonable view that if they permitted an AEO or navigator to be retrained as a pilot they would have to recruit someone else to replace him – and there was always the possibility that the AEO or navigator might fail the pilot training because the attrition rate was quite high at the flying training schools. It still is.

The AEOs who were determined that they wanted to re-train had to submit formal written applications through 'the usual channels' and all the applications that got past the station commanders eventually dropped into my in-tray because I was a link in the usual channels. I had to evaluate them all and make a recommendation on each one before I passed it along the corridor to the Air Officer Commanding, Air Vice-Marshal 'Splinters', later Air Chief Marshal Sir Denis, Smallwood. I was dismayed to see that most of the applications were lacking in substance and not likely to impress anyone. The shortest one, correctly laid out in the rather stilted formal Service language of the day, stated simply:

Sir,
I request that I may be re-trained as a pilot,
I have the honour to be,
Sir,
Your obedient servant,
Joe Bloggs,
Flight Lieutenant

That was it! No explanation, no pleading, no attempt to convince anyone that it was in the RAF's best interests that tens of thousands of pounds should be spent on re-training the writer.

I decided that I could do better than that. Purely as an academic exercise, I typed a lengthy letter explaining in some considerable detail why I thought I should be re-trained as a pilot even though I was five years over the maximum age limit. I still have a photocopy of that letter, now fading at the edges, and I am still proud of it and would not change a single word. I passed my letter through the connecting hatchway to my Boss, the Senior Personnel Staff Officer, Squadron Leader Dougie Fish, explaining to him that I did not expect the letter to go any further but I did want to make a point on behalf of all AEOs. I then forgot all about it and got on with my work. About a month later I was summoned to the AOC's office for what I expected to be one of our routine meetings to discuss personnel matters. I was ushered into the presence by the ADC, Flight Lieutenant Mike Pilkington.

'Ah, Tony, come in and sit down,' said Splinters, beaming all over his face. Now that was unusual! Air Vice-Marshal Smallwood was not noted for his affability and he had never before addressed me by my first name. He had an interesting rule about working hours. He used to say to his staff that they could start work at the scheduled time of 0800 hours or any later time they wished, as long as they got to their office before he got to his! He was one of the grand old school of AOCs. He once arrived by air at a station within his group for the annual AOC's Inspection. In those days the inspection always started with a formal parade. The Station Commander greeted him at his aircraft and they got into the car for the short drive to the parade ground. On the way there the AOC saw something, it is not recorded exactly what, that caused him displeasure.

'This station is not ready for my inspection. I'll be back in exactly seven days.'

With that he ordered the car to take him back to his aircraft. He arrived back at Mildenhall about an hour later, but many hours earlier than expected. A number of staff officers, having decided to have a few hours off while the AOC was away, were caught out and thereby incurred the AOC's wrath.

On another occasion he arrived at a station by road at 0630 hours, three hours earlier than the scheduled time, and went straight to the Airmen's Mess and ordered breakfast. A startled flight sergeant cook telephoned the Station Commander to tell him that the AOC was already on base, having breakfast. The Station Commander did not get any breakfast that day!

I sat down and waited expectantly, notebook and pen at the ready.

'I liked your letter,' said Splinters.

'Which particular letter was that, sir?' I asked innocently.

'The one asking for re-training as a pilot. I was so impressed with your arguments that I telephoned the Air Secretary, Sir Brian Burnett. He's an old friend of mine. He agreed that you should be given a chance. You start your pilots' course at South Cerney next month. Don't let me down!'

To say that I was flabbergasted would be an understatement. Some of my contemporaries were outraged when they heard what had happened; they thought I had abused my position. They were not in the least mollified when I passed the word around, discreetly so as not to upset the AOC, that I had not intended my letter to be taken seriously. I let it be known that I had forwarded all their own applications to the AOC for his attention and it was not my fault that up till then they had all been rejected. I suppose, if anything that made it worse in their eyes.

So it was that I became the RAF's oldest ever pilot student when I started my basic flying training at the age of 31. For several years afterwards I felt slightly guilty about the way I got the course which led to my third aircrew flying badge but quite a few AEOs did subsequently follow in my footsteps.

One of the tasks I was actively involved in and that kept me very busy in my final weeks at 3 Group HQ was the question of who should succeed to the vacant appointment of Officer Commanding 3 Group Standardisation Unit. 3 GSU, colloquially known as the Trappers, was a small unit responsible to the AOC for the professional standards and operational efficiency of all the aircrew in the Group. Although the RAF never had the spot promotion and 'hire and fire' mentality of the USAF Strategic Air Command, the Trappers were not popular because an adverse report could have far-reaching effects on your career. Following the recent demise of the Valiant, the post of Officer Commanding the GSU had to be filled by a Victor pilot and there was a raging argument amongst the senior staff officers at Mildenhall about the relative merits of the only two contenders. One was a highly experienced pilot nearing the end of his career and the other was a much younger and less experienced officer who was deemed to need a command appointment to help further his career. How could I, or anyone else, have known then, in 1966, that barely eight years later I would find myself appointed to that prestigious post?

The story of my passage through pilot training could fill a whole book, and perhaps it will one day. Suffice it to record here that throughout my training I was always a bit of an oddity because of my rank, age and past appointments. When I first joined the elementary flying course at South Cerney, just a few miles from Fairford where the Red Arrows were working up for their second season, all the other students, who had just completed their officer training, thought I must be a staff spy and I had great difficulty in getting them to talk to me at all, let alone use my first name.

On my basic flying training course at Leeming in North Yorkshire one of my fellow students was Chris Smallwood, son of the Air Marshal who had forwarded my application to the Air Secretary. Chris had been persuaded to join the RAF by his father but, to mix metaphors, he was like a fish out of water in the RAF and it came as no surprise to any of us when he voluntarily suspended himself from training early on in the course. That particular weekend I was going to London so I offered to take some of Chris' heavy luggage in my car to his home in Mildenhall. When I arrived to offload his belongings, I discovered to my dismay that Chris had not yet arrived in his sports car nor had he told his parents that he had suspended himself from pilot training. He had deliberately let me arrive first to break the news. The Air Marshal was incandescent with anger, to use a phrase that has very recently been used by a member of our Royal Family, allegedly.

My advanced jet training was done at Valley in Anglesey. Six out of the 20-odd students who should have been on the Gnat flying course were instead destined to be guinea pigs on a new course utilising Hunter fighter aircraft because there was a shortage of Gnats. On day one of the course the Chief Instructor apologised to the six of us and assured us that the training we would get would be just as good as if we had been on the Gnat course. He need not have worried! We were delighted to be flying the venerable but famous Hunter. Our aircraft were still painted up as front-line fighters whereas all the Gnats were in standard training command colours. The real perk, however, was that our solo flights were flown in Hunter Mk F6s – real single-seat operational aircraft. What is more our F6s had the original fully-rated engine, 10,000 lbs of thrust, not the down-rated version that many of the main force of Hunters were using. Since our aircraft were not fitted with the heavy under-wing fuel tanks that the front-line Hunters carried, the Valley F6s really did perform extremely well.

I managed to give myself one or two minor scares when flying solo in the Hunter but because we did not readily admit to that sort of thing I was probably not the only one. The best solo trip for me was the night supersonic sortie, flown on a clear moonlit night. I was briefed to climb to 45,000 feet, point the aircraft out over the Irish Sea to avoid dropping a supersonic boom over land, roll over into a 60 degree dive on full throttle and exceed Mach 1. It was quite exhilarating and eventually the ground radar controller gently suggested that I turn around and head back towards Wales as I was about the cross the border into the airspace of the Irish Republic.

On graduating from Valley I was posted to the Central Flying School at Little Rissington and I became what is usually known as a 'creamed-off' QFI – a first-tourist qualified flying instructor. The principle was that it was good for young trainee pilots to have instructors barely older than themselves. In fact, in my experience, most 'creamies' were not happy with their lot. They would have much preferred to have gone straight onto front line operational aircraft. In my case, at the age of 32, I was not a creamie in the intended sense of the word and I tended to refer to myself jokingly as a 'skimmed-off' QFI.

My first productive tour was as a QFI at the RAF College. After 18 months at Cranwell I obtained my A2 advanced instructor's category and I went on an exchange tour with the Pakistan Air Force. For most of the 1970s I was a Victor Tanker captain based at RAF Marham in Norfolk. At Marham I was once again both Station PRO and Editor of the Station magazine, secondary duty posts which I continued to hold for several years. Station commanders were by then positively keen to have stories about their stations and their personnel printed, especially when the station commander appeared in the accompanying photographs.

It was just after I arrived at Marham that I had a short story about flying read on BBC radio and I felt obliged to feature myself in one of my own news releases. Sadly, I did not hear the radio broadcast because at transmission time I was having my annual training session in the decompression chamber at the Aviation Medicine Training Centre at RAF North Luffenham in Rutland. I did, however, receive a letter from someone in Norway who asked if I would send him a copy of the script to help him with his study of English! In those Marham years I issued many news stories and had considerable success in organising media facilities on base.

For my last two years at Marham I was the Boss of the Trappers, now renamed 1 Group Standardisation Unit following the disbandment of 3 Group. After my long tour of duty on Victor Tankers I was posted onto a full-time Russian language course and spent the next decade in the murky world of intelligence, about which I must remain silent. It is the need-to-know principle at work: you do not need to know!

On 6 May 1989, exactly 24 years to the day after that first Red Arrows' display and my dinner engagement with the air hostess in Singapore, I went for an interview for what I thought was to be the newly-created post of Public Relations Officer for the Red Arrows. I was in for a surprise.

I had to take a day out from my job at RAF Sealand near Chester to attend the interview. For three years since leaving the intelligence world I had been Staff Officer for the North and West Region of the Air Training Corps: 'North and West – Biggest and Best' my Boss there, Group Captain John McMinn, always proclaimed proudly to anyone who would listen. Sadly, a few years later the biggest and best was disbanded in a cost-cutting exercise and the 180-plus cadet squadrons were transferred to other regions and the region itself was no more. Thankfully the disbandment was not put into effect until John McMinn had reached retiring age.

John and I were both RAF Retired Officers. Unlike officers in the Royal Air Force Volunteer Reserve and Royal Auxiliary Air Force, retired officers wear no special insignia. Apart perhaps from the visible signs of advancing years, I was indistinguishable from any active service squadron leader. One of the real perks of being an RO, although not everyone would see it as a perk, was that once appointed the individual could remain in service, should he or she so wish, until the age of 65. This always irked the Civil Service whose own servants were required to hang up their equivalent of flying boots at age 60. The Ministry of Defence branch of the Civil Service probably eyed the RO corps with a certain degree of jealousy because we were seen as officers who had passed their sell-by date and who, by hanging on to rank, power and privilege, were depriving real civil servants of jobs where they could hang on to rank, power and privilege. To counter that the Department of the MoD responsible for RO recruitment and careers always aimed to have the job specification for retired officer posts written in such a way that only retired officers were qualified to fill them. I changed that when I was about to retire.

From early 1989 I had been on the MoD mailing list of job vacancies. I was looking out for interesting jobs on the eastern side of the Pennines. Not that I was dissatisfied with my job at Sealand; far from it. I was, however, getting homesick for Yorkshire. I believe that all exiled Yorkshire folk sooner or later want to return to God's own county – and if they do not, then they should! It would have been polite, not to say proper, for me to have told John McMinn what I was about but I could not bring myself to tell him that I was considering a move. He was a thoroughly nice man and, apart from his habit of chain smoking which subjected me, his driver and the rest of his administrative staff to the unpleasant effects of secondary smoking, we got on extremely well together. Even John, however, would admit that he was rather possessive. Two years earlier he had moved me, with my willing connivance it has to be said, onto his Headquarters' staff from a lesser post within his command and I knew that he would try to persuade me not to leave Sealand.

Right from the outset there was considerable confusion about what the job at Scampton actually entailed. The paper shufflers had sent me two job specifications for what they presumably thought were two quite different posts at Scampton. I learned much later that there was only ever one job on offer. One of the job descriptions was for a Community Relations Officer, a retired officer post in the rank of flight lieutenant. A number of CRO posts had been created in early 1989 at major RAF flying stations dotted around the country to counter the increasing number of complaints from the general public about low flying aircraft and the noise they generated. The complainants in some parts of the country had been getting more and more vociferous; it seemed almost as though the writers were being orchestrated by some pressure group but, as far as I know, there was never any evidence to substantiate that. The RAF had decided that a group of strategically based CROs might be the answer. These officers would get to know their local communities and would visit some complainants at their homes to try and pacify them and explain why the RAF needed to fly at low level. I had read that job description with only passing interest because I was not at all interested in a flight lieutenant post, nor did that type of work appeal to me.

The other job specification was for a retired squadron leader to be appointed as the Red Arrows' PRO. That sounded much more appealing. The essential and desirable criteria listed for the post seemed to fit my qualifications exactly: I was a retired squadron leader pilot with media experience; I was, or rather had been, an A2 qualified flying instructor, although it was by no means clear why that was important; and I had graduated from various staff college courses. It seemed to me that a job which involved working with and writing about the Red Arrows was just my cup of tea. I was surely just the sort of person they needed and I put in my application forthwith. So that there could be no misunderstanding about which post I was applying for, I included with my formal application a covering letter in which I expressed my total disinterest in the Community Relations job and gave my reasons. To my great surprise an invitation to attend for an interview at RAF Scampton arrived on my desk at Sealand only a few days later, almost indecent haste I thought at the time because things do not normally move very quickly in the retired officers' world. Clearly Scampton was very anxious to fill the Red Arrows' post.

While I was in a downstairs office in the Station Headquarters building waiting to be summoned for the interview, I was handed another copy of the job description. Scrawled on the top of the form a handwritten note said, 'Mr Cunnane: for your information before the interview'. Those were the days before word processors were widely used. Reading through the form, it quickly became obvious to me that the typist at Scampton had been told to copy selected elements from the two job descriptions I had seen earlier and type them onto a new form, but the result was a botched job. There were some new items and some old ones and some that had later been crudely altered by hand without the original being sno-paked out. Furthermore, the typist had included the date, May 1988, that had appeared at the bottom of the two original job specifications. The post described in this new document bore only a passing resemblance to the one I had applied for. It was clearly a rush job but at least there was no mention of low flying complaints. Apparently I was wanted – but by whom and to do what?

The RAF has always believed in what it calls the three-prong command system whereby each commander from the Chief of the Air Staff downwards ideally has three immediate subordinates and so on, trifurcating down to the lowest level of the rank pyramid. This job seemed to be based on an inverted pyramid: the title had been changed to 'Public and Community Relations Officer' and the incumbent would have three different Bosses! The objectives were listed under three headings: RAF Scampton, Central Flying School – now based at Scampton, and Red Arrows. Under the first heading I read that the incumbent would be responsible to the Station Commander for running visits to the station 'by ex-serving members of previous resident squadrons including 617 Squadron, for liaison with the local media, administration of Command sponsored functions eg aerobatic competitions, and involvement in station charities.' Under the second heading the appointed officer would be responsible to the Commandant of the Central Flying School for the coordination of 'visits by Royalty and senior overseas military personnel to CFS.' There must be a lot of those, I mused. Finally I learned that the appointed officer would be responsible to the Red Arrows' Team Leader for 'the coordination of visits to the Red Arrows, liaison with the media on all matters concerning Team visits, lectures, and celebrity flying, and dealing with the media on all matters concerning aircraft accidents and incidents.' I thought it a little curious that dealing with accidents should be a major component of the job description but the Red Arrows had recently been through a bad patch with a series of spectacular accidents that had attracted much media attention and dented their public image. A very curious mixture indeed.

It looked as though there would be far more involved in this job than simply being the Red Arrows' public relations officer, the job that had caught my attention in the first place. I knew from my enquiries that because there were no other applicants and because I fitted precisely all the criteria in the job specification, the Interview Board was a formality and that I would have to be offered the job. There was no going back. Having barely had time to read once through the document, I was ushered upstairs into the interview room by Mrs Kathy Fleckney, the Civilian Administration Officer.

There were, as I recall, three officers sitting in judgement on me: Wing Commander John Dyer, who was in charge of the Administrative Wing and was the Station Commander's representative, one officer from CFS whose name now escapes me but who was presumably looking after the Commandant's interests, and Tim Miller, Leader of the Red Arrows. One person I fully expected to be a member of the Board in his professional capacity was missing, the Command Public Relations Officer, Keith Ansell, a professional civil servant employed in the Government Information Service. Keith had been the Command PRO when I had my short story broadcast on the BBC; he had had to get MoD approval for my story to be transmitted. I had been looking forward to meeting Keith again and so I telephoned him shortly after my interview board and expressed my surprise at his absence. He told me that he had been given the wrong date for the board and he thought it had been done deliberately so that he could not have any input into the proceedings – an example of the RAF not entirely trusting the Civil Service. Discreet enquiries I made after I had taken up the post confirmed that Keith had deliberately been kept off the appointment board.

I was scrutinised intently by the interrogators before being invited to sit down. I felt rather like the little boy in the W F Yeames painting that had so fascinated me at St James' School. I had prepared answers to questions about the Red Arrows. I would explain, if the opportunity arose, that I had flown with the Team, admittedly just for one familiarisation sortie back in 1967 when I was a student on the Central Flying School instructors' course. That, of course, did not necessarily fit me for the job but at least it showed I had had an interest in the Team – albeit 22 years earlier! As it happened, I knew quite a bit about the history of RAF Scampton from my own general service knowledge, and

I could talk at length about the Central Flying School because I was one of its graduates. There were questions that I wanted to ask the panel, given the opportunity. I wanted clarification on exactly what the job entailed; I needed to reiterate what I had put in my letter about not wanting to deal with irate members of the public on the thorny subject of low flying aircraft; I wanted reassurance about the difficulties of working for three masters at the same time. I wanted many things but my mind went blank as soon as I sat down and Squadron Leader Tim Miller launched his opening salvo.

'Why do you think you're the right person to be the Red Arrows' Public Relations Officer?'

For a few seconds, I stared blankly at Tim and I vividly remember the quickening of the heart beat and the rise in temperature that most people experience when caught out unexpectedly. I had a little panic. I had pondered that very question in the weeks between first hearing about the job and being invited for the interview but I had never got around to thinking about the answer. Was I really the right person? Surely the public relations officer for the world's premier aerobatic display team should be young and – well – female? Be that as it may, I had no answer ready for Tim's question and I had to resort to waffle. It must have been obvious to the members of the Interview Board that they had scored first. It was not a good start. At the age of 53 and having already served in the RAF for 36 years, I was applying for a new job but I had dismally failed to heed the advice I had given to countless young people and once again I had not prepared myself properly for the interview.

I cannot now remember anything more about the interview but a few days later I had a letter from Mrs Fleckney congratulating me and stating that I was 'the successful candidate' and asking when I could start. There was a form attached to the letter which had to be signed by my current Boss certifying that he was willing to let me go. That forced me into action; I could not delay any longer telling John McMinn what I was planning to do. The Group Captain was indeed very hurt when I told him that I would be leaving Sealand and I genuinely felt guilty about the way I had kept him in the dark about my plans.

5

Stitched Up!

BEFORE I STARTED THE NEW JOB AT SCAMPTON I was invited by Keith Ansell, the Command PRO, to take time out from Sealand to attend a three-day tri-service public relations course at Sunningdale. This invaluable and most interesting course used to be run in turn by the three single service Directors of Public Relations, each a one-star ranking officer. If the course had a fault it was that it tried to be all things to all people. The RAF students included some very junior officers who were destined to be Station PROs and who knew little or nothing about writing news releases and the organisation of media facilities. Others were like me, fairly well experienced in PR and about to take on a much wider range of responsibilities as Community Relations Officers. Students from the other two Services had a similar wide range of backgrounds and ranks. This diversity of talents made it difficult for the staff to run a programme that could keep all of us interested all of the time but, by and large, they succeeded. Added interest was provided by visiting lecturers from newspapers and radio and television stations who came in to tell us what they, or their news editors, expected from military news releases. Selected PROs and CROs already in post were invited to come and tell us how they were getting on with the job and give us the benefit of their experience. The senior single service officers on the directing staff told us what they expected from us and we had a series of classroom exercises where we could try our hand at writing press releases and being interviewed for radio and television.

To be honest, I found much of the course content rather boring but, more importantly, it soon became apparent to me that there was a fundamental weakness in the RAF public relations system. Without wishing to appear disrespectful to any of the incumbents during my time, the post of RAF Director of Public Relations in London seemed to be misnamed because he was not, as laymen may have imagined, the fount of all information about the RAF. The Director of Public Relations and his staff rarely issued stories to the media because that was the responsibility of the Defence Press Office, another quite separate organisation along the corridor. DPR, as our man was always known, was on the MoD Central Staffs and not in the direct RAF command chain, therefore protocol dictated he could not give orders to station commanders and as a result of that he had no authority to direct PROs and CROs or their assets. He could not, for example, direct where the RAF Bands, the RAF Parachute Team, and the Red Arrows and other display aircraft would perform. One DPR told me wryly that he seemed to spend most of his working day waiting to be summoned to the top floor, where the Minister and the senior RAF chiefs had their offices, to explain yet another PR disaster. All the DPRs in my time could do was tell us PROs and CROs the overall PR policy, such as it was, and then hope that we would be able to persuade our station commanders to let us do what was required. It would have been much more sensible, I thought, if we all worked for DPR, acting as his point of contact at the sharp end. Only as I neared the end of my 11 years in post did the system start to change but that was a long way ahead.

By happy chance the Sunningdale course I was on was run by an old friend of mine, Air Commodore Mike Barnes, another former AEO who had retrained as a pilot about the same time as I had done. When I told him I was going to Scampton he was very surprised, not that it was I who was going but that there was a Retired Officer post there. It was he, Mike told me over a beer in the Sunningdale Mess, who had persuaded the Air Force Board to establish 18 Community Relations Officers but it had never been his intention to have one based at Scampton; he intended them to be at the stations which generated the most low flying and noise complaints – Coningsby, Waddington and Leeming, for example. He told me that the Red Arrows had been trying for a couple of years or so to have a dedicated public relations post established but they had failed due to lack of money to pay for it. When I told him about the confusing job specifications I had been given, he said that he believed I had been conned into accepting a job I had not applied for. I was beginning to think he might be right.

I reported for duty at RAF Scampton at 8am on 4 September 1989 to find that I was first in, apart from the key orderly who was busily occupied switching on the water heaters in various offices so that the staff could have their early morning fix of caffeine as soon as they arrived. The Central Flying School Headquarters and the Ground Training Squadron occupied a single-story, prefabricated building that had originally been built as the Station Operations Centre in V Bomber days when it was one of the most secret places on the station. To be truthful, the whole building was a bit of an eyesore and completely out of keeping with the rest of the station.

I made my way through the maze of tatty corridors. I knew where my new office was because a few days earlier I had called in to see the officer who would be my immediate superior, Wing Commander Mike Hall. He held the post then called Wing Commander Air, the senior staff officer working for the CFS Commandant, Air Commodore Bruce Latton. My office was in one corner of the building at the end of a corridor leading to a fire exit. I later discovered that this office had, until a couple of days before my arrival, been a storeroom. No-one had wanted to use it as an office because in winter it was the coldest room in the building, being at the end of the central heating distribution pipery. It was a tiny affair just large enough to hold a cupboard, an upright chair, a desk on which stood a telephone and two empty document trays, one labelled In and the other Out, and two rather faded easy chairs. That was, in fact, all the office did contain. There was a small wooden plaque on the door bearing my name: at least I was expected. I made a note of my telephone number and gazed out of the window over the deserted airfield.

My cobwebby office window was protected by a grimy, fixed mesh security screen, one of many hangovers left at Scampton from the Vulcan days. The screen prevented me from poking my head outside but, by craning my neck, I could look towards the north and see the 'Waterfront'. The CFS flight lines at Little Rissington had been called the Waterfront when I had been a student flying instructor there over 20 years earlier. No-one seems to know the derivation of the name, possibly something to do with the parent Service of the very first CFS Commandant in 1912, but the name stuck when CFS moved to Scampton in September 1984. I could see the four large aircraft hangars that had been built in the mid-thirties, 1 Hangar the nearest and 4 Hangar, current home of the Red Arrows, the most distant. The hangars had been laid out on a gentle curve, as they had been at the many airfields constructed with commendable prescience in preparation for World War 2. The idea was to make it more difficult for enemy aircraft to destroy the entire line in a single pass with a stick of bombs.

I knew that 2 Hangar had housed the Dam Busters for about 10 weeks in 1943 and I also knew that the grave of Wing Commander Guy Gibson's black Labrador dog was located in front of that hangar. The dog had been called Nigger, which in those pre-political correctness days had no racist connotations and was a very common name for black cats and dogs. Poor Nigger had been killed when he was struck by a car just outside the Guardroom on the A15 a few hours before his master led the Lancasters into the air on Operation Chastise on 16 May 1943. Beyond the hangars, out on the airfield proper, was the modern Air Traffic Control tower built after the main runway had been extended in the mid-1950s, when I was temporarily based at RAF Hemswell, to accommodate the needs of the Vulcans. The original ATC tower between 2 and 3 Hangars had to be replaced because the controllers could see neither end of the lengthened runway from that position.

Immediately in front of 4 Hangar I could see the Red Arrows' flight line, a huge expanse of concrete constructed especially for the Team at great expense when they moved to Scampton in 1983. The distinctive red British Aerospace Hawk aircraft were being towed out, one by one, from the hangar onto the line ready for the day's activities. My gaze roamed anti-clockwise past another vast aircraft parking area in front of 1 and 2 Hangars known as Echo Dispersal, allegedly haunted by Gibson's black Labrador dog or a close relative depending upon which story you listen to. Jet Provost aircraft were being readied on Echo Dispersal for the day's flying programme. Across the airfield straight ahead beyond Echo was the escarpment known as the Lincoln Cliff, invisible from ground level. That was the direction the bombers of 617 Squadron had taken on that fateful night of 16 May 1943 and there right in front of me was the very grass from which they had taken off – long before the concrete runways had been constructed. In fact Scampton airfield goes back almost 30 years before the Dam Busters were formed.

It was in 1911 that the dream of a British military air force was born when the Prime Minister of the day, Herbert Asquith, instructed the Committee of Imperial Defence to suggest ways of creating an efficient air force. In due course the Committee recommended the formation of a flying corps comprising five main elements: a naval wing, a military wing, a reserve force, an aircraft factory at Farnborough, and a flying school. In May 1912 the Royal Flying Corps was established. The flying school element formed at Upavon on Salisbury Plain – the predecessor of today's Central Flying School. I will come back to CFS later because it features large in the Red Arrows' story.

Newspapers at the time reported that Parliament had voted £300,000 for setting up the Royal Flying Corps. The Military Wing was to have seven airplane squadrons each with 12 machines. The Royal Aircraft Factory would train mechanics, test airplanes and engines, as well as undertake the reconstruction of damaged machines. Although the Government and the military authorities had already recognised that there would be a place for aerial machines in any future wars, by the time the first World War broke out in 1914 no-one seemed to have given much attention to the question of how the mainland of Britain was to be protected from possible aerial attack. It was then that vested interests came into play. The specialized aviation requirements of the Royal Navy made it appear, to the admirals at least, that a separate organization was desirable, and so on 1 July 1914 the naval wing of the Royal Flying Corps was hived off to become the Royal Naval Air Service. After much argument between the War Office and the Admiralty, the task of defence of the homeland was passed to the RNAS in September 1914, presumably because the Zeppelins were approaching from the sea. The RNAS failed to stop the Zeppelin raids and so, no doubt to the great embarrassment of the admirals of the day, home defence duties were handed off to the RFC early in 1916.

The Zeppelins were slow, unwieldy, and highly flammable beasts. They had a maximum speed of about 140 kph and could climb to a height of some 14,000 feet. They each carried five machine guns and

2,000kg of bombs. They cruised over England for as long as eight or nine hours at a time dropping their bombs with impunity and frequently at random. Their navigation aids were not up to much. Contemporary reports suggest that many German pilots headed across the North Sea in the general direction of Lincolnshire and hoped to come across either the Wash to the south or the Humber estuary to the north. They could then pinpoint their position accurately and re-plan the route to their selected targets accordingly. Because the Zeppelins often came by night, the home defence squadrons too had to be capable of operating by night and that must have been a truly alarming prospect for those early aviators.

In March 1916 ten new squadrons were formed specifically for home defence purposes and within three months a barrage line of searchlights, anti-aircraft guns and aerodromes had been established throughout the Eastern Counties and especially around the Scampton area north of Lincoln. The flying squadrons were initially equipped mainly with the ubiquitous and once reliable BE2 and Avro 504G, aircraft which were becoming obsolescent and no longer suitable for further service on the front line in France.

The main problem facing the British pilots was that of finding the Zeppelins in the darkness. The RFC aircraft had no radio or radar and only very primitive flying instruments and so the pilots must have been extremely courageous. They used to climb to a safe height and then throttle their engine back to idle from time to time so that they could listen for the familiar drone of the Zeppelin's engines. There were more flying accidents as a result of trying to land in darkness than there were Zeppelins shot down.

The home defence squadrons usually set up their operational Headquarters in a suitably spacious civilian house commandeered by the War Office for the purpose. Each squadron had three flights of aircraft and crews detached to aerodromes known as flight stations. Because the aeroplanes in use at that time had a very limited operating range, it was found necessary to establish a system of relief landing grounds at convenient locations throughout a particular squadron's territory. 33 Squadron for example, whose HQ was in Gainsborough just a few miles west of Scampton, made use of some twenty landing grounds scattered throughout Lincolnshire as well as parts of Yorkshire and Nottinghamshire. These landing grounds mostly consisted of a single field, or in some cases two or three fields combined, for which the owner was paid a small retainer by the War Office to keep the site under grass and not ploughed. An airman was often billeted with the farmer and supplied with a telephone link to the nearest flight station so that when an aeroplane was likely to land the fields could first be cleared of livestock. Some of the more frequently used relief landing grounds boasted a permanent staff of three and a couple of wooden huts for living quarters and stores such as fuel, flares and spare parts.

By the middle of 1916 the need for front-line aircrews had grown to such an extent that training aerodromes began to spring up throughout the country. Lincolnshire's open countryside, sparse population and lack of industrial haze made it very suitable for flying operations. Furthermore, the Lincoln cliff to the north and west of Lincoln was very useful because the prevailing south-westerly winds enabled aircraft to take off from the high ground heading towards the lower ground. The aircraft could, if necessary, gain extra speed by descending after passing over the cliff edge before climbing safely away, rather like aircraft catapulted off the deck of an aircraft carrier. Although there is only an average of 100 feet difference between the top and bottom of the cliff along its length, many aircraft, in both world wars, were saved because of its presence.

Scampton's association with flying began in the latter part of 1916, initially as the home for a searchlight unit which provided light to illuminate the enemy for the aircraft of 33 Squadron. The aerodrome proper at Scampton did not come into being until the beginning of 1917 when the first aircraft arrived. The aerodrome could have been called Scampton, Aisthorpe or Brattleby, the three nearest villages just over the edge of the Lincoln Cliff, and in fact it was first called Brattleby. The aerodrome was built, if built is the right word, on land belonging to Aisthorpe Farm and it occupied the area which is now more or less at the centre of the present RAF Station, right outside the window of my new office. As it was intended for use as a training airfield, and expected to be needed only for the duration of the war, the buildings were mostly temporary wooden huts although there were six rather more substantial aircraft sheds. One aerial photograph of the site still exists.

The village of North Carlton, picturesquely situated half way up and halfway down the Lincoln Cliff just to the south west of Scampton has a magnificent old church in which can be seen a memorial to these Royal Flying Corps wings and squadrons and a brief history which I wrote in 1992 for Lord and Lady Monson who live in the village. North Carlton village is exactly in line with the modern 9,000 ft long runway at Scampton and so the Vulcans, until 1982, flew over the village at very low level. The Vulcans were replaced by the aircraft of the Central Flying School including the Red Arrows. Most of the villagers are proud to have the Red Arrows performing so close to them but, it has to be said, there are one or two who find the noise irritating. At least the Red Arrows do not make anything like the noise that the mighty Vulcans made. South Carlton, at the top of the narrow winding road leading out of North Carlton, was the site of another aerodrome, larger and more important than Brattleby, but it is now underneath the Lincolnshire Show Ground.

Flying in those first world war days was not only inherently dangerous but at times a rather carefree affair. Scampton's location on the edge of the escarpment made it an ideal site for playing silly games. The idea of one such game was to simulate a crash by disappearing from sight into the low-lying ground out to the west beyond the ridge close to what is now the busy A1500 road, known locally as Tillbridge Lane. This pastime was not without its hazards as one pilot was to discover when, after spinning spectacularly out of sight of his colleagues out on the airfield, he returned rather sheepishly shortly afterwards with a badly damaged undercarriage, having hit the ground before completing his recovery. Another jolly game was to fly low and fast over the surrounding countryside, switch off the engine and shout remarks at unsuspecting pedestrians. I can find no records of what the pilots actually shouted at the pedestrians but I am sure it was done in a very refined accent!

A curious sight which was occasionally to be observed was that of an aeroplane ejecting a chicken as it flew low over Scampton airfield. Various explanations for this strange behaviour have been suggested ranging from morbid curiosity on the part of the pilots to officially sanctioned top secret experiments connected with the release of carrier pigeons. However, for the unfortunate birds the outcome was usually the same: they would finish up on the Officers' Mess dining table. These days the two Red Arrows' soloists, the Synchro Pair, can often be seen disappearing from sight over the Lincoln Cliff but it is all legal and above board. The Red Arrows' Hawks occasionally come into high speed contact with birds, always with fatal results for the birds, but that is something the pilots try to avoid, not encourage.

The lack of inhibiting flying regulations, or a blatant disregard for them, towards the end of World War 1 was perhaps encouraged by the almost complete lack of airfield facilities. Lieutenant, later Air Vice-Marshal, Arthur Fiddament used to tell his friends how he crashed into a tree at Scampton while attempting to land in fog with the guidance of matches being struck by Mr J C Ward, the owner of Aisthorpe House. No pilot these days would even contemplate landing in fog without the aid of sophisticated precision approach aids. However, Lieutenant Fiddament had no alternative because he was running out of fuel and he had no parachute. With a very low landing speed of perhaps 30 to 40 miles an hour he trusted in luck and local knowledge of the terrain and survived to tell the tale. I cannot imagine that the light from Mr Ward's matches contributed much and such historical records as are extant do not relate how Mr Ward knew where and when to strike his matches, nor how Lieutenant Fiddament, without the benefit of radio, knew that matches were being struck to light his path.

It is a little known fact that towards the end of the 1914-18 war an ever-increasing flow of pilots began to arrive from America to complete their training before joining Royal Flying Corps squadrons. Many Americans trained at Scampton. To assist in the handling of these students a small United States Army Air Corps detachment was set up at Scampton under the command of Major Frankie Scanlon. On the staff of his unit was a medical officer, an expert jazz pianist who taught Scampton's Adjutant a good deal about syncopation. The Adjutant later put this to good use when he became famous as big band leader Jack Payne.

After the Armistice, flying training began to be scaled down until it finally ceased altogether at the end of December 1918. In April 1919 the remaining aeroplanes and personnel were moved out. Royal Air Force Scampton, as it now was, remained in existence until early 1920 when it closed down completely. Within a short time all the buildings had been removed, the field boundaries were back in their original positions and Aisthorpe Farm was back under the plough.

During the early 1930s it became evident that World War 1 had not been the war to end all wars as had been fervently hoped. The situation in Germany, where Hitler's National Socialists were fast gaining power, gave cause for concern over the future security of this country. As a result, various schemes were started to re-equip and enlarge the armed forces. From these rearmament programmes came a demand for new airfields for the expanding bomber force and one of the sites chosen was that of the old aerodrome at Scampton.

When it was announced in 1935, the year that I was born, that there was once again to be an airfield at Scampton, the local population was not exactly overjoyed by the news. However, the necessary land was requisitioned and construction work was quickly put in hand. The first building to be erected was a workmen's hut at the side of Ermine Street, the old Roman Road leading due north from Lincoln, now the A15 trunk road. Within a matter of days this hut was 'accidentally' burned down. Nevertheless, work went ahead and on 27 August 1936 Station Headquarters was formed and the station opened as part of 3 Group of Bomber Command.

Scampton airfield occupied the same site as it had done in 1918 but with the addition of some land to the south of the original aerodrome. Aisthorpe House, however, was still on the boundary of the airfield and was occupied by Mr R Fieldsend who was farming the land to the north. The house was an obstruction to flying and eventually the inevitable happened. On the night of 31 August 1937 a Heyford bomber of 9 Squadron flown by Pilot Officer Torkington-Leech crashed into the building while attempting to land. Fortunately no-one was killed although Mr Fieldsend and his daughter were slightly injured and no doubt shocked. The pilot was hurt rather more seriously. Following that accident the remains of the house were demolished and the family's land to the north of the airfield was absorbed into the camp. The construction programme was almost complete by the time war broke out. Most of the wooden huts had been replaced by permanent buildings, including the four large aircraft hangars, and dozens of married quarters had appeared in Ermine Crescent, Trenchard Square, and First and Second Avenues. All those buildings still stand today.

I was abruptly woken from my reverie by the noise of people clattering along the corridor outside my office. The staff of CFS Headquarters were arriving for their daily toil and I wandered around the offices introducing myself. I soon found where the communal coffee bar was, right at the far end of the building, adjacent to what was always known affectionately as the Greasy Spoon – the aircrew restaurant.

It was good to see there was a Greasy Spoon. Since my V Bomber days, when crews were thought to need extra sustenance to keep them going during the rigours of high-altitude flying, I had been used to the facilities of aircrew restaurants. At both Gaydon and Finningley I had been living in the Officers' Messes so I always availed myself of a full cooked breakfast before going to work. On flying days Mess breakfast was followed at about 9am by another 'full fry' in the Greasy Spoon. We always took with us into the air a large box of in-flight rations which usually consisted of well-filled sandwiches various, chocolate bars of our own choice, crisps and fruit. After a typical four-hour sortie we usually had another cooked two or three course meal in the aircrew restaurant and then, if one was quick and the flight de-briefing was short, the livers-in could race to the Officers Mess in time for late afternoon tea of toast and preserves before showering, changing and reporting to the Mess dining room for the normal three or four course dinner.

At one stage delicious chocolate marshmallows wrapped in silver foil became all the rage and most crews asked for a supply to be included in their in-flight rations box. Soon, these items of desire, often called chocolate teacakes, became the subjects of some rather unscientific in-flight experiments.

In normal peacetime flying conditions the crew cabin in the Valiants, Victors and Vulcans was pressurised to maintain the equivalent of about 8,000 feet even though the aircraft was actually flying at well in excess of 40,000 feet. This made for a comfortable working environment and there was no need for the crew to keep an oxygen mask clamped to their face. Modern airliners maintain the cabin pressure at the equivalent of about 6,000 feet for the same reasons. In so-called combat conditions, the cabin pressure in the V Bombers would have been maintained at the equivalent of 25,000 feet. The reason for this was that should the aircraft cabin be punctured due to enemy action, the subsequent explosive decompression from 25,000 feet to the real altitude of upwards of 40,000 feet would be much less dramatic than a decompression from 8,000 feet.

Since Gaydon was a training station, new crews had to practice the procedures for flying with a cabin altitude of 25,000 feet. It was uncomfortable, very cold and usually quite boring. During one of these practices someone noticed that as the cabin pressure reduced, the marshmallow inside the chocolate teacakes expanded sufficiently to crack the chocolate shell. A fair percentage of the bulk of marshmallow is, of course, made up of air bubbles trapped within the gelatinous mass. Word quickly spread and this discovery kept crews fascinated for several days. Marshmallows were stripped of their silver foil coverings and laid out on various flat surfaces in the cabin. Notes were kept and tables were constructed to show which brand of chocolate marshmallow was the most resistant to reducing air pressure. Some aircrew discovered that the expansion was so great that they could no longer put the whole teacake into their mouth in one piece. The taste, however, appeared to be unaffected!

It was inevitable that sooner or later someone would take a batch of chocolate teacakes airborne on a sortie which involved a deliberate complete depressurisation of the cabin. That 'someone' was one of the more mature instructor captains. Rapid, or explosive, decompression was a drill that was practised on training sorties when the aircraft was flying at over 40,000 feet. The student captain of the aircraft was required to initiate an immediate emergency descent to a more hospitable altitude. It was always an exciting manoeuvre which sometimes had an interesting effect on one's stomach and intestines as internal body gases rapidly expanded. When the instructor captain operated the switch to depressurise the cabin on this occasion, there was the expected loud bang and the cabin, as usual, filled with icy cold vapour. He had completely forgotten about the marshmallows on the ledge above the instrument panels. They instantly disintegrated explosively and bits of chocolate and shredded marshmallow splattered all over the windscreens and instruments panels. This rather distracted the pilots from the immediate actions they were supposed to take and so thereafter marshmallows were banned on all sorties at Gaydon. Security considerations and the need-to-know principle, together with the RAF's wish to avoid advertising, precluded me from making a news story out of these experiments – until now!

The Greasy Spoon at Scampton when I arrived on the scene was a convenience more than a necessity. It enabled instructors and students to have their midday meal in the CFS building rather than traipsing the mile to the Officers Mess. I quickly discovered that many non-flying officers used to take lunch in the aircrew restaurant because it was a good place for a bit of socialising and gossip. Naturally, as the public relations officer I soon joined in this practice and I found it was an excellent way of discovering what was going on around the station.

I had brought my own computer and associated bits and pieces from home and I installed them in my bare office. At this time, 1989, centralised pools of professional typists were becoming a thing of the past except for those serving the most senior officers who were probably too old fashioned anyway to embrace the new technology. Many junior officers were discovering the pleasures of computers, word processors and databases, and they found that it was fun to do all their own typing and record keeping. Curious is it not that a mundane task such as typing a letter, a lowly job that in the past had been done by mere typists, suddenly became suitable for commissioned officers? It is now a generally accepted fact that letting officers do their own typing resulted in a dramatic drop in productivity. It was all too easy to spend a lot of time fiddling with layouts and fonts. The finished documents might have looked pretty but did they convey more information? Of course not!

One CFS staff officer was detailed as the IT manager and in due course that secondary duty grew and grew until it consumed so much of his time that another officer had to be appointed to do his primary work. By the time I retired there was a complete Computer Squadron at Cranwell, with several rooms full of hugely expensive state of the art equipment and lots of people to operate and maintain it. So much better than half a dozen typists in a typing pool but did the work get done more quickly or more economically, I wonder. The IT man at Scampton in 1989 was in much demand because he held the budget for new equipment and software. He seemed to have a free hand to buy whatever equipment and software he fancied but, as the new boy, I got nothing from him. No-one had made financial provision in the budget for any equipment for me so I had little choice but to use all my own equipment and I continued to do so until the day I retired.

On that first morning at Scampton, before I had even met any of the Red Arrows, a squadron leader from the Operations Wing Headquarters called into my office and dropped a large pile of files on my desk.

'The Station Commander tells me that from now on you'll be handling all the noise and low flying complaints,' he said cheerily. 'Here's a few of the outstanding ones for you to be getting on with. Best of luck!'

I had been well and truly stitched up.

6

What's in a Name?

IN THE LATE MORNING OF MY FIRST DAY AT SCAMPTON I put the pile of flying complaints files to one side after giving them no more than a cursory glance and then walked along the Waterfront to 4 Hangar to introduce myself to the Red Arrows. The walk took about 20 minutes, longer than I had imagined because the large gap between 2 and 3 hangars, where once had stood the Air Traffic Control Tower, was a designated aircraft parking apron and pedestrians had to make a long detour. This is going to be great, I thought. A 40-minute round trip every time I needed to go to the Red Arrows – unless I used my own car at my own expense. I found Squadron Leader Tim Miller, whom I was meeting for the first time since he had been the chairman of my appointment board, in his office on the first floor and he greeted me with a rather quizzical look on his face. After the briefest of welcomes, we went along the corridor to the coffee bar where most of his pilots were sitting around.

While Tim was making me a cup of coffee, he introduced me to his pilots as a bunch without going around each one individually. From a very young age I have always been very bad at remembering the names of people to whom I am introduced. I can forget someone's name an instant after being told it. Even worse, I can suddenly have a mental block trying remember the name of a person I know perfectly well. Someone, I cannot now remember who, once told me that the two problems were related and that worrying about them simply made matters worse. It was always very embarrassing for me until I learned to make a joke of my shortcoming. People who know me well have got used to the fact that I may suddenly forget their name. As a new girl friend said to me on our second meeting when I had, momentarily, forgotten her name, 'I can see I made a real impression on you, George!'

A short leap ahead in time now to give you an example of the scale of my problem. One day in January 1994 that excellent photographer Lord Lichfield was visiting the Red Arrows to fly with the Team and take some airborne photographs that he wished to use in his much sought after limited edition calendars. I met Lord Lichfield first thing in the morning, escorted him to the Medical Centre for his pre-flight medical and afterwards took him to the flying clothing room to be fitted out with his equipment for the flight. I felt protocol required that I should introduce the airman to the Earl, even though there was no doubting who he was. He had already told me that he did not wish to be addressed as 'My Lord'.

'Sir,' I said to Lord Lichfield, opting for a safe but formal mode of address, 'may I introduce Senior Aircraftman Jones who will measure you for your flying helmet. Jones, this is Lord Snowdon.'

'Tony,' said Lord Lichfield with a laugh as he shook hands with Jones, 'call me Patrick – or sir if you really must – but please don't ever mix me up with Snowdon!'

No such problem with the Red Arrows' names because they are embroidered onto their flying suits. I suddenly realised, as the various pilots nodded in my direction, that I had met one of them before. It had been about seven years earlier, in the aftermath of the Falklands War, when I was serving with the Joint Services' Intelligence Centre at Ashford in Kent. This particular pilot had been shot down and taken prisoner, badly injured. When he was repatriated at the end of the war he was sent first to the RAF Rehabilitation Centre at Headley Court for medical checks. As the senior RAF officer on the staff, I was despatched by my colonel to Headley Court to debrief this officer about his experiences.

It had been a traumatic as well as a painful experience and the probing questions that I had been specifically briefed to ask him about his treatment after capture clearly caused him a lot of distress although he cooperated willingly and honestly and it was quite obvious to me that he had nothing to reproach himself about. My subsequent confidential written report was given a much wider circulation than I had been told it would get. Instead of being distributed only to senior commanders, who were meant to learn lessons from it, it was made available for all aircrew throughout the RAF to read and it undoubtedly caused considerable, and totally undeserved, embarrassment for the pilot. When we had eye contact briefly in the Red Arrows' crew room, we merely nodded at each other and I decided it would be best to let him make the first approach to me, if he wished to do so. He did not do so and right up to the day he left the Team a couple of months later at the end of his three year tour of duty, he did not speak to me. I do not criticise him for that but I never did have an opportunity to tell him my side of the story and I have always regretted that.

I wondered if word had got around the pilots about my report of his Falklands debriefing and that that was the reason I was received cautiously and with barely disguised suspicion. It was not the reason, it was something quite different and I only learned what many weeks later. I had had a predecessor about whom I knew nothing and that came as quite a revelation, especially as I found out, not from anyone in an official capacity but through a casual remark made by a clerk in Station Headquarters. It seemed to me as though there was an official conspiracy to keep me in the dark.

The person who had taken on the job back in December 1988 had still been serving as a wing commander at that time although shortly about to retire. He was appointed as the full-time PRO for the Red Arrows without any responsibility for the Station or CFS and he had turned up at Scampton during his terminal leave – additional paid leave granted to retiring personnel to enable them to clear up their affairs. The wing commander, whom I knew slightly, had served at Scampton as the commanding officer of a Vulcan unit much earlier in his career. When he arrived at the Red Arrows he was allocated desk space in a cramped corner of the already over-crowded administrative office in 4 Hangar. I was told that one of the first things he did was encourage everyone from the lowest rank upwards to call him by his first name. What a nice friendly idea, you may think, but you would be wrong, in my opinion.

These days the practice in most non-military organisations with hierarchical rank structures, such as the Civil Service and many large businesses, is to encourage everyone from the lowliest bottle-washer to the Chief Executive to refer to each other by their first names. This is definitely frowned on in the RAF. Non-commissioned personnel do not call officers by their first name, except perhaps when taking part in team sports. The reverse also used to be true but these days many officers, especially the younger element, refer to airmen and NCOs by their first names. Officers of flight lieutenant rank and below are on first name terms with each other but are supposed to call all squadron leaders and above sir. In the higher ranks it is the custom to call any officer senior to yourself sir. I was told that the new wing commander's invitation to everyone on the Red Arrows to use his first name caused quite a stir and raised a lot of eyebrows. Normal RAF protocol would have required everyone on the Team, from the Leader downwards, to call him sir. Right up until the day I retired I still called wing commanders sir even though I had been a squadron leader longer than many of them had been in the RAF. It is a simple, straightforward system that ensures everyone knows his or her place in the greater scheme of things.

Many young people these days seem to have the idea that calling someone 'sir' implies inferiority or subservience; to me it simply denotes respect for their position rather than their person. It has, for example, always been the custom for a student pilot to call his flying instructor sir irrespective of either's age or rank. As the RAF's oldest ever pilot student, I frequently flew with instructors who were junior to me both in age and rank and I called them all sir without feeling at all subservient or inferior.

In the RAF, flying instructors were entitled to call their students by first name or surname as they saw fit. Generally I called my students at Cranwell by their first name, to the annoyance of one of my old-fashioned flight commanders, but there were times when it was useful to summon your student from their crew room by surname only. The cadets on 95 Entry knew that if I summoned Martin Stoner by his first name all was well, but if I summoned him by his surname they knew that he had just flown a bad trip or had upset me for some other reason. Martin eventually served with the Red Arrows and retired from the RAF as a wing commander. When we meet nowadays, usually at Red Arrows' annual dinners, we have a little ritual on greeting each other: I call him sir and he calls me sir. We know what we mean!

The Army has always been much stricter than the RAF about the use of first names and there is still a large gulf between commissioned and non-commissioned personnel. There is an old and rather sick story which tells how a sergeant major got around his Company Commander's difficult problem of informing a private soldier that his father had just died. The CSM got the whole troop on parade and dressed them formally in three ranks.

'All those with fathers, one pace forwards MARCH!' bellowed the sergeant major, and then after the briefest of pauses he continued, 'Stand fast, Smith!! Where d'you think you're going?'

The Cranwell version of this story used to go along the following lines.

'Come in Smith, sit down,' says the flight commander soothingly to the cadet. 'Tell me, what does your mother call you?'

'Tom, sir,' says Smith, beaming, thinking that he is about to be complimented for his progress.

'Well, Tom,' snaps the flight commander, 'you've failed! Start packing.'

It seems that the wing commander PRO, my predecessor, had discovered soon after his arrival that a great deal of his time would be spent organising and hosting daily groups of visitors comprising school children, aircraft spotters' clubs, Rotary Clubs, Women's Institutes and other specialist groups, as well as a continuous stream of ordinary fans of the Team. He quickly became disillusioned because he considered such tasks, normally given as a secondary duty to the most junior officers, as menial and beneath him – or so I was told. Perhaps, like me, his Job Specification had not been properly prepared. He went off on Christmas leave apparently and was never seen again. The whole episode, which lasted only a few weeks, certainly coloured the Team's thinking about Retired Officers and caused all ranks of the Red Arrows to look upon ROs as a very peculiar breed. The post was eventually re-advertised with changes to the job specification and chain of command. It took the best part of eight months to effect those changes; that was where I came in.

Just as I was leaving the Red Arrows' crew room after an uncomfortable few minutes, Tim called after me, with a grin on his face.

'By the way, Tony, on 4th October we're having an open day to celebrate the Team's 25th Anniversary. All the major European teams will be here; there's bound to be a lot of media interest because it will be the first time that six major teams have appeared on the same programme. Your first job for us will be to organise the media at that event.'

With that parting shot, I walked back to my office at the other end of the station in a rather despondent frame of mind.

That afternoon I had a short introductory interview with the Commandant of the Central Flying School, Air Commodore Bruce Latton, who sadly died in October 2001 at an early age. The command and control arrangements at Scampton were always confusing to visitors. The Air Commodore was the senior officer on the base but he was not the Station Commander. CFS Headquarters was one of several lodger units at Scampton, the Red Arrows Team was another. The Station Commander, Group Captain Richard Howard, had been a student on the course ahead of me at the Central Flying School. He was known as a rather difficult man to get on with and if he remembered me from CFS he never let on. He managed the station, the airfield and all its facilities; CFS Headquarters and the other lodger units made use of them. To further complicate matters, the Station Commander deputised for the Commandant during his leave and other absences.

The Commandant had just a small HQ staff. The senior post, Wing Commander Air, was then filled by Wing Commander Mike Hall whose office was just across the corridor from mine. One of the wing commander's main tasks was the overall supervision of the Red Arrows' flying activities – and me, as it turned out. In the early 1990s after Mike Hall's departure, the title of the post was changed to Wing Commander Royal Air Force Aerobatic Team, always abbreviated to Wing Commander RAFAT. That title better described what the incumbent's responsibilities were but outsiders and civilians usually thought, not surprisingly, that he was the Boss of the Red Arrows. In Station Routine Orders and other correspondence there regularly appeared an announcement stating that Wing Commander RAFAT was not Officer Commanding RAFAT, which merely caused more confusion.

The Commandant welcomed me warmly and told me that they, the Red Arrows, had been waiting for me for a long time. He explained that

I would be expected to spend about 75% of my time dealing with Red Arrows PR, about 15% dealing with station PR and the rest looking after the publicity requirements of the CFS. He told me that in order to get financial provision to establish my post they had been forced to include the station and CFS tasks to 'beef up' the job. The Commandant told me to go away and write my own Terms of Reference. It did not seem a good time to mention that I was not very keen on dealing with flying complaints but it was now clear that, as I had feared, I would be working for three separate bosses.

One of the first things I learned in the next few days as masses of mail started to flood into my In Tray, was that the great British public has an insatiable desire to visit the RAF at their home bases. Scampton was especially popular for visitors because it had aeroplanes, a long and illustrious history, the grave of a famous black dog, and the Red Arrows. Almost every working day throughout my time at Scampton I received written or telephoned requests for visits – and latterly they came by e-mail as well. Every visit reported on TV or radio or in the local newspapers telling of someone or some organisation who had visited Scampton always led to a further influx of requests.

The first visit I accepted, when I had been in post only a few weeks, was from a school in Scunthorpe. The organiser telephoned to tell me that the children were doing a project on flight as part of the National Curriculum and a visit to Scampton to look at aeroplanes would help them enormously. How could I refuse such a plea? With great zest I accepted a visit by 30 pupils and a handful of teachers and parents. Carried away by my own enthusiasm, I suggested that they might like to invite a reporter and photographer from their local newspaper to come along as well to report on the visit. The organiser accepted with alacrity. The visit went off extremely well and was subsequently given extensive coverage in the local newspaper. I was very pleased with myself but I was not prepared for what happened afterwards. In the next week or so teachers from virtually every school in North Lincolnshire contacted me asking for a similar visit and I simply could not cope with the demand, National Curriculum or not. I learned a very valuable lesson from that.

There are several clearly defined groups of people who want to visit Scampton. To my mind the most important, even more important than

Red Arrows' fans, are those ex-serviceman who served at Scampton during the second world war. Now in the twilight of their lives, I considered that they had every right to visit their old station and I refused such a visit only on very rare occasions. Next in my order of importance are requests from the families of those airmen; they want to see where Dad or Granddad served their country. Another group of people merely want to visit Nigger's Grave. One particular man used to visit every year and all he wished to do was take a new photograph of the grave. On one visit he told me that he mails copies of his photographs to interested parties all around the world and he always insisted on taking a new photograph even if there was little discernible difference from pictures he had taken a year earlier. Once I cottoned on that he was making an annual pilgrimage I offered to mail him new photographs every year to save him the trouble and expense of a 200-mile round trip but he declined my offer. 'This is something I have to do myself,' he said simply.

The aircraft spotters – the so-called Anorak Brigade – make up another large group and for the most part they have no particular interest in the Station's history. I am in no position to make jokes or disparaging remarks about aircraft-spotting anoraks because I am a railway anorak although I no longer collect engine numbers. One thing the aircraft spotters have in common with train spotters is that they do collect numbers – to be precise, the aircraft registration letters painted on the airframes. Just as a child I could not underline a number in my Ian Allen ABC books unless I had seen the loco with my own eyes, so it is that the aircraft anoraks have to see the aircraft for themselves. As a general rule we took visitors into every hangar except one. 3 Hangar at Scampton was used for scheduled servicing and I had an agreement with the Chief Engineer that I would not take visitors into that hangar because they would cause unnecessary distractions for the airmen working on the aircraft. The spotters were always greatly disappointed by this exclusion and so what I had to do eventually was make a list, before the visitors arrived, of all the aircraft in the hangar. Then I would hand out a copy to each visitor and allow them, two or three at a time, to peer through the hangar doors, but without stepping inside, so that they could genuinely claim to have seen the aircraft.

Ex-servicemen's associations have very efficient grapevines and there are many such societies represented in Lincolnshire. The RAF Association, the Aircrew Association, the Bomber Command Association, the Lincolnshire Lancaster Association, and the various individual squadron associations, to name but a few, all seem to have countless branches not just within Lincolnshire but all over the country. The problem was how to deal with the sheer number of requests for visits from such organisations. We could not permit members of the public to wander around the station unescorted, not just because of security considerations but also because of the increasingly important matter of the Health and Safety Regulations. No station these days has manpower to spare to host large numbers of visitors and it is often difficult to get this across to people who wish to visit. The older ex-servicemen are the most difficult to convince. In their days, that is to say in my early days in the RAF, there always seemed to be a pool of airmen with time on their hands who could conveniently be employed to show visitors around. 'I don't need any special treatment,' was a common point ex-servicemen made in their letters. 'Just get one of the erks from the SWO's working party to look after me.' It is many years since the Station Warrant Officer had a pool of labour at his, or these days often her, beck and call.

In my first few days I discovered that visitors to the Red Arrows were being organised and escorted by two young ladies, one with an arm in plaster and the other with a leg in plaster. They were student officers from Cranwell who had been injured during the course of their initial officer training. Injured students, not always female of course, were withdrawn from formal training until they were fully fit again. As a temporary measure they were moved onto the Medical and Special Holding Flight which was, inevitably, known colloquially as MASH Flight, a term hated, and eventually proscribed, by the RAF College authorities. Those two young ladies were very keen on their job and they clearly enjoyed the relaxed atmosphere amongst the Red Arrows at Scampton, well away from the strict discipline of the RAF College. However, I considered that having damaged students to host hundreds of visitors gave out the wrong message to the public. By the time those ladies were fit enough to resume their training at Cranwell I had made alternative arrangements.

Throughout the early 90s I had the services of what are known as Holding Officers. These are young men and women, often already commissioned, who are part way through their flying or professional training and are waiting, holding, for the next course. Only rarely in the whole of my service has the RAF managed to arrange matters so that new aircrew officers could progress smoothly and without delay from one course to the next until they finally reach their first operational squadron. There almost always seem to be bottlenecks in the system. Holding Officers are often referred to as Kevin or Kev for no reason that anyone can satisfactorily explain but the individuals consider the name rather derogatory. The staff officers responsible for finding meaningful temporary jobs for these officers were only too willing to send them to Scampton to work for me. Most moved on after two or three months but some of them stayed for six months or more, fine for me but sad for them.

Often I had several Kevs at the same time and then the Red Arrows' pilots tended to refer to them as Kev One, Kev Two and so on but I always used their proper names. At one time in the mid 90s I had six holding officers all at once and the complete group became known as 'CRO Flight'. They were invaluable to me and on the whole I think they enjoyed their holding time, not least because there were regular opportunities for passenger flying. The best ones, in fact most of them, eventually got a back seat ride with one of the Red Arrows. I was hoping that before I retired at least one of my former Kevs would turn up again as a Red Arrow but it did not happen.

In my first few years, Scampton hosted around 1,000 public visitors each and every month but it put a great strain on our very limited resources finding people to escort and entertain them all. It fell to me to organise the visits and deal with all the associated correspondence but I clearly did not have time to host them all myself and do my other jobs as well. When I had holding officers available to me I used to arrange visits for up to 25 people at a time, each morning and afternoon, five days a week. I tried to limit the groups to a maximum of 25 because it was generally not practicable to look after groups larger than that safely and legally in the aircraft hangars. I evolved a standard format for most visits rather than try and tailor their particular needs. Only once did I get a complaint from someone after a visit that they had not seen what they wanted to see and on investigation it turned out that they had not asked.

The system for entertaining visitors worked well enough and was the best that we could organise with such limited resources. One day while I was showing a group of schoolboys around the Red Arrows' hangar myself, I suddenly realised I had lost their attention. Walking past along the corridor was Flight Lieutenant Rory Underwood, the England rugby star, then stationed at Scampton. He was of far more interest to the boys than my briefing about the Red Arrows, it seemed, and Rory gladly paused to sign lots of autographs. Even a couple of the Red Arrows, walking past in their red flying suits, were ignored. It is all a question of priorities I suppose.

Each standard public visit started off in the Central Flying School's main briefing room where the visitors were given a 30-minute slide presentation – Microsoft PowerPoint had not been invented then – telling them about the history of Scampton, the Red Arrows and the Central Flying School. Some of my holding officers were extremely good at giving these briefings. The visitors were then taken, or more often they drove in their own cars, to 4 Hangar for a look around the Red Arrows' home. There they were shown an excellent and never surpassed historic film about the Team made by Arthur Gibson, one of the Red Arrow's most faithful fans and a superb photographer and film maker. The small cinema, in which we could seat a maximum of 25 people because of the fire regulations, later became my office and later still, in 2001, become the Team Leader's office.

Whilst down at 4 Hangar the visitors could stand outside to watch whatever flying happened to be in progress at the time. Sometimes we would take the visitors inside to look at the exotic memorabilia displayed in a special protected showcase: solid gold and silver items encrusted with jewels, donated by foreign royalty, and other valuable gifts worth many tens of thousands of pounds in total. There was one item that always intrigued visitors. It was a short length of red ribbon pinned casually to the back wall of the display cabinet by a battered red dart. It seems that when the Duchess of York visited the Team in 1988 she looked at the extravagant gifts from King Hussein of Jordan and King Hassan of Morocco amongst others and said to the Team Leader, 'Oh dear, I have nothing to give you.' One of the pilots cheekily pointed to the red ribbon which the Duchess was wearing on her dress and said, 'Please give us your red ribbon.' She took it off there and then and it was duly pinned to the inside of the display case by a Red Arrow with a red arrow.

In addition to all the public visitors, there were several hundred privileged visitors to the Red Arrows HQ at Scampton each year. These people were known to us collectively as 'upstairs' visitors because their visit included the inner sanctums of the pilots' coffee bar and briefing rooms which were on the upper floor of the hangar. They included prize-winners from various charity events, business guests, sponsors and clients of sponsors, private guests of Squadron members, some Service visitors, and visitors who for one reason or another were deemed to have a good reason for meeting the pilots in their crew room. This last category included seriously ill or disabled children and adults, and visitors seeking meetings with the pilots in celebration of special anniversaries or events. Unlike the public visitors, most of the privileged visitors were programmed to meet the pilots. I used to meet and greet all these special visitors myself and employ the holding officers to help out with entertaining them whilst the pilots were flying.

Every upstairs visit was planned to last for about five hours and we tried to keep each group to a maximum of 10 people so that every single visitor felt special. Unfortunately, ten privileged visitors on such a visit displaced up to 50 public visitors, 25 in the morning and 25 in the afternoon, because the two classes of visitors could not be allowed to meet otherwise we would certainly have had an 'upstairs, downstairs' situation.

The upstairs visitors were always invited to sit in on one or more pre- and post-flight briefings. At midday, between sorties, they had a light finger buffet lunch with the pilots in the crew room. The RAF was never very generous in providing money for entertaining visitors so the most we could supply were small sandwiches, tiny sausage rolls and similar things, laid out on silver platters. No alcohol was permitted in the crew room during flying hours.

There was an uncomfortable moment during one of these upstairs lunches. The Chief Executive of a well-known British company, who must remain nameless to save his embarrassment, picked up a small sandwich that was curling at the edges, looked at it critically, and said in a loud voice: 'I'm pleased to see that you haven't poshed it up just because I'm here!' It was unfortunate that he chose to make his remark during a rare lull in the conversation; everyone heard him and all eyes turned towards him. The poor fellow blushed with shame. We all tried to make a joke of his solecism. However, the fact remains that the food we, the RAF, provided was inadequate and although he was unlucky to make his observation just as everyone else stopped talking, it was very bad manners to comment on it in public. We often felt embarrassed about the standard of our hospitality because whenever we were entertained by companies we were always given the five-star treatment.

I have alluded earlier to my fascination with anything to do with railways. One of my great disappointments at the very start of my time with the Red Arrows was that I was not invited to Kings Cross railway station on 7 November 1989 when the Red Arrows travelled to London by high speed train to meet Her Majesty Queen Elizabeth the Queen Mother who was about to name one of British Rail's East Coast Main Line brand-new HS125 locos, number 91004, 'The Red Arrows'. The event had been set up long before my appointment and I knew absolutely nothing about it until the day before the ceremony. No-one had thought of inviting me and it was then too late to add me to the list. The Team travelled from Newark Northgate in their red suits, naturally, and spent most of the 75-minute journey moving through the train signing autographs for passengers. The naming ceremony was carried out on the platform at Kings Cross in front of a large crowd of normal passengers waiting for trains, the Central Band of the RAF, and a host of RAF VIPs.

I could not end this chapter on the importance or otherwise of names, without making a confession. I made the point earlier that I very rarely refused a request for a visit from an ex-RAF person with Scampton connections. One request that I refused, because it clashed with a visit by a Service VIP, caused me genuine sorrow and grief three years later. The request came from a Mr W C Townsend who wrote in 1990 to say that he lived in Bromsgrove and would be passing through Lincoln on a certain day visiting relations. He wondered if it would be possible to call in and have a look around Scampton where he had served for some weeks during the war. That was all he put in his letter. I wrote back saying sorry and explained that we were short of staff and that I had a VIP to look after on that date. I suggested he wrote back if he was ever passing close to Scampton again.

It was only three years later, when I was helping to organise the events marking the 50th Anniversary of the Dam Busters and was checking with retired Squadron Leader Ted Wass, the Secretary of the Dam Busters' Association, the names of all the surviving aircrew who had taken part in the raid, that I realised Mr W C Townsend was in fact Flight Sergeant W C 'Bill' Townsend DFM. Bill was the captain of Lancaster AJ-O on the Dams' raid and he was the last to land back at Scampton at 0615 hrs. One of his Lancaster's four engines was inoperative and the windscreen was almost totally obscured by escaping oil. He was awarded the Conspicuous Gallantry Medal for his part in the operation. Sadly Bill died in 1991. He never did pass by Scampton again so I was never able to right a wrong.

7

A Short Flying Lesson and Why I Verbally Abused a Student

BEFORE I GO ANY FURTHER, this is perhaps a good point to answer a question frequently asked by visitors to the Red Arrows: why are military pilots so obsessed with aerobatics? I would not actually go so far as to agree that we are obsessed but, weather and fuel permitting, almost every RAF basic flying training sortie used to include a few minutes of 'looping and rolling' even when the lesson plan did not specifically call for them. If the student was sufficiently advanced he might be permitted a few non-assessed minutes to show off his aerobatic skills, or lack of them. Sometimes the instructor would spend a few minutes flying his own aerobatic sequence and then have to explain, when the stall turn went wrong, that he was a little rusty because he got so little time to practice. So what then is this fascination for aerobatics and why do pilots spend so much time doing them?

Aerobatics have always played a prominent part in RAF pilot training, and please note that aerobatics is the correct word for this activity. Pilots hate to hear aerobatics described as acrobatics. From the very earliest days, even before the Royal Air Force was formed in 1918, pilots of the Royal Naval Air Service and the Royal Flying Corps were taught to fly machines to their aerodynamic and mechanical limits. It had been recognised early on in the First World War that when two aeroplanes with more or less equal performance engaged in aerial combat, the better pilot would always win. The better pilot was the one who could extract maximum performance from his machine. I will try and explain things in simple terms and without delving too deeply into the technicalities, so I trust the purists will make allowances!

The wings of an aircraft generate lift, the upwards force which is used to counter-balance the weight of the aircraft. When an aircraft on the ground accelerates along the runway, all other things being equal it will take off when the speed has increased to the point where the wings are generating more lift than is required to counteract the weight. An inescapable by-product of lift is one form of drag – just take my word for that. Drag is a measure of the reluctance of the aircraft to fly through the air. Once an aircraft is airborne, and if the wings are parallel to the horizon, all the excess lift produced by the wings will cause the aircraft to climb and the amount by which the engine thrust exceeds drag will cause the aircraft to accelerate. However, when an aircraft is airborne and in a turn, if the pilot prevents the aircraft from climbing by increasing the angle of bank, the rate of turn will increase – the excess lift is 'used up' by accelerating the aircraft towards the centre of the turning circle. In the case of the Red Arrows' Hawk aircraft, if the pilot flies in a level turn on full throttle at about 350 knots, the wings generate an amount of lift roughly equal to eight times the weight of the aircraft. The pilot feels this as a force of 8g, the maximum g force permitted for the Hawk.

Maximum performance is obtained when the engine is at full power, or maximum thrust, and when the angle of attack is such that the wings are generating the maximum lift they are physically capable of generating. To put it at its simplest, the angle of attack is the angle at which the wings meet the oncoming airflow and that angle is controlled by the elevators in conventional aircraft: pull back on the control column to increase the angle; push forward, or relax the back pressure on the control column, to decrease it. If the pilot continues to haul back on the control column past the maximum angle of attack, the amount of lift being generated actually starts to fall off quite dramatically. This is known as a 'g' or accelerated stall and if the aircraft is in a turn at the time, the rate of turn reduces markedly. In these circumstances the aircraft will also start to descend because the wings are no longer generating sufficient lift to counterbalance the aircraft's weight. The pilot of a chasing aircraft would have no difficulty in getting the front aircraft into his gun sights – providing he did not also stall his aircraft.

The onset of a stall is usually indicated by the whole aircraft trembling slightly as the airflow over the wings becomes turbulent. This is known in the trade as the 'light buffet'. The Red Arrows' two soloists, the Synchro Pair, spend quite a lot of time flying for maximum performance, on the light buffet, during their part of a flying display, but more of that later. To make matters worse each wing may, and often does, stall at a slightly different angle of attack; the wing generating least lift will drop and the aircraft will then start to rotate about its horizontal axis towards the dropped wing as well as continuing to descend. This is the beginning of a vicious cycle: the aircraft will yaw towards the low wing which will then drop even further, the aircraft will continue to roll, and the aircraft will quickly enter a spin.

The best way to teach a new pilot about aerodynamic limits is to fly aerobatics. Flying a loop, for example, is really the same aerodynamic process as flying a level turn except that one is in the vertical plane and the other in the horizontal plane. Unless you are flying a super-powerful jet, your aircraft will lose speed on the upward half of a loop because it is fighting against gravity. The aircraft may be close to its minimum flying speed whilst upside down at the top of the loop. In the second half of the loop, now with the help of gravity, the aircraft descends and can be close to its maximum permitted speed at the bottom of the ensuing dive. In most aircraft there will be positive g all the way round a loop and there is no tendency for the pilot to fall out of his seat even when upside down at the top.

Flying a stall turn, not a manoeuvre flown during displays by the Red Arrows, is more dramatic than a loop. To start a stall turn the aircraft is pointed vertically upwards. Now the thrust from the engine, not the lift from the wings, has to counterbalance the weight of the aircraft. The aircraft continually decelerates as momentum is lost until the point is reached when the engine can no longer produce enough thrust to counterbalance the force of gravity. For an instant the aircraft hangs motionless in space – and, yes, at that point the pilot experiences zero gravity. It would, literally, be a hair-raising manoeuvre were it not for the fact that you are wearing a tight fitting helmet! However, just before that point is reached, to execute the stall turn the pilot applies rudder to yaw the nose of the aircraft over to the left or right as he chooses. If the pilot flies the manoeuvre successfully, the aircraft yaws through 180 degrees and ends up pointing vertically downwards, accelerating rapidly.

Clumsily flown aerobatic manoeuvres can cause the aircraft to enter a spin when, technically, the aircraft is out of control. Fortunately, that does not mean that control cannot be regained – in most aircraft anyway. As part of the basic flying training syllabus, the RAF teaches its pilots how to recognise the symptoms of approaching stalls and spins and how to recover from them. Students are also taught how to recover from fully developed spins just in case things get out of hand when there is no instructor in the other seat. Aerobatics are, therefore, an enjoyable but essential step in the training of military pilots, allowing them to develop complete confidence in their own and their aircraft's limitations.

Not all pilots like spinning although few will openly admit to being apprehensive about it. When I was a flying instructor we had to be quite certain that our students could recover from both incipient and fully developed spins before we sent them off to fly solo aerobatics. Students were not authorised to spin the aircraft deliberately whilst flying on their own – although some did. In the Jet Provost, solo students were briefed to recover at the first signs of an incipient spin when, simply by centralising all the flying controls, the aircraft would resume normal controlled flight, although that did not mean that the aircraft would necessarily return to wings level flight the right way up without intervention by the pilot.

One of the most important lessons that any flying instructor has to learn is when to take control from the student if things start going wrong. If the student makes a mistake and the instructor takes over control too soon, the student might not learn the lesson and an arrogant student might even claim that he was about to take corrective action himself. The first time I deliberately entered a fully developed spin, other than as a student myself with an instructor in the right hand seat, was in a Jet Provost Mark 3 at Cranwell in 1968 when I was a newly-qualified instructor just arrived from the Central Flying School. My squadron commander at that time, Squadron Leader Bill Jago, deliberately used to send his new instructors off to do spinning with a fairly junior student. 'It's good experience for you,' he used to say. 'Learn when to take control if the student fouls it up. Not too soon but certainly not too late!' The

Jet Provost was a very docile aircraft and usually behaved properly when handled correctly. As my student that day, Under Officer Grant McLeod, counted out aloud the eight complete spinning rotations I had briefed him to do before taking recovery action, I remember having a few qualms but the student recovered immaculately – he had been well taught by his own instructor.

Some of the less trusting, or less confident, instructors used to keep their hands and feet resting on the dual flying controls whilst their students flew spins. This was definitely frowned upon by the instructors' instructors at the Central Flying School, particularly in side-by-seat seating aircraft such as the Bulldog and Jet Provost where the student could see exactly what his instructor was doing. I never did that, even with the clumsiest of students. As I became more experienced, instead of keeping my hands firmly on my knees during spins I used to put my hands nonchalantly on top of the coaming above the starboard instrument panel, well out of the way of the control column. I did this to indicate to the student that I had confidence in his ability. When I flew with students of other instructors they would sometimes comment during the debriefing, 'My instructor always keeps his hands on the control column when I do a spin.' If I said anything at all in reply it was usually on the lines of, 'Well, that's not my way of doing it.'

I learned a lot more about aircraft performance when, in 1969, I left Cranwell and went on a one year exchange posting to the Pakistan Air Force Academy at Risalpur in the North West Frontier Province. This was a magnificent location midway between Islamabad and Peshawar, on the southern edge of the Hindu Kush range of mountains and very close to the Khyber Pass which has been in the news for all the wrong reasons since 11 September 2001. The students on my particular squadron were mainly from Iran, Iraq, and Jordan. The aircraft we flew was the Cessna T37, a truly delightful training aircraft with two small jet engines, but it had its vices to trap the unwary. It was unpredictable when spinning and was prone to entering potentially dangerous high rotational spins for no known aerodynamic reason. Even worse, if the controls were mishandled the aircraft would readily snap into an inverted spin, a manoeuvre that is both uncomfortable and disorienta-ting because the occupants are subjected to continuous negative g forces trying to force them against the shoulder harness restraints and out of the top of the aircraft – that is hair raising.

Several of the staff instructors, including the then Commandant of the Academy, learned a valuable lesson about maximum performance in December 1969 as a result of an entirely innocent suggestion I made. The Commandant had been RAF-trained before the sub-continent was split into the separate states of Pakistan and India in 1947. He was an Anglo-Indian of Irish Roman Catholic stock, Mick O'Brien by name, a very distinguished officer of the Pakistan Air Force, with a very rare A1 QFI qualification earned in the RAF and renewed by a visiting Team from CFS during my stay at the Academy. Knowing that I was keen on photography and with Christmas approaching, the Commandant suggested that we flew four T37s over the snow-covered mountains just a few miles to the north of Risalpur. I would fly as a passenger in a fifth T37 taking what we hoped would be spectacular pictures of the other four flying in close formation down steep valleys and over the high peaks. The best picture would then be used to produce a traditional snowy-white Christmas card for the Commandant and me and the few other Christians at Risalpur.

The base at Risalpur, near the confluence of the Indus and Kabul Rivers, is situated on a large plateau about 1,500 feet above sea level but it does not seem that high because the nearest sea is several hundred miles distant. After take off we headed north and maintained 500 feet above the ground but because of the steeply rising terrain we were soon actually flying at over 20,000 feet above sea level in amongst the Hindu Kush. The scenery was quite outstanding but I concentrated hard on my artistic task. After a few minutes, seeking new ideas, I suggested to my pilot that he should fly a barrel roll around the outside of the formation of four so that when we were upside down overhead them I could take a photograph through the canopy of our aircraft looking down on the formation with the spectacular snowy scenery as a backdrop. The Commandant leading the formation of four agreed with the plan.

That was our mistake! Beguiled by the breathtaking scenery, we had all forgotten that aircraft performance drops off dramatically as the height above sea level increases, for reasons that are too complicated to explain here. My pilot pulled up into the vertical to roll around the other four but our aircraft shuddered and stalled as it ran out of performance. We topped out at about 25,000 feet above sea level but only about 2,500 feet above the mountains and my pilot had no option but to centralise all the controls and hope that the aircraft would recover from the incipient spin. It did recover – into a vertical dive. On the way down we passed perilously close to the other four who, seeing us coming down towards them, scattered in all directions. That was the end of the photographic session! The local photographic shop in Nowshera, the nearest town to Risalpur on the Grand Trunk Road, told me that the film had been accidentally ruined during the processing and so, sadly, I never did see the results of my efforts. I have often wondered if Air Commodore Mick O'Brien gave instructions to have the evidence destroyed.

One day towards the end of my tour in Pakistan, an Iraqi student called Hatam flying a solo aerobatic sortie at about 18,000 feet entered a spin, presumably by accident since this particular student was not one to break the rules. For exactly 95 seconds he transmitted a Mayday distress message over and over again in English, his second language. His last words just before the aircraft struck the ground sounded like 'Dive, dive, dive', although some members of the Board of Enquiry listening to the tape recording thought it was 'Die, die, die.' There was no doubt the aircraft was in a spin when it crashed because it struck the ground almost flat at a low forward speed. The Board of Inquiry concluded that the student failed to recover from an inadvertent spin following mishandling of the controls and he then failed to use his ejection seat because he was concentrating on transmitting the Mayday message. Perhaps there was another explanation that the Board did not consider, but I did a few days later when flying with an Iranian student called Khusro.

Khusro was a difficult name for me to pronounce properly. The 'kh' has to be voiced very strongly, rather like gargling, and is similar to the guttural 'ch' in the true Scottish pronunciation of 'loch' but even stronger. Early in my tour I could not manage that and I always called the unfortunate student 'Kusro' – I say unfortunate because 'kusro' in Farsi, the Iranian language, is a particularly foul expletive with an equally foul four-letter English equivalent beginning with 'c'. I could not understand why all the students broke into howls of laughter whenever I summoned Khusro from the crew room. They put me out of my ignorance only when I was half way through my first term with them.

Khusro was an excellent, aggressive pilot and a delightful personality even though at a squadron barbecue he tried to fool me into sampling grilled house sparrow – apparently an Iranian delicacy. A few days after the fatal accident I flew with Khusro on a progress check flight that included stalls and spins as a matter of routine. He had a very interesting technique. Instead of recovering from a practice spin when I told him to do so, he took his hands and feet off the controls and looked across the cockpit at me with what I can only describe as an air of resignation.

'Inshaa'allah! Allah has control,' he said simply, raising his hands as high as he could in the confined cockpit.

'No he hasn't, I have control!' I said, hastily grabbing the controls as the T37 started to wind itself up into a very dangerous high rotational spin. I might have used stronger language than that. 'Allah may look after you but he won't look after me.'

Fearing that the deeply religious student might have thought that I was making mock of his religion, something I would never do to anyone of any religious persuasion, I discussed the incident with him during the debriefing after landing.

'You were quite right to take control of the aircraft, sir, because you are an infidel,' Khusro said in all seriousness. 'Perhaps you should consider embracing Islam?'

He genuinely believed that his God would save him from the spin should he wish to do so and, of course, no good Muslim would ever question the will of Allah. "Inshaa'allah" is one of the most common phrases used by Muslims worldwide; it may be translated as 'whatever Allah wills, will be'. There was perhaps some small, non-religious, reason for Khusro believing that leaving control of the aircraft in the hands of Allah was the right thing to do. The Cessna T37 could be so unpredictable when spinning that sometimes, but only sometimes, simply letting go of all the controls would induce the aircraft to recover to controlled flight. It was not a technique I would have put my trust in and not something we ever mentioned or taught to students. With the aid of my Pakistani staff colleagues, who were mostly Muslims, I persuaded Khusro that some things he had to do for himself without waiting for divine intervention. At the end of the academic year he graduated from the Air Force Academy and returned to the Imperial Iranian Air Force, as it was then, whilst I returned to England at the end of my tour of duty. I have often wondered what happened to him. A quarter of a decade later I returned to Risalpur, on tour with the Red Arrows.

Almost as much fun as flying aerobatics is flying in close formation with one or more other aircraft. I never developed a particular talent for formation flying until quite late in my career when I started flying Victor tankers but the very first time I taught formation flying techniques was at Cranwell with Martin Stoner in the left hand seat of the Jet Provost. By the end of that first sortie he could do it as well as I could. Naturally, at the time I put that down to my expert instruction but I knew there was more to it than that and I do not believe Martin was convinced. He was a natural pilot and I was not surprised that he eventually joined the Red Arrows after a distinguished career flying Lightning supersonic fighters.

Formation flying developed from the need of fighter pilots to give each other mutual support in combat. Because a pilot cannot look in all directions at once, a single aircraft could all too easily be pounced upon by a crafty enemy. The expression 'battle formation' was coined in the 1914-18 war to describe two or more aircraft flying together for mutual support. By flying two or three hundred metres apart, each pilot was able to cover the others' blind spots. The expression is still used today by front-line fighter pilots – and by the Red Arrows in a slightly different context.

Trying to teach students to fly in close formation is a bit like trying to teach a child to ride a two-wheeled cycle for the first time: there are a few tips you can impart but what it really comes down to is that the student either has an aptitude for it or he does not. You start off by demonstrating the position you want to maintain relative to the leader. That is the easy part. What is much more difficult is explaining how you maintain that position. The control movements needed are tiny, even in a large aircraft such as the Victor tanker, and most students tend to over-control when they first try it for themselves, resulting in large changes of position relative to the leader which in turn leads to further over-controlling, and so on until the instructor has to take over and settle things down.

'When you want to go up a bit,' Tony Ryle, my ever-patient Jet Provost instructor at Leeming, used to say to me, 'just *think* about going up and you'll find that it happens.' And, surprisingly, it usually did.

Up and down is easier than in and out. To move closer to the lead aircraft you have to bank gently towards it. That sets up a closing vector and if you do nothing else, you will very soon collide with the leader – and that is not what you want. Tony Ryle's advice to me was to squeeze the control column very gently towards the formation leader and then squeeze it again in the opposite direction before the correction seemed to have taken effect.

Most difficult of all for beginners is the control of speed. In order to maintain a stable position relative to the leader you must fly at exactly his speed. Obvious, isn't it? However each up and down movement of the elevators and ailerons increases drag slightly; the effect is cumulative and so the aircraft starts to slow down and you have to move the throttle forwards to compensate. The trouble is that jet engines cannot provide instantaneous changes of thrust: the turbine takes time to accelerate and decelerate and there is usually a sophisticated fuel control system to ensure that too much fuel is not pumped into the engine before it needs it. Thus the pilot has to anticipate the need for speed changes otherwise he will soon be moving the throttle forwards and backwards over ever-increasing distances as he gets out of sync with the requirement. The instructor can watch this happening when the student does it, but he also has time to look in at the instruments and note that although the throttle is moving backwards and forwards over quite a large range, the engine rpm are not changing. In a forgiving aircraft such as the Jet Provost with its excellent fuel control system you could prove the point to the student by rapidly moving the throttle from idle to maximum and back again several times and noting that the rpm, and consequently the aircraft speed, remained almost constant. This was definitely not advisable in the Cessna T37 because the two engines in that aircraft had a much inferior fuel control system and the engines would readily flame out if they were fed too much fuel too quickly.

In early formation practices many students tire quickly and that tends to lead to even more over-controlling. You can see the student getting tense and if he were not wearing cape leather gloves you would see his knuckles going white. While the student is getting more and more tense it is very tiring for the instructor because he cannot afford to let his attention wander for even a split second. Instructors have a joke about this.

QFI to tense student: 'Move out a bit and relax for a few minutes.

Student to QFI: 'That's all right, sir, I am relaxed.'

QFI to student: 'In that case move out and let me relax!'

What is not immediately obvious to non-pilots is that formation techniques work in all geometric planes, not just in straight and level flight, but there are other factors to be taken into consideration as well. If the formation leader starts a turn to the left, the aircraft on the right has to apply the same angle of bank as the leader but he has to climb slightly to remain in the same relative position because his aircraft will need to describe a turn of greater circumference. Since the aircraft on the right has to climb, the pilot has to increase power slightly otherwise he will be left behind. The aircraft on the inside of the turn will have to descend and reduce power slightly for the same reason. A formation barrel roll, so-called because each aircraft follows a path which can be likened to flying a horizontal path around the outside of a barrel, is one of the most difficult manoeuvres. The Red Arrows include many barrel rolls in their display routine, some with three or four aircraft either side of the Leader. The further away you are from the Leader, the greater the speed and power changes needed to stay in the correct position. In 1958 at the Farnborough Air Show the famous RAF Black Arrows of 111 Squadron, augmented by additional aircraft from another squadron, barrelled rolled 16 aircraft and looped an incredible 22 Hawker Hunters in close formation – a world record that stands to this day.

Visitors to the Red Arrows were often astonished that the pilots could perform all their aerobatic manoeuvres with as little as three or four metres between the wingtips of adjacent aircraft whilst flying through the air at five hundred miles an hour for up to 25 minutes at a time. In fact, of course, it is all relative. The speed of the formation is of little consequence: it is the speed of individual aircraft relative to the others that matters. When briefing visitors I sometimes likened formation flying to driving in formation alongside another vehicle on a motorway. You use the steering wheel for in and out and your foot on the accelerator for forwards and backwards. When the lead vehicle starts turning, the following vehicle has to adjust his speed to stay in the same relative position. I always then point out that you should never formate on another vehicle on the road because you do not know what the other driver is going to do next. Even Formula One drivers regularly get it wrong. In close formation flying, providing it has been properly briefed in advance, you do know what the lead aircraft is going to do and you trust him to stick to the brief.

8

The Central Flying School and the Birth of the Red Arrows

IN 1918, WITH THE SO-CALLED GREAT WAR, the 'War to End All Wars', out of the way, the senior officers of the newly-formed RAF quickly recognised the value of display flying for pilot training as well as for prestige and recruiting purposes. It was inevitable that sooner or later formation flying and aerobatics should be combined into a single activity and it is not surprising that formation aerobatics became a very popular part of public flying displays from the 1920s to the present day. Most, but certainly not all, of the displays were put on by pilots of the Central Flying School. The Red Arrows are, and always have been, an integral part of the CFS; not a lot of people outside the RAF know that. 'So what?' I hear you cry. Well, in order to understand how the Team functions it is necessary to understand this connection with the longest serving flying school in the world, because that is what the CFS is.

Under the arrangements made when the Royal Flying Corps was created in 1912, the cost of the flying school element was to be borne equally by the Army and the Navy, but its administration and support infrastructure were solely the responsibility of the War Office. To balance things up, a Royal Navy officer, Captain Godfrey Paine RN, was chosen to be the first Commandant. According to his personal journal, which is still lovingly maintained in the CFS Museum at Cranwell, Captain Paine was informed of his selection by Mr Winston Churchill, the First Lord of the Admiralty, and told in no uncertain terms that he must learn to fly within two weeks if he was to be confirmed in the appointment. Captain Paine, who knew virtually nothing about flying, took himself to Eastchurch and duly completed his somewhat rushed conversion under the tutelage of a much junior officer, Lieutenant Arthur Longmore, RN.

The Central Flying School opened its doors for the first time at Upavon on 12 May 1912 but, in spite of what the title might suggest, the aim of the school was not to produce pilots from scratch but to convert qualified civilian pilots into professional military pilots. To this end the first CFS students were pilots who already held a Royal Aero Club Certificate, the precursor of the present-day private pilot's licence. They were taught to fly all the types of aircraft available at the school, including such aircraft as Maurice Farmans, Henri Farmans, Shorts, Avros and Bristol bi-planes.

The ground training syllabus included 'the theory of flight, map reading, strength of materials, military and naval aviation history, practical work on Gnome and Renault engines, aircraft repair, and hints on flying.' It is nice to know that the students were given hints on flying. These days you need more than a few hints before you are awarded your wings! The standard for a pass was 50% in each subject and 60% overall, a very low target by today's standards. The first course was completed on 5 December 1912 and graduates were then, according to their end of course reports, 'able to carry out short cross-country flights and local flights of up to 20 or 30 minutes duration at heights of about 1500 feet.'

One of the 36 students on the first CFS course was 39-year old Major Hugh Trenchard DSO, then serving in the Royal Scots Greys. Having lost one of his lungs as a result of being shot up during the Boer War, the Major realised that there was little future for him in the Army. When the opportunity arose, he decided to learn to fly and he spent all of 13 days at Weybridge doing just that. One can only assume that aircrew medical standards were not as stringent in those days as they are now. Trenchard's end of course report apparently described him as an 'indifferent flyer' but nevertheless, because of his previous military background, he was posted to the CFS to be the Adjutant and Deputy Commandant before he had even fully qualified for his Royal Flying Corps wings. Since one of Major Trenchard's duties at CFS was to set the examination papers, arrange and invigilate the examinations, correct the papers and then assess the results, he regularised his situation by setting himself a flying and ground examination, correcting his own written papers, and awarding himself his pilot's wings! He later became the first Chief of the Air Staff in 1918, the first five-star Marshal of the Royal Air Force in 1927, and finally was ennobled as Viscount Trenchard.

One of the most proficient students on the first course was Lieutenant Robert Smith-Barry who was destined later to change the whole system of flying training. He eventually reached the rank of air vice-marshal. Another student on No 1 Course destined for greatness was John Salmond who became the second Chief of the Air Staff and who also, like Trenchard before him, reached the rank of Marshal of the Royal Air Force. Perhaps there is a moral here: if you want to do well, set up a new school and make sure you are on the first course.

Very soon aircraft began to take on a more warlike form and within months of its creation CFS became one of the main centres for experimental and research flying. One of the school's new tasks was to gain the confidence of commanders in the field by showing that the Royal Flying Corps was not just a fine weather Service. It was with great pride that the Secretary of State for War told the House of Commons in 1913, that CFS had 'carried out experiments in flying in strong winds.' What had actually been achieved was that an aircraft with a maximum speed of 57 mph had taken 16 minutes to cover 400 yards into the teeth of a gale. This was quite an advance, since only a year before it had been considered dangerous to fly in winds of 15 mph!

By the outbreak of war in August 1914 the CFS had contributed 93 pilots to the Royal Flying Corps. A rapid expansion then took place and by the end of that year, as the number of military pilots needed in service began to exceed the number of places available at the one school, a streaming system was introduced. All pupils carried out their *ab initio* flying at one of the Reserve Squadrons and they then passed on either to CFS or to a service squadron for advanced training. This was the first indication of how the CFS would develop into what it is today.

A major fault of the Royal Flying Corps at this time was the lack of standardisation in its training methods. Each instructor had his own ideas of how best to teach others to fly but there was no system for checking the quality of the instruction. The results, not surprisingly, were unpredictable and often unsatisfactory. One of the system's main critics was Robert Smith-Barry, by now a major serving on a front line squadron in France. In 1916, presumably as relaxation between flying operational missions and having seen many of his colleagues killed as a result of pure flying accidents rather than enemy action, he put his thoughts down on paper. He proposed the creation of a school for flying instructors where the students would have their piloting expertise brought up to the high standard necessary to enable them to teach others with confidence and ease. Smith-Barry also wanted the student instructors to be taught structured instructional techniques; today we call it teaching by objectives. Perhaps the most far-reaching of all his recommendations was the introduction of dual controls in training aircraft so that the instructor pilots could demonstrate to their students how to fly to the limits of their aircraft. As part of his written submissions, Smith-Barry wrote: 'The object has not been to prevent fliers from getting into difficulties or dangers but to show them how to get out of them satisfactorily and, having done so, then make them go and repeat the process alone.'

Smith-Barry's proposals so impressed the General Staff that he was brought home from France and given command of a training squadron at Gosport where he could put his ideas into practice. Soon his squadron was operating a fleet of dual controlled training aircraft such as Avro 504s, Bleriots and Bristol Scouts. The standard of flying improved even more after the introduction of what became known as the Gosport Tube. This was a simple tube connecting the front and rear cockpits; the end of the tube served as either an earpiece or a mouthpiece, permitting the instructor to converse easily and comfortably with his pupil. Incredibly, before the introduction of the Gosport Tube the only way an instructor could give instructions to his student in flight was to throttle the engine back and reduce speed; there were then a few moments, before the aircraft stalled, when the ambient noise was low enough to enable the pilots to shout to each other.

Pilot training became both quicker and more efficient and Smith Barry's system of teaching by objectives was adopted throughout the training school. It seems so obvious today that the first basic flying lessons should be concerned with the effects of the primary flying controls, rudders, ailerons and elevators. For example, merely pushing the rudder pedal to the left makes the nose of the aircraft move to the left, but the starboard wing is then going faster than the port wing and, therefore, develops more lift and so the aircraft rolls to the left, which makes the nose move further to the left and so on until, if left uncorrected, the aircraft would enter a spiral dive or spin. Students pilots always want to get around as quickly as possible to the exciting business of taking off and landing but without leaning the basics, sooner or later the pilot will get himself into trouble. It was because of this lack of proper instruction before Smith-Barry that there were so many pure flying accidents. The structured techniques introduced by Smith-Barry can be applied to all aircraft types and today they still form the basis of flying instruction in the RAF and all major flying schools the world over.

In 1918, when the war was over, the Royal Flying Corps and the Royal Naval Air Service were amalgamated to form the Royal Air Force and as part of that reorganisation CFS became the flying instructors' school, tasked to carry on the work started at Gosport. In 1926 the Air Ministry decided that in between courses the CFS staff should visit flying training schools to check whether the system and standard of instruction was being maintained. This was the beginning of the present-day Examining Wing. The following year a Refresher Flight was formed and pilots from air forces in many parts of the world travelled to CFS to join in the courses at CFS.

It was at about this time that the idea of a formation aerobatic team was born and a five-man team led by Flight Lieutenant D'Arcy Greig began displaying in De Havilland Genet Moths. Their repertoire was quite extensive and would do the Service justice at major air displays even today. Formation aerobatic displays by CFS instructors became a traditional item at the famous Hendon Air Displays and in 1933 a CFS team of five red and white striped Tutors led by Flight Lieutenant, later Air Chief Marshal Sir Hugh, Constantine, made a great impression with its inverted formation flying.

The idea of an annual get-together of past and present members of the staff was born in 1930. Among the 40 to 50 who attended were the first CFS Commandant, now Air Vice-Marshal Sir Godfrey Paine, Marshal of the Royal Air Force Lord Trenchard, and Air Vice-Marshal Arthur Longmore. The Central Flying School Association developed from this small beginning and now numbers about 1000, including me. The colours of the CFS Association were chosen with the school's multi-service genesis in mind: green to represent land and the Army; purple to represent the engineering branch of the Royal Navy; silver for the River Avon; and black for the unknown future. Less respectful persons apparently preferred to believe that black stood for the old tarred huts at Upavon, purple for the first Commandant's language, and green for the innocence of his Chief Staff Officer.

In 1931, the Central Flying School became one of the first RAF units to receive its own armorial bearings. The Arms symbolise the origin and work of the CFS. The pelican, the main feature, apparently represents the seat of learning in heraldic terms. The pelican is undoubtedly a strong aviator, despite its non-aerodynamic shape, but there is no truth in the rumour, freely spread about amongst the CFS students throughout the years, that it was chosen because of the size of its mouth and its poor flying performance. The crown and tower symbolise the School's naval and military beginnings; the pilot's brevet, the anchor and the sabre represent the three Services. The white and blue wavy lines serve as a reminder of the original site of the CFS which was close to the banks of the River Avon. The motto, *Imprimis Praeceptor*, is usually translated as Our Teaching is Everlasting. However, cynical students reckon the teaching is obviously not everlasting because the CFS has been running flying refresher courses for some decades now.

From the start of the second World War the CFS course was reduced from nine weeks to four and RAF Volunteer Reserve uniforms began to appear as full mobilisation took place. The Refresher Squadron began to take on an assortment of pilots from all backgrounds who had volunteered for the newly formed Air Transport Auxiliary. The ATA pilots relieved the general pilot shortage by undertaking such duties as ferrying aircraft from the factories to the squadrons. They became known, rather rudely, as Ancient and Tattered Airmen when elderly and bald pilots, very young pilots and not particularly fit pilots, some with only one eye or one arm, joined their ranks. By no means all the ATA pilots fitted into these categories and they all did a very important job of work. Early in 1940 some young ladies, who were definitely neither ancient nor tattered, arrived at CFS to be trained up for the ATA. Two of the ladies, Amy Johnson and Winifred Crossley, were old flying hands who had given aerobatic displays with Alan Cobham's Circus. One other, Jean Hughes, was only 17 years old and she became almost certainly the youngest ever pilot to pass through CFS. Now there is a good question for a quiz!

During 1939 the fighter defences of Great Britain improved dramatically from a force of about 600 aircraft, of which all but about 90 were obsolescent bi-planes, to one of 38 squadrons of which 22 were equipped with the Hurricane and Spitfire. In spite of CFS' best efforts at standardisation, it quickly became obvious that there was a lack of uniformity in the handling techniques for the new powerful aircraft which were coming into service. The new aircraft were not producing the increased fighting power and efficiency that the air marshals had hoped for because the pilots were not flying them to best advantage. To try and overcome this the Air Ministry introduced the Examining Officers' Scheme which established a flight of experienced officers to maintain a liaison between CFS and the operational squadrons and to instruct the latter in up-to-the-minute techniques. By the end of 1940, 90 pupils were being accepted in each five-week period. The modern day equivalent of these examining officers are known as CFS Agents and there is at least one for each type of aircraft operated by the RAF. The agents are there to keep in touch with CFS doctrine and to pass on their pearls of wisdom to the front line operational pilots. I was the CFS Agent for the Victor Tanker during my final years at Marham.

Some of today's familiar operating procedures can be traced back to the early 1940s. For example, on a liaison visit to the Middle East it came to the notice of the Examiners that whilst a party of Army officers was being flown from Iraq to Palestine in a Bombay transport, one of them became badly airsick and rapidly made for the toilet at the end of the cabin. Three of his friends followed to help him and thereby they shifted the centre of gravity so much that the aircraft became uncontrollable. This incident, the eventual outcome of which is not documented as far as I have been able to ascertain, highlighted the need for calculating the centre of gravity before take-off and led to the introduction of the now familiar load sheet compilation and Centre of Gravity calculations.

When I was flying in Shackletons on 38 Squadron in Malta, a jolly jape we sometimes played on a new pilot was based on that story. Shackletons often flew very long sorties – the longest I flew was almost 20 hours without landing or refuelling. There was, therefore, an Elsan chemical toilet placed near the rear entrance door, as far away from the galley as possible for obvious reasons. Towards the end of a very long sortie, when the auto-pilot was flying the aircraft and all ten crew members were getting bored and soporific and the Elsan was getting rather full, a group of three or four air signallers would decide to rush together from their usual off-watch gathering point near the galley in the centre of the aircraft, towards the Elsan. This unexpected change in the aircraft's centre of gravity usually caused the auto-pilot to trip out whereupon the aircraft nose would rear up and everyone, especially the new pilot, would suddenly wake up. What fun!

'Sorry, Captain,' one of the signallers would call out on the intercom in response to the pilot's polite request to know what was going on, 'Had to rush to the toilet. Didn't have time to warn you!'

The pilots' revenge for this was very unpleasant. When a crew member was seated on the Elsan, an unscrupulous pilot seeking retribution, or what today we would call 'a good laff', could disengage the auto-pilot and then gently start easing the aircraft's control column backwards and forwards, causing the fluid in the Elsan to start swilling about. The pilot knew when to stop because, even above the roar of the four mighty Griffon engines, he could hear the howls of anguish as the foul liquid came into contact with the unfortunate crew member's rear parts.

After the end of the second World War came the general introduction of jet powered aircraft and these, being much faster and more powerful, offered scope for more exciting aerobatics. The first leader of a jet formation aerobatic team, albeit unofficial and unauthorised, was Squadron Leader, later Air Vice-Marshal, Mike Lyne, CB, AFC and two bars, DL, MRAeS, Commandant of the RAF College at Cranwell from August 1963 until December 1964. He sent a letter to me at Cranwell in 1997 asking if he could bring some friends to see the Red Arrows.

'I took command of 54 Squadron in October 1946, having relinquished the rank of Wing Commander with the coming of peace,' he wrote. 'My first jet solo flight was on 20 September 1946 in a Vampire of 247 Squadron, just before I was appointed CO of 54 Squadron. On 24 and 25 April 1947 I flew two secret formation aerobatic sorties with two of my squadron colleagues, Flight Lieutenant C I Colquhoun and Pilot Officer I W Wood. These wholly illegal flights then continued regularly until 10 June when I confessed what we'd been doing to the Station Commander, Wing Commander C D North Lewis, DSO, DFC. To my surprise, he demanded to see a display and then, after a quick series of phone calls to higher authority, the Commander-in-Chief of Fighter Command flew in, in his own Meteor, and ordered us to display for him.

'After watching us, all sins were forgiven! A formal display programme was organised and our first legal display in public was at Blackpool on 2 July 1947. On 6 July, when I had the grand total of 23 flying hours on the Vampire, we gave the world's first jet formation aerobatic display at an international air show whilst we were in Brussels. The reception we got was excellent. Sometime after midnight, when I was worse the wear for alcohol, the British Air Attaché persuaded me to lead a mid-morning flypast at low level over Liège. This dangerous flight was made after the very minimum of flight planning and briefing, and with absolutely no permission from my superiors. After we had done it, I had a few minutes disquiet when, looking down at the ground for landmarks I could recognise, I couldn't remember which of the many roads led back to Brussels Airport. Anyone who did such a thing these days would be instantly court-martialled – and quite rightly!'

On 6 October 1997, the 50th anniversary of his formation display at Brussels, Air Marshal Lyne visited the Red Arrows HQ. On the day of his visit the Red Arrows were on end-of-season block leave so it fell to me to host the visit on my own. Air Marshal Lyne was not at all put out: he simply wanted to show some of his friends what he considered to be the result of his pioneering displays 50 years earlier and I believe he actually chose the day for his visit when he knew the Team would be away. When he arrived at Cranwell that day he was in good spirits and very proud to show off the Red Arrows' aircraft to his guests. I found him to be a quiet, dignified and unassuming man. He told me that he was greatly disappointed that the RAF was giving little recognition to the 50th anniversary of his historic flight and I told him that one of the things that frustrated me most in my job as Red Arrows' PRO was persuading the RAF to make the most of 'good news' stories.

Just before leaving Cranwell, the Air Marshal asked me if he could sit in the cockpit of one of the Red Arrows' Hawks because he had never had an opportunity to do that. I took some pictures of him in a Hawk cockpit and then left him alone with his thoughts whilst I talked to his guests. Sadly, a few days later he died of cancer but not before he received copies of the photographs I had taken of him in and around the Red Arrows. I learned later that he and his family and close friends knew he had only days to live when he came to Cranwell. He had used the excuse of bringing some friends to see the Red Arrows so that he could, for the last time, visit the RAF College. As if such a distinguished officer needed any excuse!

The 1950s and 1960s were the halcyon days of RAF jet aerobatic display teams. In the 1950s almost every fighter squadron and flying training school had its own unofficial aerobatic team. In 1955 Mike Lyne's 54 Squadron formed a team with four Hawker Hunters; from 1956 they were known as 'The Black Knights' because the pilots wore black flying suits. The most famous and the best remembered team of the 50s was that of 111 Squadron. Some RAF squadrons are very fussy about how they are called and since its formation 111 Squadron has always been known as Treble-One Squadron, or simply Tremblers, but never ever One-One-One or One-Eleven Squadron. The Team's radio call-sign was Blackjack and since 1956 they had flown all-black Hunters. The French public gave Treble-One the nickname 'Les Flèches Noires' and the name stuck. In 1961 the Blue Diamonds, flying 16 blue Hunters in an immaculate diamond shape, took over from the Black Arrows.

So much time, effort and money was being expended on these non-established tasks that the RAF eventually decided to disband all the squadron formation aerobatic teams and form a single, full-time professional team. It could not be done overnight. In 1964 CFS instructors formed a team of six Jet Provost T Mk 4s and became the first team to represent the RAF as a whole. Since the Jet Provosts were painted red, Red Pelicans seemed an appropriate name. In that same year the RAF Gnat Aerobatic Team was formed at the RAF's advanced flying training school at Valley, in Anglesey, and worked up in time to perform at the 1964 Farnborough Air Show in yellow-painted Folland Gnats. Flight Lieutenant Lee Jones was the Leader. The Team was allocated the radio call sign Yellowjack and the pilots and Team quickly became known as the Yellowjacks. The then Commandant of the Central Flying School, Air Commodore H A C Bird-Wilson, apparently hated the title and insisted on a name change. Lee Jones considered this an unwarranted interference but he had to appear to acquiesce to higher authority. For a short time the Team was known by the ridiculous name 'Daffodil Patrol'. Lee, who had no fear of 'their airships' as he called senior officers of air rank, knew that Bird-Wilson would hate the new name even more than Yellowjacks. He was absolutely right and in due course the name quietly reverted to Yellowjacks.

The following year Lee Jones was posted from Valley onto the staff of the Central Flying School. He had long wanted to run a full-time aerobatic team instead of a part-time one and so he was delighted to be given the job of forming and leading a new team to represent the RAF as a whole. The Gnat was the RAF's chosen aircraft because it was more modern, faster, and better suited to aerobatics than the only alternative aircraft at the Central Flying School, the Jet Provost. The Gnats allocated to the Team had already been painted red, probably, Lee said cynically, to make sure the name Yellowjacks could not be used again. He was asked to suggest a name for the new team. 'In that case,' he told the Air Commodore, 'let it be Red Arrows: red for the colour, and arrows in memory of the Black Arrows', and although the official name is The Royal Air Force Aerobatic Team, they have been the Red Arrows ever since and the Team has remained under the command and control of the Central Flying School.

In 1960 the Central Flying School was honoured when Her Majesty Queen Elizabeth The Queen Mother accepted the appointment of Commandant-in-Chief – an appointment which she holds to this day. In 1962 The Queen Mother received, on behalf of the School, the Cheltenham Sword which marked the granting of the Freedom of the Royal Borough of Cheltenham to CFS. 1962 also saw the presentation to CFS of Patrick the Pelican, now deceased but replaced in turn by clones Frederick, Cedric and Godfrey – the latter named, obviously, after the first Commandant. Purchased by several staff officers of CFS, Patrick and his successors resided at Birdland in Bourton-on-the-Water in the safe keeping of Mr Len Hill and latterly his son Ron. Whenever the Queen Mother pays an official visit to CFS the pelican is taken to the station and the Queen Mother has to 'meet' the pelican and be photographed alongside it, but not too close, for posterity. The last occasion this happened at Scampton was in June 1992 when Her Majesty asked the Commandant if she really had to be photographed with the bird. 'I hate these Pelicans,' she said. 'They always snap and try to bite me.' How dare they!

In their first season, 1965, the Red Arrows flew 65 displays in Britain, France, Italy, Holland, Belgium and Germany, and the Team was awarded the Britannia Trophy by the Royal Aero Club in recognition of its outstanding contribution to British prestige in the field of aviation. When the RAF decided to retain the Team for 1966, two spare pilots were established but the Team continued to fly just seven aircraft in most displays. The first display with nine pilots was in July 1966 for the benefit of HRH The Duke of Edinburgh. Lee Jones had persuaded his superiors to let him practice with nine aircraft just for that special occasion. The official end-of-season report for 1966 includes the following:

'Until late June the Team confined itself to practices and displaying with seven aircraft, the reserve pilots having to be restricted to passenger flying and a very small amount of formation flying because of the limited time available. This resulted in a lowering of the morale of the reserve pilots as they were doing nothing useful, did not feel part of the team, and could see no prospect of flying in the Team. The whole Team was particularly frustrated by the fact that since the beginning of the 1966 display season, the Team had had nine serviceable aircraft for every display but were restricted by a policy decision to flying with only seven. The Team continued to press for permission to fly nine and by the end of June it was agreed that the Team could fly nine for the display on 8 July for HRH The Duke of Edinburgh. From that moment the Team started to practice with nine. Morale immediately improved and remained excellent for the rest of the season.

'After 8 July, with two exceptions, all displays were given with nine aircraft. It is possible to maintain a nine-aircraft display with an establishment of ten aircraft with just a very small and acceptable risk of having to revert to a display with fewer aircraft. It is unlikely that a pilot without previous formation aerobatic experience could be trained to fly in a permanent position with the Team in the normal training time available. Reserve pilots are unnecessary.'

The Team had to revert to seven aircraft displays for the whole of the 1967 season because of structural problems in the Gnat's rear fuselage in the early part of the year when the Team was training. In 1968 the Team was officially increased in size to nine. Although there was nothing new in flying nine aircraft in a diamond-shaped formation, the Red Arrows' perfectly symmetrical Diamond Nine quickly came to represent the peak of precision flying and it was eventually registered as an official trade mark.

Her Majesty The Queen presented the Central Flying School with a Queen's Colour in 1969. The Queen's Colour, which is in the gift of the Sovereign and no-one else, is the RAF equivalent of a Regimental Colour. Initially there was resistance within the RAF itself to the proposal to award a Queen's Colour to the Central Flying School. I imagine this was something to do with the on-going antipathy non-CFS graduates have to those who have graduated from the school, while others may have thought that a CFS Queen's Colour would detract from the prestige of the Queen's Colour for the Royal Air Force itself. In any event, when the Queen Mother, as Commandant-in-Chief of the CFS, heard of the proposal she must have encouraged the Queen to approve the award. The CFS Commandant of the day had the dubious honour of meeting Her Majesty whilst seated in a wheel chair, having broken both ankles in an accident only a few weeks previously.

Until 1976 all the Red Arrows' pilots were Qualified Flying Instructors on the staff of the Central Flying School. The first non-QFIs were Tim Curley and Nigel Champness, Reds 8 and 9 in the 1976 Team. I do not suppose anyone, not even QFIs, ever had the temerity to suggest that only QFIs were capable of representing the RAF in a formation aerobatic team but since the Team was originally formed at the Headquarters of the School it had seemed a logical step to use QFIs on the Team. That did not stop the RAF sending pilots on the CFS course with a view to posting them to the Red Arrows immediately after graduation with no intention of using them for normal instructional duties. Dickie Duckett was one of the students on my CFS course. He was rushed through the last few weeks of the course so that he could join the Red Arrows for the final part of the winter training season. Just a week after the rest of us graduated on 11 March 1968, Dickie flew his first public display at Fairford so, to put it mildly, he must have been a fast learner. He was Red 9 in that season, Red 4 in 1969 and Red 7 in 1970 before returning as Team Leader for the 1975 and 1976 seasons. Dickie's own flying instructor when he was a student on Gnats at Valley was none other than Lee Jones, the first Leader of the Red Arrows.

Other students with me at CFS included Johnny Haddock, Richard Howard, Richard Gowring and Keith Skinner. Johnny joined the Red Arrows for the 1970 season but was one of four pilots tragically killed in 1971 when Reds 6 and 7, each with another pilot in the back seat, collided over Kemble. Group Captain Richard Howard was Station Commander at Scampton when I arrived, Richard Gowring replaced him in May 1990 and two years later Peter Edwards, who as a flying officer had been one of my flying instructors at Leeming in 1967, replaced him. Keith Skinner was, like me, a 'creamie' and he turned up at Scampton as Wing Commander Red Arrows in the early 1990s. My life has been full of coincidences!

The Red Arrows took delivery of the British Aerospace Hawk trainer in the autumn of 1979 and during that winter the pilots converted from the Gnat and worked up a display using the new aeroplane in time for the 1980 display season. In 1983 the Red Arrows moved to Scampton and the CFS HQ followed some months later.

9

Red Arrows 'Wannabes'

THE RED ARROWS ARE ORGANISED AND ADMINISTERED, as far as possible, like any other RAF flying squadron. The Team Leader is the Squadron Commander and he reports, through a wing commander staff officer to the Commandant CFS. The wing commander was known as Wing Commander Air until the early-1990s when, following a re-organisation of responsibilities within CFS HQ, the post was re-named Wing Commander Royal Air Force Aerobatic Team, or Wing Commander RAFAT for short. Apart from the nine display pilots, there is a squadron leader Team Manager, two engineering officers, approximately 65 ground technicians and administrative staff and the full-time PRO. The ground crew, known collectively as 'The Blues', because of the distinctive royal blue flying suits they wear when in the public eye during the display season, are all RAF personnel. When the Team deploys away from base they aim to take 10 Hawks; one engineering officer and nine technicians fly in the rear cockpits. The flying ground crew are known as 'The Circus' and these are much sought after jobs. For longer detachments and for tours further afield, the Team takes extra ground crew and equipment in a Hercules transport aircraft. The capacious hold of the Hercules is usually used as the mobile office for the Red Arrows' ground crew when the Team is 'down the route'.

For many years the Team Manager had always doubled as Red 10, the pilot who flew the spare aircraft to displays and the one who flew many of the guest photographers. The Manager as Red 10 was the man who did all the public commentaries at air shows and that kept him away from base for long periods during the display season. The duties of the Manager had been steadily increasing over the years. One task that had started to provide a lot of extra work for the Manager during the 1990s was dealing with the companies who were willing to 'sponsor' the Team on the overseas tours and in other ways. The annual glossy brochure, limited edition calendar and various gizzits are put together by the Manager and it is quite a time consuming business during the winter months. From time to time I offered to take over those jobs from the Manager because I saw them as part of the Team's PR output but none of the incumbents seemed to want to give up that task. I did not press the point because I was always fully occupied anyway but I understand my successor has now taken over these roles.

In June 1998, as Squadron Leader Mike Williams left the Team at the end of his tour, the job of Team Manager was split into two. Flight Lieutenant Russ Jones was posted in as Red 10 and Squadron Leader Eric Webster joined a few weeks later as Team Manager. Eric was an Air Traffic Controller by profession so he was the first non-pilot to fill the role of Manager. Russ took over all of Red 10's flying tasks together with some other professional flying duties within the squadron. Just after I retired, the Red Arrows gained their first female officer, Squadron Leader Lynn Johnson, who was appointed Team Manager. Lynn is an Air Traffic Controller by profession and came to the Team from a tour of duty as Equerry to the Duke of Edinburgh. My successor as PRO, Denise Housby, was able to make much PR capital out of Lynn's appointment, the first female to wear the Team's red flying suit.

It always seemed to surprise people when I told them that by the end of the Team's 36th Season in 2000, just 113 pilots had displayed in public with the Red Arrows. I suppose that as far as most people are concerned, the Red Arrows have been around for as long as they can remember so 113 does not seem very many. Apart from the first three years, the Red Arrows Team has always consisted of nine display pilots, including the Leader, and each one is planned to stay for three seasons. There are no stand-ins. When one of the pilots is unable to fly for any reason, the Team displays without him. If the Team Leader were ever unable to fly, then the whole Team would be grounded because there is no deputy leader, but that has never happened in my time.

The ideal changeover plot is the one where three pilots leave at the end of each season so that at any given time the Team consists of three pilots in their final year, three in their second year and three in their first year. The first-year pilots are always known as FNGs. The NG part stands for New Guy but I have never been quite certain what the initial F stands for! This 3-3-3 system gives the best overall level of expertise and, although the pilots tend not to think of this, guards against anyone getting over-confident, over-bearing, or stale by staying on for a fourth year. Most if not all pilots leaving at the end of a three-year tour with the Red Arrows are content to do so and are ready for a break from the high pressure routine. In common with some of the longest-serving members of the Red Arrows ground crew, I have watched pilots, and future Team Leaders, mature as they progress from being one of the apprehensive FNGs to being one of the most experienced and respected pilots on the Team. Some find their hair turns grey while others lose hair. Most seem to age more than the three years that have actually elapsed, and all are probably physically and mentally drained at the end of their tour. They will certainly miss the camaraderie, the thrill of performing in front of ecstatic crowds, and the glamour associated with being in the spotlight.

Only seven pilots have flown four consecutive seasons and four of those were to tide the Team over when the change from Gnat to Hawk aircraft took place in time for the 1980 Season. While I am on this subject I had better mention, for completeness, that Ray Hanna flew five consecutive seasons with the Team. He was Red 3 in 1965 and he was Team Leader for the next four years, the only pilot to lead the Team for four years.

To apply for the Red Arrows, pilots must be currently employed on a fast-jet front-line squadron, flying aircraft such as Harrier, Jaguar, and Tornado, or have recently completed such a tour. Even now, 25 years after the last all-QFI team, there is always at least one QFI on the Team. The applicants must be assessed as above the average in their operational role and they must be recommended by their squadron and station commanders. Pilots meeting those criteria are usually senior flight lieutenants in their late 20s or early 30s with at least 1,500 flying hours in their log books. Squadron Leaders are not eligible to apply because they cost too much and are usually needed to fill squadron leader appointments elsewhere.

In my decade with the Team some 500 pilots applied to become one of the elite, but only 33 made it. There were almost 100 applicants for the three vacancies on the Team in 1990; in 2001 there were less than 40. This 60 per cent reduction in just a decade is largely accounted for by the fact that the RAF is now much smaller following draw-down after the collapse of the Soviet Union and the break up of the Warsaw Pact. As a result there is now a much smaller field of pilots with the necessary qualifications, but that it is not only reason. Spending three years flying with the Red Arrows means that a highly-skilled pilot moves out of the front-line at the very time when he is at the peak of his professional capabilities and is probably in the bracket for promotion to squadron leader. Proof of this can be seen in the fact that several pilots in recent years have been selected for promotion to squadron leader during their tour with the Reds and two Leaders, Simon Meade and Andy Offer, have been promoted to wing commander before the end of their tour in command. There is a potential conflict of interest here that undoubtedly stops some suitably qualified pilots applying for the Team. Leaving the front line voluntarily to join the Red Arrows means that a fairly senior pilot on an operational squadron has to give up his position of respect and authority on that squadron to join another squadron at the bottom of the pecking order. We should all be grateful that there are still enough pilots willing to do that.

The RAF is so small nowadays, that every applicant will be known by, at the very least, one of the current Team members. Many of them will have been display pilots in their own right, often displaying their single aircraft on the same air show programmes as the Red Arrows. It is generally assumed that all serious applicants have the necessary professional skills to cope with the pure flying demands, but there is a lot more to being a Red Arrow than that. The Red Arrows do almost everything together for the three years they are on the Team. They not only fly together, they train together, socialise together, live together in hotels, make corporate and charity appearances together, and wear the same civilian dress code when making public appearances. When they travel overseas, they are ambassadors for their Service and their country. It goes without saying that they must have absolute faith in each other's flying skills but they must also get on well together on the ground. There is no place for the loner on the Red Arrows, and certainly none for an individual with irritating personal habits.

The lengthy selection procedure usually gets under way in January and is designed to weed out both the unsuitables and the undesirables. All applications are collated first by the staff of the RAF's Personnel Management Centre at Innsworth. Some pilots are weeded out at this stage, usually because the staff have other plans, not yet announced, for those individuals. Those who survive this paper trawl are invited to visit the Team during the first few weeks of the selection process, which coincides with the second half of the Team's winter training season, and have a trip in the back seat on a practice display. Not surprisingly, they all accept – subject only to operational commitments on their current squadron. This gives them their first real experience of the sort of flying and team skills required. I often used to meet them on the flight line when they got out of the Hawk at the end of a 30-minute training session and ask how they enjoyed the trip. Comments such as 'awesome', 'amazing', 'fantastic', and 'I've never been so close to so many aircraft', were commonplace. Just as important, this day trip to the Red Arrows provides all the current pilots with a good opportunity to give the applicants the once over.

The Team Leader has access to the confidential flying reports for each of the applicants and, in conjunction with his senior pilots, he eventually reduces the first list to a short list of eight or nine from which three have to be chosen. The short-listed pilots are then invited to spend a whole week with the Team. That week used to be spent at Scampton but in recent years they have flown out to Cyprus to join the Red Arrows on their annual Springhawk training detachment at RAF Akrotiri. In the course of the week, each will fly as a back-seat passenger in different formation positions on up to three routine training sorties a day. There is also a formal flying test where they have to demonstrate their own piloting skills. In the evenings they join in various social events where their demeanour and stamina can be monitored. The social functions range from the very formal, usually a cocktail party or a dinner hosted by the Commander British Forces Cyprus and attended by anybody who is anybody, to the very informal all-ranks beach barbecues. Towards the end of the week there is the inevitable interview with a selection board consisting of at least the CFS Commandant and the Team Leader. The questions do not change much from year to year and the applicants will have heard most of them before if they have done their homework properly. That does not make them any easier to answer convincingly though.

'Why do you want to be on the Red Arrows?' That one should be easy to answer.

'What will you contribute to the Team if you are selected?' That needs a little more thought.

'What impresses you most about the Team and what impresses you least about the Team?' Hmm! Tricky.

'If you had to choose three people from your short-list, whom would you choose and why?' A dodgy one that. Do you include yourself or not?

'Is there anything about the Team that you think should be changed?' Only a brave candidate would suggest anything radical.

There is no doubt that it is both a stressful and very tiring week. At the end of it the hopefuls return to their home base while the Red Arrows gather together in conclave to pick the successful ones. This is a selection process unique to the Red Arrows. No outsider, not even the PRO, has ever sat in on these discussions: many media organisations have asked to do so because they think it could make a good fly-on-the-wall documentary. We have never allowed the media in because the pilots not selected would be portrayed as failures, which is something they most definitely are not! A highly-experienced Harrier or Tornado pilot, qualified to lead operational missions in the Middle East or Balkans, can in no way be considered a failure simply because he was not selected for a place in the Red Arrows.

I have been told that the pilots usually find it relatively easy to reduce the short list to a very short list. The difficulties arise when it comes to deciding not which ones to select but which of those on the very short list should be discarded. It frequently takes as long to cast out the final one from four as it did to reduce the short list of nine to four and even then it is often a compromise. 'Flight Lieutenant A is young enough to stand a good chance next year but Flight Lieutenant B is likely to be promoted before next year's selection so this is his last opportunity to join us. Let's have B.'

Red Arrows who are staying on the Team, but not those being replaced, are allowed to veto any individual applicant as long as they explain why. It could be that the two just cannot get on together and that might lead to friction at times. Those leaving the Team at the end of the season are not allowed a veto because they will not have to fly with the new pilots anyway. Eventually, sometimes after many hours deliberation, and even heated argument, there is a consensus and names emerge. The successful applicants are told the good news by telephone or e-mail while the unsuccessful ones get a letter of commiseration – and by the time that arrives, they have probably got the message anyway!

The unsuccessful ones usually remain on the squadron from which they came and try to continue from where they left off a week earlier, no doubt suffering banter from their colleagues for having had the temerity to want to join the Red Arrows. They are allowed by the rules to apply again the following year as long as they still meet the selection parameters. Some do and are accepted into the Team on their second or even third attempt. This is getting less common because by that stage they are even more experienced in their primary role and they see their future career in the front line after all. Others feel that they cannot go through the whole traumatic procedure a second or third time. A few will have decided that it was a mistake to have applied in the first place, but they are not likely to admit that either to their friends or to the Red Arrows.

I had better deal here with the most frequently asked of all the frequently asked questions. It comes in two forms:

'Will there ever be a female Red Arrow?' and 'When will there be a female Red Arrow.'

I had a very simple and truthful answer.

'There will be a female Red Arrow when one applies for the job and gets through the selection procedure successfully.'

There is no bar on female pilots applying to join the Team but, at the time of my retirement, there were very few that had the necessary qualifications and none of those had applied. I was rather disappointed because I was looking forward to running with the stories.

When girls were first allowed to train as RAF pilots in the late 1980s, there was a suggestion in certain quarters that the procedures at the

Officers and Aircrew Selection Centre had been relaxed for women candidates to ensure that not all were rejected in the process. Whatever the reason, and it probably was not that, there are still very few female pilots in the RAF and only a few of those are flying operational fast-jets. The Red Arrows have always been adamant about one thing. Any female joining the Red Arrows must do so because she has earned her place in competition with the men, not simply because she was female. The distaff's time will undoubtedly come.

The Leader does far more than fly at the front of the formation as Red One. Some misguided people think that it must be easy for the Leader, after all he does not have to formate on anyone. When talking to visitors or to the media, I usually likened the post of Team Leader to that of a Chief Executive Officer or Managing Director. The Team Leader is the Squadron Commander, the Commanding Officer for almost 100 personnel, including all the ground crew and administrative back up – and that includes the PRO these days. He is responsible for everything that happens on the squadron, policy matters, discipline, and routine administration. In the air display season he often starts his office work when the rest of the pilots go home at the end of a series of displays. In the training season he usually arrives at work first and goes home last. The occasional bad weather day in the winter, when flying has to be cancelled, is a godsend for the Leader as it enables him to get through some of his admin 'niff-naff' in normal working hours.

The Leader has to get the Team to the display site exactly on time, plus or minus a couple of seconds. On every display he has fly the sequence smoothly and accurately with the same angles of bank, the same smooth application of g, the same rate of moving his throttle, because if he does not the rest of his pilots will have little chance of staying in close formation with him. He has to check his height and speed at the top of the loops and rolls to make sure he does not continue if there is insufficient height to complete the manoeuvre at or above the minimum authorised height. He has to keep a close eye on fuel consumption and fuel reserves; he has to watch out for unauthorised aircraft intruding into his reserved airspace; he has to make sure neither he nor any of his aircraft gets closer to the crowd than the minimum approved distance. While he is doing all that, he has to make the radio calls which act as cues to the rest of the pilots and he has to keep a close eye in his rear view mirrors to make sure that everything is in order. Finally he has to lead the Team safely back to the operating base and conduct the debriefing.

With just two exceptions, the Leader has always previously served as a member of the Team and that is now a pre-requisite. People think that this is because in order to have the credibility to lead the Team you must have demonstrated that you can do everything you will ask your pilots to do. Whilst that is partly true, it is not the whole truth. New pilots take about six months intensive training to hone their flying skills to the Red Arrows' standard. A Leader who had not been a Team member earlier in his career would need not only those six months to acquire the flying skills but also extra time in which to master the very special skills needed to run the entire squadron and lead the Team through fair weather and foul.

The two exceptions were in the first season, 1965, when someone had to lead, and 1970. Flight Lieutenant Lee Jones was the first Red Leader, but he was already very experienced in leading formation aerobatics and so he was well qualified for the job, possibly the only one qualified for the job. In 1970 Squadron Leader Dennis Hazel was the Leader for that one year without having previously been a Red Arrow. Unfortunately, after his first season he broke a leg when he had to eject from his Gnat on the final approach to landing at Kemble on 13 November 1970 and he was unable to continue training for the 1971 season. Raymond Loverseed, always known as Bill, who had just completed the 1970 Season as Red 9, was promoted to squadron leader and appointed Team leader for 1971. He was a very experienced pilot having flown such diverse aircraft as F4 Phantoms, Meteors, Vampires, Venoms, Sabres and Hunters and he had been a founder member of the 1965 Red Arrows. Sadly Bill died in November 1998 when the Dash 7 turboprop airliner he was flight testing crashed into a hillside near Ashburton in Devon just a few weeks after he had attended a reunion of Red Arrows' Team Leaders and flown with the Team, as a passenger, for the last time.

There is a selection procedure for the post of Team Leader but this is less often talked about. The Team Leader must be a squadron leader before he can be considered for the job. At any given time there are only three or four officers who meet all the requirements and, naturally, they can work out who they are, just as all the other Red Arrows, past and present, can work out who is in the running. There used to be an old wives' tale, or old pilots' tale, that you could not lead the Red Arrows unless you had been in the Synchro Pair in your first tour. Tim Miller and Andy Offer were not Synchro pilots and Andy himself was replaced at the end of 2001 by Spike Jepson, who will be the 16th Leader and was never in the Synchro Pair either. In all, only 7 of the 15 leaders so far have flown in the Synchro Pair so that appears to settle that argument once and for all. There is no formal system of asking for volunteers for the job but those who think they are in with a shout can let it be known that they would accept it if offered. Acting on his own personal knowledge, together with advice from his subordinates, the Air Officer Commanding selects who he wants for the job and asks him, either in a personal telephone call or face-to-face, if he wants it. As far as I am aware no-one has ever declined the offer.

In most cases there has been a gap of three years or more between a pilot finishing a tour of duty on the Team and returning as Leader. This is done deliberately so that the individual can have a decent rest from the stresses and strains of Team life and so that he can go back to the 'real' Air Force and look after his longer term career prospects. Squadron Leader Andy Offer was an exception. After his three years on the Team he was sent to a one-year staff appointment at RAF Strike Command having already been pre-selected by the Commander-in-Chief to return as Team Leader. In fact the one year staff appointment turned out to be little more than 10 months for, having departed in October 1998, he returned in August 1999 to start his preliminary work up.

As I joined the Red Arrows in 1989 the 3-3-3 system for rotating the pilots had been in operation for many years but it went wrong at the end of the 1990 Season when a first-year pilot, Flight Lieutenant Paul Rogers, was removed from the Team. Paul came into my office in a distressed state shortly before the end of the season and told me that he had been sacked because the pilots had lost confidence in his flying abilities.

'The Commandant has told me that he wants me to fly the last few displays but that I'll then have to leave,' Paul said to me. 'I can't understand that decision. If the other pilots have lost confidence in me, how can they trust me to fly amongst them for the last few displays?'

A very valid question, especially as the final two displays were at Rivolto, the home of the Italian Air Force formation aerobatic team, *Frecce Tricolori*, always some of the most critical spectators. The pressure on Paul must have been immense but to his great credit he completed the season in fine style and the Rivolto displays were deemed to be amongst the best of the season. Had there been any sort of safety incident in the last weeks of the season, there would have been some very awkward questions for someone to answer, and that someone would not have been Paul Rogers. Paul was asked where he would like to be posted and he opted to go and fly for what was then called The Queen's Flight and is now The Royal Squadron. Some years later, without ever succumbing to the temptation to loop and roll a BAE 146 with a member of the Royal Family on board, Paul left the RAF to work in civilian aviation and I know he is very satisfied with the way things have turned out.

Paul Rogers' replacement for the 1991 Season was Neil Rogers but they were not related. Neil should really have stayed for only two years to keep the 3-3-3 system running but at the end of his first season he pleaded to remain for the full three-year term and was allowed to do so. To my relief, the media never asked any questions about the early departure of Paul. Perhaps the fact that his successor was also named Rogers had something to do with it but, whatever the reason, it saved me having to explain why Paul had left after only one season. I am certain the media would have made a big thing out of it had they known. When I issued my usual news releases giving details of the new Team members at the start of the 1991 Season, it was one of the few occasions when I have been economical with the truth in my dealings with the media. Had they done their research properly they would have asked me what had happened to Paul and I would have had to tell them. They missed a good story but Paul has now given me permission to set the record straight.

For the next 10 years the Team was locked into a 4-2-3 changeover regime. It was, perhaps, unfortunate that the years when four pilots changed, 1991, 1994 and 1997, were also the years when a new Leader took command. It would have been preferable if it had worked out that the change of Leader coincided with the years when there was only one other new pilot, 1993, 1996 and 1999. Wing Commander Andy Offer left at the end of the 2001 Season to go to Staff College and advance his career after only two years in command and that means that the 3-3-3 regime has finally been restored.

Once, in the early 1990s, an air marshal asked me privately why I thought it was that so few former Red Arrows, supposedly the *crème de la crème* of RAF pilots, reached high rank and why so many of them left the RAF at their first exit point following their time with the Red Arrows. Dickie Duckett is now retired but he is still the only former Team pilot to reach air commodore rank, perhaps surprising in view of the high calibre of the Team pilots over the years. There is no doubt that a tour with the Red Arrows is the highlight of any pilot's career up to that point but in the course of their tour pilots inevitably get out of touch with operational flying – they may even miss out on the opportunity to be one of the first pilots on new generation aircraft. Some pilots who would dearly like to join the Red Arrows instead put their career interests first if they have aspirations to high rank in the RAF because the smaller the RAF is, the greater the competition there will be for the plum flying jobs. Those who have put the Red Arrows first often do not relish the prospect of returning to normal squadron flying with its routine and the frequent overseas unaccompanied detachments. Duty in places such as the Falkland Islands, the Balkans and the Middle East compares very badly with the excitement and glamour of the Red Arrows and the comfort of being accommodated in the world's finest 5-star hotels.

It is, therefore, not too surprising that after a highly successful career as a fast-jet front-line pilot followed by a tour with the Red Arrows, many Team members leave the air force. Curiously, many end up flying for civilian airlines. I say curiously because airline flying is often downright boring, is certainly not as glamorous as many people think, and is rarely exciting. Sadly that all changed for ever on 11 September 2001 with the events in New York and Washington so, if the airlines continue to cut services and staff, there may be fewer former Red Arrows flying airliners in future. Nevertheless, at the last count I made, Air 2000, British Airways, Cathay Pacific and Virgin Atlantic between them have had more than 30 ex-Red Arrows flying for them at one time or another, and that is more than 25 per cent of all former Red Arrows. Certainly money has been one factor that attracted any RAF pilot to the civilian airlines but stability was another. In the airlines you usually know your duty roster two or three months in advance and can organise your family and social life accordingly. That is certainly not possible whilst serving in the RAF, but then that is not why most people joined the RAF.

At the start of the 1995 Season I thought it would make a nice media story to announce to the world that the 100th pilot would display with the Team that year. It proved impossible to decide which one of the three new pilots should have the honour of being the 100th. Tim Couston would have got it had I used alphabetical order, but Richie Matthews and Sean Perrett were not happy about that. We then discussed the possibility of using seniority in rank, the oldest, the youngest, or the one with the most flying hours, but in the end I gave up the unequal struggle and accepted that this was one story I would not use!

10

A Winter's Day

I WAS OFTEN ASKED BY MEMBERS OF THE PUBLIC what the Red Arrows do during the winter. After one typical working day at Scampton in January 1994 I jotted down the following notes in my personal diary and they still serve as an introduction to way the Team operates. Now that the Red Arrows are back at Scampton once again the daily routine in winter is still very similar to this.

A surprising number of people are under the impression that the Red Arrows have little to do in winter. Nothing could be further from the truth for it is in the months from October through to April that the new pilots work up and the Team Leader, in conjunction with all his pilots, has to choreograph the next season's display. The engineers spend most of the winter months carrying out extensive maintenance on the Hawks so that they should last through the display season with just the minimum of routine servicing. During the dark winter months all ranks of the Squadron have to carry out refresher training on general service skills in order to remain fully qualified as officers and airmen of a fighting service.

Each of the Team pilots has his own secondary duty, some have more than one. The Site Survey officer visits display locations not previously used to check that they are entirely suitable. The Combat Survival officer organises dinghy drills and parachute drills. The Flight Safety officer has to ensure that everyone, aircrew and ground crew, is kept up to date on flight safety matters. Another officer organises the programme for the 50-odd lectures and presentations the pilots give during the winter to interested groups in all corners of the United Kingdom. The Entertainments officer has to make sure that everyone turns up on time for golf matches and other social occasions and that guests are properly hosted and entertained. The navigators, who are not navigators at all but two of the Team's pilots, plan all the routes the Team will use throughout the year and make sure that the Team never infringes any restricted airspace and always, but always, gets to the display sites exactly on time to the nearest second. One of the Red Arrows' pilots, a qualified examiner, has to fly with each of the other pilots once during the year to renew their instrument ratings: the Red Arrows have to fly annual test sorties just like every other pilot in the RAF. Even the examiner is not exempt: he has to renew his own qualification every year with another examiner.

During the winter months many hundreds of visitors come to the Red Arrows' Headquarters, by invitation, to see behind the scenes and, they hope, to meet the pilots. These visitors may be captains of industry from businesses that have helped the Team in one way or another during the previous season; they may be school children doing school projects on flight; Air Training Corps cadets; sick children or sick adults; people celebrating birthdays or wedding anniversaries; or just ordinary members of the public who dote on the Red Arrows and want to see them on their own ground. The pilots can never be abrupt with visitors; they must always have a smile on their face, be ready to chat and to answer the same questions they have answered many times before.

'How did you become a Red Arrow?'

'Why did you want to be a Red Arrow?'

'Have you always wanted to be a pilot?'

'Is it dangerous?'

'How close are you to each other?'

Winter is also a convenient time for me to organise interviews with newspapers, aviation magazines, and radio and TV stations: they all help to keep the Team in the public eye during the close season. Local papers and radio stations need interviews and photo sessions with pilots who hail from their circulation area – local media simply love to have 'their own Red Arrow'. Aviation magazines want to hear about the latest new manoeuvres being planned; TV stations all around the country – and overseas – want up-to-date footage for their libraries. Production teams for television programmes such as 'Surprise Surprise', 'Jim'll Fixit', and 'How Do They Do That?' descend on Scampton filling up the tiny crew room and briefing room with cameras, lights, cables, microphones and all the other paraphernalia of their profession. There is more time to do these things during the winter than in the hectic display season when time is always at a premium

Exciting? Yes. Worthwhile? Certainly. Time-consuming? Definitely. Take one typical day in January 1994 for example.

0740: The duty member of the administrative staff opens up the HQ and switches on the water boiler in the pilots' crew room. That is not all he does, of course, but it is a most important duty. The ground crew have already been busy for some time; several aircraft have already been towed out onto the flight line ready for the day's flying. The media, and public, rarely see this early morning activity. Some of the best ground photographs or videos show the immaculately polished red aircraft being towed out of the brightly lit, centrally-heated hangar into the winter gloom.

0750: I was sitting in my car at the Main Guard Room waiting for a photographer and reporter from a well-known Yorkshire newspaper. The reporter is one of the lucky few each year selected for a trip in the back seat of one of the Hawks; the photographer will cover events from the ground. Several weeks ago I booked an 0800 hrs medical for the reporter. Blood pressure, heart, ears and sinuses all have to be examined. His weight, height and leg measurements need to be checked to ensure that they are all within the laid down limits for safe operation of the Martin Baker ejection seat. The RAF doctor has no access to the reporter's own GP's record. I have already briefed the reporter that he must answer all the doctor's questions about his health honestly. Concealing details about a cold or previous illnesses could be dangerous.

Apart from the media, there are dozens of requests each year from members of the public requesting a flight with the Red Arrows. The letters are often ingenious, sometimes very touching, but the answer always has to be no. The Hawk is an operational fast jet aircraft not a toy; it is potentially dangerous for unqualified persons and in any case if the Team said yes to one individual request what would they say to all the others?

Once the Medical Officer has declared the reporter fit to fly, he will be issued with all the special flying clothing needed for a flight in a Hawk. The kitting out will take the best part of an hour. After that there will be a detailed briefing with his pilot. He will not be ready before 1100 at the earliest. Plenty of time for apprehension and for thinking, 'Perhaps I shouldn't have had that fried breakfast after all!' I had warned him about that well in advance. A sensible breakfast is what is needed so that you are not flying on an empty stomach. If there is one thing worse than being airsick, it is trying to be sick when there is nothing in your stomach.

0800: The Synchro Pair, Reds 6 and 7, arrive at the Squadron. They are already dressed in most of their flying equipment because they travel to and from their homes on base like that. It saves time. It is not true, as some wags suggest, that they sleep in their flying suits – or so I am told. These two are the 'soloists' in the second half of the display. In the early part of the winter they often fly as a pair working out new routines to thrill the crowds. Synchro Leader, Red 6, has to check the weather with the Duty Met Officer on the telephone: the main station briefing is not until 0815 and that is at the far end of the station. No time for Synchro to go there in person although the Team Leader and Team Manager will be at the main briefing with the rest of the Station's pilots. In the meantime Synchro 2, Red 7, will be telephoning Air Traffic Control to find out which runway will be in use at base, which alternate airfields have been booked, and to be briefed on any air traffic matters that might affect their flight. One of the Synchro Pair talks on the intercom to the engineers to see which aircraft have been allocated to their flight. During the display season each of the nine display pilots has his own aircraft, with his name painted on the side, but in the winter that is not possible because on any given day several aircraft will be on scheduled maintenance in the hangar.

0815: The Synchro pilots brief each other. This is a formal briefing but certainly not a formality. Synchro Leader is in charge and has the final say on exactly what the flight profile will be but it is very much a team effort, a team of two in this case. Together they review what happened on the previous flight, decide what changes or refinements are needed, and go through what they are going to do on the coming flight down to the minutest detail. After signing the Flight Authorisation Sheet, the legal document which codifies what they will do during the flight, they zip up their anti-g trousers and go downstairs to Flight Line Control where they check their aircraft's documentation. The Senior NCO in charge briefs them on any pertinent engineering matters, perhaps explaining how any faults reported on the previous flight were rectified. Pilot and NCO confirm that the aircraft has the correct fuel load on board. There may be some 'red snow' items in the aircraft log. These are faults which the engineering officer considers will have no impact on the proposed flight and can safely be deferred until later; they are highlighted in red so that the pilot can be briefed about them. If he is not happy, the pilot can refuse to accept a red-line entry but because of the trust between ground crew and pilot that is a very rare event. Finally, the pilot signs the log indicating that he is satisfied that the aircraft is fit for flight. From that moment the pilot, the captain, has sole responsibility for the aircraft.

0825: The pilots walk out to their aircraft parked on the apron a couple of hundred metres away. It is still not fully daylight this January morning. There are some snow-covered ice patches around following a recent wintry shower and the wind is quite blustery. The pilots glance up at the sky as they walk, visually checking on the cloud base. Was the Met Man right? Is the lowest cloud really 1,600 feet above the airfield? It is difficult to be sure in the half-light.

Distant sounds of shooting followed by amplified birds' distress calls indicate that the station's Bird Control Unit is out at work. Actually, it is one man in a yellow Land Rover. He does not shoot the birds; he fires into the air in their vicinity to frighten them off. But Scampton's resident birds are wily birds; they know it is only a trick and they have learned to keep out of the way of aircraft. Many of them fly around the airfield at very low level totally ignoring the mechanical Hawks with their attendant noise and smoke. Unfortunately, every now and again a bird fails to get out of the way. A bird strike is potentially dangerous: it can damage the canopy and hinder the pilot's vision; in the worst case it can cause airframe damage or engine failure.

Out on the flight line the see-off airmen have already completed most of the pilots' pre-flight checks. This is not standard RAF practice but on the Red Arrows everyone trusts everyone else and it saves the pilots several minutes at the start of every flight. The airmen greet the pilots and perhaps have a few jokes with them while they help them strap into the ejection seats. Within seconds the pilots are ready. The canopies close and the pilots are then snugly sealed into their pressurised offices. Thumbs up from the ground crew, the engine igniters tick rhythmically and the Rolls Royce Adour engine roars into life. All around the married quarters area people, some of them still in bed, hear the noise and check their watches. Synchro Leader calls Air Traffic Control for taxi clearance. Runway 05 is in use, that is the north-easterly runway, and there will be a strong crosswind component from the right on take-off.

0833: A Hercules transport aircraft, arriving empty from its base at Lyneham in Wiltshire, lands. It is here to pick up a Scampton-based British arms control team bound for Kiev. Fat Albert, a soubriquet for the aircraft not the pilot, has to clear the runway before 0840, Synchro's scheduled take-off time. The Hercules captain reports on the radio to Air Traffic Control that he saw the runway lights at three miles from touch down on his radar controlled approach. That means the cloud base is about 1,000 feet, OK for Synchro, but the visibility is not too good. When the Synchro pair are flying directly towards each other for their opposition manoeuvres, they have a closing speed of 12 miles per minute, that is one mile in just 5 seconds. If the visibility is only three miles, and that when looking at powerful runway lights, the pilots will have a maximum of 15 seconds from first sighting each other until they cross, hopefully in the middle of the runway.

The pilots wave the chocks away and Synchro are on the move, taxiing past the four pre-World War 2 hangars, past Nigger's Grave, past my former office in CFS HQ, past Foxtrot Dispersal in the south eastern corner of the airfield where other ground crew are waiting to receive the Hercules, and eventually turning right onto the 9,000 foot runway that was especially built in the mid-fifties for the V Force.

0840: The Synchro Pair take off in close formation. Picturesque condensation trails stream from the wing tips as the aircraft rotate and get airborne – the trails indicate that humidity is very high so there is a possibility of mist and fog forming. This is the start of Slot 1. There are six half-hour slots every day reserved for the Red Arrows. During each of those periods no other aircraft, military or civilian, is allowed inside a cylindrical section of airspace known as Restricted Area 313. R313 is five nautical miles in radius centred on the Scampton Air Traffic Control tower and extends from ground level to 9,500 feet above the ground. Synchro traditionally fly the early slot: It gives the rest of the pilots an extra half hour in bed. There is no surveillance radar at Scampton these days but there is at Waddington just a few miles away on the other side of Lincoln. The controllers there will keep a very close eye on R313 for the next half hour and remind any transiting aircraft of the need to stay well clear.

0900: The other Red Arrows' pilots have arrived at the Squadron in the last 30 minutes, one of them with just seconds to spare. Also present is a flight lieutenant pilot from another station who has applied to join the Red Arrows at the end of the 1994 season. He will fly with the Leader today to get a first hand impression of what the job is like. There will be many more like him in the following weeks. I arrive from Sick Quarters with the newspaper photographer and reporter just in time for the briefing. The reporter has passed his medical and the adrenalin is beginning to flow. At exactly 0900 one of the pilots rings the bell on the wall, the signal for the met briefing to start. Everyone congregates around the coffee bar to listen to the Met Man but, as they listen, they glance surreptitiously out of the windows every now and again as the Synchro pair roar past.

The winter weather at Scampton is rarely straightforward. The airfield perches on the edge of the Lincoln Cliff with no higher ground to the east until the Urals. Today, apparently, the low stratus may or may not clear; there is a 'prob 30', thirty percent probability, of radiation fog forming if the stratus layer does break and the wind drops off; the bitterly cold cross wind may or may not go out of limits later in the day; runway braking action was reported as good by the Hercules pilot but there were icy patches in places – watch out in case of an aborted take-off! The air temperature is plus 1 degree Centigrade but the wind chill makes it feel like minus 10 degrees. There are likely to be snow showers from late morning onwards. One of the pilots needs to know yesterday's highest temperature at Akrotiri in Cyprus. He keeps a chart going which compares the Scampton temperatures with those at Akrotiri. The Team deploy to Cyprus every April for final rehearsals in guaranteed good weather and without many of the distractions they get at Scampton. It cheers everyone up to learn how much warmer it is in Cyprus than at Scampton

0905: The Team's Executive Officer, Red 9, who prepares the daily flying and ground programme for the Boss, welcomes the pressmen and the visiting pilot and reminds everyone that an important group of 'upstairs' visitors is expected at 1140. The term 'upstairs' is used to differentiate between those visitors who meet the pilots in the crew room and have a buffet lunch with them, from the masses of ordinary visitors who do not go upstairs into the inner sanctum. If the pilots had to meet and chat to every visitor they would never get any work done. Eng 1, the First Line Engineering Officer, reports that there will be seven serviceable aircraft for slot 2.

'OK', says the Boss calling his bluff, 'Subject to a last-minute weather check, we'll fly the front seven in slot 2. Brief at 25 past.'

The Boss then takes a coffee along to his office where he spends a few minutes looking through his paper-work. The admin corporal has already sorted the contents of the Squadron Commander's in-tray so that the most important papers are at the top and the 'niff-naff' lower down. The corporal has to be adept at sorting the wheat from the chaff and the Boss trusts him.

0910: The reporter barely has time to finish his coffee before I whisk him off downstairs to the Flying Clothing section where he will be kitted out with everything from thermal underwear and socks, to flying boots and helmet and everything in-between. It is important to wear non-flammable clothing next to the skin in case of a fiery accident and in winter it is most important to wear a number of layers of clothing to protect against hypothermia whilst waiting for rescue in the event of an ejection over wild country or into the sea. The reporter pales slightly as he ponders this information. The grinning photographer hangs around watching and taking photographs of his colleague, although some will not be suitable for publication – not in a daily newspaper anyway.

0925: Exactly on the dot, the pre-flight briefing for slot 2 starts. Accurate timing is provided by a radio-controlled wall clock that is synchronised with a time signal transmitted from Rugby. One of the pilots has some private guests who sit in the back row listening intently as the Boss briefs the sortie. It sounds like a different language to them. The briefing is short and to the point – it has to be because take-off is scheduled for 0955. The Synchro pilots pass through the briefing room on their way in and give the Team Leader a favourable weather report. Those two grab a coffee and then take over the briefing room for their own debriefing of Slot 1. The CFS Commandant was watching the first sortie from the comfort of his car out in the middle of the airfield and he now arrives to sit in on the debriefing; it is all part of his supervisory duties. Synchro will fly again in Slot 3, take off at 1110, but before then they have to try and find time to give a short interview to the newspaper reporter.

0955: 'Reds rolling go!' commands the Leader on the radio.

Exactly on time to the nearest second the brakes are released and the seven red aircraft roar down the runway. Acceleration is always better in low temperatures. In the meantime the newspaper reporter has finished his kitting out. He feels very conspicuous clumping awkwardly around in heavy leather boots and a g-suit, the elasticised garment which fits tightly around the waist and lower limbs. When the aircraft accelerates against the force of gravity, high pressure air from the engine's compressor is forced into the g-suit: the more the g, the greater the pressure. This has the effect of squeezing the arteries in the lower abdomen and legs thereby preventing all the blood rushing down to the toes. On this flight he will experience at least 4g, when every part of his body, internal and external, will weigh four times normal. You cannot accurately describe this to someone: it has to be experienced. The Red Arrows pull up to 7g in their display, Synchro Pair sometimes more than that but passengers are not supposed to be subjected to more than 4g because they have not had the specialist training that aircrew get.

1000: While the seven are airborne I settle the photographer and reporter down in front of a TV set to watch a passenger video brief about the ejection seat and emergency drills. The film lasts 15 minutes and has to be seen by every passenger who flies in the back seat of a Hawk. It is very comprehensive: it aims to cover every possible eventuality and, because of that, it can be alarming for a nervous passenger. As the video finishes the Team Manager, call sign Red 10, comes in to brief the reporter about his forthcoming sortie. This allows me to go back to my office and start dealing with the morning mail and the many calls that will have been stored on the answer phone by this time.

1030: The seven have landed from Slot 2, taxied in to dispersal, closed down, and reported any snags to the ground crew. Then they go upstairs to their crew room for a cup of coffee and a biscuit. In the meantime the Red Arrows own video man, who has been filming Slot 2 from his spot in front of Air Traffic Control, places the video cassette in the machine in the briefing room and winds it forward to the correct start point. The bell rings again and the pilots settle down for debriefing. The Leader gives his first thoughts about the sortie and then runs the video, stopping frequently to freeze-frame the picture and study in detail exactly who was out of position and why. There can be no argument: the video-camera never lies. The debriefing can last up to an hour in the early part of the training season; it is rarely less than 30 minutes even at the end of the display season. Every single practice sortie and every single public display is recorded on video and debriefed in this way. Only when the Leader is sure that every lesson that can be learnt has been learnt does the debriefing end.

1050: Red 10 and his passenger walk out to the flight line and pose for the obligatory picture by the nose of the aircraft. There had been a short delay because the passenger had decided that he needed a last minute nervous pee – it is not easy wearing a g suit! It takes about 10 minutes to get the reporter properly strapped in; in spite of his pre-flight coaching, he is all fingers and thumbs, but that is quite normal. When the pilot is satisfied that his passenger is happy, he climbs into the front seat and quickly straps himself in. Once a passenger is strapped in it is best to get moving as quickly as possible. In any case they must be airborne before 1110 which is when Synchro are due to take off in Slot 3. There are no delays. Fifteen minutes later they are airborne and clearing off out of the circuit to fly northwards to Yorkshire to have a look at the reporter's local area. The Hercules, having completed embarkation of the arms control inspectors and their accoutrements, takes off just after Red 10 and sets course for the Ukraine.

1105: In the meantime I have driven to the Guard Room to greet the day's 'upstairs' visitors who have already been identified and checked by the security staff. On this occasion they are nine senior executives from a well-known company that has provided the Team with a lot of support behind the scenes during the previous season. This visit is all we can give them in return for the help and support they give the Red Arrows; it may not seem much but they are delighted to be given a privileged view behind the scenes. The Ministry of Defence does not allow companies to use their connection with the Red Arrows for overt advertising purposes. The visitors are taken to a small museum-cum-briefing room in the Central Flying School HQ, at the far end of the airfield from the Red Arrows' hangar. There they are given a short slide presentation about the history of Scampton, CFS and the Red Arrows by one of my Holding Officers. There are two reasons for going to CFS to do this: one, to keep the visitors away from the pilots while they are still debriefing slot 2; two, the CFS is an interesting place in its own right.

1110: The Synchro Pair are airborne again on their second sortie of the day – Slot 3. The reporter, perhaps without yet realising it, has missed his opportunity for an interview; he and Red 10 are heading, at 450 mph, past the Humber Bridge and into God's Own County.

1140: The upstairs visitors arrive at the Red Arrows' HQ just in time to see Synchro Pair taxi back into dispersal. The other pilots have finished their debrief and are ready to welcome their guests. There are only a few minutes for socialising because the time is rapidly approaching for Slot 4. Seven aircraft will fly again. The engineers are doing a good job keeping aircraft serviceable; each aircraft has already flown two sorties and the day is not half over.

1155: Once more the bell rings. The visiting pilot will be flying a second sortie with the Team Leader. In addition, the Commandant of CFS has decided to fly with Red 4 to see how he is getting on. Red 4 is one of the season's new pilots. It is a little off-putting having such a senior officer flying in your rear cockpit but it is all part of the process of becoming a Red Arrow. With overall responsibility for the Red Arrows, the Commandant regularly flies with the Team and, just as regularly, watches their progress from the ground. This time the upstairs visitors are occupying the back two rows of seats in the briefing room. Just outside they can see a single Hawk taxiing back onto the apron: that is Red 10 and the reporter returning from their foray into Yorkshire. A few flakes of snow are blowing around in the easterly wind – the Met man was right about that.

The visitors, huddled into warm top coats, watch Slot 4 from the best position on the airfield, Display Datum directly in front of Air Traffic Control alongside the video man. The whole display is centred on Display Datum as the name implies. Datum represents the VIP enclosure at a public display. It is where the Synchro Pair aim to cross in front of each other. Datum is where the Manager usually stands to give his public commentary. Datum is very cold today.

'How long do they fly for?' someone asks plaintively.

Never mind him... Datum is the place to be!

1300: Everyone, including the Synchro Pair, is back in the crew room by 1300hrs. The visitors help themselves from a light finger buffet with still half-frozen fingers. I am keeping an eye on the newspaper photographer who is taking fly-on-the-wall pictures. The reporter, having changed back into civilian clothes, joins in with everyone else; he is a much braver man now that the sortie is over. To his intense relief he was not airsick, just a little queasy. For a few minutes he had been allowed to handle the controls for himself and had flown himself around a sort of loop and barrel roll. There will be much to tell his colleagues back in the news room.

All the visitors are invited to sit in on the debrief. They do not understand everything that is said but at least they can watch the video and marvel at how finicky the pilots are about each other's perform-ances.

'I told you he was out of position', whispers one visitor knowingly to his colleague. It is only a practice of course.

1400: The photographer is anxious to get back to his office and develop his films and the reporter has to let the sub-editor loose on his words. They hope to print the story tomorrow. They promise to send me a copy of the paper; the Red Arrows always like to read about themselves – as long as the reporter has got all his facts right! I had told the reporter in advance of his visit that he should let the photographer do the driving on the way back to Leeds; you can get surprisingly tired after experiencing high g for several minutes when you are not used to it. He had not believed me then but he does now.

1425: The slot 4 debriefing has barely ended but it is already time for another pre-flight briefing. Synchro Pair did not fly in Slot 5 at 1340 because of a passing snow shower. The weather has now improved and the Team Leader has decided to fly slot 6, take off at 1455. All nine aircraft remain serviceable but this time the Synchro Pair will fly in their accustomed positions in the stem of the Diamond Nine as Reds 6 and 7 directly behind the Leader. Reds 3 and 5 will stay on the ground so there are spare aircraft in case one goes unserviceable on start up. Another reason for keeping two pilots on the ground is that the Leader has not yet flown all nine aircraft together. The first nine ship formation is a psychologically important sortie for all the pilots but especially for the new pilots and the Leader will not fly it until he is entirely satisfied that the pilots are ready. The resulting seven-aircraft formation, the right hand side of a Diamond Nine, looks a bit lop-sided but is good practice, in particular for two of the new pilots, Reds 2 and 4. The upstairs visitors have gone into the hangar to take a close look at the aircraft undergoing scheduled servicing and to drop in on the Red Arrows' souvenir shop.

1455: Seven aircraft airborne again. The spares were not required so the ground crew tow them back into the hangar. The upstairs visitors were expected to depart at 1500 but, when invited, could not resist the temptation to watch Slot 6. This time they watch from in front of the Team's HQ and get a quite different view.

1530: The last formation sortie for the day is over. As the pilots walk back to the crew room from their aircraft they pause on the grass to chat to a group of visiting children and sign autographs. They cannot afford to stay outdoors long because they are hot and sweaty from the cockpit and it is bitterly cold outside in the wind talking to the children. The last thing any pilot needs is a running cold which would prevent him from flying. The visiting children will have a close look at one of the Hawks in the hangar; one or two of them may be allowed to sit in a cockpit and have their photographs taken. All the other visitors have left. As the final debriefing for the day starts, the ground crew begin towing the aircraft back into the hangar. Already the sky is darkening. The temperature which had struggled up to a maximum of two degrees just after midday is again hovering on zero and more snow is forecast. A single Hawk remains out on the flight line; one of the pilots has to fly down to Exeter Airport to give an evening lecture to a local aviation society. It will be a night landing at Exeter, but that should not be a problem as the weather is much better in the south west. The pilot will stay overnight before returning early the following day, weather permitting, in time to fly slot 2 with the rest of the Team.

1615: Time for the Team Leader's weekly meeting with the Manager and me to discuss the following week's PR events and schedule of visitors. There will be upstairs visitors every single day. Additionally, an independent TV company is due to be with the Team for two days making a seven minute item for a new BBC series. Two days' work for a seven minute item is about par for television but, when I last spoke to him, the Director had still not decided exactly which shots he wants to include. It was not easy to convince him that Red Arrows' time is just as valuable as his and that he had better have his story board prepared before he turns up. The meeting goes on until 1730 when the Boss and the Manager go to their own offices to start dealing with the day's accumulated business.

240 air nautical miles to the south west, Red 9 is just landing at Exeter airport; his day is not yet over. By this time most of the other pilots have either gone home or adjourned to their 'quiet' room to get on with fan mail and secondary duties. The last person to leave the Red Arrows' HQ is the admin clerk who locks up at 1815. The end of another typical winter day for the Red Arrows.

.....But not quite. The engineers are still working in the hangar. They cannot finish until enough aircraft are serviceable for the following day's flying programme and that is often around midnight.

11

Red Faces Day and Red Suit Day

PEOPLE ARE OFTEN SURPRISED TO LEARN THAT the pilots stay in one formation position for a whole season. They move around during a display, of course, as the formation changes from one shape to another, but Red 2 is Red 2 for the whole season. The reason becomes apparent when you learn about the training that goes into the display.

The Team Leader is the final arbiter on who flies in which position but there are rules of succession to help him. Actually they are not so much rules as conventions, born out of many years of experimentation and experience. It has long been the custom in the RAF that aircraft flying on the right hand side of a formation leader should take the even numbers. In the Red Arrows' trade-mark formation, the Diamond Nine, that means that Red 2 flies immediately to the right of the Leader with Red 4 on his right, out on the wing. Red 8 is also on the right hand side of the formation, behind Red 2. Reds 3, 5 and 9 slot into the equivalent positions on the left hand side of the Diamond Nine. In what the Red Arrows call the stem, the two aircraft directly line astern of the Leader are Red 6, the Synchro Leader, in the centre of the diamond, and Red 7, Synchro 2, right at the back.

For the last decade or so two of the new pilots each year have been allocated to the Red 2 and Red 3 positions, closest to the Leader, because they are deemed to be easier than any of the others. 'Easier' is, of course, a relative term. In earlier years Team Leaders used to think that it was a good thing to put two of the new pilots down the back of the formation, in positions 8 and 9, out of harm's way and where any mistakes they might make would not have a serious impact on the rest of the formation. Whether that was right or not is debatable but from

1990 onwards it was no longer a practicable proposition because the rear group of four aircraft, Reds 6 to 9, started carrying out their own complex manoeuvres in the second half of the show and Leaders wanted two of the more experienced pilots in the 8 and 9 positions. The last pilots to fly their first year at the back of the formation were Andy Wyatt who was Red 8 in 1990 and John Newton who was Red 9 in 1989.

There is another convention. Unless a pilot becomes part of the Synchro Pair for his second and third years, he will spend all his three years on the same side of the formation. After spending the first season flying immediately on the right hand side of the Leader as Red 2, it is easier in the second year to move out one place and fly at Red 4 than it is to move over to the other side of the formation. The picture Red 4 sees out of his cockpit during a display is not all that dissimilar to the picture he saw as Red 2 and he is able to give the new Red 2 advice when necessary. The flying techniques will be similar and, furthermore, his neck and shoulder muscles will have become accustomed to twisting over to the left. This really becomes important when flying formation barrel rolls.

As I explained in an earlier chapter, a barrel roll is so called because the path the aircraft describes through the sky can be likened to the path around the outside of a long horizontal barrel as you progress from one end of the barrel to the other. A quarter of the way round the manoeuvre the aircraft is at its highest point with its wings perpendicular to the ground. Halfway round the aircraft is upside down with wings parallel to the ground; three-quarters of the way round it is at the lowest point of the manoeuvre with its wings once again perpendicular to the ground. All being well, the aircraft finishes the manoeuvre pointing in same direction and at the same height above the ground as when the roll started.

Now imagine flying a barrel roll in close formation, where all nine aircraft are rolling to their left. On the right hand side of the Leader, Reds 2 and 4 have to fly a larger barrel than the Leader because they have more distance to cover if they are to remain in the same relative position with respect to the Leader. It follows, therefore, that Red 2 has to go faster than the Leader and Red 4 has to go faster than Red 2. Exactly the opposite applies on the other side of the formation, Reds 3 and 5 describe a smaller barrel than the Leader and so they have to reduce speed slightly. Reds 6 and 7 in the stem have it relatively easy because all they have to do is, literally, follow the Leader. If you are unfamiliar with aerobatics and this all sounds very complicated, it is!

A little bit of trivia for those readers who like that sort of thing. The Red Arrows always barrel roll to the left when they are a group of nine aircraft. Not a lot of people know that! As Team Leader Simon Meade once put it:

'If we routinely did some rolls to the left and some to the right, it would only need one pilot to roll the wrong way for any reason, a momentary lapse of attention perhaps or a minor distraction, and we would get into an awful mess. Every pilot knows that all our barrel rolls are to the left – we've practised them that way all winter so we're mentally attuned.

'There is an anecdote,' he added, with a wistful smile, 'that a Leader once screwed up his position relative to the Display Datum and blandly announced on the radio that the next barrel roll would be to the right in order to regain position. The story goes that the Leader was thoroughly debriefed by the rest of the Team on his change of plan soon after landing! It would've been nice to have been the proverbial fly on the wall at that debriefing. Of course, we could include both left and right hand rolls in the programme but, since the vast majority of the public wouldn't notice, it makes sense to keep things simple and safe.'

A pilot who has flown as Red 4 in his second year will normally spend his final year as Red 8, right at the back of the formation on the right hand side. Similarly Red 3 progresses to Red 5 and finally to Red 9. This sequence does have an added advantage. Suppose Red 2 was unable to fly on a public display due to illness. It would be virtually impossible to fly the formation with a gap in the number two position because Red 4 would have no-one to formate on. Even if it were possible, the shapes would look most peculiar. However, because Red 4 was the previous year's Red 2, it is easy for him to slip forward into the number two position and fill the gap. Having the gap out on the wing at the number four position is less noticeable to the public and is certainly much safer. In the past some Leaders, when faced with a gap due to sickness or aircraft unserviceability, elected to drop the equivalent position from the other side of the formation. This had the merit of maintaining symmetry but recent Leaders felt that it was short-changing the public and they generally prefer to fly eight rather than drop a serviceable pilot and aircraft. Either way, it is a decision for the Leader alone.

Another trivia item. The only pilot to have changed sides in recent years was Barry Cross who, having started as Red 3 in 1992, became Red 4 the following year and Red 8 in his final year.

For the last 10 years or so, the Red Arrows have also introduced some manoeuvres in the second half of the show with groups of five and four aircraft to give even more variety to their programme. In fact, for some years now the second half of the show has started with the Five-Four Split where the Diamond Nine gracefully splits into two sections in front of the crowd. Names have developed over the years to describe these smaller groups of aircraft. The front five aircraft, Reds 1 to 5 inclusive, are known as Enid, an allusion to Enid Blyton's Famous Five. Older fans should recognise this reference but younger children seem never to have heard of Enid Blyton's books about the five adventurous children since these days her works are considered by some misguided individuals to be not politically correct. As I have revealed earlier, I came from a working class family and, like most of my friends, in my pre-teen years I read every Enid Blyton book avidly as soon as it was published. Not once did I feel deprived because we lived in a grotty inner-city area rather than 'in the country' and my family never had a gardener, a cook, or a car.

When Enid splits off from the rest of the Team, the back four aircraft are referred to collectively as Gypo, pronounced with a soft g and rhyming with hippo. No-one is quite sure when the term was first used to describe Reds 6 to 9 and, because the word is only rarely written down, no-one knows whether the word should be spelled gypo or gippo. I always use the former spelling.

In June 1998 the Red Arrows gave a display at RAF Cosford, near Wolverhampton, where the RAF was holding an Equal Opportunities Recruiting Exhibition. Various government ministers attended as well as the Chief of the Air Staff. As usual Red 10, Flight Lieutenant Russ Jones, gave the public commentary and in the course of his commentary he made several references to Gypo. The morning after the display I got a call from a very senior civil servant whose name, fortunately, I cannot remember. He introduced himself as the person responsible for advising senior officers about ethnic affairs.

'Squadron Leader, I was present at Cosford yesterday during the Red Arrows' display,' he said. 'It was all very embarrassing!'

'Oh,' I said, nonplussed. 'I'm not aware that anything went wrong.'

'Your commentator made several references to "gypo" and in the circumstances that was extremely embarrassing for the Minister.'

'What is wrong with that?' I asked, but I could guess what was coming. 'We've used that word for years and years and never had a complaint about it. Did the Minister tell you he was embarrassed?'

'No, but I'm certain he was. What do you think the word means?' asked the civil servant, with a trace of irritation in his voice.

'I know what it means,' I replied, trying to keep calm. 'The word refers to the rear four aircraft when they're flying separately from the rest of the formation and it's so called because the officer who used to lead that group of aircraft in the late 1960s had a rather swarthy complexion. His fellow officers always called him Gypo. I know the officer well and he never had any complaint about the nickname.'

'So the word is a derogatory term for non-white people?'

'Not at all,' I retorted. 'The officer in question is as English as they come – he just happens to have a swarthy complexion.'

He was not impressed so I told him that I would represent his views to the Team Leader and hung up. I logged onto the Internet and did a search on Yahoo for the word 'gypo'. Within a few seconds I found over 1,200 references, none of them in the least objectionable, many of them referring to a popular music publishing company in the USA. The Team Leader was not prepared to make any changes and so we continued, and continue, to use the word. There has never been another criticism.

The whole order of succession hinges on the composition of the Synchro Pair, Reds 6 and 7. The concept of a Synchro Pair was introduced at a very early stage of the Team's life to provide added excitement and variety in the second half of the show. All the well-known international aerobatic teams now have their equivalent of a synchro pair.

Nowadays, Synchro Leader, who is Red 6, is always a third year pilot. It has been so since 1985. The departing Synchro Leader is always replaced by his number two, Red 7. That is a sensible convention for to have credibility as Synchro Leader you need to have flown as Synchro Two. The new Synchro Leader is allowed to choose his own number two, subject to the agreement of the Team Leader. That is also sensible for if you are going to allow another aircraft to fly head on to you at a closing speed of about 1,200 kph and a lateral spacing of about 30 metres, as the Synchro pilots do, I think it is reasonable to allow you to choose who that pilot should be. In his second year, therefore, Red 7 will be considering who he wants to be his replacement in the following season when he will be Synchro Leader. He has to choose from amongst the first year pilots. The first year pilots almost without exception want to be in the Synchro Pair for their second and third years and so they have to be jolly nice to Red 7 throughout their first year with the Team. The third new pilot in those years when the Team Leader is not changed, takes the slot left vacant by whichever first year pilot has moved into the Synchro Pair. Got it?

The Team Leader makes his announcement of team positions for the next season during the annual visit to the Channel Islands in September. The aim is for the incoming pilots to join the Team in time to go on this four or five day detachment and it is their first away mission with the Team. The Red Arrows are extremely popular in the Islands and they have displayed there every single year since 1965. In fact the Channel Islands is the only location which has had a Red Arrows display every single year, 74 in all up to the end of the 2000 Season. Usually the wives, partners and girl friends go along to the Channel Islands as well – at their own expense I might add and not in the back seat of the Hawks. This is often the only occasion in the season when the Team's 'girlies' see their men at a public show.

The first really important date for the new pilots is the day of the official End of Season Guest Night. This is a formal dinner held every year, usually in early October, at which the departing members are officially dined out. On the stroke of midnight those who are leaving cease to be Red Arrows and they relinquish all the responsibilities and privileges of being in the Team. At the same moment the incoming pilots become Red Arrows and after many months of anticipation, typically 10 months since they put in their application to join, they have at last achieved the first part of their goal. They are part of the elite few and now the real work starts. The day after the dinner most of the Team, pilots and ground crew, go off on well deserved end of season leave for two or three weeks, unless there is a winter tour, but more of that later.

The new pilots do not get any leave at this stage, nor does the Team's senior pilot, usually the Executive Officer. They stay behind and start practising in small formations. Initially they fly at three or four thousand feet above the ground so that if anyone falls out of the formation there is plenty of space in which to recover safely. This sort of formation flying will be nothing new to most of the FNGs. Most of them will have spent quite a lot of time flying in close formation with two or three other aircraft whilst serving on their operational squadrons but then formation flying was a means to an end, now it is the whole raison d'être.

Usually everyone has a good time in this interregnum; there is no real pressure on the new pilots and it is all rather exciting and exhilarating. However, it is a bit like the long school summer holiday: all good things have to come to an end. The FNGs know it will all be different when the Team Leader and the rest of the Team return from leave and so it is.

I always considered it part of my job to advise photographers and cameramen how and when to get the most effective shots. Some of the most atmospheric video and television footage can be obtained around Slot 1, if the companies can be persuaded to pay their crews overtime to work at such an early hour. My favourite was to have a camera positioned outside the hangar on the taxiway, turning over or whatever digital cameras do, as the huge main doors slowly rolled sideways to reveal the Hawks within, nestling close to each other in two neat rows. The sodium lights in the hangar contrast sharply with the blue and green runway and taxiway lights outside, ensuring that pictures of the aircraft being towed out are surprisingly colourful and particularly effective. Sometimes early morning mists and fog swirl around adding to the ethereal scene. There is one safety man on each wing tip until the hangar walls are cleared, another sitting in the cockpit operating the aircraft's wheel brakes, and one man driving the small yellow tractor.

The aircraft are towed out one at a time, so a film crew has several opportunities to get it right. There can be some fine sunrises in mid-winter and another effective shot is one or the other of the Synchro Pair silhouetted against the rising sun as it, the Hawk, whooshes past at six miles per minute, its smoke trails then appearing to be black whatever colour they actually are.

Visitors cannot fail to notice the Red Arrows' precise time-keeping and often ask why the pilots bother with such accuracy for training sorties. It is all a question of discipline. The Red Arrows time all their activities by the clock because once the season gets under way they aim to start the show exactly on the stated time plus or minus a couple of seconds. Adhering to this sort of discipline during the winter, even for non-flying events, gets them into the required frame of mind for the display season.

The Red Arrows did once keep the Queen Mother waiting in Clarence House for almost half an hour and she noticed! The policemen and guardsmen on the gate into Clarence House were clearly looking out for us and, therefore, they all knew that the Red Arrows were late. I dread to think what the officers of the Household Brigade thought of us! The pilots were hustled quickly into an ante-room where they changed into their red flying suits ready for the official photograph later with the Commandant-in-Chief.

'I hear the traffic was particularly bad this morning,' Her Majesty said with an impish smile as she entered the drawing room. 'Shall we do the photograph first so as not to keep the photographer waiting any longer?'

We took that to be a royal reprimand! The late arrival was nothing to do with exceptional traffic congestion. The Team Leader, John Rands, made his humble apologies and explained that they had simply miscalculated the time it would take to drive from Scampton to Central London. After the photographs were taken we all moved back into the drawing room where we were served light refreshments. The Queen Mother was obviously delighted to be entertaining and chatting to the Red Arrows and she displayed a remarkable knowledge of the Team's history, past and present. At one point, when I was pinned up against a sofa, she said to me, 'Would you be so kind as to look behind the sofa. You will find some of the many gifts I have received from the Team in the past. I got them out earlier today so that you could all take a look at them.' For the next few minutes I lifted out and held up for viewing paintings and photographs of the Red Arrows that she had been presented with over the years since 1965.

The atmosphere was by this time remarkably relaxed. One of the pilots, who had better remain nameless, suddenly said, 'Boss , why don't you tell Her Majesty the gorilla joke?'

There was an appalled silence followed by nervous giggles. The gorilla joke was in very bad taste and certainly not repeatable in front of the Lady in Waiting let alone the Queen Mother. Turning to John Rands the Queen Mother said beguilingly, 'Oh do please tell it to me, Squadron Leader.' With barely a moment's pause, JR told the Queen Mother another entirely clean joke that had nothing whatsoever to do with gorillas. I am quite sure the Commandant-in-Chief knew that John had been set up.

Red Arrows pre-flight briefings for training sorties are formal and follow a standard sequence. Visitors sitting in on the briefing often think, because it is so formal, that it has been laid on for their benefit, but not so. The Team Leader first of all announces what the aim of the sortie will be and what particular manoeuvres they will be concentrating on. Another pilot will have checked with the Flight Line Controller to find out which aircraft are available and which position they want them to fly in.

The engineers have to try and balance out the wear and tear on each aircraft. Some pilots use up more of the aircraft's fatigue life than others, not because they are ham-fisted but because aircraft in some formation positions naturally experience more g forces. Generally speaking the Leader uses up least and the Synchro Pilots use up most. During the display season each pilot flies his own aircraft and his name is painted on the side so he knows he has gone to the correct aircraft. The pilots like to have their own aircraft because each airframe has its own little quirks and idiosyncrasies. They cannot do this during the winter, when a lot of scheduled maintenance has to be carried out on each aircraft in turn, so the aircraft are pooled and allocated as they become available. Some days there will be no spare aircraft and the Leader then has to decide which pilot will drop out if one of the allocated aircraft becomes unserviceable before take off. In Red Arrows' jargon, that pilot is 'the loser'.

The Leader briefs each phase of the flight in detail from the start up, taxi and take off procedures, to the recovery and landing phases and everything in between. To the uninitiated, the briefing sounds like a long stream of unintelligible jargon but every word is essential and each pilot concentrates fully on what is being said. Any visitors who may be sitting in on the briefing must keep silent – they are not permitted to ask questions at this stage, partly because it would be distracting but mainly because it would delay things. At some point during the briefing, the squadron QFI will postulate an airborne emergency that could arise and, having given all of them time to consider their own actions, one of the pilots will be nominated to describe exactly what he would do if it happened to him. This is not just a test of the nominated pilot's knowledge, but an invitation for all the pilots, including the Leader, to join in a discussion about the options available in various emergency situations.

There is always a section of the pre-flight briefing devoted to the vital matter of escape manoeuvres. If any pilot starts to gets dangerously out of position for any reason, whether it is due to a slight miscalculation on his part or a problem with the aircraft, he has to know how to depart from the formation expeditiously, without endangering either himself or any of the other pilots. In a full display sequence there are about two dozen separate manoeuvres; each pilot has to know instinctively what to do if something goes wrong at any point in any of the manoeuvres. Visitors were usually surprised when I told them that only the Team Leader looks where he is going, indeed he is the only one who needs to know where he is in relation to the ground because everyone else is concentrating on maintaining the correct formation position. Pilots quickly learn the sequence of manoeuvres off by heart but as they gain in experience they will find that they have time to cast the occasional glance away from the Leader's aircraft to see exactly where they are in relation to the ground.

The pilot who has the worst position from which to escape if something goes wrong is Red 6 in the Diamond Nine. He has an aircraft on either side of him, the Leader immediately in front and Red 7 close behind. In an emergency Red 6 has only two escape routes – up and down and he has to remember that if the emergency occurs when the formation is inverted, up and down are reversed. In those circumstances he has to push the control column forwards quite hard, generating negative g, to make the aircraft climb out of the formation before rolling the aircraft the right way up again and dealing with the emergency. The worst thing he could do if he had an emergency at the top of a loop would be to pull back on the control column to take him out of the formation because by so doing he would be aiming the aircraft towards the ground thereby dramatically reducing his chances of a safe recovery.

The Leader concludes each briefing by telling the pilots what time he wants them to check in on the radio. The whole briefing has lasted for about 15 minutes and check-in time is usually about 10 minutes later. The pilots make their way to the flying clothing section where they collect their flying helmets and other equipment and then walk out to their aircraft. Some prefer to walk alone, some in small groups, one or two first disappear into the toilet. Most are deep in thought about the forthcoming sortie.

Incidentally the pilots do not formate on the aircraft nearest to them; they all formate on the Leader. This is another way in which the Red Arrows differ from most of the other aerobatic teams. Pilots two or more places out from the Leader have to watch the Leader while at the same time trying to ignore what the intervening aircraft are doing and that takes some getting used to. When the Leader calls 'pulling up' or 'rolling now' on the radio, the way he enunciates the exact syllable on which he expects the command to be acted upon, is the signal for all the pilots to put in the appropriate flying control movements simultaneously. Different Leaders have a different way of giving the orders and everyone has to learn how each Leader does it. In this way the whole formation seems to move as though it was but one aircraft. Other teams operate on a follow-my-leader system whereby each pilot keeps station on the aircraft nearest to him. In that way the formation changes and manoeuvres seem to flow in a sort of slow motion Mexican Wave. The Red Arrows do not claim that their method is better than the other but it certainly makes the show look crisper and, we think, more professional. The Red Arrows method requires every pilot to have absolute trust in all the others. At the start of a loop, for example, on the word of command all the pilots simultaneously pull the control column back and apply about 3g. Anyone who does not, for any reason, will be left a long way behind.

One of the Team's own video cameramen always stands exactly at Display Datum, whether it is a practice or a public display. Only by filming from the Datum can the pilots watching the video at debriefing assess how accurately the show was flown. The video would also be used if any unusual incidents occurred during the sortie. The cameraman's job is to record all the activity, not artistically as a TV director would require but often in wide shot with the horizon visible so that the pilots can review their performance as the public would have seen it with the naked eye and without binoculars. Thus the cameraman has to have a detailed knowledge in advance of what the Team Leader is going to do next. Every sortie by two or more aircraft and every public display is recorded on video and debriefed afterwards. There is but one exception – the final show of the season is not normally debriefed because there is little point unless something out of the ordinary has happened.

In the training season the whole cycle of pre-flight briefing, flying and post-flight debriefing takes about 2 hours and there are three such cycles every day, weather permitting. It does not leave much time for doing anything else. Nevertheless, the pilots still have to carry out many other tasks. They all have squadron secondary duties and they all have ground training of one sort or another to undertake, like any other RAF officer. They also have to answer their own fan mail!

At the end of a good flying training week it is obvious to everyone who sees them that the pilots are physically and mentally drained. I once noticed one of the new pilots with red raw eyes at the end of his first full week of training and I asked him if he had a cold.

'No! I've flown 15 half-hour sorties this week and I don't have time even to blink when I'm flying because if I do, when I open my eyes again I find I've dropped out of position.'

As the winter training season progresses the Team Leader gradually increases the number of aircraft flying together until everyone apart from the Synchro Pair is on board. Initially, the Leader does not fly any particular sequence but concentrates on perfecting individual formation shapes and the all important changes from one shape to another. Sometimes he will fly just one side of the formation, a left hand side or a right hand side, and sometimes he will fly second and third year pilots in the stem, positions which would normally be occupied by the Synchro Pair, so that the new pilots can get used to having other aircraft close around them. Whenever someone is flying in the 'wrong' position or a formation is incomplete, the manoeuvre's name is prefixed by the word 'amateur' in the briefing and on the radio during the sortie. This is done as an aide memoire to everyone that something is not standard.

In the meantime Reds 6 and 7 have been practising on their own working out their own sequences for the second half of the show. The new Red 7 has, first of all, to be checked out at flying accurately 100 feet above the runway and then at 150 feet inverted. Only when he and Synchro Leader are comfortable do they start flying in close formation with each other. It is later still when they start practising the head on and other more complicated manoeuvres. Synchro manoeuvres are made to look exciting but the pilots will tell you they are safe because everything has been worked out in great detail. When the two aircraft fly head-on towards each other they are each travelling at about six miles a minute so the distance between them reduces at the rate of one mile every five seconds. Looked at from head on, the Hawk has a very small profile so in anything less than perfect visibility it can be quite difficult for the pilots to see each other when they start the run in. They each have fixed points on the ground, worked out in advance and providing they start their run over their check point and fly the correct heading and speed, adjusted for wind, they will meet at or near display Datum.

One aircraft, the Synchro Leader, flies what is called the predictable path and the other aircraft aims to miss. It is as simple as that. Actually there is one refinement – they call it fudge. To make it look to the punters on the ground as though Reds 6 and 7 are exactly on a collision course, the aircraft furthest away from the crowd flies slightly higher than the other one. Because of the viewing angle this creates the optical illusion that they are at the same height. You can only see the height differential if you can get to a viewpoint at one end or the other of the display line – and you cannot do that at most air displays.

Depending on how the weather has behaved, usually by late January the Team Leader and Synchro Leader are ready to start working out the intricate timing that is needed to ensure that the second half flows smoothly. When that is done the stage is set for the first nine aircraft practice of the winter.

The Team Leaders I worked with always made the point at the pre-flight briefing for the first nine that it was just a normal sortie. There was nothing new to learn and as far as the new pilots were concerned they would notice nothing different. Perhaps so but, nevertheless, it is a significant sortie for everyone and more so for the new pilots. For them it is the first time they will have flown in such a large formation and, if all goes well, at the end of the sortie they will feel for the first time that they really do belong to the Team. The Leader often arranges for this important sortie to be the last one of the day so that everyone may relax properly after it has been flown and debriefed. This is one sortie that I and the rest of the Team's support personnel would always go out to watch.

As the pilots walk in from the first nine there is always much mutual hand-shaking in the good old fashioned British way. Everyone now feels that the winter is over and spring and the display season are on the way. From this point on most of the practice flying will be in nines, as long as sufficient aircraft remain serviceable. There are no new moves to be learned but there is a lot of polishing to be done.

By late March or early April, the Team is ready to fly off to Cyprus for last minute rehearsals when the display sequence is polished to perfection. Why go to Cyprus? For the good weather factor – and to avoid being distracted by visitors and all those other duties that have to be done at home. Towards the end of the Cyprus detachment, when the Team Leader is satisfied that the display is as good as he can make it, he invites the Commander-in-Chief to watch a practice display. The CinC is the sole authority for granting the Team's licence to display in public – known as Public Display Authority. PDA is granted by the CinC on behalf of the UK Civil Aviation Authority but it is recognised throughout most of the world and only rarely is the Team required to fly what is known as a 'validation display' for show organisers.

The CinC, himself a highly experienced pilot, has to satisfy himself on two counts: first, that the display is of the high standard expected from the Red Arrows and secondly, and more importantly, that the display is safe both for the pilots and for the spectators on the ground. The PDA sortie does not always go as planned and sometimes, but quite rarely, it has to be re-flown. As soon as the CinC announces at the end of the sortie debriefing that he will award the Team its licence, off come the green standard issue flying suits that the pilots have worn all winter and on go the pristine bespoke red flying suits which just happen to be hanging close by. Thus, this day has become known as 'Red Suit Day'.

And so ends another training season – but that is not quite the end of training. Even during the busy summer season, if there are five consecutive days when the Team does not display in public, a relatively rare situation, the Team must practice in private to regain currency. Safety is always paramount.

12

WHAM!

THE RED ARROWS' CONNECTION WITH RUSSIA and the former Soviet Union goes back to 1990. For decades before that, the Soviets had been seen as the number one enemy of the west and so when it was suggested that the Red Arrows should penetrate the Iron Curtain to visit Leningrad, as St Petersburg was called then, and give displays in the Ukraine and Hungary there were many raised eyebrows. But that is what happened. It was a wonderful PR opportunity and it almost happened without me, the PRO!

For many years the internal planning document issued by the Team Manager for every display or series of displays has been known as the WHAM – an acronym for What's Happening Manager. WHAMs not only give full details of the planned flying programme and aircraft fuel requirements, but also all the other logistics details that may be needed both at home and down the route. Information on planned PR activities, entertainment, gifting requirements, dress codes, and hotel information are all there. WHAMs for overseas displays also include names and telephone numbers of local contacts at British Embassies and High Commissions and a curious item called Warp.

Normally GMT, or as we are supposed to call it these days UT, is used for all civil and military aviation times throughout the world. The RAF has always referred to GMT as Zulu for reasons which are now lost in antiquity. The Red Arrows, however, prefer to deal in local time wherever they are and so the Manager has to have two columns for times in overseas WHAMs, one for local and one for Zulu. To make sure the pilots remember to change their watches at the appropriate time, whenever there is a time change it is annotated in the WHAM by the word Warp. To everyone except the Red Arrows this causes no end of confusion, especially when, as sometimes happens, the two columns do not tally.

Everyone on the detachment, including the ground crew and the crew of the support Hercules, has his or her own personal copy of the WHAM so no-one has any excuse for not doing the right thing or for not being in the right place at the right time in the right form of dress. The preamble for WHAM 11/90 written by Team Manager Squadron Leader Andy Stewart and issued on 18 June 1990, started off thus:

'This WHAM covers the trip that would not have been possible until this year (and I'll believe it when we get there!). This is not so much a WHAM as a "Whatever Makes You Think I Know What's Going On?" The goal posts have moved so many times, and will doubtless continue to do so, that the best advice is to stay flexible and keep your sense of humour at all times.'

WHAM 11/90 had more blank spaces than most. This was to be the first time British operational military aircraft had flown behind the Iron Curtain. Details were difficult to obtain from the Soviets. The British Air Attaché in Moscow had described his efforts to obtain clearances and timings for the proposed shows as like 'swimming in treacle'. Almost literally at the last minute, the Red Arrows were given clearance to proceed by the Ministry of Defence in London but it was not the sort of clearance that gives one confidence.

'The Soviets haven't said you can't go so that's the nearest you are likely to get to an approval,' said the Ministry of Defence official reassuringly, but not altogether convincingly, from the security of his London office. 'Just make sure you get air traffic control clearance before entering Soviet territory.'

Right, we thought, we'll do just that! Not that there would be much we could do about it if the Soviets took exception to our presence. The version of the British Aerospace Hawk flown by the Red Arrows is not armed. In my mind's eye I could see the stories in the world's press: 'Red Arrows impounded in Soviet Union'.

The primary purpose of the tour was to give air displays in Kiev, capital of the Ukraine and then still part of the Soviet Union, in support of a British trade exhibition. Overall command of the detachment was vested in Air Vice-Marshal Mike Pilkington, Air Officer Commanding Training Units, an old friend of mine from much earlier in our careers when we were both flight lieutenants at RAF Mildenhall. Mike was then ADC to the Air Officer Commanding No 3 Group; now he was an AOC himself.

The plan was to fly to Leningrad on day one and stay two nights. No display was planned for Leningrad because there was no suitable air show or other event to justify one but a whole day in the northern capital was set aside for cultural activities. The following day we were to fly south to Kiev, keeping well clear of the Moscow area which would have been on the direct route. This was quite a disappointment because we all wanted to visit Moscow but the Soviets would not hear of it. Russians have always, throughout their history, been very protective of their capital city and to the Soviet military chiefs it was probably unthinkable that ten military single-jet aircraft, albeit unarmed training aircraft, should be allowed anywhere near Moscow. There would be one, possibly two, displays at a small training airfield near Kiev followed by time off to make appearances at the ongoing Anglo-Soviet Trade Exhibition in the city. Then it was off to Hungary for a display at Budapest International Airport before returning to Scampton via a refuelling stop at an RAF base in Germany. The display in Budapest was not part of the original plan but since the most economical route home from Kiev passed through Hungary an offer to display at the airport was readily accepted by the Hungarians.

'Danish pastries with tea or coffee will be served as soon as we're airborne'.

Those were the final words of Corporal Carl Morgan's pre-flight briefing to the passengers on ZD621, the British Aerospace 125 executive jet of 32 Squadron which was to lead the formation of 10 Red Arrows' Hawks throughout the tour. We passengers smiled at each other as we settled into the comfortable VIP seats. How civilised and how very British.

The date was 20 June 1990; the time 8.10am. There were five passengers on board. The senior man was Air Commodore Bruce Latton, the Commandant of the Central Flying School, who would be in charge of the detachment until we reached Leningrad.

Squadron Leader Roger Matthews, the Senior Medical Officer at RAF Scampton, carried mysterious bagsful of potions and pills designed to ease the queasiest of stomachs and to purify the foulest of waters. I believe, but was never able to confirm, that he had also packed onto the support Hercules aircraft stocks of pure British blood so that none of us would be contaminated with Soviet blood should we need a transfusion. I can personally confirm that he also carried several large bottles of Glenfiddich malt whisky – presumably for medicinal purposes.

Then there was Squadron Leader Mick George, at that time one of the most accomplished Russian interpreters the RAF possessed. Until shortly before the Soviet Tour, Mick had been the Senior Air Traffic Control Officer at Scampton and he now served on the newly-formed Joint Arms Control Implementation Group, also based at Scampton. Mick and I had first met each other over 10 years earlier when we were learning Russian at the RAF's language school at North Luffenham in Rutland. Later, when I was serving at a Signals Unit in Berlin, Mick was on the staff of the Berlin Air Safety Centre, the joint British, American, French and Soviet organisation which controlled all aircraft entering and leaving that divided city. Although Mick was not aircrew, his excellent knowledge of Russian and his familiarity with international air traffic control procedures were sufficient qualifications to make his seat on the tour unchallengeable. The fourth passenger was Warrant Officer Roy Fleckney, Red Arrows' Adjutant and Cash Imprest Holder. He was a very important passenger because he carried an attaché case stuffed with large amounts of hard currency sufficient, hopefully, to finance the entire detachment.

I was the fifth passenger and I felt rather like an intruder. Our Command HQ had gathered together a small party of UK media folk and was flying them out to Leningrad in Air Marshal Pilkington's VIP aircraft. I was neither consulted about the composition of that party nor invited to join it. Having previously worked in the intelligence world, I had at first assumed that there was either an ulterior and devious motive for not taking me along, or a different ulterior and devious motive for taking Mick George along. Adhering to the need-to-know principle, I did not delve into this at the time. I now know that I was wrong on both counts; it was simply that no-one even thought of inviting me along until

I asked. Had I not pressed my case and slightly exaggerated my ability to speak Russian, there is little doubt that I would simply not have been invited along.

The Red Arrows found a place for me in the Commandant's executive jet but I had the distinct impression that my late inclusion created a bit of a nuisance because all the hotel bookings had to be changed. No-one gave me any briefings about what I was supposed to do, what I was allowed to write about, and what I should not write about. Nine months after starting the job of PRO for the Team I was still largely left to my own devices to do as much or as little as I wished. I carried a simple automatic camera, my own property needless to say, with a bagful of films I bought with my own money from Boots in Lincoln, and a stack of notepaper taken from the CFS stationery store.

But why was a small executive jet to lead the Red Arrows? The principle was straightforward, but never practised before. Unlike the current export versions of the Hawk, the version used by the Red Arrows was quite old and had very limited navigation aids, barely sufficient to meet the international requirements for flying in controlled airspace. It was unthinkable that the world famous Red Arrows might cause a diplomatic incident by wandering off course inside the Soviet Union and so it had been decided that there should be a Russian speaker somewhere within the formation in case of difficulty with the Soviet air traffic controllers. The BAe 125, with Mick George on board, was chosen to lead the formation on the transit flights to Leningrad, Kiev, Budapest and then back to Scampton via RAF Wildenrath. For the all-important flight across the Soviet border into Leningrad, Mick George would transfer to the Team Leader's back seat thereby ensuring that if the Red Arrows and the BAe 125 became separated for any reason, the Red Arrows would still have a Russian speaker within their formation. Tim Miller's back-seater would join us in the executive jet for that leg.

Tim had already practised flying in formation with the BAe 125 and had discussed speeds, heights and rates of climb and descent with Flight Lieutenant Paul Mulkern, the Captain. It turned out that the performance of the two types of aircraft was compatible so no problems were envisaged in maintaining formation. Corporal Morgan had barely completed his briefing before the captain asked us all to leave the aircraft. There was, he told us, a minor snag with one of the Hawks that would delay take off by an hour or more. The Danish pastries were returned to the aircraft's cold store, the passengers disembarked and we ambled along the Waterfront to where the Red Arrows and the Hercules were parked. Things turned out to be a bit more complicated than we had been led to believe.

The MDC, miniature detonating cord, in one of the Hawks had exploded as the canopy was being locked down. The MDC is there to shatter the Perspex in the aircraft canopy immediately a pilot initiates the seat ejection sequence. The ejection seat then has a large hole through which the ejection seat can leave the aircraft cleanly and safely. On this occasion the MDC had fired inadvertently. The pilot, Flight Lieutenant Martin Cliff received several minor, but painful, burns around his face caused by what is known as 'MDC splatter', small burning fragments of the fuse that makes up the cord. He should have had his helmet visor lowered to protect his face but, perhaps in the excitement of leaving for the Soviet Union, he had omitted to take that elementary safety precaution. He needed medical treatment and his aircraft needed a new canopy.

The doctor, Roger Matthews, examined Martin's injuries and decided that he might also be suffering from shock. Roger declared Martin unfit to fly his Hawk to Upsaala. A quick change of plan was needed. It was highly undesirable to delay the entire Team and Tim Miller certainly did not want to arrive in the Soviet Union one pilot short. In any case, it would be a logistical nightmare trying to get clearance for a single Hawk to transit alone to Leningrad. Air Commodore Latton decided that he would fly Martin's aircraft and that Cliffy would take the Air Commodore's place in the BAe 125.

The support Hercules, XV199 from 30 Squadron at RAF Lyneham, parked at the side of the Red Arrows hangar, was also having its own technical problems as evinced by the sight of an airman clinging precariously to the top of the rudder. The Hercules, variously known as Ascot, the Bomber, and Fat Albert, would be carrying out its regular Red Arrows role of following on behind, but not far behind. It was loaded to the gunnels with technical equipment, food, bottled water, additional ground crew, and Roger Matthews' blood supplies. No Red Arrows major detachment is complete without the Hercules and it turns up, regular as clockwork, down the route often before the Red Arrows pilots have had time to board their coach to the next hotel.

The BAe 125, the 10 Hawks and the Hercules eventually took off almost two hours late. The first leg was to the Swedish Air Force base at Upsaala, not far north of Stockholm, home of a Viggen Squadron, good friends of the Red Arrows. The BAe 125 and Hawks maintained loose formation at 31,000 feet and the flight was uneventful. The Hawks broke away at the latter stages of the approach to the airfield to do a typical break and landing while our aircraft made a more sedate approach suitable for VIPs.

Apart from the pilots of 3 Squadron, the British Defence Attaché, Group Captain Page, was on hand to greet and assist. The Swedes were fascinated that we were about to fly across their border to the Soviet Union. Air Commodore Latton told Mick George to get on the telephone straight away to the Soviet air traffic controllers in Leningrad to discuss arrival procedures. The Swedes looked at each other with raised eyebrows and Group Captain Page blanched. The Soviet border was only just across the Baltic Sea from Sweden but it might as well have been at the other side of the world as far as telephones were concerned. It would probably have been easier to use the Prime Minister's hot line in Downing Street! Mick and the Air Attaché did their best but failed to make any contact with the Soviets. The Swedes looked at us with an 'I told you so' sort of expression on their faces. There was nothing more we could do except take off on the revised schedule and rely on radio communications once we were airborne.

Over lunch the Commandant and Tim Miller managed somehow to persuade Doc Matthews, probably against his better judgement, that Martin Cliff was fit enough to fly his own aircraft on to Leningrad. It was important from a PR point of view for all nine Red Arrows to arrive together and it would have been embarrassing to explain why one pilot was travelling in a transport aircraft.

As soon as lunch was finished it was time to say farewell to the friendly Swedes and board our aircraft for the long awaited leg to Pulkova Airport, Leningrad. Tension and excitement had been steadily mounting for some time. We got to the take off point and requested take off clearance. We were held on the end of the runway at Upsaala for 25 nail-biting minutes, fuel reserves depleting, temperature rising, before the Swedes somehow managed to obtain ATC clearance for us to proceed. Had there been just another couple of minutes delay the Hawks would have had to taxi back to the flight line to take on more fuel. As it was, the departure was uneventful. The formation passed through several thick layers of cloud causing the Hawk pilots to work hard to avoid getting separated from the rest of the formation before we all levelled off at 31,000 feet in brilliantly clear skies. At 6pm Leningrad time, still only 3pm at Scampton, the formation passed almost directly over the centre of Helsinki heading east. The Soviet border was now very close and all the aircraft in the formation were sticking close together..

'Hope the IFF is working properly,' muttered one of our passengers, referring to the Identification Friend or Foe radio transponder equipment that identifies aircraft to ground controllers. We giggled nervously at his little joke.

Penetration of the Iron Curtain, when we reached it, was a bit of an anticlimax. We had half expected a Soviet fighter escort to be waiting for us but none was forthcoming. The air traffic controllers seemed to be expecting us. They understood English quite well as long as they were not asked anything complicated. From then on the pilots had to get used to measuring heights in metres instead of feet. The Leningrad weather was given as more than 10 kms visibility, cloud base 1,200 metres, runway in use 28 Left, runway surface dry but with thunderstorms threatened. The formation had planned to fly a continuous descent from high level right down to airfield height but, frustratingly, clearance was granted in steps so that, with only 24 nautical miles to run, the formation was still at 9,000 feet altitude and just skimming the tops of the cloud. It was going to be difficult to manoeuvre the large formation onto the runway centreline in such a short distance with a high rate of descent. Then, suddenly, the clouds broke again and all was clear below with no sign of the promised thunderstorm. The Hawks requested permission to pull ahead of the BAe 125 at this stage of the approach so that they could proceed independently for a run and break. I do not think the controllers ever really did understand that request but the Reds did it anyway, leaving dense trails of patriotic red, white and blue smoke all over the airfield. The Red Arrows had arrived!

The BAe 125 made a more sedate instrument approach and after landing a few minutes behind the Red Arrows quickly caught up with them on the taxiway. All eleven aircraft then proceeded at a stately pace through the extremely crowded civil airport to a military dispersal several miles away where the Air Attaché, Air Commodore John Cheshire, and the Assistant Air Attaché, Squadron Leader John Elliott, another old friend of mine from Victor tanker days at Marham, were waiting to greet us. The first thing that struck all of us was how friendly the Russians were. Their faces were beaming, and they were anxious to shake hands and to try out their few words of English. Fuel bowsers were instantly available for refuelling the aircraft something that often does not happen at UK airfields. Customs and immigration officials were on hand to dole out reams of paper and even they were able to smile. Apparently handing out the forms was more important than collecting them in or reading what we had written on them. It was then that it dawned on us that we were being treated like VIPs, not like tourists or possible enemies.

The Red Arrows ground crew, who had travelled as usual in the back seat of the Hawks, set about the Hawks' after-flight servicings while the pilots and other support personnel soaked up the atmosphere and signed autographs. Eventually we were invited to board a fleet of military coaches which took us to the airport terminal. There we met up with Air Vice-Marshal Mike Pilkington, who had travelled ahead of us in the 32 Squadron VIP Andover together with the few members of the British media and a PR team from British Aerospace.

'Hello, Mike,' I said as we greeted each other warmly for the first time in 25 years. 'Long time, no see.'

'You can't call the AOC Mike,' said one of the Reds, aghast at my breach of protocol.

'Oh yes he can,' said the AOC with a grin.

Formalities over, we were driven off in a long convoy, led by a police car with flashing lights and siren. Each coach had at least one Russian interpreter on board and from ours we learned that we were now a *delegatsiya* and as such entitled to a police escort to ensure we were not held up in traffic jams. For a while we thought that red traffic lights in Russia meant go until we realised that every traffic light at every junction was red until after we had passed when, presumably, the normal sequencing was resumed. It was fascinating to note that many ordinary vehicles tagged onto the end of our convoy so that they, too, could take advantage of the police escort.

We eventually arrived at the Soviet Officers' Club in down-town Leningrad, a faded but once grand building with an imposing façade outside and sweeping staircases and lofty decorated ceilings inside. The Club was crowded. Whether it was always so or whether people had turned up especially to see us I do not know but we were certainly the centre of attention. We were led by our hosts and interpreters to the front of a long queue to collect our dinner. We then sat down at tables that had been held ready for our arrival. The food was no more than adequate but better than many of us had expected. Most of us found it embarrassing that the hundreds of other diners were watching us, not simply because we were British but because we were being fed meat. I was not the only one, I suspect, who ground his way through the gristly, tasteless meat when we would normally have left it untouched on the side of the plate.

After dinner, we were ushered back into our coaches for another long bus ride with the same police escort. We arrived at a military hotel in a really shabby part of town and parked at a rear entrance. The hotel, of appalling modern architecture, would rate barely one star by western standards but who cared? There was a TV in every room and the world cup was being shown live. We had adequate supplies of British beer, freshly delivered from Albert, and I doubt if any import duty had been paid. I was fascinated to meet my first *dezhurnaya* – the archetypal, unsmiling, large Russian ladies who sit bolt upright on small chairs and guard all hotel corridors. They watched us dashing from room to room, making quite a bit of noise as we unpacked, drank our beer and checked for late amendments to the WHAM. There seemed to be no other guests in our part of the hotel and soon we settled down for the night.

The next day was set aside for touring and PR opportunities in and around Leningrad. Our host for the day was Lieutenant General Boris Yurevich Nikiforov, Commander-in-Chief of the Soviet Air Force

Leningrad District. It was typical of the Soviets that they made sure our two-star detachment commander was outranked by their general – or were they just making sure we felt welcome? At each location Intourist had laid on one of their VIP guides to explain everything to us through one of their own interpreters.

The city's original name was St Petersburg, after its founder, Peter the Great. Even in 1990 many of the locals still called the city simply Peter. In 1914, at the start of the first world war, the name had been changed to Petrograd to avoid the hated German suffix 'burg'. In 1924, following the death of Lenin, the city had been renamed Leningrad, *grad* being a contraction of the Russian word meaning city. Leningrad is on the shores of the Baltic and is an important naval base and port but, being so far north, it is ice-bound on average for four months every year which must seriously reduce its usefulness as a harbour.

Leningrad city centre was still shabby and uninteresting on second acquaintance. Most of the buildings and all of roads were in desperate need of renovation. The majority of the shops appeared to be empty of goods but the occasional long queue indicated a shop that did have something to sell. Soviet shops were not privately owned and most stocked a single commodity, indicated by one-word signs on their windows: meat, milk, vegetables, furniture, chemist, and so on. It must have been extremely frustrating for the shoppers who could spend all day moving from one queue to another.

There were, however, some spectacular places for the tourist to visit in and around Leningrad. We were taken to two of them: Tsar Peter's Winter Palace in the city centre, housing the world-famous Hermitage Museum and Art Gallery with its fabulous treasures including many original Rembrandts, Monets, Cezannes, van Goghs and Rubens paintings, and, 28 km west of the city, Petrodvorets, Peter the Great's magnificent Summer Palace. At both places we were given VIP treatment.

The following morning before leaving the hotel I went in search of the *dezhurnaya* on my corridor. I wanted to give her one of the large bars of Cadbury's fruit and nut chocolate I had brought with me as gifts. I found her in an office at the end of the corridor and she showed no signs of discomfiture when she realised that I could clearly see that she was sitting in front of a complicated telephone switchboard with a jumble of patch-cords and tape recorders. Presumably this was where the KGB monitored conversations in the hotel rooms. The woman was absolutely delighted with the chocolate and quickly secreted it within the ample folds of her dress – but not before she had looked around guiltily to see if anyone had noticed. The Assistant Air Attaché told me later that she would undoubtedly have sold the chocolate rather than eating it herself.

There was a general reorganisation of aircraft seating before leaving Leningrad for Kiev. The British Ambassador, Sir Rodric Braithwaite, and Lady Braithwaite hitched a lift in the BAe 125 with the Air Attaché, while the Doctor and I transferred to the support Hercules. In addition we had picked up a couple of Soviet interpreters who flew in the Hercules. They could have been KGB, I suppose, but at least they were friendly and helpful. It was obvious that the Soviets did not want us to over-fly certain areas and so there had to be lengthy negotiations about the precise routes to be flown. The weather was excellent, the flights uneventful, and the entire detachment arrived at Borispol in mid afternoon.

Borispol, situated about 50 kms east of Kiev, the capital of the Ukraine, was both the civil international airport for Kiev and a Soviet Air Force base. It quickly became obvious that the Ukrainians were very proud of their country and had no great love for their near neighbours, the Russians. We now know, of course, that as soon as the opportunity presented itself, the Ukraine split from Russia. It was made quite clear to us as soon as we arrived, that the locals preferred us to refer to the *Ukrainian* Air Force rather than the Soviet Air Force. They even provided their own interpreters who seemed to spend as much time with the Russian interpreters as they did with us.

Kiev itself was the third largest city in the Soviet Union, after Moscow and Leningrad, and the Ukraine was the third largest republic in the union, after Russia and Kazakhstan. The Ukraine was one of the four original republics that formed the USSR immediately after the 1917 revolution. It has more than 50 million people and stretches over 1,300 km from east to west and over 800 km from north to south. Although everyone could speak Russian, Ukrainian was given equal prominence in all public places, in newspapers, and on radio and television.

Ukrainian has a strange mixture of Cyrillic and English letters and it sounded to me, an English student of Russian, familiar yet almost totally incomprehensible.

We were met at Borispol by another 3-star officer, Lieutenant General Nikolai Petrovich Kryukov, deputy Commander-in-Chief of the Soviet Air Forces Kiev District. Also in the line up were a large number of military personnel and a delegation from the Antonov Aircraft Design Bureau based at another airfield close to Kiev. The Antonov design team whisked the Hercules crew off almost immediately for a trip in the Soviet equivalent of the Hercules, an AN12 transport aircraft which they had specially flown in for the occasion. Wing Commander David Guest, the Captain of the Hercules, spent much of the hour-long trip at the controls of the aircraft and he reported later that he found it unsophisticated compared with the Hercules. They flew 180 kms to the north of Kiev to take a close look at the still very hot nuclear power station at Chernobyl before returning to Borispol. Had they known in advance where they would be going, the Hercules crew might have been less enthusiastic about the trip. Shortly after landing, the Hercules crew entertained the Antonov group with a familiarisation flight around the local area which ended with the Hercules' speciality, a tactical short landing. I was there taking photographs when they returned and it was clear that Antonov crew were most impressed.

After that we were all taken to an air force briefing room to do some pre-flight planning for the air displays. The walls of the room were covered with charts and diagrams comparing the performance of Soviet fighters with NATO fighters. Whilst the diagrams had obviously not been put up for our benefit, no attempt had been made to hide them. One of our pilots was caught surreptitiously trying to take a photograph of one of the posters while others clustered around him trying to hide what he was doing. A Ukrainian pilot saw what was happening and smiled, saying that there was no problem photographing anything we wanted. The data on the charts was accurate as far as it went and clearly showed the superiority of many of the NATO aircraft over their Soviet equivalents.

Eventually, just as everyone was beginning to feel rather tired and grubby, we boarded a fleet of luxury coaches for the long drive into Kiev city centre, with yet another police car with flashing lights leading the procession. Our hotel, the Libyed, was located right in the centre of Kiev, one of three major Intourist Hotels in the city. It was a fine hotel by any standards and would probably rate four stars from the AA or RAC.

The two air displays by the Red Arrows took place overhead Chaika, a small grass airfield about 10kms NW of the city centre, used mainly by the Soviet equivalent of our Air Training Corps as a flying club and for model aircraft flying and go-kart racing. To get to Chaika from Borispol took the Red Arrows seven minutes and involved flying at low level over part of a magnificent forest, across the river Dneiper and around the northern outskirts of the city.

On the Saturday the weather was poor with a lot of low cloud and rain and so the Red Arrows could only perform a rolling display. Squadron Leader Mick George delivered the public commentary, his own translation of the Red Arrows Manager's text. He travelled from Borispol to Chaika in a Soviet Mi-8 helicopter and was accompanied by Warrant Officer Fleckney who carried a large pile of Red Arrows Brochures, in English and Russian, plus stickers and other publicity material. With the benefit of hindsight, we should have had the glossy brochure printed in Ukrainian rather than Russian but the public did not seem to mind.

The Soviets had not advertised the event in advance, for reasons best known to themselves, and so the crowds at Chaika were small, hundreds rather than thousands. In fact there were probably more casual observers at Borispol watching the Team take off and land than there were at Chaika. This was rather disappointing because, like any artists, the Red Arrows perform best when they have a large audience. However, those who were there were in raptures – they had never seen anything like it before. As the Red Arrows cleared off to the east, Mick George and Roy Fleckney were besieged by autograph hunters and souvenir-seekers and eventually the airport officials had to come to their rescue so that the helicopter could take off for the return flight to Borispol.

After the debriefing back at Borispol, the Red Arrows pilots met a group of MiG-29 fighter pilots who had been flown in from a nearby air force base and an interesting and lively question and answer session ensued. The MiG pilots were interested in how the Red Arrows pilots are selected and they seemed very surprised to learn that the RAF do not pay them extra money whilst they are serving with the Team! Although of course we did not know it then, we would meet several of those pilots the following year at Scampton when they formed part of the Russian Air Force aerobatic team, the Russian Knights, and four of them would be killed in December 1995 on returning to Russia from displays in Malaysia at the same air show as the Red Arrows.

That afternoon we were all taken for a cultural tour of Kiev although most of us would have preferred to have been left to our own devices to wander around the city centre shopping for souvenirs. Our hosts had laid on a special visit to a Museum of Folk Architecture and Rural Life on the south-western outskirts of the city and it would have been churlish not to have gone along. The museum was set in rolling, green countryside that could easily pass for England at first glance. Within these grounds were set over 200 rural farmhouses, barns, windmills and cottages representing all parts of the Ukraine from the Crimea to the Carpathian mountains. They were spread out along an 11 km trail of paths. The buildings, and their very life-like interiors, showed Ukrainian life from the 15th Century to the present time but in truth it was difficult to tell the difference, in spite of the valiant efforts of the Intourist guide and his pretty interpreter. Unfortunately, long before our group reached the end of the 11 km trail, we had broken up into many small groups and the guide and interpreter were eventually left talking to themselves. I found it rather sad and I felt rather guilty but I suppose this is an occupational hazard for guides everywhere.

Later that afternoon most of us had, at last, an opportunity for doing some shopping but there was depressingly little to buy apart from the inevitable *matrioshki*, the famous wooden Russian dolls with other smaller dolls inside and, curiously, musical instruments. Two of the Red Arrows ground crew bought accordions – not that they could play them but they seemed too cheap to ignore! Later Red 5, Flight Lieutenant Dom Riley, not to be out-done, bought a cello for £12, while others bought trumpets, bugles and cymbals at knock-down prices. Later still, fortified by some beer, there was an impromptu musical concert on the 15th floor of the hotel in a lobby close to our rooms. Unfortunately, although everyone played with great gusto and enthusiasm, not a single person knew how to play the instruments they were clutching so the appalling noise can be imagined. What the Ukrainians thought of it I cannot imagine: perhaps they thought it was decadent western music. Dom Riley's cello stood, very inconveniently, in the small toilet compartment at the back of the BAe 125 during the flights back to Scampton, the only place Dom deemed safe enough for his prize!

On Sunday the weather was even worse. This time I went along in the helicopter to Chaika and at times we were forced down to 100 feet above the ground by low cloud, rain and mist. The Airport Director at Chaika, an Air Force full Colonel, decided that since I was a pilot he and I should get airborne and do a weather check. He could not speak a word of English. He ordered an ancient Antonov AN-2 biplane, rather reminiscent of an overgrown Tiger Moth, to be prepared for an immediate take-off. The Colonel borrowed a huge cape from another Russian officer standing there and draped it around my shoulders. We then barged our way through large crowds in the Air Traffic Control building and outside into the pouring rain. A civilian mechanic, not a pilot, had taxied the aircraft from the flight line to the front of the tower. As we boarded, the Colonel occupied the left hand pilot's seat and I was invited to take the right hand seat. The civilian stood behind us on a step looking distinctively apprehensive, as well he might.

It quickly became apparent that the Colonel was not very familiar with flying this type of aircraft, or possibly any type, and he had to be repeatedly prompted by the civilian. Once airborne the Colonel handed control over to me just as we went into thick, turbulent, rain-bearing cloud. It was some time before I identified all the instruments I needed for maintaining a safe climb and even longer before I realised that all the instruments were calibrated in metres for height and kilometres per hour for vertical and horizontal speed. I found conversation difficult in my halting Russian partly because of the Colonel's strange dialect but mainly because I was having to devote most of my attention to flying that incredible monster of an aircraft. In this fashion we flew around for a full hour, in and out of thunderstorms and torrential rain, not once catching sight of the ground, seeking the hoped-for clearance from the west. A great deal of rain came in through the windscreen seals and liberally covered the instrument panels and me. Then the Colonel, who had been fiddling with a radio compass, indicated by hand signals that I should start a descending left hand turn; he closed the throttle to make quite sure I understood his wishes. We descended in a continuous spiral from a height of 2,000 metres right down to 200 metres above the ground before we came out of cloud over the forest. I can only assume that one of the other two on board knew where we were because I certainly did not.

We landed, to my not inconsiderable relief, and the Colonel complimented me on my flying ability! We walked back to the terminal building to polite but prolonged applause from the drenched onlookers who must have thought this was part of the entertainment. The weather was clearly unsuitable for a Red Arrows display. By this time the Soviet general had arrived with Air Marshal Pilkington and the crowd had grown to several thousand. Amongst them I met some teenage boys who told me they had cycled 80 kms just to see the British Red Arrows. Word had obviously gone quickly around the Ukrainian grapevine since yesterday. The General and Air Marshal were naturally keen for the display to go ahead but it was obvious a new time would have to be negotiated with the Civil Airport authorities. The airport had its own General who was more concerned with airline schedules than with the Red Arrows' display – which he was not going to see anyway. All these negotiations between Generals and our Air Marshal took place in the crowded air traffic control with dozens of ordinary citizens eavesdropping! Mike Pilkington later wrote in his report:

'I reflect now on the unlikely spectacle of a Soviet 3-star general and myself in the Control Tower at Chaika studying meteorological charts and re-planning together as fellow airmen the re-staging of, as he termed it, the operation of the Squadron. I believe the significance was not lost on him, or the 50 or so ordinary people breathing down our necks either. He certainly pulled out all the stops – even to the extent of arranging for the civil airport to be closed for movements for the second time that day.'

At last the weather started clearing from the west and a new display time of 6pm was set. Most of the crowd wandered off for a couple of hours to do what ever they do on a Sunday afternoon in Kiev but they returned in time to see an excellent flat display. The crowd were extremely enthusiastic and we off-loaded another large batch of brochures, souvenirs and stickers and received in turn many souvenirs from the Ukrainians in the crowd. The Team Leader's debriefing of this display took place in the lobby on the 15th floor of the hotel using our portable video playback equipment. Bemused tourists and hotel staff watched in astonishment, but at least it was quieter than the musical performance of the night before!

Monday 25 June dawned mild and sunny with no sign of the clouds and rain that had threatened to ruin the Red Arrows displays on the previous two days. Whilst waiting to board the coaches from Kiev to Borispol, Wing Commander David Guest, the Hercules Captain, told me that his crew had spent the previous evening having dinner at the house of the Borispol Base Commander. Wing Commander Guest had produced a bottle of Glenfiddich for the Colonel to try. 'Very like Russian vodka to my mind', said the Colonel. David was not sure whether that was a compliment or not.

Out on the airfield while the official farewells were being made, I found that I still had a 10 rouble note in my possession. I could have changed it back into Sterling with the Assistant Air Attaché but, since it was worth barely £1, I decided instead to give it to one of the Soviet guards who had been protecting our aircraft overnight. The guard, obviously of Far Eastern origin, quickly stuffed the note inside his jacket. I told John Elliot what I had done.

'You shouldn't have done that, Tony,' he said earnestly. 'That guard will be in serious trouble if he's found with a 10 rouble note in his possession because it's more than he earns in a month. They've nothing to spend money on and his officers will assume he has stolen it.'

The BAe 125 and the Reds taxied out at 0950 local time for a take off exactly on schedule at 1000hrs for the flight to Budapest. On the climb it had been arranged for the Hawks to join up in close formation on either wing of the BAe 125 for photographic purposes. The late Arthur Gibson, the well-known and sadly missed freelance film-maker, photographer, and friend of the Red Arrows for many years, had moved from Air Marshal Pilkington's VIP Andover to the BAe 125 for this purpose.

Just after the formation had levelled off at around 30,000 feet the first Hawks appeared on the starboard side of the aircraft and all six passengers in the BAe 125 moved over to that side to get a good view. We heard an anguished shout from the flight deck and Corporal Morgan came rushing back to see what was happening. The auto-pilot had failed to cope with the rapid change of lateral trim and the co-pilot flying in the left hand seat had fought to stop the aircraft rolling to the right. Before the steward could report back to the co-pilot what was happening, we noticed more Hawks coming up on the port side and the inevitable happened – an undemanded roll to the left. We passengers became rather better behaved after that!

The flight to Ferihegy Airport in Budapest took 90 minutes. This time the BAe 125 led the formation of 10 Hawks right down to the runway threshold at 300 kts and 500 feet for a spectacular arrival. An enthusiastic and very friendly group of Hungarians greeted us on the apron. Also there were the British Defence Attaché, Colonel Nicolas Davies, and the Air Attaché, Wing Commander Malcolm Gaynor, and his staff. There was a short press conference in the very modern airport buildings before we were taken to the Hyatt Hotel in Budapest city centre.

We were all immediately surprised at the beauty of this city and the friendliness and cheerfulness of its inhabitants. We were told that in recent months the Hungarians had gone to considerable expense removing all signs of Russian occupation. There was not a red sign or Russian poster in sight and we tactfully removed from our uniforms and flying suits all the Russian badges we had been given in Leningrad and Kiev. The Budapest Hyatt was worth five stars even by Western stand-ards. Because it was still early in the day, having warped our watches back two hours from Kiev time, we were taken on a city tour with one of the charming secretaries from the British Embassy acting as courier. No generals, no military, no police escorts here. There simply was not enough time to get more than the merest flavour of what is undoubtedly a fascinating city. Many of us resolved to go back there on holiday.

The Red Arrows display was set for 6pm over the airport. There had been much advance publicity on Hungarian radio and TV and in the local press so quite a large crowd was expected. It is just as well we set off early from the hotel because long before 6pm all approach roads were jammed solid with traffic heading for the display. The airport authorities asked for a 15-minute delay because of the traffic chaos. The Hungarian police finally estimated that 15,000 people were inside the airport while another 15,000 were outside trapped in their cars. This was by far the largest crowd seen in Budapest for many years.

The weather was brilliantly clear and for the first time on this tour the Red Arrows were able to do their full looping display in front of an enthralled crowd. The Red Arrows motto ÉCLAT means brilliant and this really was a brilliant occasion. The pilots do not readily congratulate themselves, as anyone who has attended one of their de-briefings knows, but this time even the pilots were satisfied and they climbed out of their aircraft grinning from ear to ear. General Borsits, a Hungarian air force officer hosting the British Ambassador and Air Marshal Pilkington, offered to buy the Red Arrows, lock, stock and barrel. We believe the Air Marshal refused the offer. That evening the British Embassy Defence Staff hosted a dinner in a local restaurant for the entire RAF detachment. There was a splendid Hungarian three course meal, unlimited supplies of local beer, and an authentic five-piece gypsy orchestra to provide the music. A good time was had by all.

The following day it all started to wind down. First, there was the transit flight from Budapest to RAF Wildenrath in West Germany where we stopped to refuel and pick up our duty free allowances. No VIP escorts here – and very few smiles either! Then it was the final leg across the North Sea to Scampton. The difference on this leg was that the ten Red Hawks took the lead with the BAe 125 flying close astern so that Arthur Gibson could do some more aerial photography. The Reds landed first at Scampton, followed by the BAe 125 and a few minutes later by Albert the Hercules. The local customs officers met us, of course, but as far as I know no-one had exceeded their allowances so they did not trouble us for long.

So ended a historic tour for the Red Arrows and the RAF, the first visit by military non-transport aircraft behind the Iron Curtain or what was left of it. We had all been surprised by the genuine warmth of our welcome in Leningrad, Kiev and especially in Budapest. We did not meet any surly, grumpy Russians, Ukrainians or Hungarians. No-one tried to make life difficult for us – not even the *dezhurnayas*, who, in the past, had been notorious for making life difficult for foreign guests. If the inhabitants of Leningrad looked less happy than the others, well who could blame them? *Glasnost* had arrived but *perestroika* was still awaited in that once prosperous city.

The Red Arrows had shown the Soviet and Hungarians something they had never seen before: precision flying and skills of the highest order. They wanted the Red Arrows to go back but it has not happened. The Red Arrows invited the Soviets to visit RAF Scampton but at the time that did not seem likely to happen. None of us expected to see the Soviet Union break up but of course that is exactly what did happen a few months later.

The RAF missed a great PR opportunity. Although there were some TV and radio interviews and newspaper reports about the Red Arrows within the Soviet Union and Hungary, there was very little reportage back home. While the Red Arrows resumed their UK display programme I did some interviews about the tour for the Lincolnshire media and I wrote a two-page article for the RAF's own in-house magazine Air Clues but that was about it. The British Aerospace film crew that accompanied us wherever we went made a rather good 20 minute film of the tour but it was never shown publicly. There were few stories that I saw or heard from the media group that had gone on the tour.

It was almost as though the RAF were not interested in generating good news stories. From that day on, I decided that if the Red Arrows were ever to get the media coverage they deserved I would have to arrange it myself, bypassing both our Command HQ and the Ministry of Defence. Never again did I ask anyone in those corridors of power for permission to do anything.

13

A Tale of Three Cities

One dark and wet Friday afternoon early in 1991 the Scampton Station Commander, Group Captain Richard Gowring, telephoned and asked me to meet him at 4.30 outside the MT Hangar which was in a corner of the airfield not far from the Red Arrows' hangar. Some BBC people wanted to have a look at the hangar with a view to broadcasting a band concert from within. Naturally I said I would be there but I was mystified by the choice of venue. It turned out that the BBC had planned to record one of their popular 'Friday Night is Music Night' programmes from RAF Coningsby on Thursday 16 May, the anniversary of the Dam Busters' Raid in 1943. It so happened that the date coincided with the delivery to British Airways of a brand-new Boeing 747-400, registration GBNLT but always known simply as Lima Tango, that was to be named 'City of Lincoln' by the Lord Lieutenant of Lincolnshire out on the airfield at Coningsby. The Jumbo jet would be parked nose to nose with the other 'City of Lincoln', the Lancaster of the Battle of Britain Memorial Flight permanently based at Coningsby. Unfortunately, the Acting Station Commander at Coningsby had decided that he would be unable to offer the necessary facilities for the band concert because of the on-going Gulf War. Many of Coningsby's personnel, including the Station Commander, were still away on active service in the Middle East so one could understand his reluctance to have a public concert on base.

The BBC researchers and engineers were dismayed when we showed them inside the MT hangar. It was exactly what you would expect an MT hangar to be: dirty, dark, cold, and full of MT vehicles and their smells. In any case the BBC wanted a space large enough to contain the BBC Concert Orchestra, the Central Band of the RAF, and an audience of about 1,000. Our MT hangar was obviously much too small. The researcher was getting desperate and asked if there were any other hangars at Scampton that might be more suitable. I suggested 1 Hangar – it was under-utilised at that time and the few aircraft that usually spent the night in there could easily be accommodated in one of the other three aircraft hangars just for one night.

We drove in convoy to 1 Hangar at the other end of the airfield in driving rain and went inside. Instantly the BBC folk were delighted with what they saw. It was much larger than the MT hangar, it was clean, and it had its own efficient heating system. Group Captain Gowring committed himself there and then to hosting the band concert. What we did not know at that time was that the BBC wanted the British Airways Jumbo and the Battle of Britain Flight Lancaster to be at Scampton for the concert, the Lancaster inside the hangar with the audience around it and the Jumbo just outside the hangar on Echo dispersal. When I questioned this requirement for aircraft to be in position at a radio concert, the BBC researcher assured me that, although this was one of a series of radio concerts, they always tried to make their sets look as pleasing and impressive as possible for the audience. Whilst this seemed a bit over the top for 1991, I remembered reading that in the 1930s and 1940s BBC radio announcers and news readers used to wear formal attire in the evenings for addressing their unseen audience. The theme for this programme would be the two City of Lincoln aircraft in a programme coming from the City of Lincoln itself and it was, therefore, important that the audience at the recording could see both aircraft and get up close to them even if the audience on the radio could not.

I thought it worth pointing out there and then to the BBC representatives that Scampton is not actually in the city of Lincoln, any more than Coningsby is. The confusion this quirk of geography causes is something which, from time to time, annoys the councillors of the West Lindsey District Council in whose bailiwick Scampton really is. West Lindsey DC has its headquarters in Gainsborough which is twice as far from Scampton as Lincoln. Most ordinary people do not worry themselves about local politics but I learned soon after starting work at Scampton that there is a long standing jealousy between the District

Council and the City Council, always denied by both councils, and that civic protocol is all important – to the councillors at least. For example, the Mayor of Lincoln is not permitted to attend a function at RAF Scampton wearing his official Chain of Office without getting the prior permission of the Chairman of the District Council. The BBC researcher was not fazed by this intelligence but, as Community Relations Officer, I would have to make sure that the Chairman and councillors from West Lindsey DC were invited to the concert and they would no doubt make sure that the Mayor and Corporation of the City of Lincoln did not get all the glory.

The week before the concert was recorded David Jason, Del Boy from the popular TV series 'Only Fools and Horses', came to fly with the Red Arrows. During the Gulf War, David and his co-star Nicholas Lyndhurst had done a lot of welfare work on behalf of British forces in the Gulf. They had, for instance, bought a three-wheeler yellow Reliant and had it painted up like the Trotters' vehicle in the TV series. They had then filled the vehicle with goodies, including food and videos, and had it flown out at their own expense to the Middle East. Some time later the Commander-in-Chief of Strike Command had invited David and Nicholas to lunch at his headquarters in High Wycombe. During the meal the CinC asked them if there was something he could do by way of recompense for their generosity. David Jason replied that what he would really like was to have a trip with the Red Arrows. The Strike Command CinC was a little put out. He had expected, and hoped, that the pair would have asked for a trip in a Strike Command aircraft such as the Harrier or Tornado. That would have made a good PR story for his command. However, he did the decent thing and arranged matters with our CinC.

Unfortunately Nicholas was appearing in the West End at the time and his manager would not allow him to undertake what he, the manager, perceived as a dangerous activity. No such problem with David. He thoroughly enjoyed his 30 minute flight in Red One's back seat, a full nine aircraft practice of the display routine.

'David discovered where the radio press-to-transmit button is,' said Adrian Thurley after the flight. 'After that I could hardly get a word in edgeways to control the display. David kept transmitting "Come in number two", "you're too close Red 3" and similar remarks. It was amazing. I've never flown a civilian passenger who was so at ease as David was.'

There were no media present because David had requested that it should be a private visit. I was out of the flight line with my own camera when they landed and watched as he rushed along the flight line with seemingly boundless energy shaking hands with all the pilots. He then disappeared into the ground crew coffee bar and regaled them with jokes and stories non-stop for about half an hour. It was greatly appreciated. What a good thing it had been the last sortie of the day because the Hawks' turn-round servicings were delayed for quite some time.

There was much excitement around the Station and the local area as soon as word leaked out that the 'City of Lincoln' Boeing 747 would be coming to land at Scampton immediately after the naming ceremony at Coningsby. The 747-400 version was still quite a rare bird in 1991 and it would be by far the largest aircraft ever to touch down on our runway. There had to be many measurements and calculations to make sure the runway surface was strong enough to take the weight and the taxiways wide enough to accommodate the aircraft. All was well and the aircraft landed safely after flying around the local area at low level to make sure as many people as possible could get a good view of it. I was surprised to discover that the main undercarriage legs of the 747 are steerable and that enables the aircraft to turn in its own length – literally. I met the crew on Echo dispersal when they disembarked and took them down to 4 Hangar for refreshments and to meet the Red Arrows while the British Airways engineers worked on the aircraft. That was the start of a long Red Arrows' association with the airline's 747 Fleet.

The band concert was a great success and Lima Tango was a really impressive sight parked on Echo dispersal, lit with sodium floodlights. It had been delivered from the factory in Seattle just a few days earlier. The Lancaster looked equally imposing inside the hangar placed centrally amongst the audience of over 2,000 packed into the hangar to listen to the concert, more than twice the originally planned number and there was still room to spare. I did a lengthy interview for BBC Radio Lincolnshire who were transmitting the programme at the same time as Radio 2. A huge crowd gathered around to watch and listen as I was interviewed – the first time I had been interviewed in such conditions. Afterwards anyone who wanted, and most people did, had conducted tours of the pristine Jumbo. What a pity it was not television. The station got a lot of excellent PR out of the concert but the real stars were the two City of Lincolns aeroplanes. As soon as the last visitor left the Boeing, the aircraft took off for Heathrow and six hours later was on its way to Los Angeles on its very first commercial service.

The Three Cities of Lincoln event started me off on an idea that was to come to fruition two years later. Throughout 1992 I was conscious of the fact that the following year would be the 50th anniversary of the Dams' Raid and I felt sure that Scampton would be involved in some way in whatever events were being organised to mark the occasion. How wrong I was! When I made enquiries, I discovered that neither the RAF as a whole nor Scampton had any plans at all to mark the anniversary. I got in touch with the Dam Busters' Association to find out what their plans were. I spoke to Squadron Leader Ted Wass, who is both the Association's secretary and, as I learned when I got to know him, the greatest living expert on all matters to do with the Dams' Raid and the personnel of the wartime 617 Squadron although he had not joined the Squadron until late 1943, shortly after it left Scampton. Ted put me firmly in my place during our very first conversation when I mentioned that we were considering how the station could celebrate the 50th anniversary of the Dams' Raid.

'Squadron Leader', he said gravely, 'We do not *celebrate* an event which cost the lives of 53 of our colleagues and countless lives on the ground'. I felt quite humble and I never made that mistake again.

I had often wondered why the surviving Dam Busters aircrew never came on visits to Scampton. When I asked Ted for the reason he eventually, and rather reluctantly, admitted that they had not been made welcome the last time they had been to Scampton. That was when I confessed to him about my unfortunate letter to Bill Townsend in 1990. Try as I might, Ted would not be drawn further on the subject but he assured me that it was nothing to do with my letter but went back to an incident several years before I arrived at Scampton. I assured Ted that they would be honoured guests in 1993 and at any other time.

Ted told me that the Association always have their annual reunion at the Petwood Hotel in Woodhall Spa, a beautiful country hotel in a quiet village 18 miles south-west of Lincoln and about five miles from Coningsby. The hotel had been requisitioned by the RAF in 1943 to serve as 617 Squadron's Officers' Mess when the Squadron left Scampton almost immediately after the Dams' Raid. There is now a well-known Dam Busters' exhibition permanently on view in the hotel. The hotel certainly has better accommodation and facilities than can be provided at Scampton so I am sure they are better off there.

In spite of the fact that the RAF apparently was not intending to do anything about it, the Station Commander, the Church of England Padre, the Reverend Andy McMullen, and I thought that it would be very appropriate for the 50th anniversary of such a well-known and nowadays controversial war mission to be marked by means of a religious service with a theme of reconciliation and forgiveness. Accordingly, on 10 March 1992 I sent the following fax to the BBC Songs of Praise office.

'16 May 1993 will be the 50th anniversary of the famous Dam Busters raid by No 617 Squadron led by Wing Commander Guy Gibson who was awarded the Victoria Cross for his part in it. The raid was mounted from this station and the precise 50th anniversary occurs during your "on air" time – the crews were briefing for the operation at about 7pm on 16 May 1993.

'I wonder if you would be interested in producing a "Songs of Praise" from here to commemorate the event. I am in touch with the surviving members of the crews who flew in the raid. We are considering various plans at the moment including a concert with music provided by the Central Band of the RAF in one of the large hangars that housed the Lancaster bombers during World War 2.

'For your information, Richard Todd who played Guy Gibson in the film "Dam Busters" lives locally. Guy Gibson's black Labrador dog, Nigger, was killed in a road accident outside our main gate just a few hours before the crews took off on the raid. Nigger's grave is here in front of the hangar where it has always been, still tended carefully by a local civilian.'

A few days later a fax came back from the Reverend Roger Hutchings, Editor of Songs of Praise.

'You certainly persuade me that this is a suggestion we should consider carefully. It would be particularly good to broadcast a live Songs of Praise on the 50th anniversary and I am sure it would be very popular with our viewers. The problem is this. We would not normally be transmitting on 16 May, which is two weeks before Pentecost, when we normally produce one special programme for that festival within our repeat series, Praise Be! Thus a transmission on May 16 would mean a considerable re-jigging of our schedules.

'I would like to find time to come and see the base, and a possible venue, and to discuss the possibilities.'

Roger Hutchings visited Scampton some weeks later. Based on my experience with the concert in 1991, I was confidently able to tell Roger that there was room in the hangar for 2,500 people including the Central Band of the RAF. Three would still be sufficient room for the world's last flying Lancaster, from the Battle of Britain Memorial Flight, and a Tornado from the present-day 617 Squadron, together with a Red Arrows' Hawk and other Scampton-based training aircraft, to form a colourful backdrop for the TV cameras. All the surviving aircrew from the Dams' Raid, including some travelling from New Zealand, Australia, Canada and USA, would be in the area for their annual reunion and so could take their place in the congregation.

Roger was instantly sold on the whole concept. Then by happy chance came an opportunity to include in the programme the other 'City of Lincoln' aircraft. Following that first visit to Scampton by Lima Tango, an entirely Lincolnshire-based crew of British Airways were, quite independently, organising a charity flight for 250 disabled and under-privileged Lincolnshire children. Lima Tango would return to Scampton and take the children on a two hour flight including low level flypasts over all the major towns and villages in the county. It soon became apparent that the charity flight could be run on the same day as the 50th anniversary 'Songs of Praise'. Lima Tango could be parked just outside the hangar and the children and flight crew could be part of the congregation. This would add an extra dimension to the programme.

With more than 10 months still to go, the Station Commander obtained the approval of the Air Officer Commanding to go ahead with the plans and I was appointed Project Officer. I had several meetings with the Dam Busters' Association committee and together we started working out a programme for the day. I put out a news release nationally inviting people to contact me if they wished to be present. I gave a large number of interviews on radio, TV and in newspapers. Letters started pouring in asking either for more information or making firm bids for tickets. I decided that I would have to give priority to those people with Scampton or 617 Squadron connections. Although the tickets would be free, we needed to issue them for security reasons and to avoid over-crowding on the day. I started a database on my own computer in my office. Within four weeks I had allocated over 1,000 tickets.

Then in July someone at a high level in the MoD banned the Songs of Praise programme. There was outrage in the local press and the nationals quickly picked up on the story. I had to write several hundred letters telling people that the event would not now take place. The BBC were very disappointed. Barely a month later the MoD gave in and announced that the programme could go ahead after all. Several national newspapers reported the about turn. One of them said:

'We're delighted to report that a dotty decision by RAF chiefs has been shot down in flames. Apparently anxious not to upset the Germans, the defence bosses said it would be inappropriate for the BBC to do a live show from the RAF base at Scampton. Now, after a bombardment of criticism from ex-airmen, the MoD has done a smart about turn and the programme will go ahead. Wizard prang!'

Once again my word processor had to work overtime as I sent out hundreds more personal letters advising people that the event was back on. By early winter I had allocated all 2,500 tickets but letters continued to arrive by every delivery of post. I could not spare the time to answer each one individually so I had to run off a standard letter saying that there were no more tickets. The number of requests was so great that it was quite pointless trying to maintain a reserve list. Eventually word spread that all the tickets had been allocated but there was still a trickle of requests coming in as late as two weeks before the programme. I estimate that I could have allocated over 6,000 tickets in all. Less than a dozen people in total returned their tickets for re-allocation, and that was mostly because they were unable to attend due to illness. In other words, the 2,500 lucky people who were allocated tickets were so committed to the event that they put the date in their diaries months in advance and made sure that nothing would prevent them from attending.

Right from the outset I wanted the Red Arrows to be involved in the programme because I knew it would attract enormous publicity that could only be good for the Team. Curiously the Team pilots were not all that enthusiastic, perhaps because the Sunday in question was scheduled to be a day off in a very busy period. Initially the Producer, Christopher Mann, was also ambivalent because, as he rightly said, the Red Arrows had nothing to do with either Bomber Command or World War 2. I told him that his viewing figures would go up considerably if it became known that the Red Arrows would be appearing. Talking viewing figures to television producers is much like talking votes to politicians. Christopher agreed to let the Red Arrows fly over the hangar right at the very beginning of the programme as their tribute to 617 Squadron and to represent the present-day Scampton. He decided that after landing they should quickly make their way into the hangar in their red suits where the television cameras would pick them up as they joined the congregation.

Building the Red Arrows into the programme format gave us the argument we needed to get permission from British Airways' management, the Civil Aviation Authority and our own RAF bosses for Lima Tango to fly over Lincoln in close formation with the Red Arrows. The Red Arrows were always more enthusiastic about flying in formation with Lima Tango than they were about appearing in Songs of Praise.

On the morning of the programme, Lima Tango departed from Heathrow, rendezvoused with the Red Arrows at the southernmost point in Lincolnshire and then flew northwards in close formation at 1,000 feet above the ground, passing directly overhead the RAF Stations at Wittering, Cranwell and Waddington, before finally flying over the 900 year old Lincoln Cathedral and landing at Scampton. For this special formation flight, the Civil Aviation Authority insisted for safety reasons that Lima Tango should have on board no cabin crew and no passengers but just three qualified pilots: the Captain in Command, one of BA's most experienced 747-400 pilots; the First Officer, an experienced 747 pilot who was a former RAF fighter pilot and who would fly the aircraft as it formated close behind the nine Red Arrows; and the Red Arrows' senior flying supervisor, Wing Commander David Hamilton, as overall safety officer.

'Shortly after taking off from Heathrow and before joining up with the Red Arrows,' said David afterwards, 'I had to leave the flight deck and go back for a call of nature. I then took the opportunity to take a walk through the cabins. It was the weirdest sensation I have ever had – walking alone through both decks of that enormous aircraft and finding nothing but hundreds of empty seats. It was a great relief to get back to the flight deck and find that there really were two pilots on board as well!'

Adrian Thurley leading the Red Arrows said: 'It was quite an economical way to fly because the huge bow wave which precedes a 747 was literally pushing us along through the air and I found that we had to reduce power quite considerably to maintain the assigned true air speed of 330 knots.'

The British Airways cabin staff, all from Lincolnshire, arrived independently at Scampton and met up with the dozens of helpers, including doctors and nurses, who were to look after the children on the flight. Amongst the children were 20 youngsters in wheel chairs and each had to be accompanied by a nominated adult at all times for safety reasons. In the early afternoon Lima Tango took off from Scampton with 413 persons on board, the largest number of people ever to be loaded onto a single aircraft at an RAF base. BBC Radio Lincolnshire, broadcast live from on board the aircraft during the flight and listeners to the programme were able to ring in to the radio station as the aircraft passed overhead and talk live on air with the crew and passengers.

What none of us knew then was that a car from the Lincolnshire Police traffic division, parked up in a layby close by the entrance to RAF Scampton, had caught Lima Tango on a hand-held speed gun as it passed overhead. The officers, who had doubtless been lying in wait for this special arrival, issued a Fixed Penalty Notice stating that the aircraft had been clocked at 368 mph in a 30 mph zone. The ticket was passed to the owner, British Airways, at Heathrow Airport and it eventually reached the pilot, Captain Peter Lewis. Peter passed it to me since, as he said, I was the organiser. The action was widely reported in the national and regional media and in the end the Head of the Traffic Division issued a statement saying that no further action would be taken. Good PR for all concerned.

At 6.16pm 'Songs of Praise' went live on air in a specially extended 45 minute slot. The opening did not go as planned. The programme presenter, Sally Magnussen, was positioned out on the taxiway close to the Air Traffic Control Tower. In the background of the shot looking towards Lincoln city the aircraft hangar with Lima Tango's tail fin towering above it could be seen clearly. The Red Arrows were supposed to approach from the direction of Lincoln and roar at low level first overhead the hangar and then over Sally's head as she came to the end of her introductory speech at exactly 6.16 and 30 seconds. As the programme went live on air and the Director gave her the cue through a hidden radio earpiece, she was supposed to start walking towards the camera and talk to camera.

'Hello and welcome. These last few years have seen many anniversaries of events in the second World War. Some say these glorify war and we must never forget the awful toll of lost human lives. But there were also tales of extraordinary bravery and courage as men gave their lives for the defence of the country and its values, and it was here, 50 years ago to the day, that Lancasters of 617 Dam Busters Squadron took off on one of the most daring and ingenious raids of the second world war. Tonight many hundreds have gathered in the hangar behind me to remember all those who lost their lives on that night. Today, RAF Scampton is the home of the Red Arrows who, together with the Central Band of the RAF, welcome you to Scampton and salute the Dam Busters in their own special way.'

Unfortunately, a very rare timing error meant that the Red Arrows were overhead exactly 60 seconds early, and they flew over the hangar and Sally during the opening announcement from the continuity studio in London. I had assured the Producer, Christopher Mann, that the Red Arrows could time their arrival to an accuracy of plus or minus two seconds. He had not been impressed and had pre-recorded the Red

Arrows' flypast and Sally's opening speech at the Dress Rehearsal. The tape was on a quick start machine ready to roll at exactly the right time. Everyone in the hangar heard the Red Arrows fly overhead the hangar early and they realised what had happened but I reckon none of the viewers at home knew there had been a problem.

Most of the 2,500 people in the hangar had some connection either with Scampton or RAF Bomber Command during World War 2. All the surviving Dam Busters aircrew were there. Marshal of the Royal Air Force Sir Michael Beetham, President of the Bomber Command Association, was there to represent the whole of Bomber Command. In addition all the children who had flown on Lima Tango earlier in the day were in the congregation. The Red Arrows pilots did manage to enter the hangar on cue so that the cameras could pick them up as they joined the congregation. I think I detected a guilty look on the face of the pilot who had been responsible for the ill-timing of the flypast. The programme included prayers of reconciliation from British and German ministers and Richard Todd read out a letter from the Minister of the church nearest to the Mohne Dam. It was all very moving and tasteful. The live programme was watched by 8 million people in UK and was subsequently repeated on BBC World Service satellite TV enabling millions more in many countries throughout the world to see it.

What a pity the RAF hierarchy had so little foresight and were so grudging about a good news story of peace and reconciliation. It has become the fashion to write knocking stories about distinguished people and famous events. With the benefit of hindsight it is possible that the Dam Busters raid might not have taken place, who can say? However, I remember listening to the news of the raid on the radio – was it the morning after? – and I can remember everyone around me that day was talking about it, the brave aircrew and their sacrifices and the belief that it would shorten the war. They were my heroes then and I was proud to meet the survivors when they came to Scampton for Songs of Praise.

Sadly, two of the aircrew who had been enthusiastically working with me and the Dam Busters' Association died before the programme went on air.

Basil Feneron was a flight engineer and he flew in Lancaster F for Freddie piloted by Canadian Flight Sergeant Ken Brown. They made eight separate runs against their target, the Sorpe Dame, and after each one the pilot had to slam the four throttles fully open to climb out of the valley. F for Freddie landed back at Scampton at 0533 hrs, unscathed and Basil flew in 12 further raids with 617 Squadron. He died on 18 November 1992.

David Shannon always looked younger than his years, even when he visited Scampton in March 1993, but he was just 20 years old when he piloted his Lancaster in an attack on the Eder Dam after the Mohne had been breached. He had already been awarded the DFC for his actions when flying with 106 Squadron. He was awarded the DSO for his part in the Dams' Raid and the medal was pinned on his chest by the King himself on David's 21st birthday. The King remarked, 'How well preserved you look for your age!' Before the war ended Shannon had collected another DSO and another DFC. He died on 8 April 1993 just five weeks before the 50th anniversary.

14

The Russian Knights Visit Scampton

'HOPE TO SEE YOU IN SCAMPTON,' had been the cry as we said farewell to the Soviet pilots at Borispol in the Ukraine in June 1990 when the Red Arrows started home after their highly successful six day tour of Leningrad, Kiev and Budapest. It was the sort of thing you often say on leaving new-found friends even when you do not expect it to happen. But in this case it did happen – just fifteen months later. The Russian Knights aerobatic team, flying the mighty Sukhoi-27 fighter bombers known to NATO as Flanker, did come to Scampton.

In Russian folklore a young warrior famous for his strength and ability to defend the Motherland was called a *Veetyaz*, roughly equivalent to an English Knight. Hence the name for the Team, *Russkiye Veetyaze*, Russian Knights. But was it a Russian Aerobatic Team or a Soviet Aerobatic Team? So much had been happening on the international stage, especially in the three short but eventful weeks before the scheduled start of the visit, that we were by no means sure. The Soviet Union was rapidly disintegrating and the entire world was watching with bated breath. However, no-one at Scampton really cared about the politics – all that mattered was that they were coming.

I was heavily involved in planning the station's arrangements for the Russian Knights' visit. Knowing how fond the Russians are for ceremonies, I recommended to our Command HQ that the Russians should be greeted with a VIP formal arrival ceremony to mark what would have been an historic occasion even without the break up of the Soviet Union. My suggestion was greeted with not a little scepticism and alarm; apparently no PR lessons had been learned from the Red Arrows visit to the Soviet Union. Long gone are the days when RAF stations used to have regular parades, so long gone that most officers and airmen never parade again after graduating from initial training schools. However, that was not the sort of parade I wanted. I reckoned there should be a marching band and a saluting base from which the leading players could make their speeches of welcome. It would be nice, I hinted, if our senior officer outranked the senior visitor. I wanted a formal line up of Red Arrows' aircraft and pilots opposite the Soviets. I wanted the pilots to walk across the tarmac from opposite sides of the dispersal so that they could be photographed and filmed greeting each other halfway – a symbolic token of friendship. I wanted lots of media on hand to record it all.

Some months before the actual visit by the Russian Knights, a small Soviet delegation flew in to RAF Scampton for a preliminary planning meeting. Probably without realising the irony of the situation, the station hierarchy had decided to park the Soviet AN-72 transport aircraft on a remote and normally disused dispersal that for many years had been the place where Blue Steel missiles were loaded onto Vulcan bombers. Still there on the dispersal, and probably still connected to the mains supplies, were the high pressure water hydrants that were designed to flood the dispersal rapidly in the event that the extremely volatile fuel for the missiles leaked out during the loading process.

The prospect of any Soviet military aircraft on the ground in Lincolnshire was so unusual that I invited the local media to Scampton to cover the event even though we had no clear idea what to expect. All the local print and television media sent representatives. The local BBC radio station sent along Chris Jones, their popular presenter and friend of mine, to do a live outside broadcast from their radio car. As a result, Chris made broadcasting history. Out of the Soviet aircraft popped a three-star general. We had not been expecting such a high powered visit. I persuaded the Soviet general to be interviewed live through an RAF Interpreter. I was astonished that the General readily agreed to do the interview and some of his aides seemed quite worried and whispered hurriedly into his ear. I assured them that Radio Lincolnshire was a family radio station and that there would be no political questions. And so, for the first time ever we think, a serving Soviet general was interviewed live on a western radio station without any advance notification and without a script. It was a great success and Chris was a minor celebrity in the BBC. I imagine political and defence news reporters around the country were rather miffed at a missed opportunity.

Later, we took the visitors to the Officers' Mess for lunch. While I was in a toilet cubicle having a short rest, I overheard part of a conversation in Russian in the adjacent wash room.

'Comrade General,' someone, presumably a KGB man, said in a hushed voice, 'be very careful what you say in front of Major Cunnane, the public relations officer – he can speak Russian!'

That Russian had broken one of the most elementary rules of espionage: if you have something private to say, make sure you say it in private. The most intriguing part of that anecdote is that I had not uttered a single word of Russian that day; I had no need to, because there were more than enough official interpreters around. Someone had done their homework though. I then had to remain in the toilet until I was quite certain that all the Russians had left the wash room.

I got agreement for the arrival ceremony that I wanted. Conscious of the fact that when the Red Arrows visited the Soviet Union in 1990 our senior officer was outranked by the escorting Soviet three-star general, it was arranged that our Commander-in-Chief, Sir John Thomson, a three-star air marshal, would head the welcoming committee for the Russian Knights. Once again Chris Jones was on hand with the BBC Radio Lincolnshire radio car broadcasting live during the early part of the morning, drumming up interest and excitement for his listeners. At that time of day Radio Lincolnshire has a larger share of the listening public than BBC Radio 1. Lincolnshire is still to this day known fondly as Bomber County and the Lincolnshire folk seem to have an insatiable appetite for aviation stories of all kinds. From time to time I buttonholed other station personnel to be interviewed by Chris. He is a master at this sort of thing; he can always think of something useful or sensible to say when his interviewee dries up.

It was a warm early autumn morning but the visibility was rather poor – anticyclonic gloom the meteorologists call it. The Red Arrows' Hawks were drawn up in a line along one side of Echo Dispersal. The pilots stood around in their red suits waiting expectantly. The

Commander-in-Chief was already there with all the usual hangers-on. The security and intelligence men kept themselves to themselves trying, and failing, to look inconspicuous. The forty-odd professional musicians of the Band of the RAF Regiment marched smartly onto Echo Dispersal playing the official march of the Central Flying School, 'Those Magnificent Men in their Flying Machines' followed by the Dam Busters' March. They took up their allotted position close to the dais, resplendent in their ceremonial uniforms. Almost 100 members of the media were on hand to record every historic second, while the public roads outside Scampton were blocked with countless sightseers who filled every lay-by and vantage point for miles around. Station families and their excited children, let out of school for the occasion, lined the taxiways around the dispersal. A Royal Visit would not have attracted more attention.

The first surprise was that the huge IL-76 transport aircraft carrying the ground support personnel landed first. That was not part of the plan! So I had already imparted wrong information to the radio listeners but at least Chris Jones and I had something new to talk to the listeners about. As the aircraft moved slowly and cautiously past the CFS HQ building and along the taxiway in front of the hangars, its wingtips overlapping the taxiways at both sides, it was supposed to turn left and park at the northern end of Echo Dispersal. That is exactly what the marshaller indicated with his wands but, inexplicably, the Ilyushin turned to the right and nosed in between numbers 1 and 2 hangars. It came to a rather abrupt halt, rocking slightly on its enormous undercarriage, as the pilot suddenly realised he had turned into a dead end. What is more, not only was there no way out, there was insufficient gap between the ends of the two hangars for his aircraft so it was just as well he had stopped where he did.

'Everyone knows that the Soviets turn towards the moving wand – exactly the opposite of what we do,' said someone in a loud voice.

A bit of a sweeping statement that! We learned afterwards that he was wrong anyway. Why is there always a know-all on such occasions? What possesses some people to swear blind that something is so when they know full well they have just made it up?

'I wonder if he has reverse thrust so that he can taxi backwards like the Hercules?' someone else asked of no-one in particular, but no-one volunteered an answer.

After a few minutes, when you could almost see the 'thinks bubbles' emerging from the cockpit of the aircraft, the engines wound down and a curious silence descended on the airfield. Everyone standing around realised that the Ilyushin had turned the wrong way but, broadcasting live on the radio, I merely informed the listeners that the Russian transport aircraft was now in position. All right, I was dissembling: in position, yes, in the right position, no. There seemed no point in causing embarrassment for our visitors. A few minutes later a Russian officer, who turned out to be an air traffic controller, descended from the aircraft and was met by one of the RAF Russian interpreters. They had no interest in sorting out what was to be done about extricating the Ilyushin from its spot. They drove off to Air Traffic Control in some haste, presumably leaving the aircrew to ponder their future careers. Fifteen-love to the RAF.

I was assured by someone that the Sukhois were almost at Scampton so Chris Jones and I continued our radio chat whilst peering continuously through the gloom towards the north east. We had by then been broadcasting live on and off for almost an hour and I had used up all the pearls of wisdom I had prepared. Time passed and still no news. Even Chris Jones ran out of things to say and so he temporarily handed back to the studio for a musical interlude. Eventually word reached me that the Soviets were thought to be approaching the east coast close to Spurn Point, not far north east of Scampton, and we were quickly back live on air.

'The Russian Knights will be with us very shortly,' I said confidently on the radio. 'The RAF air defence radar has them on screen descending near to Cleethorpes. Four F3 Tornados from RAF Coningsby flew halfway across the North Sea to the United Kingdom boundary to meet our visitors and they are providing an escort. At the speed they are travelling they will be with us, overhead Scampton, in two or three minutes.'

It was more like six minutes before the six gleaming red, white and blue Sukhoi Su-27s of the Russian Knights appeared through the autumnal haze overhead Scampton, flying in a very tight formation. The four Tornado F3s from Coningsby had split themselves, two onto either flank of the Sukhois, in traditional escort formation. The Sukhois performed a very low, very slow, and very tight orbit over Scampton airfield. This was obviously one-upmanship on their part because they were able to manoeuvre more slowly than the Tornados in the tight turn. The two Tornados at the bottom of this impromptu flypast were barely 100 feet above the ground and, as the airspeed reduced perilously close to their stalling speed, the Tornados were forced to break formation and accelerate away very noisily to a more sensible speed. To the non-experts on the airfield it all looked very exciting; to the experts it was both shambolic and embarrassing – which is, presumably, exactly what the Russians intended. However, with the possible exception of the Tornado crews, we all thought this was a brilliantly cheeky move on the Russian Knights' part. Fifteen all!

We learned afterwards that the arrival over Scampton was late because the Russians had deliberately ignored air traffic control instructions and hand signals from the Tornados. Just as the Red Arrows had conveniently failed to correctly interpret Air Traffic Control instructions on the approach to Leningrad 15 months earlier, the Russians were now playing a similar game. They had obviously planned in advance to deviate from the approved route in order to make a low flypast directly over the Tornado base at Coningsby. There had been confusion and alarm at Coningsby when, a for a short while, controllers thought the Sukhois were intending to land there. Bearing in mind the fragile state of the Soviet Union at the time, senior officers at Coningsby may have thought that the Russians were intending to defect. However, having made a spectacular low flypast, the Russians lit up their afterburners and obediently joined up with their escorts again and continued towards Scampton. Thirty-fifteen to the Russians!

The SU-27s taxied into their positions facing the Hawks and their pilots disembarked. The Russian pilots stood rigidly to attention by their aircraft facing the Red Arrows pilots. Lieutenant General Nikolai Timofeyevich Antoshkin, Commander of the Air Force of the Moscow Military District climbed nimbly down from the single seat of the leading SU-27 and greeted our Commander-in-Chief warmly.

'Russian fighter pilots do not fly in transport aircraft', said General Antoshkin in English, beaming broadly at the assembled VIPs and media. What a splendid sound byte to start the visit! Our Air Marshal had arrived at Leningrad as a passenger in a rather elderly transport aircraft. Forty-fifteen to the Russians!

Air Marshal Sir John Thomson escorted General Antoshkin and politely motioned him to mount the dais first. The Bandmaster raised his baton, the musicians moistened their lips, ready to play the traditional RAF General Salute as soon as I gave the signal. General Antoshkin, with his own interpreter close by his shoulder, had other plans. He moved quickly and purposefully towards the microphone, while Air Marshal Thomson, his aides and his interpreter were still getting themselves into position. The Russian launched straight into his welcoming speech, his voice booming out over Echo dispersal. I gave a surreptitious signal to the Bandmaster and the band quietly stood at ease. Talk about one-upmanship. Game to the Russians.

'We were not sure we would be welcome,' continued the General in what must have been the understatement of the year. He had reverted to Russian and he spoke in short sentences, pausing after each one so that his interpreter could translate. Spontaneous applause from all sides greeted each remark and the General beamed appreciatively. 'You will notice that we have replaced all the Soviet symbols on our uniforms and on our aircraft with Russian insignia.'

I must admit I had not noticed and I doubt if many others had. The photographers and television cameramen took the hint and pointed their cameras at the Russian aircraft. One furtive looking guy dressed in an old anorak, really and truly, not a word of a lie, sidled up to me and half pulled a small 35mm camera out of a bag.

'I'm from you-know-where,' he whispered into my ear. 'I'm just going to try and get a few cockpit shots while everyone is meeting and greeting. OK?

He might as well have had 'Spy' tattooed on his forehead. I shrugged my shoulders.

'Be my guest,' I said to him in a non-committal way. I pointed towards one of the Sukhois. 'One of the aviation magazine photographers has beaten you to it anyway.'

The 'spy' looked worried and dashed off towards another aircraft.

The General continued for several minutes and then stood back, gesturing our Commander-in-Chief forward to make his speech, which should have been a formal welcome but turned out to be an ad-libbed reply to the General's remarks. The Air Marshal gave his RAF interpreter a hard time by delivering long, involved sentences one after the other without pausing often enough or long enough. However, interpreters are used to that sort of thing and there is an unwritten code amongst interpreters that you do not embarrass each other if translations of such lengthy unscripted tracts are not 100% accurate. After the speeches there was an exchange of gifts and then the Band Master decided it was his turn to take the limelight. Acting on his own initiative, he marched his men between the lines of aircraft to a reprise of the Dam Busters' March. As soon as the band had passed him, Adrian Thurley strode smartly across the tarmac to meet the Russian Knights' Squadron Commander, Lieutenant Colonel Vladimir Pavlovich Basov. They came to a halt facing each other a few paces apart, saluted, and then advanced for a hand shake and embrace. Red Arrows pilots do not normally embrace other men in public but this was clearly an exceptional occasion. Hundreds of shutters clicked to record this momentous act while the remaining Red Arrows pilots marched across the apron to greet the rest of the Russian Knights in similar fashion

Suddenly, without anyone apparently seeing it happen, Squadron Leader Thurley was seated in an SU-27 giving an interview to a British TV camera crew while a Russian TV crew that had disembarked from the stranded Ilyushin filmed them. For once the red Hawks were left deserted, all eyes were on the Sukhois.

It soon became abundantly clear that the Russians were perfectly happy for anyone to clamber all over their aircraft and take as many photographs as they wished. Presumably any secret equipment had been removed and so there was nothing to hide. What followed was a serious outbreak of *glasnost* followed by six days of highly infectious *druzhba* – friendship. Politics were forgotten: this was like any other squadron exchange visit – pilots talking to pilots and comparing notes and to hell with politics.

The Russians did not waste any time. Barely half an hour after the Sukhois had landed, the pre-planned programme of events, that had been through so many drafts and re-writings, was discarded for good. The Commander-in-Chief was deep in conversation with the General through two interpreters, one RAF and one Russian, at one end of Echo Dispersal. Air Commodore Latton, Commandant of the Central Flying School, having climbed into the rear cockpit of one of the two-seat Sukhois to have a look around, found himself being strapped into the ejection seat by the Russian crew man while Colonel Basov strapped himself into the front cockpit. Basov was categorised as a 'Sniper', the highest category in the air force. A few minutes later the aircraft roared down the runway and pulled up into the vertical. It had not been refuelled so it had on board only what was left of the fuel taken on at their base near Moscow. The first most of the Scampton air traffic controllers knew about this unscheduled flight was when the Sukhoi passed their control tower, its nose pointed to the heavens. The visibility had improved and the sun was shining brightly.

'We pulled straight up into a loop from take-off,' said Air Commodore Latton somewhat breathlessly to the media immediately after the flight, describing what we quickly learned was the Russian Knights' speciality. 'As soon as we cleared the ground we started pulling to the vertical. Normally you would expect to accelerate to three or four hundred knots before starting to loop but this aircraft continues to accelerate in the climb. We reached the vertical before the under-carriage travel indications had gone out. It took some time to get accustomed to an altimeter reading in metres and an air speed indicator in kilometres per hour but I guess we went over the top at about 250kts at about 4,000ft. Naturally we continued to accelerate on the way down. I was most impressed with the way the aircraft performs at low speeds. The tremendous amount of lift from the wings and the huge power of the engines enable the aircraft to turn well within the airfield perimeter.

'Then the Colonel handed over control of the aircraft to me,' continued the Air Commodore, 'Colonel Basov and I could not speak each other's language although while taxing out before flight we'd had a few moments to agree some hand signals for "I have control" and "You have control". I could find no means of selecting the afterburners from the rear cockpit so I pointed the aircraft into the vertical and waited for the Colonel to select afterburner as the speed reduced. He did!'

I was told that the Russians were going to the Officers' Mess for lunch and that later the Russian Knights would be practising their display over Scampton. I passed that information on to the media and most of them chose to go off base for a pub lunch in nearby Welton with the Command Public Relations Officer. Reporters and photographers are usually most insistent upon getting their victuals at the right time and are likely to get sulky when deprived, but this time it backfired on them. I decided to hang around on Echo Dispersal and assist the RAF Police to keep an eye on the families and friends who by now were all milling around the Russian aircraft and 'chatting' to the Russian ground crew by means of hand signals and smiles.

The Russian general and our Commander-in-Chief returned to Echo Dispersal from the Officers Mess much earlier than expected and climbed into the two-seat Sukhoi. I saw this happening and quickly grabbed the only media people in sight, a reporter and photographer from an East Anglian regional newspaper who had brought their own packed lunches and were downing them in their car in the car park. They got exclusive pictures of the two three-star officers strapping into the Sukhoi and a few minutes later having the time of their lives looping and rolling overhead. The rest of the media, including the official RAF photographers, arrived back on base as the two Commanders climbed out of the aircraft. The Commander-in-Chief was not very pleased with the Command PRO at this missed PR opportunity. The furtive looking man in the anorak was still clicking away taking innumerable photographs of the Sukhois' wheels and undercarriage bays – except by this time he was so engrossed in his work that he no longer bothered to be furtive about it. He was happy!

We learned that the Russian Knights' first ever public performance of their display routine had been just one week earlier at their home base for the benefit of their families and their own local media. The practice they flew at Scampton was, therefore, only their second performance. Curiously, this was rather similar to the genesis of the Red Arrows. The Red Arrows very first display was at their own base for the media and families, while the first proper public performance was a few days later at Clermond Ferrand in France.

The Russian Knights performed as a group of four aircraft with a separate singleton display. To start the display, the four took off together and pulled straight up into the vertical. As soon as the wheels were clear of the ground the fourth aircraft dropped back into the so-called 'box' position directly astern the leader, reaching that position before they all went over the top for a perfect Box Loop. After a series of steep turns, rolls and loops they cleared off to allow the singleton aircraft to take off and do his solo display. At Scampton the singleton startled everyone, not least the air traffic controllers again, by taking off downwind with 20kts of tailwind and he still pulled straight up into a loop. It was truly amazing watching such large aircraft fly such tight manoeuvres, so close together with such precision.

The following afternoon the Russian Knights flew a practice display at RAF Finningley and Squadron Leader Andy Stewart, Manager of the Red Arrows, flew in the box with Lieutenant Colonel Vladimir Petrovich Bukin, Chief Inspector of Pilots at Kubinka.

'For a fly-by-wire aircraft I found the handling surprisingly heavy – not unlike the Phantom F4,' said Andy afterwards. 'Although the flying controls were very responsive, large stick movements were needed. We never used more than 5g during the display but the aircraft is cleared to 9g. Engine response was fast and extremely smooth – the transition from full cold power to reheat was barely perceptible. I was always aware of the vast size of the aircraft – particularly sitting back in the box position. The most surprising part of the flight was the female automatic voice warning system – she seemed to give warnings every few seconds of height, angle of attack, fuel consumption. Even in these enlightened days when we in the RAF have female pilots I found it rather unnerving!'

I learned more about General Antoshkin as the visit continued. He was held in very high regard by his officers. In fact it is probably not an exaggeration to say that he was revered by them. Before being appointed to the three-star appointment as the Commander of the Air Force of the Moscow Military District in 1989, he had held a similar, but two-star, appointment in the Kiev Military District and so he was in the Ukraine throughout the Chernobyl affair. A copy of *Krasnaya Zvezda*, Red Star, dated 9 February 1991 came into my hands and there was a long article about General Antoshkin.

'The Chairman of the Kiev Military Division State Commission summoned General Antoshkin on 26 April 1986, the day of the Chernobyl accident, and told him, "Everything depends on you, the military. The crater in the damaged reactor must be sealed with sand." What was not clear was the answer to several important questions. What was the level of radiation above the reactor? Could men work there? How could they be protected? How to transport the sand to the crater?

'Antoshkin flew himself several times around the reactor in his helicopter,' continued the Red Star article. 'He convinced himself there was only one way to deliver the sand – to hover over the crater at a height of 200 metres, open the helicopter doors, glance into the throat of the crater and aim the sand into it. Dosimeters in the area had gone off the end of the scale. Antoshkin and his crews dropped 50 tons of sand on the first day alone and soon he had 60 of his helicopters operating over Chernobyl. On the morning of 1 May Antoshkin reported back to the Chairman of the State Commission that the reactor was sealed. The General then went home to see his wife; she did not recognise him. In that short period he had shed tens of kilograms of weight and it took six months for his blood count to return to normal. Eight months later he was made a Hero of the Soviet Union. It was only then that Antoshkin and his wife and two children were able to move out of the single-roomed apartment provided for a two-star general by the Air Force and into a rather larger apartment.'

Before leaving Russia, General Antoshkin had learned about the Queen Mother's honorary appointment as Commandant-in-Chief of the RAF's Central Flying School from some briefing notes about the Team I had sent to the British Embassy in Moscow some months earlier for onward transmission to the Russian Knights. Without the knowledge of anyone in the RAF, the General had then written to Buckingham Palace asking if it would be possible for his Team to meet the Queen Mother and accept a gift. It was a nice idea but the Queen Mother's Private Secretary had replied that a visit would not be possible because she would be on holiday in Scotland during their stay in Britain. However, the Queen Mother would be delighted to watch a flypast over Birkhall House, her residence on the Balmoral Estate. When this message eventually filtered through to the RAF it had, in effect, become a Royal Command and it caused a flurry of activity at high level. The RAF decided that the Russian Knights could not be permitted to flypast without an escort because of the very hilly terrain in the Balmoral area. Naturally the Red Arrows were given the job.

Once the Russian Knights had settled in at Scampton, General Antoshkin asked how it would be possible to deliver his gift, a replica of a traditional Russian samovar, to Birkhall. Time was short and so I was asked if I would drive up overnight and deliver the gift to Sir Alistair Aird, the Comptroller of the Queen Mother's household. The arrangements were quickly made. To share the long drive, I took with me Pilot Officer Russ Fraser, a young Holding Officer who was working for me temporarily while waiting for the next phase of his flying training. I had first met Russ when he was a cadet with the Royton Air Training Corps Squadron and I had gone to the Squadron on a staff inspection with Group Captain John McMinn. I told Russ that we would travel in comfortable civilian clothes but take our formal uniform with us so that we could change before entering the Balmoral Estate. There was just a possibility that we might meet someone important – perhaps even the Queen Mother. I briefed Russ on how to greet royalty.

After passing through the beautiful town of Ballater, only a few miles from Birkhall House, we turned into the Estate's narrow approach road and started looking for a suitably secluded place amongst the trees where we could change into uniform. We thought we had found the ideal place but, just as we were pulling into the side of the road, I noticed someone I took to be a British Telecom workman working at the top of a telegraph pole. He waved cheerily at us and we drove on without stopping. A few hundred metres further on, out of sight of the telephone man, we pulled into a sizeable clearing on the side of the road. There was no-one in sight and so we got out of the car and quickly changed into uniform. We were expected at 1030 and we had about ten minutes to spare as we continued the drive along winding avenues towards the house. Suddenly, after going round a sharp bend, we were brought to a halt facing someone we took to be a game-keeper. He was standing in the middle of the road and had a shot gun cradled in his arms. He came up to the car and I wound the window down.

'You must be Squadron Leader Cunnane and Pilot Officer Fraser,' he said, as he peered in. 'We watched you getting changed!'

There was no-one else in sight so I have no idea who 'we' were. Somewhat abashed, and wondering where the hidden cameras were, we showed him our identity cards.

'That man up the telegraph pole must have been one of the security guards, I suppose?' I asked weakly, hoping fervently that he would be very discreet with any negatives or video footage. It did not bear thinking about what the Red Arrows would do with pictures of Russ and me without trousers in a forest clearing if they got their hands on them!

'He might have been,' grinned the game-keeper. 'Keep right on for another hundred yards. You'll come to a car park near the stables behind the house. Park there and Sir Alistair will meet you.'

He waved us on, still grinning broadly. We found a parking space and looked around. Sir Alistair Aird came out of the house almost immediately and introduced himself. We showed him the large box in the boot containing the highly ornate samovar.

'Ah, it's electric,' he said thoughtfully, peering inside the container.

'Yes sir,' I replied. 'The outside is a replica of a traditional Russian samovar but this is a modern electric version. You will see that General Antoshkin has had the emblems of the Russian Knights and the Red Arrows engraved on it as well as the Royal Cipher. We had the electrics checked over at Scampton. Our engineers recommend that you don't permit the Queen Mother to plug it into the mains – it's not safe.'

'I will certainly make sure that is passed on to the Housekeeper,' said Sir Alistair. 'I think the best thing to do is place the samovar on a lace cloth on a small table out on the front lawn and then you can formally present it to Queen Elizabeth before the flypast. Would that be all right do you think?'

I replied that it certainly would be all right.

We were taken inside the house and given a cup of tea, served from a silver tea pot on a silver salver of course. We then asked to go to a bathroom so that we could make ourselves look tidy. In the meantime one of the staff found a suitable lace cloth and table and placed them on the front lawn. When we had combed our hair, I having decided that we would not wear our service hats, we joined Sir Alistair on the lawn where he was carefully placing the samovar on the table. I then saw that a small lady was approaching from the house. With a shock, I realised that it was the Queen Mother. She must have been waiting inside the house until we came out onto the lawn. Sir Alistair formally presented me and then Russ to the Queen Mother and I had to explain all about the Russian Knights and General Antoshkin's gift. I lifted the lid, showed the Queen Mother the internal electrics, and recommended that she did not allow her staff to plug it in.

'It is so kind of you to make that long drive from Lincolnshire just to present me with this gift,' said the Queen Mother. 'How long is it before the flypast is due?'

'They will be overhead at 11.30, Ma'am,' I replied. 'The Red Arrows are leading and they're always on time.'

'I know. I do so enjoy watching them. We have about 20 minutes to wait then. Would you like me to show you my gardens?'

The Queen Mother led the way across the lawn, down a few steps, over a ha-ha, and into her private garden. I suddenly noticed that Sir Alistair had silently withdrawn from the scene and the three of us were all alone. For ten minutes or so Her Majesty proudly showed us her flower beds, explaining how much she enjoyed spending time in this quiet garden, then she excused herself and disappeared towards the house leaving Russ and I alone in the garden. A few minutes later we started to make our way back up to the front lawn. As we did so a rather unkempt looking man came out unexpectedly from behind some bushes and confronted us. It really was amazing how people kept silently appearing and disappearing. It was almost as though this man had been waiting off stage ready for his cue to make his appearance. He was supporting a large artist's easel over one arm. I assumed he was another secret service agent although he did seem rather old for that sort of job.

'Good morning,' he said, holding out his spare hand to be shaken. 'You must be the gentlemen from the Red Arrows. I'm the Duke of Hamilton and I'm very pleased to meet you.'

I racked my brain swiftly and decided that the correct form of address was 'Your Grace'. If I was wrong the Duke did not correct me. We chatted as we made our way slowly back to the front lawn, then he looked at his watch and said, 'Oh dear, it's almost time. I'd better go and change. Excuse me please.'

No sooner had he disappeared into the house than the Queen Mother re-emerged, accompanied this time by two corgis, and once more joined Russ and me on the lawn. From various other doors and gates, people silently appeared and lined themselves up to the right and to the left of the main entrance. A television crew from Grampian Television in Aberdeen appeared and also a still photographer, Colin Gower, an old friend of mine and one-time picture editor of the Daily Express. They kept at a discreet distance.

'I've invited my house guests and the staff to come out and watch the flypast,' said the Queen Mother, gently waving at each group in turn. The ladies all curtsied gracefully and the gentlemen bowed deeply in obeisance. 'I invited the television crew here so that everyone in Scotland can see the flypasts and I've asked the Headmaster at the village school to let the children out to watch.'

Whilst I was explaining to the Queen Mother where the formation would come from and the fact that they would fly past twice, I noticed the Duke of Hamilton, now immaculately dressed in a morning suit and looking much more ducal, come out of the front door and take his place in the line up of house guests. He smiled in my direction. That had been a pretty smart change of clothing in more senses than one.

I peered into the distance towards Ballater, hoping that Squadron Leader Thurley would be on time. The Queen Mother saw the formation before either Russ or I did.

'There they are,' said the Queen Mother pointing excitedly. It was another five seconds or so before the aircraft came into my vision.

The Red Arrows followed very closely by the Russian Knights, looking enormous by comparison to the British Hawks, swept over the town of Ballater and down the valley at 360kts and 500ft above the ground. Exactly on time to the nearest second, the formation flew directly over the spot on the lawn where the Queen Mother was standing. The Commandant-in-Chief raised her right hand in salute. Russ and I had moved back a few paces so that the TV crew would be able to film the Queen Mother without having us in shot. The corgis at Her Majesty's feet looked up disdainfully at the unusual noise.

Adrian Thurley then manoeuvred his 17 aircraft formation, nine Red Arrows, six Su-27s and two photographic chase Hawks, around a wide right hand circuit over Balmoral Castle for a second flypast. The Royal corgis totally ignored the aircraft this time round. The Queen herself was said to be watching the flypasts from another part of the Balmoral Estate. Calm once more descended upon Royal Deeside.

'That was magnificent,' said the Queen Mother turning to Russ and me. 'It brings a lump to the throat and a tear to the eyes. Please tell all the pilots, RAF and Russian, how much I admire their skill and precision.'

I promised to do just that and Her Majesty withdrew. The audience was over. Sir Alistair led Russ and me back to a side entrance into the house. We quickly changed back into civilian clothes and we left a large pile of Red Arrows' brochures and stickers for the Housekeeper to distribute amongst the staff. We then set off on the long drive back to Scampton. The same guard was on duty as we drove down the avenue. He flagged us down.

'Have you got any brochures left, please,' he asked. 'There's half a dozen of us here and we're all Red Arrows' fans but the ones you just left with the Housekeeper will all have been snapped up by now.'

We handed over the rest of our gizzits. I was very impressed with the internal communications!

After the flypasts over Balmoral, all the aircraft landed at RAF Leuchars for yet another press conference. On Saturday there were public displays for the At Home days at Leuchars and Finningley and then it was time to wind down and really relax for the first time in five days.

During the course of the Russian Knights' all too short visit, eight senior RAF officers were lucky enough to fly in the two-seat Sukhoi 27. On the final day of the visit there were flights for eight of the Russians in Jaguars and Tornado GR1s flown in to Scampton especially for the purpose. The Russians made no secret of the fact that they were very disappointed not to be offered sorties in a Tornado F3 or a Harrier. I never found out what excuse the RAF gave.

At parties in the Officers' and Sergeants' Messes at Scampton that last evening, more speeches were made, gifts exchanged, and hand aerobatics performed as the relative performance of Russian and British aircraft were discussed with passionate fervour. At one stage, when dinner had been cleared away but we were all still seated, more or less, a Russian colonel came to sit alongside me. I had never met him before so I assumed he was one of the many officers who were travelling on the Ilyushin support aircraft. He knew who I was because I had just made a short speech explaining how I had delivered General Antoshkin's gift to the Queen Mother.

'Hello Major Cunnane,' he said affably in good English but using the Russian equivalent of my squadron leader rank. 'You used to fly Victor tankers from Marham and Leuchars.'

It was a statement not a question. Although I was taken aback by his forthright approach, I managed to refrain from giving him the satisfaction of asking him how he knew, so I simply said yes.

'We met many years ago flying in the Faroes-Iceland gap, although maybe you did not know it,' he continued, obviously enjoying having the ascendancy over me and knowing full well that I had no idea what he was going to tell me. 'You were on Operation Dragonfly. I never imagined that we would meet as friends. I was the captain of a TU-95 bomber, what NATO calls a Bear, and your Victor tanker was refuelling two Phantom F4s from Leuchars before they came looking for me.' He paused, then continued slyly, ' ….but the F4s never found us.'

He then mentioned some details of an incident that had occurred on one particular sortie I had flown and that convinced me that either he was in the TU-95 as he claimed, or he had taken the trouble to read about the incident in a Soviet Air Force report.

It was just as well we had not invited the Defence Intelligence Staff to the party! I regret that I cannot remember the colonel's name; I am not even sure he told me his name. Just for the record, in case the Defence Intelligence Staff read this, no classified information passed between us and I never met the colonel again. Well not so far, anyway. I would have made a very poor spy.

The farewells the following morning were emotional – just as the Red Arrows' farewell to Kiev had been. The Russians seemed genuinely reluctant to leave. They were seen off by most of the Station's personnel either lining the dispersal or watching from outside the hangers. One final flypast of all six aircraft and the Russian Knights disappeared, climbing steeply into the low stratus. The noise of the Sukhois could be heard for several more minutes: memories of their visit will last far longer. Sadly, some of the pilots would never be seen again in the UK.

The following year there was a follow up to the story about the Samovar. The Queen Mother came to Scampton in June 1992 to present, on behalf of the Queen, a new Queen's Colour to the Central Flying School. I was in charge of the media arrangements and not slated to be presented to the Commandant-in-Chief. The Russian Knights' Samovar had been returned to Scampton to take its place in the CFS Museum because the Queen Mother thought that it would make a fine exhibit for the public. During her visit to the Museum, whilst looking at the Samovar again, the Queen Mother had eye contact with me at the far end of the room where I was shepherding the media and keeping them at a respectable distance. Her Majesty left the group of VIPs and came over to me, much to the delight of the media and the surprise of the VIPs and me.

'Good morning Squadron Leader,' she said. 'How nice to see you and the samovar again. I followed your advice and never did plug it in but I am sure it will have pride of place here in this museum. How is that nice Mr Fraser who came with you to Birkhall.'

'He's almost finished his flying training, Your Majesty,' I said. 'He's done very well and is hoping to be posted onto Harriers shortly.'

'Do give him my very best wishes when you next speak to him.'

I was amazed at the Queen Mother's memory. Although her aides had probably briefed her that she might bump into me, there was no way they would have thought of briefing her about Russ Fraser. The Queen Mother must have remembered his name without any prompting. I tried to speak to Russ later that day. He was stationed at RAF Chivenor in Devon but he was in the flight simulator when I rang the crew room. His flight commander answered the phone

'When Russ comes out of the simulator will you ask him to call me. Tell him I've got a personal message for him from the Queen Mother.'

The flight commander thought I was winding him up and I had some difficulty persuading him that I was not but he did pass on the message and I spoke to Russ an hour later..

15

Scampton to Close –
Where Will the Red Arrows Go?

Following the break up of the Soviet Union and the dismantling of the Warsaw Pact, it became apparent that there would have to be large-scale reductions in the strength of the armed forces. As part of the RAF's 'draw down', there was great pressure to reduce support costs so that there would be minimal effect on the front line. Indeed, a study entitled Front Line First spelled that out quite clearly. Thus, most of the RAF's money would be allocated to Strike Command while Support Command, to which CFS and the Red Arrows belonged, would have to make the most significant economies.

Airfields cost a lot of money to maintain; the fastest and easiest way of saving millions of pounds in one fell swoop is to close down a whole airfield, especially if you can sell off the real estate. This does not mean that you disband all the units based at the airfield, you simply redeploy them to other bases. It is not so straightforward with the civilian staff who usually do not wish to move home. The RAF's big problem with closing down one of the flying training airfields is that it seriously reduces the runway time available to train pilots. Pilots have to practice lots of circuits and landings and it takes only four or five student pilots going round and round the circuit to fill any given runway to capacity. On top of that has to be added the number of more advanced students who are learning how to fly bad weather instrument approaches. An aircraft practising a typical radar circuit turns onto the runway final approach heading at eight to ten miles from touch down and if the exercise is to have maximum value the aircraft must be given priority to land, or go around again, at no less than three miles from touchdown. Fitting in everyone's requirements can become a nightmare for the air traffic controllers and for the harassed flying instructors who have to try and get as many approaches into a sortie as possible while still finishing the sortie at the scheduled time.

It is for this reason that the RAF has always made used of what are called Relief Landing Grounds. RLGs are airfields that provide a runway for students to practice on but they usually have no resident aircraft. The RLG has to be within a few minutes' flying time of the main flying training school otherwise valuable time and fuel is expended in transiting between the two. In the early 90s Scampton had the use of two RLGs, the former Lightning base at Binbrook and the civil airfield at Sturgate near Gainsborough; Cranwell had the use of Barkston Heath. Both Scampton and Cranwell could also use Waddington, on the southern outskirts of Lincoln. Waddington is not an RLG but training aircraft could use it on an opportunity basis for circuit flying because for much of the time the airfield was not very busy. The Red Arrows did not use the RLGs but the CFS aircraft operating from Scampton had to make use of them, especially during the winter months when the Red Arrows used up so much of the available flying time.

My diaries tell me that the first media story about possible closures of airfields in Lincolnshire came in July 1990 when the local newspapers reported that the Government was looking to save £600 million on defence spending that financial year. At the time there were nine RAF stations in the county, Barkston Heath, Coningsby, Cranwell, Digby, Donna Nook a bombing range near Mablethorpe, Nocton Hall Hospital near Lincoln, Scampton, the recruit training base at Swinderby and Waddington. An MoD spokesman said that any closures would not take place for another four or five years. The first enquiry to come my way about the possible closure of Scampton came from the Lincolnshire Echo, the County's daily newspaper, in January 1992.

'A rumour that RAF Scampton was to close was denied yesterday,' reported the Echo. 'Squadron Leader Tony Cunnane said, "Every RAF station's future is being reappraised but RAF Scampton is under no more immediate threat than any other RAF station."'

I was quite pleased by the way I had worded that statement; it managed to quell the rumour without actually saying anything useful. What more can a PRO, or his bosses, want?

Allegedly a notice appeared in the corridors of the MoD Main Building in Whitehall about this time which stated, 'Would the last person to leave please switch off the lights'. The rumours about airfield closures in Support Command really started to gain momentum in 1993. There was no question of Cranwell, the home of the RAF College, closing. That would be unthinkable. The other two large airfields in our Command, Linton-on-Ouse in north Yorkshire and Valley in Anglesey, were unlikely to be selected for closure because they were the main flying training schools and there was no obvious place for either to relocate their activities. It was, therefore, widely recognised that either Scampton or Finningley, the navigation and non-pilot aircrew training school, would have to go and most people reckoned that the axe would fall on Finningley. Accumulated wisdom within the lower ranks in the RAF was that it would be relatively easy to relocate the various units at Finningley to other bases within Support Command but that it would be well nigh impossible to relocate all the disparate flying units based at Scampton.

Bill Corke, a well-known reporter with a great sense of humour, reported in the Sunday Sport in November 1993 that:

'As part of the on-going defence cuts Britain's crack flying squadron The Red Arrows is to have its wings clipped and will be re-named The Red Arrow. There will be modifications to the Team's show. A new manoeuvre will be introduced – Loop-de-Loop in which the pilot will land his plane and run around it. Diamond Formation, a breath-taking feat, will now be performed by the pilot's wife who will display her engagement ring in a marquee at air shows. For the Concorde manoeuvre the pilot will simply shout "Vive La France" as he flies past.'

As part of the economies, Support Command was disestablished at the end of March 1994 and was replaced a few days later by two new commands, Logistics Command, based at Brampton, and Personnel and Training Command, based at Innsworth. The flying training stations, including CFS and the Red Arrows, were allocated to the latter. I was very pleased that I did not have to answer the inevitable PR questions about how splitting two commands into three, each with its own HQ and staffs, could lead to savings. As it happens, Logistics Command lasted just over five years and on 29 October 1999 it became part of yet another newly established organisation.

The definitive word about closures came in July 1994 when it was announced that both Finningley and Scampton would eventually close, a decision that stunned most aircrew in the RAF. The announcement prompted the Lincolnshire Echo to start a remarkable media campaign which they called the 'Save Our Scampton' or SOS Campaign. Almost every working day for the next 12 months or so Julie Wetton, a charming and persistent reporter at the Lincolnshire Echo, called me with the latest rumours and snippets she had gathered and every day I faxed a summary of our conversation to the MoD and Command HQ. I enjoyed my daily chats with Julie and I listened to all her stories with great interest. She knew that I would never tell her anything that I was not supposed to but she also knew that I would report all her stories and rumours to the MoD. Barely two weeks later, on 28 July 1994, I sent a fax to the MoD giving a run down of the rumours that were already circulating about the new home for the Red Arrows. Here are just some of them.

An expert in Sleaford, who preferred to remain anonymous but who regularly provided the Sleaford Standard with stories, confidently announced that the Red Arrows would be moving to Barkston Heath, the RLG about five miles south of Cranwell. Several Red Arrows' self-styled experts telephoned various Oxfordshire media to report that the Team would be moving to RAF Brize Norton. A newspaper in Cirencester telephoned to ask me to comment on a report that the Team would be moving to RAF Fairford, where they started out in 1965. BBC Radio York and a couple of north Yorkshire newspapers reported that we would be moving to RAF Leeming, while a reporter on the Western Daily Post rang me to say that the Chairman and members of the Newquay Council were very unhappy to learn that the Red Arrows would be moving to Newquay Airport, formerly RAF St Mawgan, because we would seriously interfere with their civil aircraft movements. Would I please comment and also explain why the Newquay Council had not been involved in consultations about the move. The Marketing

Manager for Exeter Airport called me to say that the management was willing to provide a home for the Red Arrows and asking to whom he should write to make a firm offer. At the other end of the UK a newspaper in Elgin asked me if I could confirm that the Team would be moving to RAF Lossiemouth.

The facts of the matter are that a formal study was initiated and every RAF airfield was considered as a base for the Red Arrows. It could have been news of this study leaking out that led to the wild assumptions. It was highly desirable, but not essential, that the chosen base should be part of Personnel and Training Command and not Strike Command so that there would be no command and control complications. Account had to be taken of the Red Arrows' need for six 30-minute training slots every working day in the winter months and that would mean barring the airfield to all other movements for three hours a day. Not a single airfield was willing to accept that limitation without a fight. Many airfields were ruled out because of their location at the extremities of the UK. The Red Arrows need to be based reasonably close to the major air display locations otherwise there will be a lot of transit flying, expensive in terms of fuel and wear and tear on aircraft. In that respect Brize Norton or Fairford might have been ideal since the majority of air displays are south of Birmingham. For the same reason bases in Scotland were non-starters. Taking everything into consideration, we were not surprised to learn that the study concluded that for one reason or another there was no airfield in the whole of the UK more suitable than Scampton.

The SOS campaign quickly gained a lot of support from local councils and institutions. Quite early on I did give some advice off-the-record to Julie Wetton. I told her that the Echo was making a mistake basing its campaign purely on nostalgia about the Dam Busters. I reminded her that many historic RAF airfields had been closed in recent years. If the SOS campaign was to have any hope of success, I told her, it would have to be based on economic grounds. It is worth making the point here that, with few exceptions, RAF personnel have no particular attachment to an RAF station so most of the Service personnel at Scampton watched the campaign with little more than passing interest.

The closure was of far more importance to the civilian staff who would be out of a job when the station closed.

In October 1994 Air Vice-Marshal Johnnie Johnson, the World War 2 fighter ace, joined the fray. In a letter published in two national newspapers and copied to us at the Red Arrows and, for all I know to the Chief of the Air Staff himself, he wrote:

'I think the mandarins in Whitehall, and by that I mean the Treasury and not the Royal Air Force, take no notice of history or of the feelings of people. Scampton should be saved. The base has a long and illustrious history. I would have thought that if they wanted to reduce the number of operational bases there are many which are far less worthy than Scampton.'

It was nice to have his support but on this occasion his logic was flawed. The Lincolnshire Echo then came up with an alarming story, 'Pollution Scare at threatened base', claiming that the land at Scampton could be contaminated with chemicals. The report claimed that MoD had already confirmed that the base was formerly the home 'to the nuclear missiles carried by the Vulcan aircraft' and that large amounts of fuel and chemicals were still stored at Scampton. An MoD spokesman added, rather unwisely in my opinion, 'there is no truth in allegations that widespread radioactivity contamination exists at RAF Scampton'. That statement implied perhaps not widespread but *some* radioactivity contamination? Surely any radioactive contamination is a cause for concern and the campaigners quickly latched onto this lapse. The SOS campaigners got hold of an environmental expert who reckoned that it would cost between £2 and £3 million to clean up 220 cubic feet of land contaminated with radioactivity. The paper then pointed out that Scampton covers 889 acres, but left it to its readers to work out how many cubic feet there are to an acre.

The Gainsborough and Horncastle MP, Edward Leigh, said he would demand answers from the Armed Forces Minister, Nicholas Soames. 'If the MoD offloads Scampton and it does need decontaminating, it makes closing the base totally uneconomic. We are not talking tens of thousands but rather tens of millions.' Then, mixing his metaphors he added, 'It would be outrageous if the MoD washed its hands of Scampton once it was closed.' We knew what he meant.

Soon the Echo raised the stakes and introduced the transatlantic factor. Details of Whitehall's proposals to close Scampton were faxed to American defence experts in Washington prior to a meeting between them and the Chief Executive of the Lincolnshire Training and Enterprise Council. The Chief Executive was quoted as saying that he had learned that at a meeting of American veterans, 20% of them had signed the Echo's SOS petition – they were the ones who remembered Scampton and the Dam Busters and knew of the Red Arrows being based there.

The SOS campaign was brilliantly run but really it had been doomed to failure from the outset. The MoD had apparently made its mind up that Scampton would close. The Echo printed a bitter but heartfelt editorial on 24 March:

'The battle to save RAF Scampton will never be forgotten. The people of Lincolnshire have long memories, like most rustic folk, and for years to come they will talk about the day the Government turned its back on the county. Nicholas Soames says he has fully considered all the facts and that the case for Scampton's closure remains proved. But every single argument put forward by the Save Our Scampton group was ignored. Local clubs and organisations were actually told the date that facilities would close. Servicemen from another RAF base started to move into Scampton's married quarters. We asked the Ministry of Defence for assurances that the decision had not been made. We were told everything which was happening was forward planning in case of closure.

'We have to ask the question: did the MoD ever have any intention of listening? Or had they made the decision – in the county's opinion, a bad decision – and come hell or high water they intended to stick with it. It would appear that when the MoD steamroller starts to move, nothing and nobody can stop it.'

On 16 May 1995 the Eastern Daily Press proudly proclaimed the news that the Red Arrows were moving to RAF Marham near Kings Lynn. An editorial commented:

'Confirmation that the Red Arrows are to move to Marham will be welcomed with anticipation and pride in Norfolk, a county whose links with the Royal Air Force are unusually strong. Although its famous home at Scampton is shortly to fall victim to defence cuts, the future of the world's premier aerobatics team was guaranteed in last year's Defence Costs Study. Marham, the RAF's biggest base, and Norfolk, with uncluttered airspace and a relatively sparse population, are obvious long-term homes for the Red Arrows.'

There was that famous phrase yet again – the world's premier aerobatics team. That announcement in the Eastern Daily Press and in other newspapers was to cost a Lincolnshire man a lot of money. He claims to be the Team's number one fan, and on reading the news of the Team's move to Marham he promptly moved home from Lincoln to Kings Lynn.

'People may think I'm mad chasing them about but I'm their number one fan,' he told the Lincolnshire Echo. 'Wherever they go, I go, and I'll follow them to the four corners of the earth if I have to.'

Sadly for that man, no sooner had he moved into his new home in Kings Lynn than the MoD announced that the move to Marham would be delayed at least two years, 'for operational reasons', and that in the meantime the Team would be moving to Cranwell.

'As soon as I heard the news I got back on the next train to Lincoln,' the fan said. 'If they're staying in the County, then I'm staying in the County.'

Soon afterwards we learned of another plot, and I phrase it that way deliberately. We were not officially told of the new plot but the gist of it simply emerged; no-one I asked knew where the story originated but we had all heard it. The Red Arrows would, according to this new plot, move to Marham as originally planned but all the training flying would take place at Sculthorpe, a base with a very long runway that had been used by the US Air Force for many years but was now inactive. There was a major flaw to that plot that we could see immediately but no one outside the Red Arrows had apparently thought of it. The idea was that the Red Arrows would take off for the first slot in the morning, practice overhead the airfield at Sculthorpe and then land there. In the meantime, the ground crew would leave Marham as soon as they had seen off the Red Arrows and travel to Sculthorpe by road aiming to be there in time for the Red Arrows when they landed about 35 minutes later. The problem was that the distance between Marham and

Sculthorpe as the Hawk flies is 15 nautical miles but the distance by road, narrow twisting Norfolk roads, is 27 miles and the journey would take an hour. It was an ill-conceived idea and it we heard no more about it.

There was an official announcement on 26 August 1995. The Red Arrows were to be based temporarily at the RAF College Cranwell for up to two years while the MoD searched for a permanent home for the Team. One very curiously worded report from a usually reliable source that I found on the Internet stated:

'The team will not, however, be able to fly over Cranwell. Instead, they will be accompanied by fire engines and ground controllers to their old base of RAF Scampton, Lincolnshire, which closes next month, to practise their precision aerobatic routines. The team, which needs a six-mile wide cone-shaped area free of all other aircraft in which to fly, originally planned to move to RAF Marham in Norfolk, but other squadrons complained of a possible clash with training. After the transfer, a daily convoy of fire engines, emergency trucks and ground controllers will leave RAF Cranwell to drive the 25 miles to the deserted base at Scampton and stand by in case of problems. They will then drive back to Cranwell where the Hawks of the Red Arrows will land and the crews return to their quarters.'

The report was largely accurate. An MoD spokesman that day announced, 'The aerodrome and buildings at Scampton won't be disposed of until 1998. Most of the family quarters will be retained by the RAF for people working at Cranwell and Waddington. The Arrows can only do their intricate manoeuvres over RAF premises in the interests of safety. Keeping the Scampton runway open as a stand by will cost an extra £1.6 a year.'

By and large the population close to Cranwell were delighted by the news of our imminent arrival. The problem with Cranwell was the same as with all the other airfields: the station could not afford to stop its own flying for six 30-minutes periods daily to give the Red Arrows sole use of the skies overhead. There was now the delicate PR problem of explaining why, if Scampton was to be closed because it was no longer needed, the Red Arrows were going to continue their training flying there. Curiously, the local media never asked that question, probably because they were so pleased that the Red Arrows were staying. Neither did the media question the cost of maintaining the runway at Scampton, necessary in case any of the Red Arrows needed to use it in an emergency. The media might also have asked how the MoD hoped to sell off the base to business concerns when the Red Arrows would be roaring overhead six times a day in winter. But they did not.

It was clear, to us at least, that the decision to close Scampton had been taken hastily and without giving due thought, or any thought, to the consequences. One very senior officer whom I met socially four years later cornered me and asked, 'Are they still blaming me for closing Scampton?' I was forced to be honest and say that many people were, but of course that did not mean that they knew the inside story of what had led to that decision. 'Suffice it to say,' replied the very senior officer with a resigned look on his face, 'It was not my decision. I tried to warn people of the difficulties that it would create but I was over-ruled.' I looked at him askance but he merely smiled and refused to be drawn. It was that need-to-know principle at work again.

A frequently-asked media question at this period was, 'How much does it cost to run the Red Arrows?' I had often asked the question myself but the answers I got, when anyone bothered to answer, ranged from £6 million to £34 million which indicated to me that no-one really knew – or cared. I used to turn the question back on the media and say, 'You're asking the wrong question. You should be asking how much would be saved by disbanding the Red Arrows?' I then pointed out that if the Team were to be disbanded, the pilots and ground crew would be deployed elsewhere and not sacked so there were no savings there. The aircraft would be moved to the flying training school at Valley where there were always shortages, so there were no savings there. The RAF had already decided to close Scampton and try and sell it off into the private sector so there were no savings there even if the Team was disbanded. The only real savings would be in consumables such as fuel, oils and spare parts.

Had a decision to disband the Team been taken at the time the Defence Costs Study was published, I think the MoD might have got away with it without too much of an outcry because of the wide-ranging defence cuts which followed that study. However, so much positive publicity about the Red Arrows was generated once the announcement that Scampton was to close was made that it was then too late to tell the great British public that the Red Arrows would be sacrificed. There would have been outrage – and not only in the UK. The statement that the Red Arrows would move to Cranwell as a temporary measure was, I suspect, made in desperation just four weeks before we set out for the Middle East and South Africa on the first part of what became known, inaccurately, as the world tour. At least we would now have a home to come back to.

Very soon, a lot of people became concerned about another home that might be needed. Nigger, Guy Gibson's black Labrador, had lain in his grave just outside 2 Hangar for 52 years. Many thought that, if the base was to be sold off or abandoned, he should be exhumed and moved somewhere safe. 'Grave Doubts Over Final Resting Place' was just one of the newspaper headlines that appeared in the spring of 1995. There was a flood of letters to newspapers, Scampton and the MoD offering suggestions about what to do. The main worry most people had was that if Scampton base was left unattended, then vandals would get in and wreck the grave. Suggestions included: making a shrine on the side of the A15 at the exact point where the dog was run over in 1943; moving the remains to the Petwood Hotel in Woodhall Spa where the Dam Busters transferred after leaving Scampton and where their annual reunions are still held; reuniting the dog with his Master in the graveyard in Holland where Guy Gibson is buried; moving the dog to East Kirkby, the home of the well-known aviation heritage museum and the airfield from which Gibson took off on the mission from which he never returned.

Inevitably the arguments started up again between those who maintain that the dog was never buried outside the hangar and those, including me, who maintain that he was. I had on one of my files a photocopy of part of a letter written by Flight Sergeant 'Chiefie' Powell in 1986, shortly before he died. Powell was the man who collected the dog's body from a cell at the Guardroom at Scampton's main entrance soon after the accident. Powell had drawn on the back page of his letter a sketch map indicating exactly where he had buried the dog – and that was exactly where the grave's headstone now stands. I had intended to save that letter when Scampton closed down but, sadly, when I remembered and went to collect the file, I was too late. It, along with hundreds of other Scampton files, many of them of great historical interest, had been destroyed as part of the closing down procedures.

I had a letter from a helpful person who said that he knew of someone at Sheffield University who was an expert at locating human bones hidden under the ground. He had, apparently, recently helped the police in finding buried bodies connected with some gruesome murders. The Station Commander, Group Captain Chris Burwell, declined to take up that offer and I agreed with him. From a PR point of view it could have produced the wrong result.

In the end, it was decided to leave the dog at peace where he was buried until such time as RAF Scampton was sold off. Group Captain Burwell was mightily relieved because that meant he no longer had to make, or be associated with, such a controversial decision. In the event, that tuned out to be a very wise decision. Nigger is still there today and his grave is lovingly tended, as it has been now for many years, by a local resident, Mervyn Hallam.

16

African Safari

IN DECEMBER 1994, WHEN EVERYONE was beginning to come to terms with the impending closure of Scampton, the first hints of an extended overseas tour in the autumn of 1995, perhaps to South Africa, started to filter through to Rumour Control at the Red Arrows' HQ at RAF Scampton. Even though South Africa was now legitimate in the eyes of the world and defence companies in many parts of the world were eyeing up sales prospects, it did not seem even remotely possible that the Red Arrows could be going there. However, these rumours made a nice change from worries about the Team's future home and, rumours or not, it did not stop everyone getting out their atlases to work out how the Team might get there and how many intermediate stops might be required. The Hawks, without any air-to-air refuelling capability, would need to land and refuel roughly every 800 miles. The general consensus was that a journey down the western side of Africa would not be possible for political as well as operational considerations, but a transit down through the Middle East and East Africa certainly looked possible and several countries looked particularly inviting.

I had been to South Africa as the guest of British Airways in 1992 when I had flown to Johannesburg and Capetown and back on the flight deck of a Boeing 747-400. Captain Peter Lewis, who had been on the flight deck of Lima Tango, The City of Lincoln, when it first flew to Scampton in 1991 was my host on the South African trip. I had immediately been captivated by Capetown and the prospect of a return trip with the Red Arrows was appealing. None of the Red Arrows had been to South Africa and I probably started boring the Team with my stories of how much they would enjoy it if only we could get there.

The biggest problem was how the RAF could justify sending 11 Hawks, one support Hercules and about 60 people 6,000 miles in autumn when that was traditionally the time for saying goodbye to time-expired pilots, welcoming the new pilots and generally working up for the next season. Bearing in mind that the Red Arrows are established primarily to give public displays in the UK and those European countries where reciprocal military team visits are possible, it would be difficult to justify the cost of sending the Team to the southern hemisphere unless tangible benefits for either the RAF or what was becoming known as 'UK plc' could be identified.

As the months went by, it began to look more and more likely that the tour was on. The whole concept was the brain child of the Head of the Defence Export Services Organisation, Charles Masefield. DESO is a department of the MoD that acts as an intermediary, bringing together representatives of British defence-related companies and potential customers overseas. Mr Masefield, later Sir Charles Masefield, reckoned that British companies attending major aviation exhibitions overseas would benefit greatly by having the Red Arrows as a star attraction. Fortunately British Aerospace, the makers of the Hawk, and Rolls Royce, the supplier of the Hawk Adour engine, were especially keen on the idea. Displays would be given in those countries where there were suitable international aviation exhibitions and the timing of those meant that the Red Arrows tour would have to be split into two quite separate entities, one to Africa and one to the Far East. By August 1995, the rumours had come to fruition but even then, no-one realised, or even thought it really likely, that before the following Spring the Team would have travelled to, and displayed in, Africa, Malaysia, the Philippines, Brunei, Singapore and Australia – and moved base to Cranwell.

The main country in the first tour would be Waterkloof air force base, just outside Pretoria, where the South African Air Force was planning to celebrate its 75th birthday with a major international air display in October, the first since pre-Apartheid days. En route to South Africa the Red Arrows would give displays in both Greece and Turkey for major exhibitions, at Doha in Qatar and at Seeb in the Sultanate of Oman. The second tour would follow almost immediately after the first and take in Malaysia in December for the Langkawi International

Maritime and Aviation Expo, known as LIMA95 for short, and Asian Aerospace in Singapore in January 1996. Later, Australia was added to the itinerary and provided the opportunity to take in Brunei and the Manila en route.

The first official news of the tour was given out to the media in a News Release, issued by the Defence Press Office just six weeks before the date set for departure. In it the Chief of the Air Staff, Air Chief Marshal Sir Michael Graydon said:

'Since 1965, the Red Arrows have demonstrated a standard of excellence which the public in the UK has come to recognise as the hallmark of the Royal Air Force. Moreover, during their many displays abroad they have been outstanding ambassadors for their Service, for British Industry whose technical capability is epitomised in the Hawk aircraft which they fly, and for the UK. I am thus delighted that they have been chosen to represent the best of British Industry by undertaking this tour.'

Flight International took this opportunity to publish an article entitled 'Made in Britain', based partly on another interview with Sir Michael Graydon.

'The last couple of years,' wrote Flight International's Douglas Barrie, 'are unlikely to be singled out as particularly auspicious in the RAF's distinguished history – senior resignations tinged with swingeing cuts in hardware and personnel have left their mark on morale and on the Service's standing in the public eye. As if this were not enough, the Red Arrows display team – one of the Service's sacred cows – appears to be under threat, with the Team rendered homeless by the closure of RAF Scampton. There was even a rumour that the aircraft were to be mothballed. This is firmly dismissed by Air Chief Marshal Sir Michael Graydon who says that the future home of the RAF's pre-eminent display team has been under consideration at ministerial level. He is acutely aware of the importance of the Red Arrows and the slightest suggestion of the demise of the Team he says "fills me with horror."'

I suspect that the Red Arrows were better pleased with the publicity that accrued from that article than the air marshals.

In the end, Charles Masefield cajoled and bullied sixteen defence-related companies to club together in a unique sponsorship deal and around £3 million was raised, or promised, before final flight planning began. There were, however, to be no logos painted on the side of the Hawks, on the Team's flying suits, or on ground equipment; the Air Force Board had been quite adamant about that and the Red Arrows were delighted with that decision. The RAF financiers had worked out that £3 million would be sufficient to pay all the Red Arrows' costs over and above their normal European operating costs. In all the news releases issued by me and my colleagues at Command and in London, we stressed that the tour would not cost the British taxpayer a penny. If we had really wanted to make the most of this, we could probably have proved that the tour would actually save the taxpayer money because we would be out of the country for about four months, with all our expenses being paid for from what we came to call the 'Pot of Gold.'

The Chief of the Air Staff issued an edict to the RAF's Director of PR that one of the main aims of the tour as far as he was concerned was to get a lot of good PR for the RAF in the UK national media. I attended numerous meetings in London about public relations and how we might achieve publicity for the Team at home. The trouble is that it is not really national news if the Red Arrows give a display in Cape Town or Harare: there has to be something extra to attract the attention of the UK media.

The two pilots due to leave the Team in early October 1995 at the end of their 3-year stint, Red 6, Sean Chiddention and Red 9, Benny Ball, had to stay an extra 5 months, but they did not find that any great hardship! Their replacements, Andy Offer, the 1995 solo Harrier display pilot, and David Stobie, ex-Hawk solo display pilot, had reported for duty as scheduled in September and they accompanied the team throughout the tour flying occasionally in the rear cockpit of one of the 11 Hawks or, more frequently and less comfortably, in the back of the support Hercules. The winter training for the new pilots would have to be fitted in as and when possible and it was accepted that there might be a need to delay the start of the 1996 European display season.

It was decided at a fairly early stage that the best way of achieving maximum PR for the Red Arrows would be if I and my colleagues from the MoD and Command HQ were to travel ahead of the Team. That way we could liaise with the sponsoring companies' resident agents in-country and work together doing publicity interviews and setting up press conferences before the Team's arrival. If we had travelled in the support Hercules aircraft with the ground crew we would always have arrived at the destinations after the Team. The big advantage of this arrangement, from my parochial point of view, was that I could travel in comfort by civil airlines. My first port of call would be Doha.

There were two critical dates that constrained the planning of the first part of the tour: a very important display in Oman on 2 October at which HRH The Prince of Wales would be the guest of honour, and the need to arrive at Waterkloof, 4300 nautical miles to the south of Oman, only 48 hours later in time for the VIP opening of the South African Air Force's 75th Birthday Celebrations. Having to transit 11 single-engined aircraft across the thousand of miles of inhospitable territory south of the Arabian peninsula, with virtually no radio or navigation aids, was not something to be undertaken lightly.

The original 1995 Display Season ended in late September with displays in Turkey and Greece and it was convenient and economical to continue from Athens through the Middle East without re-starting from Scampton. A wave of tummy troubles afflicting pilots and ground crew, caused by unscrupulous hotel staffs in Ankara filling mineral water bottles from the ordinary taps and then sealing the bottles to make them look authentic, made life unpleasant for several days. We know for a fact that was happening because one of the ground crew saw it for himself. The whole detachment immediately changed hotels but the damage was done. The Red Arrows flew from Athens to Akrotiri, then two more legs to Tabuk and Riyadh in Saudi Arabia, where the engineers had to change an unserviceable engine and tail plane on one aircraft, and finally on to Doha Capital of Qatar.

I arrived in Doha a few days before the Team and gave several interviews to newspapers and magazines. I also did a 60-minute 'Desert Island Discs' type of programme on Qatari Radio's English language programme. I had to choose my six records from a rather limited library of western music but the presenter and I recorded the programme in one continuous take. I took the opportunity to explain the history of the Red Arrows and the reason for our visit to Qatar, and gave the listeners a detailed description of the display they would see. There was a lot of local publicity and a great deal of excitement amongst the ordinary Qataris as they awaited the arrival of the Red Arrows.

There was no air show as such in Doha, just a display by the Red Arrows at which members of the Qatari Royal Family and many Government ministers were the guests of honour. The display was centred on the splendid Hotel Sheraton right on the beach front, which was where we were all staying. All six lanes of the entire 10km stretch of the Corniche, the main thoroughfare from the centre of Doha, became one huge parking lot. A very late change of plan, caused by the imminent arrival of a detachment of USAF aircraft which needed the apron parking slots, meant that the Red Arrows had to leave Doha earlier than planned. They could not fly on to Oman straightaway, as originally planned, because all the hotels there were fully booked for a Gulf Co-operation Council meeting. Instead the Team had two unscheduled nights in Bahrain before flying to Seeb International Airport in Oman.

I flew from Doha to Seeb on Gulf Airways. It was a great pleasure to be back in Oman for the first time since my tour of duty there in the mid-1980s. There was no PR I could do because the media were not allowed to be told in advance of the Red Arrows' visit or of the presence of the Prince of Wales. That is the way they do things in Oman. As in Doha, the Red Arrows were the only performers and the display was private and not open to the public. There were only a few hundred spectators, including Omani Royals and most of the Diplomatic Corps and military brass. The Prince of Wales took time out to talk with every single member of the Red Arrows after the display, before departing with his entourage, in a fleet of helicopters which literally blasted the 11 Hawks with sand, dust and flying debris. The Red Arrows' ground crew were not amused at that but it wasn't the Prince of Wales' fault.

After the Seeb display, which was in late afternoon to avoid the ferocious heat, there was no time for entertainment or rest. I headed off to the civil airport on the other side of the main runway and took an overnight flight to Johannesburg via Abu Dhabi. The Team took off from Seeb at last light for Riyadh where they made a night landing. It was nearly midnight before the ground crew had serviced all the aircraft and readied them for the next day's very long haul. Leaving Riyadh, the Red Arrows had an extremely tiring three-hop day – the first two legs, to

Jeddah and then Addis Ababa, took the formation over very isolated terrain with few navigation aids. The Garmin satellite navigation equipment that was on loan to the Team proved to be worth its weight in gold and from time to time civil airliners they passed en route obliged by transmitting position reports to the air traffic control authorities by short wave radio, equipment not fitted to the Hawks.

The airport facilities at Addis Ababa were poor. The parking ramp in particular was littered with all kinds of rubbish, a real hazard for small jet aircraft. The airport authorities would not accept the departure flight plan until the landing fees had been paid in full – and in cash! Fortunately, a representative of the British Embassy was on hand to fork out. But Addis had one final surprise for the pilots. As the 11 aircraft accelerated down the runway for take off, dozens of people suddenly and alarmingly appeared from the long grass immediately alongside the runway as they stood up to wave goodbye to the British fliers. No-one had thought to warn the pilots that many local people live in the long grass! That is the sort of distraction you can do without when making a close formation take off.

The flight from Addis Ababa to Nairobi took the Team through the Inter-Tropical Convergence Zone, a phenomenon much loved by meteorologists, and across the Equator. The weather progressively worsened. Approaching Nairobi, the Hawks had to climb to 43,000 feet to keep above the dangerous frontal cloud, but the descent into Jomo Kenyatta International Airport was something of a nightmare. John Rands split his formation into two sections for the penetration to the airfield. The weather turned out to be even worse than forecast. The aircraft were in thick cloud continuously until they broke out, in torrential rain, just 400 feet above the ground and about one nautical mile from the runway. A fine piece of precision close formation flying by all the pilots.

The following day there were two long legs to be flown, from Nairobi to Lilongwe in Malawi and then on to the South African Air Force base at Waterkloof, midway between Pretoria and Johannesburg. As the Red Arrows approached the border between Malawi and the Republic of South Africa, in anticipation of a friendly interception by SAAF fighters at the border, Squadron Leader Rands mischievously obtained ATC clearance for a cruise climb to 47,000 feet. The SAAF Cheetahs that came up to meet the Red Arrows could not reach that height and so the Hawks obligingly descended to a more modest 32,000 feet to be escorted to Waterkloof. One up to the RAF!

Sadly the pilots were so tired and mentally drained when they arrived at Waterkloof that they felt unable to give the media the interviews I had set up. Particularly frustrated was the ITN television crew who had set up a live satellite link back to London and found they had no-one to talk to other than me. In fact they were so disappointed that they left without even talking to me and valuable live coverage on UK national television of the Red Arrows arriving in South Africa was lost. Later that same afternoon, having barely had time to meet and greet their hosts, the Team was airborne to practice. This was essential for two reasons. Firstly it was required by the Display Regulations which called for all participants to demonstrate their routine so that flight safety officers could be satisfied that no display contravened their rules. Secondly, the airfield at Waterkloof is what is known in the trade as 'hot and high' – ground temperatures well into the upper 30s Centigrade and an altitude of 5,500 feet above sea level. In these conditions jet engines give considerably less thrust than at sea level in temperate climates. Turning circles get physically larger and looping manoeuvres use up more height and are more difficult to fly.

While the Team was airborne on the practice the Command PRO who was accompanying me decided to give an interview to a lady reporter who was putting together a package for an English language radio station that covers most of Africa by short wave. I stayed in the background until I heard the following exchange.

'How do you think the Red Arrows will cope with the hot and high conditions here in Johannesburg?' asked the reporter.

'Well, we've displayed in a lot of hot countries on the way here,' said my colleague, rather patronisingly, having misunderstand the question. 'I think our pilots know how to cope with high temperatures and the height is no problem – it was even higher when they passed through Nairobi. Plenty of liquid and the right clothing is so important!'

I stepped in quickly to rescue the astonished reporter and completed the interview. That was how my colleague learned about hot and high conditions and how dramatically they can affect aircraft performance, let along the comfort of people. The practice display showed that the 20-minute UK display would take 23 minutes at Waterkloof and the flying programme timings would have to be adjusted to take that into account. Other overseas performers had to make similar adjustments to their own displays and timings, even the Russians' mighty Su-27s.

On the first day of the show 27 Chiefs of Air Staff were present, including our own, Sir Michael Graydon. In the following three days the Team displayed five more times. According to official estimates, over half a million people attended the air days at Waterkloof and countless thousands throughout the Republic watched the extensive live TV coverage.

'I have never displayed in front of such enthusiastic and friendly people as those we found at Waterkloof,' John Rands said afterwards. 'Displaying hot and high was a new and fascinating experience.'

One of the little things that kept Red Arrows' personnel amused was estimating how long it would take any South African citizen to introduce the subject of the Rugby World Cup into any conversation. 75 seconds was about average. You could easily wind up patriotic South Africans by innocently asking them which World Cup they were referring to. Whilst the official reason for the Red Arrows' presence at Waterkloof was to help the SAAF celebrate its 75th birthday, high level representatives of the British companies funding the tour were much in evidence in their companies' display areas and they were delighted with the Red Arrows' presence and performances. Having the Team appear in their bright red flying suits on the display stands of the companies that had contributed to the Pot of Gold acted as a magnet, so much so that companies occupying adjacent stands eventually became a little peeved that we were taking attention away from their products.

From Pretoria the detachment moved south west for a few days in Cape Town and everyone immediately fell in love with this delightful city and its friendly people. On arrival the Red Arrows and the support Hercules made a spectacular and rare joint flypast through Kloof Nek, the gap between Table Mountain and Signal Hill, and then over the city itself. John Rands reported that as they passed through the gap he could see thousands of people waving. The display over the historic waterfront area with Table Mountain looming dramatically in the background was received ecstatically and traffic in large parts of the city came to a complete standstill. During the display a large cargo ship started majestically steaming its way out of the harbour. The Cape Argus reported what happened thus:

'Over the Team Manager's radio came the warning, "large ship in the mouth of the harbour". Seconds later Reds 6 and 7 passed the ship, flying so low it appeared the captain on the bridge could have looked into their cockpits. Asked later whether the ship had posed any problems, Squadron Leader Rands said that although it had been in the way of the Synchro Pair it had not posed a major threat. "If you hit a big ship like that, you shouldn't be doing the job," he said. And then he added as an afterthought: "And you'd better see an optician straight away."'

We knew what he meant!

A surprise arrival at Capetown was the British Airways 'City of Lincoln' Boeing 747-400 on a scheduled service bearing the Scampton Station Commander, Group Captain Chris Burwell. After Cape Town everyone started to relax knowing that they were, in effect, starting the long journey home. First there was a low level transit around the Cape of Good Hope and Cape Agulhas en route to Durban. Hands up all those who, like me, thought that the Cape of Good Hope, not Cape Agulhas, was the southernmost point of the continent.

Once again I flew ahead of the Team, this time an early morning two-hour flight to Durban. Shortly after arriving at my hotel I was taken to the Presidential Suite in the splendid Rugby ground to gave a live interview on late Breakfast Television, seen throughout the Republic. Quite why the interview was transmitted from the Presidential Suite was not made clear to me but I think the interview went well. I agreed to return for another television interview, especially for the Durban area, later in the day and that was when the trouble started. A well-meaning PRO in the South African Air Force had told the media that the Red Arrows would perform over the towns of George and Port Elizabeth on the low level transit flight from Cape Town to Durban. Unfortunately, the Red Arrows had no such intention – they had not been asked to do so nor did they have enough fuel to do it anyway. Virtually the entire population of each town stopped working to throng the streets, looking in vain for the Red Arrows. There were a lot of disappointed and angry citizens. I was trapped in the middle of the second TV interview at Durban when the news broke.

'It had been announced that the Red Arrows were going to fly over George at midday,' asked the interviewer. 'Why didn't they do it?'

For a stunned moment I could not think who George was and then I remembered, just in time, that it is a town not a person! Not one of my more comfortable interviews but fortunately this one was being recorded. At the time I had no idea that it had been announced that there would be a display over George so I had to make some quick telephone calls before I was able to resume that interview.

The confusion over the display-that-never-was created so much ill feeling that it almost cancelled out all the beneficial PR. The Port Elizabeth Herald printed a scathing report headed 'Missing the Target.' Never in the history of British aviation have so many been disappointed by so few, Winston Churchill might have said, according to that newspaper. It continued, 'The Red Arrows appeared for only a few flashing seconds and so undid much of the good work of the Queen's visit to the city last March. Let us hope that they have learned from this debacle and that in future they stick to their schedule and their promises.'

The following day the same newspaper stated that I 'had apologised profusely for the fiasco.' It continued, 'Tony Cunnane said that, battling in the face of strong coastal winds and flying at sea level which uses up more fuel, the Red Arrows had no choice but to take the shortest possible route to East London.' In fact I never spoke to that newspaper. Having unilaterally decided that it was the Red Arrows at fault, the media were not prepared to make any apologies, particularly since they would have had to lay the blame on their own air force. I did hear some time later, from a reliable South African source, that the top echelons of the SAAF were extremely miffed that the Red Arrows displays at Waterkloof had almost entirely eclipsed the displays by SAAF aircraft. Certainly the Red Arrows got more publicity in the media than all the rest of the participants put together.

When the Team arrived at Durban someone had arranged for them to be met and blessed by Phemelele Ngcongo, a sangoma, which is a polite word for female witch doctor. The sangoma's name in the strange Zulu language, which is full of tongue clicks, was completely unpronounceable by the Brits. The ceremony, which lasted about three minutes but seemed a lot longer, bemused the Red Arrows and the airport workers and media alike but it provided some unusual pictures for the media. During the subsequent press conference, John Rands was quoted in the Durban Mercury as saying that 'a stable extrovert with an appetite for adrenaline and a capacity for beer is what makes a good fighter pilot.'

The display over Durban was centred on the splendid beach and watched by an enormous crowd and caused the nearby civil airport to be closed down for 20 minutes. The Team Manager's commentary, relayed over a public address system, was heard by tens of thousands of people along several miles of the promenade. The following day was a rare day off, spoilt somewhat because of a temperature of 42 degrees Celsius, a 40 mph wind blowing like a furnace, and humidity of almost 100%.

I then went my own way again and flew to Harare, capital of Zimbabwe while the Team spent a few days in the dry north of the Republic at Hoedspruit, home of the SAAF's own aerobatic team, The Silver Falcons. I was made very welcome in Harare but it was difficult to obtain any advance publicity for the Team. I was invited to the offices of the Harare Herald and spent about an hour telling a reporter all about the Red Arrows. I was very conscious of the fact that the reporter spent most of his time making surreptitious glances towards the man I assumed to be the News Editor at the other end of the room and little time making notes of what I was telling him. The next day his lengthy report was spread over three columns but there was hardly a mention of the Red Arrows. Most of the article was about the Air Force of Zimbabwe and their participation in the 'historic air show at Charles Prince Airport.' Perhaps they had heard how the Red Arrows had stolen the show at Waterkloof and did not want the same to happen at their air show.

The Red Arrows eventually arrived in Harare from Hoedspruit. Air Commodore Bostock, Commandant of CFS, later reported that the Harare display took place 'before a modest crowd by South African standards' but there was a great deal of good will.' Performances by aircraft of the Air Force of Zimbabwe were noisy and spirited, he continued, but hardly within normal safety regulations accepted within Europe. I learned that the Air Force of Zimbabwe, AFZ, is so-called so as not to be confused with the neighbouring Zambian Air Force, ZAF.

The following day a side trip was made to the Victoria Falls for a photo-shoot. Unfortunately, the Falls were not at their best because there had been a drought for several years. Nevertheless a spectacular picture of the Red Arrows flying over the Falls was obtained by the Team's own photographer, Peter Mobbs, flying with Red 10. I write picture in the singular because, although Peter was using the motor drive in his camera, the Hawks were travelling at 400 miles per hour and as a result there was only a single frame that had the Red Arrows centrally placed over the Falls. There was no time or fuel to go around again for another attempt. Peter spent some anxious days until he could develop his film but he need not have worried. His superb picture appeared in several of the UK national newspapers and was seen around the world in newspapers, brochures and magazines. Up until the day I retired I was still getting mail from members of the public asking where they could get copies. If only one PR photograph had come out of the whole tour, this one would have made the tour worthwhile. What a pity that Peter was an RAF serviceman and so he got no royalties from his work!

'The journey north from Zimbabwe was relatively uneventful with light winds and stunning scenery' said Squadron Leader Rands. 'I was mesmerised by the greenness and beauty of Kenya and Ethiopia. In the many trips I have flown over the Mediterranean and the Alps I have never had such superb visibility as we found over Africa. It was a little compensation for the stiff legs and numb bum after 15 hours in the cockpit over three consecutive days!'

The detachment arrived back home on 19 October having flown 23,000 nautical miles. The Hawks had amassed a total of 631 flying hours and the support Hercules 75 hours. The Hawks then underwent an extensive series of engineering inspections and servicings. Just 35 days later, on 23 November, the Red Arrows took off from Scampton for what was expected to be the very last time. That final departure from Scampton was an emotional occasion, more so perhaps for those left behind. The media were there in force to film the events for posterity and John Rands led his pilots on one final flypast over 4 Hangar, the Team's home since 1983. The Hercules support aircraft took off just a few minutes after the Hawks had disappeared from sight and sound. What we thought at the time would be the very last aircraft to leave Scampton, shortly after the Hercules, was a Chipmunk flown by Station Commander, Chris Burwell, on his final day in command.

17

The Far East and Australia

THE 7,500 MILE ROUTE TO LANGKAWI, a holiday island off the north west coast of Malaysia, took the Team through Saudi Arabia, where the Red Arrows gave their first ever display in the Kingdom, the United Arab Emirates, Pakistan, India and Thailand. This time the transit was rather more leisurely and relatively uneventful with no urgent appointments to keep. The detachment had two days off in Langkawi before a very public practice display on 4 December followed by proper displays on seven consecutive days at LIMA 95, the Langkawi International Maritime and Aeronautical Expo.

Britain's Minister for Defence Procurement, James Arbuthnot, was at Langkawi. At a press conference he was asked by a local reporter why British pilots were demonstrating the Hawk. The Royal Malaysian Air Force operates the advanced Hawk 100 two-seat trainer and the Hawk 200 single seat fighter variant. Why were the Malaysian pilots not flying the Hawks?

'The Red Arrows pilots are probably the best in the world', said the Minister. 'Everyone is keen to see them. Their aerobatics show what the Hawk aircraft can do when operated to the limits. LIMA 95 is one of the world's finest international aviation exhibitions, an excellent shop window for British industry. One of the highlights, if not *the* highlight, is the Red Arrows, sponsored by 16 British companies and showing what is the very best in Britain.'

I was not able to go to Langkawi and so a lady PRO from Command HQ, who was going to share the onerous task with me, had to manage on her own. An unfortunate road accident on the island put an end to the tour for one of the pilots and created a precedent for the Red Arrows.

Three of the pilots were in a stationary hire car waiting for a gap in the traffic to turn right when they were struck from behind by a lorry. The rear offside corner of the car was so badly damaged that any passenger in that seat would probably have been killed. As it was all three occupants suffered cuts and abrasions but Flight Lieutenant Sean Perrett, Red 3, suffered a complicated collar bone fracture as well. He spent several days in the brand-new Langkawi hospital before being flown home to England. During the Christmas holidays Sean was operated on and a titanium plate was bolted in to hold the two ends of bone together. Sean had flown his last tour sortie with the Red Arrows.

This accident should have reduced the Red Arrows to eight aircraft which would have been most unfortunate at such a prestigious event. However, travelling with the detachment were the two replacement pilots for the 1996 season, Dave Stobie the new Red 3 and Andy Offer the new Red 2. Since joining at Scampton in September they had been getting in a little practice as and when it could be programmed. Dave Stobie, was both a Qualified Flying Instructor and a Qualified Weapons Instructor. More importantly in this context, he was a former Hawk solo display pilot and had performed at over 30 displays all round the UK during the summer months of 1994. The Team Leader, John Rands, in consultation with the CFS Commandant, Air Commodore Bostock, decided it would be possible to modify the first half of the display to allow Flight Lieutenant Stobie to fly in the number 3 slot but ultimately the decision was made by the Team Leader.

'It was not an instant solution,' said JR afterwards. 'The plot just evolved. As always in such matters, it is a balance of risks and possibilities. If I had thought I was flying a pilot who was a danger to himself or, more importantly, to the other pilots it would have been a non-starter. But I was clear in my own mind that what we were doing was safe and sensible and the best decision available to me. In the event, Stobes' flying was immaculate'.

Thus, Flight Lieutenant Dave Stobie became the first ever 'green-suited' pilot to display in public with the Red Arrows and if ever there was a difficult question for a Mastermind contestant that is it – or rather that is the answer. There was no time to integrate Stobes into the intricate, high energy manoeuvres which form the second half of the display and so that was flown by the remaining eight pilots and Stobes made a discreet exit at the halfway point. The displays for the remainder of the tour followed this pattern.

About 1030 one morning, as the pilots were chatting to delegates at the various British exhibitions on Langkawi airfield, there was an announcement over the public address system stating that the Red Arrows would open the flying display shortly. The Team Manager, Squadron Leader Mike Williams, was dispatched to have the announcement corrected, only to be told by the organisers that the King of Malaysia was coming at 1130 to watch the Red Arrows and that they had better be ready to display! The display had originally been scheduled for late afternoon and the ground crew were some miles away relaxing in their hotel. Needless to say the Team did take off within the hour and gave a superb performance for the King.

The Hawks were left at Butterworth in Malaysia over the Christmas and New Year period because it was neither financially nor operationally sensible to fly them all the way back to UK. It was a different matter for the pilots and ground crew who returned to the UK by British Airways to join their families for the holiday period. They made the return journey in early January and then spent a week getting back into practice. After that it was the long haul to Australia, transiting via Jakarta, Bali, El Tari, Darwin, Alice Springs, Adelaide, Canberra and thence to Sydney where they arrived to a rapturous welcome on 23 January.

It was fortuitous that the Red Arrows display in Sydney was scheduled for 26 January because that is Australia Day and a public holiday. The Team gave a spectacular display over the harbour area and Australian police reported that 1.2 million people watched. I claimed that, on behalf of the Red Arrows, as a world record for the largest number of spectators ever at any single air display show anywhere. It seems likely that most of the people would have turned out whether the Red Arrows were there or not. Apparently the Harbour Bridge area on Australia Day is something like Trafalgar Square on New Year's Eve – but warmer. I cannot, therefore, claim that all those people turned up specifically to see the Red Arrows perform, but see them perform they did, and no-one so far has challenged my world record claim.

I arrived in Bandar Seri Bagawan, the capital of Brunei Darussalam, a couple of days before the Team. It was the Holy Month of Ramadan so the Sultan was unable to appear in public and there was little I could do in the way of PR. However the display was watched by the Sultan's teenage son, Prince Abdul Maten. The Sultan himself watched from the privacy of the Royal Hangar on the other side of the airfield. The Team Leader was later granted an audience with the Sultan.

The display at the Villamor Air Force Base in Manila was intended only for locally invited guests because members of the public were not supposed to be allowed into the airfield restricted area. However, many thousands of onlookers turned up at the gates and eventually a young Philippine Air Force Officer shrugged his shoulders and ordered the gates to be opened. 'This is a free country,' he said to the guards. 'Let them in!' The grateful people swarmed in. The lucky ones at the front of the throng found shelter from the blazing sun in the VIP pavilion. When the VIPs, including several Government Ministers and high ranking military officers, arrived at the pavilion from a reception on another part of the airfield, they stood out in the blazing sun and made no attempt to move the interlopers out of their seats! Can you imagine that happening at a VIP event in UK? It is not recorded what, if anything, happened to the young officer but I reckon he deserved congratulations for his sensible decision.

The Red Arrows appearances in Singapore caused a few problems. For a start the flying displays were very much secondary to the exhibitions in the main hall, quite unusual for an international show but imposed upon the organisers by the geography of the site. The airspace set aside for flying was over the sea but perilously close to the Singapore International Airport. Viewing of the flying from the area in front of the exhibition halls was seriously hampered by an avenue of tall trees and had the Red Arrows and other display aircraft operated to their normal base heights many of the manoeuvres would have been hidden from the spectators. The display organising committee insisted that there should be no over-flight of the crowd at all and this meant that the Red Arrows would have to alter some of their manoeuvres, not least the standard crowd rear arrival. By this time the 1995 Team had already flown 140 public displays using exactly the same choreography that had been approved by the Commander-in-Chief on Red Suit Day back in April. Last minute changes to the approved display routine carry with them potential flight safety risks. Even flying to higher base heights has it problems because the Team Leader and the Synchro Pair have got used to the view they get at the lower height limit and there is a completely different perspective at other heights. To compound the problems, the organisers wanted the Red Arrows to occupy the stage for no longer than 15 minutes, a reduction of about 6 minutes on the standard show.

It is true to say that the pilots were extremely angry that these limitations and restrictions only came to light a few days before the first scheduled show. The show organising committee had been told well in advance, as are all Display Organisers, of the Team's mandatory display parameters but they apparently decided not to insist on the Singapore rules until the Red Arrows were already on the island. One can only surmise why they took that course of action. As the Red Arrows' end of season report stated:

'The whole episode highlighted the potential conflicts when a sponsored team performs on an international stage, and flight safety dictates that future sponsored appearances must be conditional upon an early acceptance by the display organisers of the Team's modus operandi and in the absence of this, a clear option to withdraw, regardless of sponsorship interests.'

An uneasy compromise was reached on this occasion because it was unthinkable that the Red Arrows should withdraw at such a late stage. To have done so would have caused a considerable loss of face for the organisers, embarrassment for the British companies sponsoring the Red Arrows, and huge disappointment for the thousands of spectators who wanted to see the Red Arrows. It is, perhaps, significant that the Red Arrows have never appeared at the Singapore air shows again.

The Red Arrows finally arrived back in the United Kingdom on 20 February 1996 to land for the first time at their new home, RAF Cranwell, Lincolnshire. Straightaway they had to begin preparations for the 1996 season, the opening displays of which were barely 12 weeks away. The overall statistics for the 1995 season and for the two overseas tours are impressive. The Team passed through 16 countries in four continents, Europe, Africa, Asia and Australasia, and the tally of countries in which the Team has displayed increased to exactly 50, with the first-ever displays in Qatar, Saudi Arabia, South Africa, Zimbabwe, Australia and the Philippines. In all, each pilot travelled about 52,000 miles, the equivalent of twice around the Equator.

'I'll have many lasting impressions of these tours,' John Rands told me when we all gathered together at Cranwell for the first time, 'but the first, and probably the most lasting, was the sheer exuberance and sense of achievement we experienced when we arrived in Pretoria. All the months of uncertainty and planning were over. We were there – we'd done it – and we were on schedule! We'd made an incredible two day, six sortie, dash south from Oman, where we had performed in front of the Prince of Wales, to arrive exactly on time to the minute at Waterkloof on the outskirts of Pretoria. But the journey was not without its challenges. Hot and high operations at several African airfields with temperatures of 35 degrees Celsius and an altitude of 6,000 feet above sea level tested the aircraft and pilots to the limits. It was even more demanding at Nairobi. We descended through thick turbulent cloud from over 40,000 feet to just 400 feet on the final approach to Nairobi. Not very pleasant. Without the Garmin GPS satellite navigation equipment it would have been very hazardous flying over vast tracts of Africa. For long periods we would have been out of range of all navigation aids.'

Were there any low spots? 'Undoubtedly the fatigue,' said John Rands. 'It sounds very glamorous to be travelling around the world visiting all these exotic places. But the frequent time changes, forever booking into and out of hotels, rushed meals, being caught in horrendous traffic jams in places such as Manila, Bangkok and Singapore, and wondering whether we would get to the aircraft in time for the display – all these things contributed to an ever growing sense of fatigue. I also feel both very grateful and desperately sorry for the ground crew. They worked very long hours: they started before the pilots each day and finished after them, often working in extremely hot and humid conditions. The saddest thing was that most of them did not get a chance to see the Victoria Falls in Zimbabwe because it was dark by the time they had finished working on the aircraft and we had just a one night stop. Sydney was one of the nicest cities I've ever visited, clean, fun and friendly. The display over Sydney Harbour on Australia Day was the most amazing experience – more so because of the huge crowd.'

'One of the most impressive logistical achievements was getting two new tail-planes delivered to Oman in less than 48 hours after ordering them,' said Flight Lieutenant Mark Northover, the engineering officer. 'Splendid teamwork by the Hawk Engineering Authority and the 38 Group Hercules people. We had to change an engine in Brunei. The Hercules had to go back to Singapore to collect the new engine and as a result missed the trip to the Philippines. We flew to Manila, a long leg from Brunei over the shark-infested South China Sea, with just 10 Hawks and the ground crew in the rear cockpits. It sounds very dramatic – changing tail-planes and engines – but it wasn't at all. These, and other components wear out from time to time and have to be changed – we can't always have the luxury of doing the work at base. Apart from those fairly major items we had only minor technical problems to deal with. In total the Hawks flew about 1,100 sorties during the tour – that is from the time we left Scampton back in September until the day we arrived at Cranwell. We never had less than 10 of the 11 Hawks serviceable and we flew every sortie and every display on time. I think that is a remarkable tribute both to the ground crew and to the reliability of the British Aerospace Hawk aircraft.'

Air Commodore Simon Bostock, who accompanied the Team on both tours said, 'Few would disagree that the 1995 Season was one of the finest ever, and the manner in which all members of the Squadron faced daunting challenges was nothing short of superb. The highly successful tours just completed are a fitting reflection of their worth and all members of the Red Arrows, but above all the Leader, deserve great credit.'

On 29 March 1996, just 40 days after arriving at Cranwell for the first time, the 1996 Red Arrows flew their first nine-ship practice. For good measure the Team included in that practice a flypast at RAF Waddington for the official opening of WAVE, the Waddington Aircraft Viewing Enclosure, on the side of the busy A15 trunk road.

But the touring was not over for the year. The Team was tasked to appear at the Indonesian Air Show in June 1996. Once again the tour was sponsored by DESO. I am sure it is true to say that hardly anyone on the Team wanted to trek all the way out to the Far East again and there was criticism in the UK media when the tour details became known although, because of the action of protest groups objecting to the sale of Hawks to Indonesia, there had been no official PR about the trip. The main purpose of the Red Arrows' attendance was indeed to assist British Aerospace in their endeavours to get a further contract for Hawk sales.

The days spent in Jakarta were quite pleasant for us. The display organisers had gone to enormous trouble with all their arrangements and I have to say the end product was better than the set up in Singapore. The Team were invited first to a grand reception 'to meet the Red Arrows' hosted jointly by British Aerospace, Rolls Royce and Marconi. Dr Habibie, then the Minister for Research and Technology but later to become, for a short while at least, President of Indonesia, and Michael Portillo, then Secretary of State for Defence, were both present. Dr Habibie spoke at the Reception for 60 minutes; one of the British Embassy staff next to me commented that this was the short version of a much longer speech that all the diplomats had come to know almost off by heart. Dr Habibie said that in future the Indonesian Air Show would be held biennially. It would be known as the Asia-Pacific High Technology and Aerospace Show and he expected the Red Arrows to attend. Two days later the Red Arrows were guests at a Grand Dinner in the Jakarta Hilton to celebrate Dr Habibie's 60th birthday.

Because of the Red Arrows trip to Indonesia several important UK shows had to be cancelled at quite short notice and the organisers of those shows were not best pleased. All aircraft landed back at Cranwell on 10 July having flown 18,000 nautical miles, seven public displays and one practice display, 362 Hawk sorties amounting to 492 flying hours, without any major unserviceabilities. The support Hercules used 60 flying hours and remained serviceable throughout.

The ongoing political problems in Indonesia meant Dr Habibie's dreams of an Asia-Pacific High Technology and Aerospace Show came to nought but I doubt if even he expected to become President one day. The Red Arrows have not been back to Indonesia.

18

Complaints

ONCE I ACCEPTED THAT I HAD BEEN STITCHED UP on the matter of low flying and noise complaints, I went about the task with good grace, although it always remained one of my less satisfying jobs. Until the Red Arrows moved out of Scampton at the end of 1995, there were two quite separate elements to this part of my work. Firstly I was expected, quite rightly, to deal with any complaints relating to Red Arrows' activities wherever those activities took place. Secondly, I was made responsible for dealing with all complaints received at Scampton relating to any flying activity anywhere in the country by any type of aircraft. After the Red Arrows moved to Cranwell I dealt only with complaints about the Team; all other complaints were handled by the Operations Squadron staff.

At the risk of upsetting my erstwhile colleagues, let me explain how to go about making a complaint about RAF flying activities should you need to do so. Individuals may lodge their complaint with any military unit but it is usually easiest to contact the nearest RAF unit, the address and telephone number of which can easily be found in the telephone directory under the heading 'Royal Air Force'. Thus any complaints about the Red Arrows at air displays, or whilst in transit between airfields, are usually received first at the nearest RAF base but they eventually found their way onto my desk for action.

I tried to avoid taking initial telephone calls from complainers myself, partly because I needed time to check up on the activity being complained about and partly because I wanted the complainer to have time to calm down! I much preferred dealing with letters because they gave me time to look into the substance of the complaint instead of having to appease an angry person on the telephone without knowing the background. Although I used to work very long hours, even I did not always know exactly what the Red Arrows were doing at any given time.

I make no criticism of the complainant for being angry; I can get angry myself when someone or something annoys me. I do, however, feel sorry for the Railtrack and airlines' customer relations folk who literally have to face the wrath of passengers when their transport is delayed or cancelled. There is usually no point in taking your anger out on such people: they are not the cause of the delays, they are there to assist you to get over the inconvenience caused by the delay. With that in mind, during my time at Scampton all low flying complainers who identified themselves as such were put through to an airman or airwoman in the Station Operations Centre during the airfield operating hours. The clerks there had been specially briefed by me on how to deal with the calls. There was a proforma to be filled in so that all the important details I would need later were logged. The airman, I refuse to use the word airperson, would politely tell the caller that I would return their call as soon as I was available. Out of airfield operating hours the complainers were connected with the Station Duty Officer who would take similar action. It was always very noticeable that people were liable to be more rude and impatient with airmen and airwomen than they were with officers. That says something about human nature, I suppose.

The RAF's first and most important principle for dealing with complainers is that they should be dealt with courteously. Personally, I have always taken the view that if a member of the public takes the trouble to contact the RAF, the very least we can do when talking or writing to them is treat their complaint sympathetically. When someone did manage to get through to me on the telephone to lodge a complaint about the Red Arrows, I always started off with an apology.

'I am so sorry you've had cause to complain about the Red Arrows,' I would say. I would then make sure the caller knew my name, appointment and my direct telephone number. I always offered to call the person straight back to save their telephone bills. If I was writing a letter to a complainant, I always started that off with an apology. I did not have to agree with the complainant but I did always investigate their complaint impartially.

Dealing with complaints was, fortunately, never a particularly time consuming task. One of my colleagues for many years was Flight Lieutenant Maggie Pleasant, the Community Relations Officer at RAF Leeming in North Yorkshire, a very busy Tornado base with a main runway running more or less parallel to the A1 trunk road and very close to a number of villages. Tornados are extremely noisy aircraft and Maggie had to deal with more public complaints in the course of a typical working day than I did in a typical working month. I sympathised with her, up to a point, but then, as I have explained earlier, I never wanted to be a CRO anyway. Maggie, presumably, did. I know for a fact that she was an outstanding CRO.

Rather surprisingly I found that many complainers do not believe any action will be taken as a result of their complaint; they make the telephone call or write a letter in the heat of the moment to get it off their chest and assume that will be the end of the matter.

'I didn't expect anyone to write to me,' complainers often told me, almost apologetically, after receiving a letter from me. 'I don't really want to make a fuss or cause any trouble. I complained because I was angry at the time but now you've explained what was going on, I'm satisfied.'

So was I when that happened. I had put myself on the high moral ground and that is a good place to be.

Complainers can usually be slotted into one of two main types. First, there are the one-off complainers who have been genuinely upset or frightened by some unusual air activity and secondly, there are the regulars who complain frequently, usually about a particular type of activity. This latter type is much more likely to telephone and ask for the same officer each time. If they have been in touch with me before, they already know my name and telephone extension. They also know what the answer is going to be but they feel they have to let the RAF know they have not gone away. The fact is that CROs, even I, cannot promise an instant fix for a complaint. At best we are only messengers; we do not control the activity being complained about.

The most annoying complainers, and the least convincing, are those who try to be too clever. For example, those who are familiar with RAF low flying operations know that in most parts of the United Kingdom the minimum height above ground that is permitted for many aircraft types is 250 feet. To be strictly accurate and pedantic, except when taking off or landing these aircraft should not be flown closer than 250 feet to any object in any plane – this is known as the minimum safe distance, or MSD. For all practicable purposes with fixed wing aircraft the nearest object is likely to be on the ground unless you can envisage an aircraft flying at, say, 500 feet above the ground but less than 250 feet horizontally from some object. This could theoretically occur if a pilot chose to fly around the top sections of the Belmont television mast in north east Lincolnshire at a horizontal distance of less than 250 feet, but that is not very likely. It is quite amazing how many complainers make exaggerated claims about aircraft height.

'It was definitely less than 50 feet'.

'It was lower than roof top level'.

'It was almost brushing the tops of the trees in my garden'.

'I could feel the heat from its exhaust.'

'I could see the pilot quite clearly inside his cockpit.'

So what? You can see the pilot in a Hawk cockpit when the aircraft is flying at 500 feet above the ground.

'I was in the RAF for 15 years so I know what I'm talking about,' said one particularly irritating individual.

'I'm a pilot and I'm now in my 40th year in the RAF,' I replied suavely. 'What's the point you're trying to make, sir?'

Stunned silence from the other end.

When regular complainers make ridiculous claims about the height an aircraft was flying, they are usually doing so because they know the pilot will get into trouble if it can be proved that he was breaking the rules. In almost every other case what people are really complaining about is the noise or a perceived danger and those are perfectly legitimate reasons for lodging a complaint – but it does not necessarily mean that any rules were broken. I was always far more prepared to listen sympathetically to a person who claimed to have been frightened by the unexpected passage overhead of a Red Arrow than a person who claimed the same jet passed overhead at tree top height. Exaggerated claims about the height, or lack of it, do not enhance the complaint and merely cause the person taking down the details to treat other claims with a large pinch of salt.

The pilots of the Red Arrows are highly disciplined and very professional, as I think I had made clear in the earlier chapters of this book. The type of flying they do is exciting enough without any need to break the rules. They fly in aircraft that are instantly recognisable and they are well aware that any misdemeanour will quickly be traced back to them. In all my time working for the Red Arrows I know of only two occasions when what I could only describe as a sudden rush of blood to the head persuaded a pilot to descend below the permitted minimum height and on both those occasions the pilots were disciplined and threatened with dismissal from the Team should there be a further infraction.

Estimating height by visual clues only is not easy, even for experts. A popular competition at air shows in years gone by involved guessing the height of aircraft flying over the display area. In practice, unless you have been specially trained to observe low flying aircraft, which you would have been if you were a member of the estimable Royal Observer Corps before they were stood down, you will make some very wild guesses. With all my experience I still would not wager very much of my own money on guessing heights. One yardstick I was able to use to help me was to compare the height of the aircraft above the ground with its wingspan. I know, for example, that the Hawk measures 34 feet from one wing tip to the other so I can easily visualise what a Hawk would look like if it really was flying at less than 50 feet above the ground. Even this method loses all accuracy when the height is more than three or four times the aircraft's wingspan.

If there is one type of complainer I hate more than any other it is the name-dropper. When you have just been caught speeding, what is the point in telling the traffic policeman that you are a friend of the Chief Constable – is it not more likely to alienate the policeman? Even if you are a friend of the Chief Constable, is it remotely likely that he will intervene on your behalf? One member of the Red Arrows, who was wearing his red flying suit at the time, hesitantly tried such an approach with a traffic policeman only to be told that the Chief Constable in question was already dealing with one of his own Detective Chief

Superintendents who had been caught in a speed trap. There is always the possibility of course that the policeman was looking forward to telling his colleagues that he had nabbed a Red Arrow, which is just one of several reasons why most of the pilots wear an anonymous jacket over their flying suits when out and about in their cars. Name dropping is a futile tactic to employ and I never allowed myself to be brow-beaten but low flying complainers are prone to employ this tactic.

'After the last incident your Station Commander sent me a letter assuring me that it would never happen again.'

Do they imagine I do not keep my Station Commander informed of what I have done? Who do they think usually drafts the letters that the Station Commander signs?

'I intend writing to my MP,' is another common ploy.

'Thank you for letting me know,' I would reply politely. ' I will inform the Station Commander.'

Sometimes, if I was in a benevolent mood, I would offer them the postal address of their MP.

I sent a summary of every complaint, other than the most trivial, and a copy of every letter I wrote to complainers, to the appropriate department of the Ministry of Defence in London for their records – and most Community Relations Officers do likewise.

Members of Parliament, or their secretaries, must get letters of complaint on a wide range of topics every day from their constituents. MPs cannot possibly be expected to know all the whys and wherefores of every subject that crops up and so they usually forward flying complaints to the appropriate Minister's department where the staff deal with them. A small number of complainers, not satisfied with my explanation, subsequently did write to their MP. One individual even wrote to the Prime Minister to complain about me. He addressed the PM as 'Dear Tony', and took the opportunity to express his total support for all his Government's policies before getting around the real purpose of the letter. Even that letter ended up on my desk together with a Photostat of my original letter to the complainer. We call them PEs – parliamentary enquiries – and they are a form of what I call circular correspondence. I would draft a reply, usually a paraphrase of my original letter, for the MoD official, who then translates it into parliamentary language for the Minister for the Armed Forces to send back to the MP who received the original complaint. The MP usually then simply sends a copy of the Minister's letter with a short covering note of his own to the original complainant who is, presumably, gratified to have several letters on Westminster-headed notepaper. In most cases I eventually received for my files copies of all the letters involved in this circular correspondence so that I and my Station Commander knew how the complaint had been handled at each and every level. Talk about the paperless society!

No MP or official at the MoD ever changed the sense of anything I had written and no changes to the Team's flying practices were forced upon us as a result of a complaint. I mention that not for my personal satisfaction but because it indicates that the Red Arrows do have very strict operating procedures and that they do not disregard them.

For some years at Scampton I had two very persistent complainers, one was a name-dropper of a sort and the other a self-styled expert.

The name-dropper reminded me, every time she called to complain about aircraft low flying over her house on the run-in to the East Coast bombing ranges, that she was the wife of the local police constable. She always complained to me because Scampton is the nearest proper RAF to those ranges. I always wanted to say to her, 'thank you, I'll bear that in mind if I'm ever in your area.' I did send her a short and formal follow up letter after every conversation but I did not accept her frequent invitations to visit her and watch the aircraft. Perhaps she was lonely? I might have got more than I had wanted.

The other regular complained about Tornados from RAF Coningsby over-flying his house at 50 feet. It was always 50 feet.

'I'm glad I've discovered you, Squadron Leader,' he said brightly on his first call to me when I had been at Scampton only a few days. 'I used to complain to the Community Relations Officer at Coningsby but he never believed me and he never did anything. Now I'm going to call you every time I have a complaint.'

Thank you very much, I thought. I checked with my fellow CRO at Coningsby and he confirmed that this man was, or had been until then, the bane of his life. The Coningsby CRO had regularly checked with the Tornado squadron commanders who confirmed that their aircraft were always at least 250 feet over the ground in the vicinity of the complainer's house. This man would go on at me at great length, sometimes for up to half an hour. I believe he, too, was lonely and merely wanted someone to talk to so I occasionally indulged him and we talked about all manner of aviation subjects. He was obviously in his 70s and enjoyed talking about the war years, as do I. Occasionally, when I was particularly busy, I would put the telephone loudspeaker on and carry on with my other work. Every five minutes of so he paused for me to make some comment. This platonic relationship continued right up until the end of 1995 when Scampton closed. I had intended to telephone him to let him know that I was moving to Cranwell but I forgot. Presumably he reverted to calling the CRO at Coningsby, by this time a civilian lady, but I never bothered to check. If he reads this, let me say to him, I am sorry but you used up an inordinate amount of my time.

Complaints about the Team, from any source, were few and far between and mostly from outside Lincolnshire. Most of the inhabitants in the Scampton area had lived locally for many years and, by and large, they were delighted to have the Red Arrows near by. I received many letters to say just that. Every now and again someone from the Scampton local area did lodge a complaint and most of those concerned one or other of the Synchro Pair flying overhead the Cliff villages or over nearby Welton and Hackthorn.

The main runway at Scampton runs roughly north east/south west and there is a slight downhill gradient at the northern end. Just off that northern end, beyond the long bend in the A15, is the tiny village of Hackthorn and just off the other end of the runway are the delightful North and South Carlton villages. There is no way the Red Arrows can avoid flying over those villages in the course of a normal training sortie because the display line runs along the line of the runway and extends several miles beyond each end. It must have been extremely noisy for those villagers in the Vulcans days, up to the end of 1981. On full power for take off or for a missed approach, the Vulcan engines made a very distinctive noise that seemed to rip through the air and could be heard for miles around. There was then a period of just over a year when Scampton base was on care and maintenance and the airfield itself was closed. The Red Arrows arrived in 1983, the Central Flying School shortly afterwards, and from then on the number of sorties flown from Scampton increased enormously but the aircraft were smaller and less noisy that the Vulcans.

Long as it is, the Scampton runway was not long enough one morning for a Jet Provost training aircraft. Somehow the pilot managed to let the aircraft run gently but ignominiously down the slope and off the end. It finished up in the front garden of a house in the village. The pilot and his student were not injured and were quickly collected by the crash crews who were able to approach the scene from the airfield side via one of the crash gates. I was despatched by the Station Commander to go round via the main road, apologise to the occupants and ascertain whether there was any damage to their property that might lead to a claim for compensation.

From the village side it took me some time to identify exactly which garden had gained a Jet Provost. I parked on a side road, found the correct house and knocked on the front door. There was no reply but I could hear noises from within so I went through the garden gate and round to the back, half expecting to see the occupants examining the aircraft. A man came out of the rear patio doors just as I was contemplating the Jet Provost, which was resting drunkenly amongst the flower beds at the far end of the long garden. The man was dressed in a velvet smoking jacket. He looked quite flustered and was nervously smoothing his hair down. All he needed was a cigarette in a long holder and he could have passed for Noel Coward.

'Good morning, sir,' I said. 'I'm Tony Cunnane, the public relations officer at the airfield. I've come to apologise for the Jet Provost that has finished up in your garden.'

He looked to where I was pointing and gasped. Even though there must have been considerable noise from the fire engines and ambulance immediately after the crash, the man was obviously unaware until that moment of the aircraft in his garden, or that anything untoward had occurred. Turning back towards the patio doors, he shouted loudly to someone inside:

'Frederick, darling, do come and look. We have an unexpected visitor.'

I did not stay for morning coffee.

The Tucano, which gradually replaced the venerable Jet Provosts from 1989, is a turbo-propeller aircraft and although it is not exceptionally noisy in terms of decibels it does make a particularly irritating noise which can clearly be heard even when the aircraft is flying several thousand feet above the ground. Tucanos started generating noise complaints almost from the day they arrived, which was about the same time as I arrived at Scampton. The MoD were aware of the problem and I was able to assure people that something was being done to reduce the nuisance. It was still being done when CFS moved out in 1995 and Scampton closed down.

I had scant sympathy for noise complainers who had recently moved into the Scampton area and only then discovered they were living in the vicinity of a busy airfield. When I am searching for a new place to live I do not rush straight into a purchase just because I have found a house that meets all my needs and desires. I check on Ordnance Survey maps to see if there are any nearby military or civilian aerodromes; I visit the area in the morning and evening rush hours to see if there are any regular traffic snarl-ups; and, if there is a nearby pub or club, I check at closing time to see if there is any noisy activity. Only when I am satisfied on all those counts do I start thinking about committing myself to the purchase. It is a case of *caveat emptor*. If you are foolish enough to move into a house close to a busy airfield you should expect noise. Of course, I never said that to them! As I was writing this chapter I watched a news item on Yorkshire Television which showed a small group of people who had been queuing outside the main gate at Scampton for up to 14 days to buy surplus RAF married quarters on the station. Some of the houses are so close to the taxiways that you could reach out and almost touch the aircraft from the bottom of the garden as they taxi past. I hope those people have done their homework properly. On the other hand, of course, they may be really keen fans of the Red Arrows.

From time to time I had phone calls at both Scampton and Cranwell from people who were considering buying property in the local areas. They usually wanted to know if there would be much noise from low flying aircraft. I did not think it right and proper to give them direct advice that might have put them off because I did not want to get into trouble with the Estate Agents. However, since they had had the commonsense to make enquiries, I always sent them a letter explaining the Red Arrows' pattern of flying together with a map showing the local flying areas and the approach and landing paths. I thought that was the least I could do and it was then up to them to make their own decision.

I felt very sorry for one family who had lived close to Scampton since just after the last Vulcans had departed. They had been trying to sell up for some years when I first had contact with them. Every time someone went to view their very desirable property, either the Red Arrows or one of the other Scampton-based aircraft flew low overhead on the approach to landing. Eventually, I got a particularly angry phone call on a summer Monday morning.

'I thought you would like to know that we had a couple viewing the property yesterday. It was a beautiful day as you know. The couple were delighted with the house and had just agreed to go to the Estate Agents in Lincoln and make a firm offer. As they were leaving, the Red Arrows roared overhead and that was the end of that sale.'

My sympathy for the vendors evaporated somewhat after that telephone call. The Team had been away for several days and, unfortunately or fortunately depending on your viewpoint, had returned to Scampton on the Sunday afternoon for a run and break at just the critical moment. A few weeks after that incident we moved to Cranwell and I heard nothing more from that particular family, but it was not the end of the matter. Early in summer 2000, shortly after it had been announced that the Red Arrows would be returning permanently to Scampton, I had a written complaint from the head of a different family at that same property. They had just bought it having been told, allegedly, that Scampton airfield was closed. They had, it seems, finalised the deal while the Red Arrows were away on their annual spring detachment to Cyprus. Recognising that this might soon lead to a legal battle and was no longer a PR matter, I quickly handed the whole affair off to the MoD for the legal experts to deal with it.

The village of Welton, barely three miles east of Scampton as the Hawk flies, poses a problem which needs careful handling. In 1988, the year before I started, one of the Red Arrows aircraft had crashed into the village, narrowly missing one of the schools which was full of children at the time. Fortunately, and miraculously, no-one was injured. At the time there was the inevitable outcry about aircraft practising at low level over a built up area and there were vociferous calls from some of the residents for low flying over the village to be banned. The fact is that the aircraft that crashed onto the village had been involved in an incident a few miles away. The pilot had ejected as late as possible from an uncontrollable aircraft and the empty aircraft had landed on the village. A ban on low flying over Welton would not have prevented the accident. When an aircraft has a catastrophic failure it rarely descends vertically unless it happens to be in a vertical dive when the catastrophe occurs. Most people in Welton accepted that and were grateful that they had had a lucky escape. As it happens many RAF Scampton personnel had young children attending the schools in Welton and, as far as I am aware, no parent moved their children to other schools in the area. From time to time throughout my first period at Scampton and again from 2000 when it was announced that the Team would be returning, a small number of villagers continued to raise the spectre of the Welton crash.

At the end of the letters I sent to everyone who complained about Red Arrows activities at either Scampton or Cranwell and who lived reasonably close, I included an invitation to come and meet the Team and see for themselves how we operate. Very rarely did anyone take me up on the invitation. However one man who lived just one mile from Exeter Airport very quickly did accept.

In the summer months the Red Arrows quite often operate out of Exeter Airport because it is a convenient staging post for displays in the south and west of England and because the airport authorities always make us feel so welcome. This particular man claimed that his exotic ostriches and emus stopped laying eggs after the Team flew low over his exotic animals farm while departing from Exeter for a display at Middle Wallop. When I called him on the telephone he told me that he regularly complains to the Airport authorities, especially about helicopter flights and the occasional Concorde charter flights. The man acknowledged that he could not prove that it was the Red Arrows that had caused his birds to stop laying. He accepted my invitation, sent with the approval of the airport manager, to meet us at the airport a few days later at a Civic Reception being held in the Airport Terminal. He brought three friends along and they all chatted amiably with our pilots and the airport staff. When one of the Reds expressed a genuine interest in the man's exotic birds and animals, he excused himself, went back home and returned later with a pack of 8 kilos of emu meat, or it might have been llama steak, I forget now, as a gift for the Red Arrows. I understand the man never again complained to Exeter Airport and for that the managers there were very grateful to me. A victory for PR if not for the animals.

Another group of complaints concerns the smoke used by the Red Arrows during displays. Strictly speaking it is not smoke at all because smoke is created when something burns. What the Red Arrows emit is vapour, created by injecting neat diesel oil into the hot efflux from the jet's exhaust pipe. Someone must have discovered, long before the Red Arrows were formed, that if you inject diesel into the hot air coming out of the back of a jet engine, the diesel instantly vaporises and creates a brilliant white 'smoke'. The red and blue coloured trails are made by adding small quantities of harmless vegetable dyes to the diesel oil before it is injected into the jet stream. The Red Arrows, and countless other display aircraft throughout the world, have always called it smoke and I do not suppose any amount of legislation about smoke emissions into the atmosphere is going to change that. 'Reds, smoke on go!' sounds so much better than 'Reds, vapour on go!'

The diesel oil is carried in the fuel tank bolted underneath the fuselage on the Hawk's centreline. Within the tank are two small containers to hold the red and blue dye. Expert fans of the Team know that there are three small tubes protruding into the jet pipe at the rear of the Hawk's fuselage and it is from these that the diesel, with or without the addition of coloured dye, is injected into the jet efflux. A lot of people assume that there are three pipes because we use three colours. Not so! All three pipes are connected in parallel to provide redundancy and the same colour comes out of all three.

There is no doubt that some people find the smell of our 'smoke' unpleasant although many others, including me and most of the ground crew, do not mind it. In 1989 and 1992 independent surveys were done to check whether or not there are any health hazards from breathing in the Red Arrows' smoke. Both reports were inconclusive, but they made the point that the diesel and dye products exhausted into the atmosphere were diluted to such an extent that they were almost immeasurable at ground level. That of course, being inconclusive, was not really a scientific proof that there was no danger to health but I have never come across anyone who could prove that their health had been impaired by inhaling the vapour. Some people have complained that their cars, their houses, and even their washing hanging out on the clothes line, have been covered by greasy flecks coming from the Red Arrows' smoke but these claims have never been proved either.

One claim, from someone living near Scampton, was different. The complainant telephoned me to say that some nasty greasy stains had appeared on his car after the Red Arrows had flown over during a practice sortie. Later, several people on base also reported stains on their cars. There was an official inquiry and it was eventually proved that the deposits emanated from effluent coming out of the cooling towers at the large power stations near Newark-on-Trent A fault in one of the cooling towers had allowed some form of waste product to escape into the towers where it merged with the steam and was blown on the strong westerly wind towards Scampton. It was pure coincidence that the Red Arrows happened to be practising over the airfield at the same time.

The Red Arrows do not use smoke purely for cosmetic reasons. In their very first season white smoke only was used. During the winter of 1965/66 all the Gnats were fitted with additional equipment which allowed the use of red, white and blue but this modification was opposed by the 1966 Team pilots on the grounds that the technical problems introduced were 'of greater magnitude than any likely improvements to the display.' They were overruled, however, and the three-colour system was used in the 1966 season but still with many niggles which irritated pilots and ground crew alike. Even when the pilots operated the correct switches, sometimes the wrong colours appeared and sometimes no smoke at all, making the display look messy and insufficiently rehearsed. The problems continued throughout the 1967 and 1968 seasons and the CFS Commandant eventually concluded that, 'All the European aerobatic teams now use coloured smoke, with varying degrees of success, therefore it is considered essential that the engineering staff solve this problem.' They must have done so because thereafter there were no more adverse comments about the smoke and three colours have been used ever since. It seems unthinkable now to have a Red Arrows' display without the three colours.

There is no doubt that the red, white and blue patriotic trails greatly enhance the show but there are several other reasons for making them. For example, when the Synchro Pair are flying directly towards each other, at a closing speed of 12 miles per minute, it is very difficult for one pilot to see the other, especially in reduced visibility, because the head-on aspect of the Hawk is very small. By smoking from each end of the display line, each of the pilots can see the other at a much greater range and the Team Leader with the main section can more easily keep track of where the Synchro Pair are. The main section often uses smoke cunningly to conceal a formation change from the public while single aircraft will often give a burst of white smoke on final approach to landing, especially in strong cross-wind conditions, to enable following aircraft to 'see' the wind and judge the turbulence.

There is no doubt that there are people who find the noise of the Red Arrows passing overhead or performing at an air display nearby intensely irritating and I can feel sympathy for them. When such a person complains I always point out that we are in the business of giving pleasure to millions and that the number of complaints is vastly exceeded by the number of compliments we get. I think it is unreasonable for someone to expect our activity to cease simply because they have complained, but some people do expect that. If you live close to a major football ground you would not expect the team to move out to another location just because the cheering annoyed you. Or perhaps some folk would? It is worth my pointing out that the average number of spectators turning out at an air display featuring the Red Arrows greatly exceeds the number of people who can fit into the largest football ground.

One of the most popular English locations for Red Arrows displays is Dartmouth and the Team displayed there on 21 occasions up to the end of 2000, including their official 3,000[th] display on 23 August 1995. The displays usually coincided with the Royal Regatta and over the years the Red Arrows displays came to be seen as an integral part of the Regatta festivities. Of course, it is never possible to please everybody. In

September 1997 a squadron leader serving at RAF Boscombe Down wrote to tell me of a letter to the Editor of a west country newspaper. It was called 'Misdirected Arrows'. The squadron leader thought that someone from the Red Arrows might like to reply. What follows is an extract from that letter.

'Saturday night's poor splodge of colour upon an already predicted grizzly sky cost Dartmouth £3,500, merely because the Red Arrows took it upon themselves to fly over our much soaked bodies. The amateur plane that flew through a real storm overhead a few days earlier provided a more stunning display – for free. In this day of computer wizardry and laser aimed flight it was surprising that the "crème brûlée" of the RAF could do no better than stain the sky. If my radio could tell me at breakfast time that the skies would be miserable at 1800 hrs, the RAF must have been well informed. That they decided to slowly ink our clean Dartmouth air was not to amuse 10,000 pairs of eyes, but so that they could claim their fee.

'Perhaps someone with a military background could explain to me, a mere local pleb, why the Red Arrows compared so poorly with infuriating low-flying jets which frequently intrude upon the peace as they perform their stunning feats in the more confined valleys of Dartmoor, the Lakes and most of our national parks. Sure those red fellows must have the brains to think up inspiring acrobatics for every type of weather. After all, we do live in a predominantly wet country.

'Take note Dartmouth paymaster: in this après-Thatcher market we ought not to pay them for such a bad breach of contract.'

Wow! That told us. The newspaper printed a reply from another local inhabitant.

'.....As far as your correspondent is concerned I could only laugh at his comments. Firstly, how can nine aeroplanes do aerobatics without being able to see each other. These aeroplanes are flown by humans and not, as your correspondent seems to think, by computers. Secondly, had the display gone ahead, 70 per cent of the action would have been above the cloud – not much use to the spectators. Had there been an incident I suspect that your correspondent would have been the first to write in to complain about the death and destruction in the town. My wife knew all the four pilots killed at Kemble airfield in the 1970s and had to attend their funerals, which is why safety first is a wise policy. In any case insurance can be taken out against cancellation, something I am sure the committee investigated.'

The second letter made many of the points that I would made but not in the style I would have chosen. I thought it incumbent upon me to write an open letter to the Editor.

'The Red Arrows were, of course, fully aware of weather conditions at Dartmouth on 29 August. The Leader elected to fly to Dartmouth from Exeter Airport and, at the very least, make one flypast for the large crowds. In fact, conditions were such that he was able to make two flypasts before returning to Exeter. There were several television crews at Dartmouth and I know from their reports to me that the Red Arrows' very brief appearance was very much appreciated. The Display Organiser has not made any complaint as far as I am aware.'

I have never heard the Red Arrows described as 'crème brûlée' before: 'crème de la crème' certainly! The fact is that the display organiser would still have been charged the Ministry of Defence fee even if none of the aircraft had taken off from Exeter and he knew that because it is clearly laid out in the contract. The fee represents part of the cost of taking the Team to Exeter Airport and, incidentally, it goes into RAF central coffers and does not come to the Red Arrows.

I must mention one complaint that I found difficult to take seriously. A lady living in a village close to Scampton called me one Monday morning in 1991 to complain about UFOs air-to-air refuelling overhead Scampton.

'It really is very dangerous,' she said. 'If they have a collision at that height they could crash and wipe out most of Lincolnshire.'

I asked her to explain what she had seen.

'There were several small space ships orbiting directly overhead Scampton airfield last night about midnight. Suddenly their mother ship appeared and they took it in turns to refuel.'

'What happened next?' I asked.

'When they had all refuelled, they flew off into orbit again and disappeared. The mother ship flew around for a few minutes before it also flew off into orbit.'

Mindful of MoD policy, I apologised to the lady. I explained that the matter was nothing to do with RAF Scampton since the space ships had not taken off from our airfield but I said that I would inform the appropriate department of the Ministry of Defence in London. In those days there was a department that dealt with UFO sightings and that day I had my first and only contact with it.

Finally let me relate a story about a very unusual complaint that came my way in August 1998. I was told by a friend in the north east of England that stories were circulating in newspapers in the Sunderland area to the effect that one of the Red Arrows had shed a turbine blade during the Sunderland display on 1 August. Allegedly this blade then struck the roof of a house and caused a considerable degree of damage. No-one contacted the Red Arrows to lodge a complaint. I contacted one of the policemen who had been called in to investigate and he told me that a blade recovered from the roof space of the house in question had been identified as part of the metal blade fitted to a garden hover mower – it even had bits of grass still stuck to it. I was able to reassure the policeman that none of our aircraft had suffered an engine failure on that day. I know from personal experience that if a jet engine throws a turbine blade there is absolutely no way the pilot would not have known about it immediately. Had it happened that day to one of the Red Arrows, he would have gone straight away for an emergency landing at Teesside International Airport. I passed my version of this story to the Sunderland Echo and to their credit, and my relief, they published it word for word and in full.

There was a curious corollary to this story which makes one wonder about the motives of the house owner. Towards the end of that display at Sunderland, Red 6 had a glancing bird strike. He broke out of the formation and made what we call a precautionary landing at Teesside Airport. A precautionary landing is one where, although there is no immediate indication of a major problem, there is reason to believe that a problem may arise if the aircraft does not land as soon as possible. Red Arrows pilots always make a precautionary landing after a bird strike because it is possible that some of the birds remains may have gone down the air intakes and that could lead to a failure of the engine shortly afterwards. On this occasion, however, a post flight inspection on the ground at Teesside showed that the bird had stuck the leading edge of the port wing. There were minor traces of blood but the wing surface was not even dented. It seemed to us that someone was suggesting that the bird strike and the hole in the roof were somehow linked and perhaps there was thought of compensation. Whether the piece of hover mower blade caused the damage to the house roof or not was of no concern to the Red Arrows. The bird strike was a red herring if you will pardon the pun.

19

The Cranwell Years

THE CRANWELL YEARS WERE NEVER REALLY A GREAT SUCCESS as far as the
Red Arrows are concerned, but that was not the fault of anyone already
based at Cranwell. Everyone on the base from College Commandant
downwards made us feel very welcome and did what they could to help
us operate efficiently. There had been a lot of changes since my previous
tour of duty at the College over 30 years earlier. When I was a flying
instructor at Cranwell the College had only two main functions: one was
to train officer cadets and the other was to train pilots. Then the whole
of the College staff were geared to those two tasks. However, in the
intervening decades the College had assumed a whole gamut of
additional roles and units and I found that people tended to keep to their
own particular corner of the base and only rarely venture out. The
people themselves were different too. In the 1960s almost everyone wore
blue uniform; when the Red Arrows arrived in early 1996 a fair
percentage of the working population at Cranwell were civilians and by
the time we left Cranwell again at the end of 2000, a goodly percentage
of the aircrew were also civilians of one sort or another. One could walk
around the roads on base and rarely see anyone in RAF uniform. When
we at the Red Arrows invited service personnel from other sections to
come and pay us a social call, as often as not we had to explain where
the Red Arrows HQ was located. The reverse was also true. Yes, this may
have been our fault but the fact is that everyone was so busy with their
own business that there rarely seemed to be the time or the inclination
to visit other sections.

Almost from our first day at Cranwell the rumour mongers started
their work again asserting that it was only a matter of time before

Scampton was re-opened as a permanent base for the Red Arrows. In fact the Red Arrows remained at the RAF College not for a maximum of two years, as originally announced by the Minister for the Armed Forces in 1995, but for just under five years. Much of that extra delay was caused by the change of government in 1997 and the extensive Strategic Defence Initiative, SDI, started by the new Secretary of State for Defence, George Robertson. The Defence Secretary said that there were to be no piecemeal moves of squadrons and units before the final SDI report was published. That seemed to me to make a lot of sense. For once the MoD was going to define the tasks before buying the equipment or redeploying units and personnel. It may be thought odd that a simple matter like the basing of an RAF squadron should be affected by a General Election but it is all a matter of political protocol. Since a Government Minister had been involved in the closing down of Scampton and the subsequent move of, amongst others, the Red Arrows, a Government Minister had to be involved in the next move.

Shortly after the 1997 election, all RAF PROs, for Public Relations Officers is what we still were then, were summoned to a meeting at RAF Brampton near Huntingdon, to meet the newly-appointed Minister for the Armed Forces, Dr John Reid. Within minutes we were spellbound by his eloquence and obvious enthusiasm for his new task, and I am not necessarily indicating my personal political preference when I state that. Walking informally from side to side of the auditorium, making eye contact with as many people as possible, with no need for a lectern, and speaking for about an hour without any notes whatsoever, he amazed us with his depth of knowledge about anything to do with the RAF. It was not just his knowledge of major defence matters, that we expect of a Defence Minister, but he spoke about many really minor internal air force matters that we would not have expected him to know of at all, let alone in his first few days in office.

Dr Reid told us several anecdotes that clearly indicated that new winds of change were about to start blowing. He started off by telling us something that was blindingly obvious, but something that I for one had never really considered. In the 1950s, when I joined the RAF, National Service was still in force and World War 2 was not long ended. The services were huge and almost everyone in the UK knew a relation or friend who was either in, or had been in, one of the armed services. There was no need to explain then to the great British public what the forces were for; it was obvious to all. In the late 1990s statistics showed, said Dr Reid, that only about one person in 20 knew anyone in the services. The armed forces were out of fashion. There were far fewer people in uniform, there was no longer an obvious enemy and it was, therefore, much more difficult for him, as Minister for the Armed Forces, to get money out of the Treasury for defence purposes. It was essential, therefore, that we PROs did our very best to keep the services in the public eye as much as possible. I remember thinking, rather smugly, that no organisation did that better than the Red Arrows.

Dr Reid also told us that on his first day as Minister he worked very late on his own in his office at the top of the MoD Main Building in Whitehall. At about 1am, feeling in need of a break, he telephoned down to the MoD Duty Press Officer on the ground floor and asked for the morning newspapers to be brought up. Not an unreasonable request one would have thought since the daily papers had already been on the streets for several hours. Dr Reid told us that it took several minutes for the Duty Press Officer even to answer the telephone. When asked why, the unfortunate officer replied that it was a sleeping duty because nothing much happened in the middle of the night. Dr Reid then asked for the morning papers to be brought up to his office.

'Sorry, Minister,' the DPO continued haplessly, 'the papers don't arrive in the building until about 8am – but a digest of current defence stories, compiled by the staff, will be on your desk by 10am.'

Dr Reid told us that he was appalled by this news.

'How am I supposed to prepare myself for breakfast television and radio interviews if I don't see the newpapers until mid-morning?' he asked us.

There was, of course, no acceptable answer to that. You could hardly expect the Minister to descend from his office in the early hours and wander along Whitehall looking for a newsagent.

'Things have changed now,' he said, grinning at us as we digested this little story. Then he became more serious. 'I can only do my job if you PROs keep me informed of what you're doing. I don't want to read or hear in the media, or be asked questions by a reporter, about any defence matter that I have not been briefed about. Good news or bad, I want to know it in advance so that I can either defend our position or make capital out of it.'

You could see the brows of the assembled PROs furrow as we digested that gem. We knew that there was no real mechanism at that time for junior officer PROs at stations to pass stories to the Minister's office, whether through the normal chain of command or not. The PROs' job was never the same again. I must admit, however, that my own way of working changed very little. I had always kept the MoD fully informed, through our Command HQ, of any planned Red Arrows' activity that might come to the attention of the national media and I had always sent copies of my news releases to both. Whether they were read was, of course, a different matter.

There followed major upheavals within the MoD publicity machine and I will not go into them here as they were not my concern. I was delighted to learn that PR was at last being taken seriously while being resistant to the new terminology that came in – the evidence of advancing years I suppose. I made jokes about the new job titles and then used them anyway. Shortly afterwards Simon Meade asked me to write to the RAF's Director of PR asking for a definitive statement of the role of the Red Arrows. This might seem an odd request but the fact of the matter was that no-one had ever written a Mission Statement for the Red Arrows. It had still not arrived when I finally retired – of it had, no-one showed it to me.

Throughout the Cranwell years the Red Arrows carried out most of their practices overhead Scampton and that added, typically, 10 minutes flying time to each sortie – an increase of about 30%. The extra cost of that alone in terms of fuel used and aircraft life expended must have been considerable. To that sum must be added the cost of maintaining the 9,000 feet of runway at Scampton serviceable for emergency landings, and the cost of providing Air Traffic Control services, fire, crash and medical cover. What cannot be quantified is the cost of the inconvenience to the Team.

At Scampton the entire Red Arrows squadron had been accommodated in 4 Hangar and everyone knew everyone else. At Cranwell the Red Arrows squadron was split between two sites about 300 metres apart.

The ground crew were housed in two side-by-side hangars because there was no single hangar available that was large enough. Those hangars had been out of daily use for many years until the Red Arrows arrived and there was no heating inside. A considerable sum of money had to be expended to bring the hangars up to an acceptable state for all-the-year-round aircraft maintenance. The pilots and administration personnel were in an old building near the Junior Cadets' Mess. The rooms in the HQ were small and there was nowhere really adequate for entertaining corporate guests, nor was there anywhere to display the Team's many trophies. Two external Portacabins had to be brought into use because there was insufficient room inside the main building for all the pilots to have desk space.

As I have explained before, in the early part of the winter training period the Synchro Pair's first sortie of the day has to be supervised by the Team Leader and, occasionally, by the Wing Commander and the CFS Commandant. Those three officers did not have time to spare to go the 25 miles by road north to Scampton through the early morning Lincoln rush hour to supervise the first slot and then drive another 25 miles south to sit in on the debriefing. It was, therefore, agreed from the outset that the Red Arrows would have sole use of the Cranwell airfield for the first slot of the day, from 8am. That was not a great inconvenience to the other flying units at Cranwell because only rarely did they wish to start flying before 8.30. However, because many of the Synchro manoeuvres are orientated on specific points on the ground, their second sortie of the day also had to be flown overhead Cranwell so that they could benefit from the lessons learned in the first sortie and that barred the airfield to all other traffic for half an hour mid-morning. That was inconvenient for the other users but they had to plan around it. The third Synchro sortie of the day was normally flown overhead Scampton.

Quite apart from the two Synchro sorties that were flown over Cranwell, every time the Red Arrows took off or landed, the circuit at Cranwell had to be cleared of all other aircraft movements. The main section also aimed to fly three sorties each day so this was an added irritation for the other flying squadrons who had to arrange their flying programmes to avoid those times. It became a common sight to see aircraft queuing at the take-off point or orbiting clear of the airfield waiting for the Red Arrows to take off and land. More wasted time and fuel and more frustration for all the aircrew. It is a well documented fact that frustration leads to accidents, on the roads as well as in the air. It quickly became apparent that with the best will in the world, Red Arrows' operations had the potential to create a flight safety risk. All operators were reminded of this at regular intervals and, thankfully, the professionalism of all concerned ensured that there never was a serious incident.

About midway between Cranwell and Scampton by air are two important places that have to be avoided by the low flying Red Arrows: the Strike Command airfield at Waddington and Lincoln city centre. A one-way, clockwise, avoiding route was designed for the Red Arrows' transit flights between Cranwell and Scampton. Northbound from Cranwell the aircraft would fly to the west of Waddington and southbound, on the return to Cranwell, they would fly to the east of Lincoln. Since the prevailing winds favoured the use of Cranwell's westerly runway this meant that the clockwise route was the most expeditious. When the wind favoured use of the easterly runway, the transit times were increased by two or three minutes at each end of the sortie. The circular route had a valuable plus from the PR point of view – it reduced the amount of low flying over nearby villages by half.

To enable the Red Arrows to debrief as quickly as possible after landing back at Cranwell following practices overhead Scampton, a live television link using an ISDN high quality telephone line was set up to relay pictures straight from the Team photographer's video camera at Display Datum back to the flight planning room in the Red Arrows HQ. There the pictures were to be recorded onto a normal VCR and the tape would be ready for viewing as soon as the pilots came in. That was the theory, but for some inexplicable reason the company contracted to install and maintain the video link could never make it work reliably throughout the five years we were based at Cranwell. The total number of times a usable tape was received via the link must have been less than 50. One aircraft, therefore, had to land at Scampton at the end of almost every practice to pick up the cassette from the video camera. Furthermore, because Red Arrows take offs and landings at Cranwell also had to be videotaped, a second airman had to leave his other duties twice each sortie to go out onto the airfield with a camera.

The single aircraft landings at Scampton initially caused a lot of scare stories about flying emergencies and for the first few weeks I regularly received telephone calls from various media outlets asking what had happened. It never seemed to amaze me how many people were willing to sit around the Scampton airfield perimeter ready to telephone stories to the media. I assume they get paid for the tip offs they give. The scare stories stopped once I had briefed all the local media what was going on; that meant that some subsequent real emergency landings at Scampton went unreported by the media and for that I was grateful. The practice of landing to pick up a video tape did, of course, lend credence to those people who continued to insist that it had been a mistake to close Scampton in the first place.

In May 1996 I was just beginning to learn about the World Wide Web and I was wondering how to go about getting a Red Arrows' presence on the Internet. Quite fortuitously, and actually while I was sitting in an arm chair in my office pondering that very question, I received a telephone call from Tim Callaway, a freelance aviation journalist with whom I had had a few dealings at Scampton. Tim's Father, Alan, was an air traffic controller at Marham when I was there in the 1970s. Tim introduced himself as the MD of Deltaweb Publishing. He wanted to set up and run a dedicated Red Arrows web site and he was willing to do it for six months as a free trial. Yet another of those coincidences that have cropped up so often in my life. Suffice it to say that the web site went live a few weeks later and quickly started gaining readers in many parts of the world. A couple of years later Tim won the contract to run the RAF web site and shortly after I retired the Red Arrows site was merged into that and is still going strong. The many thousands of words I wrote for the Red Arrows site are still all there in the archives. The site is at www.raf.mod.uk/reds.

In April 1997 I was invited by BBC Radio Leeds to be the subject of a programme called 'Real Lives'. This 60-minute programme, which goes out every weekday afternoon, is another one in what I call 'Desert Island Discs' format. Radio Leeds, which is actually heard throughout West Yorkshire, wanted me because I was a local boy working for the

Red Arrows – and programmes about the Red Arrows were always guaranteed to get a good audience. After my 'Desert Island Discs' effort on Qatari Radio in a real desert setting I was getting into the swing of this sort of thing. I thoroughly enjoyed myself and the whole programme was recorded 'as live', which means it went through from start to finish with no stops and no re-takes. It was broadcast a couple of days later but I did not hear it because Radio Leeds is inaudible in most parts of Lincolnshire. The presenter promised to send me a tape of the programme but I am still waiting for it to arrive. If he reads this book I hope he will contact me to say sorry!

Another Far Eastern tour took place in the autumn of 1997. Following a highly successful second appearance at the Dubai Air Show, the Red Arrows moved on to Islamabad, capital of Pakistan on Sunday 23 November. I flew out to Islamabad in advance of the Team to help the Defence Adviser at the British High Commission organise the displays at Risalpur and in the capital itself.

The Hawks and support Hercules were parked on the VIP apron on the Pakistan Air Force Chaklala area of Islamabad International Airport. I could not recognise Chaklala from the days of my exchange tour in the late 1960s because it had changed so much. In 1969 Islamabad was a very new capital and the international airport did not exist. The most significant feature of the new airport is that there is no parallel taxi track; all aircraft have to back track after landing until they reach an access taxiway about halfway along the 9,000 ft length of runway. It is quite interesting watching the big jets, such as the Boeing 747, carrying out a 180 degree turn in the width of the runway prior to back-tracking – it cannot be good for the undercarriage especially when the aircraft is fully laden!

On the morning of 24 November 1997 the Team was to fly a display at the Pakistan Air Force Academy at Risalpur in the North West Frontier Province, about 100 miles west of Islamabad. This was a very nostalgic trip for me because I had not visited the place since I had been stationed there 28 years earlier. I met some old friends – and I do mean old! The Commandant of the RAF Central Flying School, Air Commodore Gavin Mackay, his ADC, Flying Officer Vania Pearson, his Senior Staff Officer Wing Commander Dick Johnston, the Team Manager Squadron

Leader Mike Williams, the Team's video man SAC Colin Searle and I, all travelled to Risalpur in a Pakistan Air Force Y12, a Chinese-built, twin-engined passenger aircraft.

Unfortunately the visibility at Risalpur was very poor, as low as two or three kilometres looking into sun. This was a great shame because the entire population of the Academy, cadets, staff and families, had turned out to watch and they were all dressed in their best uniforms and finery. It was obvious that a great deal of hard work had been put in to make the public viewing area look attractive. Simon Meade led the Red Arrows over the crowd for a crowd rear arrival arriving exactly on time, naturally, and pulled up into the traditional Diamond Nine looping arrival. The Hawks disappeared from sight at the top of the loop – not because of cloud but simply because of the poor visibility. After three or four tentative manoeuvres, with the Hawks visible only as they passed in front of the crowd, it was obvious that it would have been dangerous to continue, not least because of the very high ground a few miles to the north of the airfield, and so, regrettably, the rest of the show had to be cancelled and the Hawks returned to Islamabad.

The Commandant of Risalpur very kindly conducted me on a tour of my old haunts around the airfield but so much had changed in the intervening 28 years that I hardly recognised anything. I had hoped to meet up with a fellow instructor of mine who had just retired as Chief of the Pakistan Air Force but unfortunately he was in his village west of Peshawar and could not be present.

The afternoon display at a park in central Islamabad was, not to put too fine a point on it, spectacular. The President of Pakistan, all the Chiefs of Staff and their subordinates, virtually the entire Diplomatic Corps and a public crowd estimated to be in the region of half a million, turned out to watch a display celebrating the 50th Anniversary of both the country and the Air Force. The display line of about 3,000 metres had been laboriously marked out in two unique ways. Every 75 metres along its entire length three-foot high poles topped by red markers had been hammered into the ground and, to give even more visibility, a metre-wide ditch had been excavated by hand along the whole length. There was obviously no shortage of manual labourers. Never has a Red Arrows display line been so comprehensively marked out!

The show opened with two F6 jets, Chinese-built MiG19s, trailing the Pakistan National Flag at the end of long lines and closely followed by 21 Swedish-designed but Pakistani-built Mushak piston training aircraft flying an immaculate figure 50 formation. It could not have been easy keeping 21 elementary training piston-engined aircraft in perfect position for such a complicated formation. One of the pilots was Flight Lieutenant John Dearden, the current RAF exchange officer with the Pakistan Air Force.

Then followed displays by a part-time team of four Cessna T37s and four Mirages, and a solo display by the Pakistani ace F-16 pilot who ended his very impressive performance with a vertical climb and 11 vertical rolls before gently and gracefully falling off the top. It was then time for the Red Arrows and I know the Pakistan Air Force will not mind me saying that this was what everyone was really waiting for.

The display went perfectly until a few minutes into the second half when Gary Waterfall, Red 3, suffered a fairly dramatic bird strike which badly damaged the nose of the aircraft and front section of the engine. At that time the formation was just outside gliding range of the international airport but, fortunately, Gary's engine kept going and he landed quite safely. The airport had been closed to all non-display traffic for the duration of the display for just such an eventuality. Gary, of course, had not seen the birds approaching but Red 1 had.

'I had no time to avoid them or warn the other pilots,' said Simon afterwards.

The display, which was received ecstatically by the huge crowd, continued to its conclusion with the remaining eight aircraft.

From Pakistan the Team moved on to India en route to Langkawi in Malaysia but sadly, a display scheduled for Hindan Air Force base on the outskirts of Delhi had to be cancelled due to very poor visibility. That was particularly unfortunate because 1997 was, of course, also the 50th Anniversary of the foundation of India and the Indian Air Force and we did not want to create any disharmony between the two countries. We put matters right two years later when the Red Arrows again passed through the continent en route to the Far East.

Back home again I was asked to do a third 'Desert Island Discs' type of programme, this time for BBC Radio Humberside on the afternoon

24 December 1997. This Christmas Eve programme really was transmitted live. Most of the Radio Humberside staff had been to their Christmas party at midday so when I arrived at the studios in Hull town centre at 2.45pm some very merry broadcasters greeted me and introduced me to a very new, very young, and very sober young man who was to be my host and presenter. He had obviously drawn the short straw. I had been asked to take my own CDs along because the station did not have the sort of music that I wanted to be played. When we went on air there were only the two of us and a nice lady answering the telephone and making us copious cups of coffee in the whole building. The presenter, whose name I regret to say I cannot remember, impressed me greatly with his skill for not only was he speaking to me and playing my records, but he also had to read the news summaries, the weather forecast and details of road conditions.

For the 1998 season, which included the 80th anniversary of the formation of the Royal Air Force on 1 April, someone, I know not who, decided that the vertical fin of all the Red Arrows aircraft should be emblazoned with the legend '1918-1998'. Although this looked fine, apart from the fact that the figure 1s were represented by capital Is for some reason, I thought it was a mistake because every PR picture we took that year was dated and could not be used in subsequent years. If there is one thing display organisers do not like for their brochures, it is out of date pictures. One lady visitor to the Squadron shortly after the first aircraft came out of the hangar with the new tail fins was heard to comment, 'I never realised the Red Arrows had been going since 1918.'

It has always saddened me that there are so few Red Arrows displays in Scotland. When I retired there had been only 109 displays in that country out of a grand total of 3478. I deliberately decided not to make a PR story out of the Red Arrows 100th display in Scotland, at Tain on 30 June 1999, because I anticipated trouble if it became publicly known that there were so few displays in Scotland. The fact is that there are very few air shows in Scotland and the Team can display only when they are invited to do so. One splendid Scottish display was at Stromness in Orkney on 21 July 1998 during Stromness Shopping Week, which is apparently famous in that part of the world. It was actually the Team's second display in Orkney, the earlier one being at Kirkwall in September

1982, so Shetlanders, where the Red Arrows have never displayed, could perhaps claim that the Orcadians were getting more than their fair share. The Stromness display was flown at one end of the island well away from habitation but the organiser, Calum McInnes, called me afterwards to say that the island had just had its first ever traffic jam when virtually the entire population, and that is not all that many, stopped what they were doing to drive out to watch the display. The Team flew a superb show in brilliantly clear weather. The cost of the display was met by house-to-house collections and village fund-raising events over many months. I really do hope the MoD put the income to some good use.

For the sake of completeness I had better mention that out of the 3478 displays I just mentioned, 107 were flown in Wales and only 28 in Northern Ireland, the latter for what I suppose are obvious reasons.

20

This Is Your Life

PROBABLY THE MOST COMPLICATED PR EVENT I ever conceived and organised had its genesis with a telephone call I received at Cranwell from Tony Charles on the afternoon of 1 May 1996. The Red Arrows were away in Cyprus on a Springhawk detachment shortened because of the Australia and Far East tour but it had still been quite a busy day for me. At 8am there had been a photo shoot on the flight line with the Band of the RAF College posing in front of one of the spare Red Arrows' Hawks. The Director of Music wanted a series of pictures to go on the sleeve of a forthcoming CD which would include a new piece dedicated to the Red Arrows, 'The Diamond Nine March', composed by their Director of Music, Flight Lieutenant Duncan Stubbs. As is the way with photo shoots, it took the best part of two hours to get shots that the photographer was happy with. Later in the morning I had a meeting with Tim Callaway and Crispin Driver from Deltaweb Publishing who had come to tell me more about their proposal to set up an internet site for the Red Arrows. In between, I dealt with some of the never-ending flow of letters that found their way into my in-tray and answered the usual stream of telephone calls from members of the public requesting information, brochures, or visits. In the early afternoon I had to remain close to my office in case Group Captain Tom Eeles from the Defence Export Services Organisation called in with a Venezuelan Air Force three-star General who was on a fact-finding visit to the RAF College. Perhaps a tour to Venezuela was in the offing. They did not call in and by about 4pm I was just thinking of having an early finish when Tony Charles called.

I had never heard of Tony Charles, much to his chagrin, but I learned later that he is a well-known entertainer, stage name Luci, and amongst other things he does an amazingly accurate visual and vocal imitation of Prince Charles. Tony and I had a very strange conversation during which he kept lapsing into a confusing mixture of what sounded to me like real Italian and English with a heavy Italian accent. He asked me for a lot of information about the Red Arrows for a 'secret' project BBC Television was proposing to do. From his guarded line of questioning, some instinct told me immediately that he was talking about a programme for 'This Is Your Life' but he would not be drawn. The Red Arrows had been involved in three 'This Is Your Life' programmes in the past six years so I knew the score, that secrecy was all important. I sent Tony the material he asked for – the 1996 colour brochure, hot off the press, and all my current news releases, thousands of words in all. He rang again a few days later.

'Thanks very much for all the PR material. It's great and just what I needed. Would it be possible for me to visit you at Cranwell? I need to talk some things over with you.'

'We're talking about the Red Arrows taking part in This Is Your Life aren't we?' I said. He admitted that was so.

'Let me guess,' I continued. 'You must be thinking of Ray Hanna, am I right?

I had flown in Ray's back seat on a formation training sortie from Kemble in 1967 when I was on the CFS course and Ray was in his second year as Leader of the Red Arrows. I had not seen him since although in the intervening years he had become famous in both the military and civilian aviation world. I knew that Ray was now running his own aviation business, The Old Flying Machine Company, based at Duxford Airfield in Cambridgeshire, that he owned and flew a famous World War 2 Spitfire, MH434, and that 1996 was the 60th anniversary of the first Spitfire flight. Those seemed to me to be good enough reasons to make a programme on Ray's Life. Tony Charles refused, wisely, to be drawn further on the subject of the programme on the telephone so we arranged to meet at Cranwell on 15 May, a date when I knew most of the Red Arrows, apart from Team Leader John Rands, would be off base playing at a golf tournament at Lindrick. The fewer people who were around to ask Tony, quite innocently, what he was doing, the better.

When the Team returned to base from Springhawk on 8 May, resplendent in their new red suits, I told JR what I had arranged. He seemed as enthusiastic as I was and told me to get on with the arrangements. Tony visited me as arranged and confirmed that Ray Hanna was to be the subject of a 'This Is Your Life' programme and that it was natural to involve the present-day Red Arrows in his story. He seemed very surprised, and I think rather sad, that I had correctly guessed not only the programme but the subject. Tony told me that Thames TV now made the programmes under contract for the BBC but he was a freelance and worked for neither. As a long-standing friend of the Hanna family he thought that it was high time Ray Hanna got some public credit for all that he had contributed to the British aviation scene over the past 40 years or so. Tony, through his professional contacts, had put the idea of a programme about Ray to John Graham, the Producer of This Is Your Life, and John had quickly been sold on the idea.

From the Producer's point of view the 'hit', when Michael Aspel surprises the subject, is all important. They have to have a 100% guarantee that the subject will be where they want him, when they want him.

'We're planning on making the hit at Fairford on 21 July,' said Tony. Fairford was the venue for the Royal International Air Tattoo, the biggest air show in the UK. 'Ray will be there with his Spitfire and so will the Red Arrows so it should be easy to arrange a surprise meeting.'

'Oh no it won't,' I said, glancing at my diary. 'The Reds will be flying the Tattoo displays from RAF Brize Norton this year. The show organisers have told us that there is no room for the Red Arrows to park at Fairford because there will be so many visiting aircraft, but you weren't to know that. The only Red Arrows on the ground at Fairford will be Red 10 and his videoman. It will look very suspicious if we suddenly have to try and get the Tattoo organisers to change their arrangements and there's no way you'll persuade Ray to go to Brize Norton on that day. There's no good reason for him to go, but there's every reason for him to be at Fairford. He'll be doing business there.'

That flummoxed Tony Charles but suddenly I had a brainwave.

'Why not do the hit here at Cranwell?', I suggested helpfully. 'Ray Hanna has a long-standing invitation to visit us here and fly with John Rands. I am sure we could get him here – but obviously not on 21 July. Are you committed to that date?'

'I'm not sure,' said Tony. 'They normally record the programme as quickly as possible after the hit. That way the subject doesn't have time to get over the shock and change his mind, or get too used to the whole idea. I think Thames TV had it in mind to film the whole programme at the International Air Tattoo. If we did the hit here at Cranwell we would probably have to do all the filming here.'

Obviously we could not make a decision on that there and then. Tony knew some of the filming deadlines but not all. The two of us went along the corridor to have a word with JR in his office, where he was slowly working his way through a mountain of mail that had accumulated during the three-week detachment in Cyprus. I asked him what he thought about doing the hit and the programme at Cranwell. JR liked the idea. As he said, it is always easier to do things on your own patch.

'I think we should do the programme from College Hall,' I said, warming to the idea. 'It's a splendid building inside and out and probably has all the facilities the TV company would require.'

I also knew that it would provide great PR for the RAF as a whole. The three of us then spent a few minutes comparing diaries and trying to find a suitable date. That was not easy, especially as we had no idea what the TV company's diary looked like. Fitting late engagements into the Red Arrows' summer schedule is always difficult but 1996 was made far more complicated by the tour to Indonesia. The Team were scheduled to depart from Cranwell on 12 June and were not due back until 10 July. JR and I identified three dates when the Red Arrows could make themselves available. Our favourite was 12 July when the Team had to fly an in-season practice at base for currency reasons prior to two public displays the following day at Brize Norton, coincidentally, and Yeovilton. Another possible date was 17 July when the Team returned to base after a scheduled display at Valley in Anglesey. The only other available day as far as we could see would be 2 August but that was a poor third choice because it clashed with a Red Arrows' Families Day and the Central Flying School Association's annual meet at Cranwell, when the whole camp would be swarming with retired air marshals and other VIPs. We left it to Tony Charles to discuss the Cranwell idea and the possible dates with Thames Television and instead turned our attention to some of the logistics of getting Ray Hanna to the right place at the right time.

'It won't be easy,' said JR. 'I know for a fact that Ray is just as busy as the Red Arrows are during the display season so his diary is probably very full. There's another problem. He's very proud to be a founder member of the Red Arrows but for Ray that was all a long, long time ago. These days, as you know,' he added, looking at me, 'he shuns publicity about that time of his life. My invitation for him to come and fly with us has been on the table for three years but he's always found some excuse for not coming.'

JR suggested that he should renew his invitation for Ray together with Mark, his son and business partner, to come to Cranwell on the chosen day in their own aircraft and fly with the Team on a practice display.

'I would tell Ray that this was his last opportunity to fly with me before I finish my tour as Team Leader,' said JR. 'He might go along with that. If we rope Mark in to help, and to fly Ray here, that should make sure he gets here.'

That seemed a good idea. We decided that we could dress Michael Aspel up in one of the Circus' blue flying suits and arrange for him to make the hit as JR and Ray got out of the Hawk at the end of the display. Then we would get them and the rest of the Reds across the campus to College Hall where there would be an audience of mainly RAF families for the recording of the show. I suggested we could also involve the Band of the Royal Air Force College in some way so that they could give the first televised performance of the new Diamond Nine March. Tony Charles had by this time got quite excited and could wait no longer to put the revised plans to the Producer. He spoke to John Graham on the telephone from my office and obtained his very provisional approval for our plot. It was early evening, much later than originally intended, when Tony Charles left Cranwell to return to London and I left for home.

When I arrived at work early the following morning I started keeping a private diary for this project. Tony Charles had stressed that secrecy was all-important; if word leaked out to the subject that he was being set up, the whole programme would be cancelled. One of the major problems, as I saw it, was that the Red Arrows tended to meet up with Ray Hanna several times each year at air shows. Great care would be needed to make sure that word did not accidentally slip out during the course of one of those meetings. I decided that I would keep all my notes on the project in my briefcase which went everywhere with me. I needed a code-word for the programme's subject in case someone saw my papers by accident. I chose the name 'Phil', completely at random – it was simply the first name that came into my head. However, this choice was to have an amusing side effect that I did not learn about until the day of the programme.

That same morning, John Rands called into my office to tell me that our preferred date, 12 July, was no longer possible. It was only two days after the scheduled return from Indonesia, and there was every possibility that the Team would be jet-lagged, or even delayed in transit. Because of that the planned displays at Brize Norton and Yeovilton had been cancelled by the RAF Participation Committee. There was, therefore, no need to fly a practice at Cranwell on the 12th. I called Tony Charles to give him this information and he told me that he had just learned that Michael Aspel was not available on 2 August. Two of our three possible dates already had to be discounted. This was getting complicated!

The next thing I had to do was get permission from the AOC and Commandant of the College for the use of College Hall so I telephoned his Personal Staff Officer to make an appointment.. The PSO did not answer her telephone and just I was about to hang up the Commandant, Air Vice-Marshal Tony Stables, answered the phone himself. I asked him if he could spare me five minutes to discuss a major matter. He invited me over to his magnificent suite of offices on the first floor of College Hall and I explained what was being proposed. He was enthusiastic about the concept of using the College Hall for the programme and he gave me his full authority to make whatever arrangements were necessary.

'Tell the whole story only to those who really need to know,' said the Air Marshal. 'Tell everyone else that I've given my approval for the use of College Hall and that will be the only authority you need to get done whatever you need to be done. Make sure the chosen date goes into the College Diary as soon as possible, though, to avoid any double-bookings.'

I was grateful for the air marshal's instant approval and the free hand he had given me to get on with the arrangements. There is nothing like tossing the name of a two-star officer into the conversation when you want to get something done! For once I was willing to ignore my aversion to name-dropping!

A few days later I had a telephone call from Mandy Lee, the Production Manager for Thames Television, to say that they had gone firm on 17 July for recording the programme and that she and her producer would like to come to Cranwell on 31 May to have an on-site meeting. They would bring with them Alec Lom, the script writer, Avril Norton, a researcher, and Nigel Spong, the Facilities Engineering Manager. I readily agreed and told Mandy that I now had formal permission for them to use College Hall. Mandy then said that Mark Hanna was having difficulty in getting hold of his Father's diary to check for other commitments on 17 July. Thinking back later when the plot thickened, I should have realised that was a pretty flimsy excuse bearing in mind Mark and his father were business partners. Mandy was worried about making too many arrangements, and spending money, before she was certain that Ray would be available. I told Mandy to tell Mark that John Rands would write to Ray formally inviting him to come to Cranwell to fly with the Team. I thought a written invitation from JR would ensure that Ray would make himself available.

In the meantime I continued making secret arrangements. I fully briefed the Station Commander, Group Captain Jake Jarron, and the CFS Commandant, Air Commodore Simon Bostock. Both were content to let me get on with the planning, the former more so than the latter. One of my worries as the days passed was that word would leak out accidentally. It was too dangerous even to acknowledge that we, the Red Arrows, were doing a This Is Your Life programme because word would inevitably have leaked back quite innocently to Ray Hanna through the air show grapevine. Instead, I decided to let it be known that the BBC was preparing a major full-length documentary about the Red Arrows.

Everyone believed that because there were often TV crews in and around the Team's HQ.

I arranged with Duncan Stubbs for the College Band to be available and added that the BBC would like to use his new march in the programme. He was, naturally, very keen on that. I spoke to the College Hall Officers' Mess Manager, Alan Waby, and explained that the television company would be taking over the entire Mess for 24 hours. He would have to arrange to feed the living-in staff and cadets elsewhere but he would also have to provide food for the TV crew and a large number of guests. Alan was concerned about the Mess staff. There was a major reorganisation in progress and several staff were likely to be made redundant. I said that the television company would pay all expenses and overtime for the staff. Like the excellent manager that he was, once he knew that the Commandant had approved the filming, Alan simply told me to let him have a list of requirements and he would make it happen.

On 30 May while I was at Cranwell waiting for the arrival of the planning team from Thames Television, John Rands was at Duxford on business and bumped into Ray Hanna as well as his wife and son Mark. In a quiet corner, when Ray was well out of earshot, Mark told JR that the family were not all that keen about the programme and had not realised that things had progressed so far. It seems that in the recent past Ray and Tony Charles had had a major disagreement about something. Mark and the family feared that if Tony turned up when the programme was being recorded, Ray would walk off the set and refuse to take any further part.

JR telephoned me straightaway to tell me of the family's fears and I passed on the news to the Thames production team who had already gathered in my office. John Graham decided to talk to Mark Hanna at the office of the Old Flying Machine Company. To John's dismay, Ray himself answered the phone. With a quick bit of thinking, John passed himself of as a friend of Mark and Ray handed the phone over to his son. Somehow Mark got his father out of the office while he had a lengthy conversation with John, who eventually persuaded Mark that all would be well and that Tony Charles was not going to be at the recording of the programme.

There was more difficulty about dates. The Hanna family could not make any dates in July because some or all of them would be away on holiday. The Hannas wanted to put the programme off until October but that was no good for the Red Arrows because by then the display season would be over, the pilots would have gone on leave and there was no way we could convincingly invite Ray to come to Cranwell. We eventually settled on 23 September as the date for the recording, the day after the final UK display of the season at Southport using Blackpool Airport as the operating base.

The Thames people were delighted with everything they saw in College Hall. Alec Lom gave me a long list of things to do, including making contact with all the Red Arrows who had flown with Ray, especially the ones who had flown with him in 1966, his first year as Leader. Alec also wanted me to make contact with Air Vice-Marshal Johnny Johnson, the World War 2 Spitfire fighter ace, and Raymond Baxter, former RAF Spitfire pilot and television personality. I knew how to contact all of them.

Finally we went out onto the flight line to see how we could arrange the 'hit' with Michael Aspel. I had already worked out what I thought should happen. Fortunately for an event such as this, the Red Arrows can close the airfield for all other aircraft movements. That would immediately get around one of the major problems associated with filming on airfields – unwanted aircraft engine noise. I suggested that we built the hit around the Red Arrows' return to base from Blackpool. I would arrange for Ray Hanna and his son to be out on the flight line ready to watch the Reds as they made the traditional end-of-season celebratory flypast. I would tell Ray that the TV company was there purely to film this final return to base and that they were going to interview John Rands before they all went off again for Ray's trip with the Reds. I thought that I could persuade Ray to agree to give a rare interview. As JR climbed down from his aircraft, Ray Hanna would move forward to greet him and then Michael Aspel would appear from nowhere and spring the surprise on Ray. Simple!

John Graham and the rest of his team thought this was an excellent plot and Alec was tasked to write the script accordingly.

I had a three-week break from all these arrangements while I went off to Indonesia with the Team and it was while we were in Indonesia that we heard the splendid news that John Rands had been awarded the OBE in the Queen's Birthday Honours List. A very well deserved honour for a very fine Leader, and a nice fellow to boot.

On 1 July, my first day back in the office while the Red Arrows were still transiting across the Middle East, I had a telephone call from Alec Lom. It seems that Mandy was still having difficulty getting confirmation from Mark Hanna that his father had definitely agreed to come to Cranwell. Everyone involved with the production was now getting anxious. Would I please get John Rands to talk to Ray as soon as possible after he got back to Cranwell. Alec also asked me to telephone Ray's wife, Eunice, make myself known to her, explain roughly what the plot was, and apologise on behalf of Alec for not contacting her himself as promised. I telephoned Eunice a few minutes later and it was quickly obvious that she knew all about me although we had never met.

'Oh, Tony,' said Eunice in a despairing sort of way. I could tell that bad news was forthcoming. 'I've done something really awful. I've told Ray about the programme.'

For a few seconds I was speechless.

'Why on earth did you do that?' I asked lamely.

'I – we – the family – were all worried about what Ray would do if he meets Tony Charles and learns that he was the instigator of this programme. We think that it's best if you tell Alec that Ray will have to be in Saudi Arabia on the 23rd on business and so he cannot do the programme. It's only a little white lie. Then it will be too late to reorganise things and they'll call it all off.'

'I'm sorry, Eunice,' I said, thinking quickly. 'You're going to have to tell Alec the truth yourself. A lot of people have already put in a lot of work to make this tribute to Ray. All Ray's 1966 Team were coming, and Raymond Baxter, and Johnny Johnson, and goodness knows who else they had lined up. We don't want to waste any more of all those people's time. Thames won't do the programme now, anyway. They never do the programme if the subject learns about it in advance. I think the least you can do is tell Alec yourself before he finds out from someone else.'

Eunice reluctantly agreed. She must have telephoned almost immediately, but she did not tell Alec the whole truth and nothing but the truth because Alec rang me a few minutes later and asked me what the Red Arrows would be doing on 15 September.

'A last minute problem has cropped up with Ray,' said Alec. 'I've just heard from Eunice that our subject has to be in Saudi Arabia on business on 23 September.'

I decided that Alec deserved to know the truth. Reluctantly I told him that Eunice had spilled the beans to her husband but she had thought she was doing it for the best. Not surprisingly, Alec was very upset and he told me, rather coldly I thought, to do nothing more until he had spoken to the Producer. Later John Graham rang me himself and told me that, reluctantly, the programme was cancelled. He thanked me for all my work and asked me to thank, on Thames Television's behalf, all the people at Cranwell who had contributed to the programme without even knowing it.

'Wait a minute, John,' I said suddenly. I had had one of my inspirations. 'Before you cancel anything, give me half an hour and I'll get back to you with an alternative proposal.'

John agreed to wait, but he did not sound very enthusiastic. Even as I put the telephone down after John had agreed, I began to wonder what I was letting myself in for. What I had in mind was not something that I had just dreamed up; it was an idea that I had been nurturing for some days but I had not expected to have an opportunity to develop it for several years hence. Thoughts raced through my mind as I tried to consider all the pros and cons but it actually took only about ten minutes before I telephoned John back.

'John, I want to suggest that you go ahead almost exactly as we had planned except...,' I paused and took a deep breath, '...I think John Rands should be the subject of the programme instead of Ray Hanna.'

There was a long pause at the other end before John said, 'Go on, Tony, tell me what you have in mind.'

'JR is an absolutely ideal subject for your programme,' I said. 'He's served with the Red Arrows for six years; he was the youngest Red Arrow ever, I think, certainly he's the youngest ever Leader; he's flown over 600 public displays, 350 of them as Leader – that's probably more than anyone else; he's led the Team on an unprecedented world tour; he's just been awarded the OBE by the Queen; and the Queen Mother, our Commandant-in-Chief, knows him and I bet she would send a personal message to be read out at the end of the programme. The Red Arrows have never been so popular around the world and in the UK as they are right now. It could be the most wonderful double bluff. There he'll be, like a lamb to the slaughter. He'll expect to see Michael Aspel when he lands on 23rd September after his final UK show – the only thing he won't know is that he's the subject not Ray. Personally, I can't think of anyone who deserves a This Is Your Life more than JR does.'

After I had stopped talking, John Graham paused for a few seconds before he said: 'I like it. Can you fax me your proposal as soon as possible and I'll put it to the BBC. I have to get their approval – we just make the programmes for the Beeb you know. What about JR's wife? Is she on board with this?'

'You're the only person so far who knows about this idea. I haven't discussed it even with the Commandant and I don't intend to. I'll go and see Karen Rands on the way home, she lives just round the corner from me in a little village near Scampton. The Reds are having a day off in Bangkok today on their way home from Jakarta. If any of the neighbours see me, I can just say I'm passing on the latest situation report from JR.'

I telephoned Karen and told her that I would like to call in before the children came home from school so that I could discuss a proposal for a television programme. I had assumed, wrongly as it turned out, that JR would have told his wife that we were planning a This Is Your Life programme about Ray Hanna.

'Karen,' I said as soon as we sitting down in her lounge and had exchanged the usual pleasantries, 'what I'm about to tell you must go no further – not to your children and certainly not to JR.' We even referred to John as JR to Karen.

'That's all right,' she replied. 'I can keep a secret.'

'I expect JR has told you about a television programme we're doing with Ray Hanna?'

'No – that's news to me. But let me guess. You want to get JR on This Is Your Life – am I right?'

I was astonished. 'How did you know that?

'I didn't – call it woman's intuition if you like. As soon as you mentioned Ray Hanna just now I knew I was right.'

My mind was racing. Should I tell her the whole story and risk her being disappointed that JR was the BBC's second choice, or should I conceal that part of the story. I decided on the latter course of action, for the time being at least.

'I'm not very keen on the idea,' said Karen. 'I'd an idea that you might come up with something like this and I've been thinking about what I might say.'

'Look at it this way,' I said. 'JR has earned this special tribute. He's been an outstanding Leader. Yes, I know he'll be very embarrassed about it but I imagine most subjects of This Is Your Life are embarrassed at first. His parents and your children will be very proud of him and his many friends, in and out of the RAF, will want to contribute to the programme.'

'What do you want me to do?' asked Karen.

'I want you to meet the programme researcher. It's really crucial that you don't mention this to anyone yet. No-one but you and me and the programme producer's small team know about this.'

That evening I put together a complete story board for John Graham and I faxed it to him first thing the following morning. John rang back a day later and gave the green light for the new programme. I told Karen the news and I think she received it with mixed emotions. I assured her that I had passed on her misgivings to the Producer.

When I got home I telephoned Wing Commander Andy Stewart. Andy had been the Red Arrows Team Manager until 1991 and he now worked for the RAF's Director of Public Relations in the Ministry of Defence. As such he had easy access to the Chief of the Air Staff, Air Chief Marshal Sir Michael Graydon. Being rather neurotic about security, I had decided that this was one conversation that was safer carried out from my own home where I could not be overheard.

I told Andy about the Ray Hanna plot and how it had gone wrong. I then told him what was being planned in its place and I asked him to speak to CAS as soon as he could, tell him what was being planned and ask him for his approval. We would want CAS to be at the recording of the programme so we needed to get the date in his diary quickly. I suggested to Andy that as far as everyone else was concerned we could say that CAS was coming to the Red Arrows to take part in a PR film that the BBC was making. No-one would see anything unusual in that because it was well known that Sir Michael was a great friend of the Red Arrows and he must have given his approval to the citation which had led to the award of the OBE to JR – if he had not actually written it himself. A couple of days later Andy rang me to say that CAS had given his approval and would come to Cranwell for the recording of the programme.

Thereafter, things started to move rapidly and I found myself leading not a double life but a triple life. I could count on the thumb of one hand the people at Cranwell who knew about the JR plot – there was only one – me! There was a slightly larger number who knew about the Ray Hanna plot; and there was a growing number of people who knew that we were planning a film about the Red Arrows.

I arranged a meeting between myself, Karen and Avril Norton, the researcher for the JR programme. I picked a day when the Red Arrows were well out of the way – flying from Aberdeen to Exeter between air shows – and we agreed to meet at the Mill Lodge Hotel at the top of Canwick Hill on the southern outskirts of Lincoln where we could get on with our business without danger of being seen by anyone who knew us. After I had introduced them to each other, Karen had a long chat with Avril and, thankfully, Karen was reassured and agreed that the programme should go ahead. Karen then went home while Avril and I went back to Cranwell to start detailed work on the story.

I was amazed at how much work was necessary. First of all there was a major and unforeseen problem at Cranwell on our chosen date. Monday 23 September was set to be Black Monday, the day when the senior entry of student officers hear their fate and are told whether they will be graduating or not. On the evening of Black Monday there is always a huge party in College Hall Mess. I went across to the College to meet the Director of Initial Officer Training, Group Captain Beney. I gave him the story about This Is Your Life without telling him who the subject would be. Much as I dislike name-dropping, I had no alternative: I told the Group Captain that I had the Commandant's full authority to make such arrangements as I saw fit and that the Chief of the Air Staff would be present.

The good Group Captain was very helpful. He quickly decided that rather than postpone Black Monday and make a Black Tuesday instead, he would move all his students out of the College Hall Mess on the Sunday evening into the York House, the staff officers' Mess. That would leave the whole of College Hall free for the TV company to build their sets and do whatever they wanted. The production team was delighted with this. I persuaded John Graham that it would a great PR gesture if Thames Television could provide some beer for the York House Mess to help the Black Monday party go with a swing. They did in fact eventually donate £500 as a token of their appreciation to the student officers for moving out of their own Mess.

One day our two-star Air Officer Commanding, Air Vice-Marshal John May, was on base at Cranwell and I thought it was about time I came clean about what was being planned. I told the AOC, and the CFS Commandant who was with him at the time, the full story as we walked from the Red Arrows to the CFS Headquarters. The AOC thought it was a great idea and told me I had his full approval to continue making whatever arrangements I felt necessary. This rather irked the Commandant and took the wind out of his sails because he would rather have been involved in the decision making processes before I had started making arrangements with the Chief of the Air Staff.

The next few weeks were a whirl of activity. From time to time I gave JR an update on how plans for This Is Your Life Ray Hanna were progressing. I made sure that JR knew everything that was being planned – except the identity of the subject! One day I had a heart-stopping moment when JR told me that he had just bumped into Ray Hanna at Duxford. Neither JR nor Ray had apparently said anything to each other to give the game away. I was fairly sure that Ray did not know that the programme was going ahead with JR as the subject but I could not be certain. I found that the secret diary I was keeping had become absolutely invaluable otherwise I would never remember what I had told and to whom, particularly because of my problem of remembering people's names.

As the date of the recording approached I began to have worries about another little problem. I had told Mandy, the Production Manager, that I would provide an audience of 200 to fill all the available seats in the College Hall dining room which was being transformed into the theatre for the recording. The audience would have to be in their seats for the rehearsal at 1715hrs. Where was I to get 200 people at tea time on a Monday afternoon?

Word was already spreading around the whole of Cranwell Campus that something big was afoot. I decided that I might just as well add to the rumours by sending out invitations to all the squadrons at Cranwell inviting them to apply for tickets to the filming of a BBC programme about the Red Arrows. I had the Station Commander's approval to let people come in working clothes, including flying suits, because then they could come straight from work. I thought it likely that people would eventually guess that we were doing a This Is Your Life programme but that it was extremely unlikely that they would guess the name of the subject. In order to keep tabs on how many people were likely to attend, I made it a ticket-only affair. I printed the tickets myself and got one of my Holding Officers to issue them from my office. I need not have worried; I could have easily made up an audience of double the number required.

It was after my invitations were sent out that I realised most people were assuming that This Is Your Life was coming to Cranwell. Rumours were rife about who the subject was and there were some very wild guesses. Some devious people thought that I was bandying around the name of the Red Arrows as a red herring. Others thought the subject would be the College Commandant, Air Vice-Marshal Stables, because we were filming at the College; some thought it would be Raymond Baxter because he had been at the Red Arrows a few weeks earlier; some thought it would be the Prince of Wales because he had done his flying training at Cranwell. The rumour that gave me most amusement was that the subject would be the Duke of Edinburgh. Why did that amuse me? Because, when I first started my secret diary and when Ray Hanna was still the subject, I used the nickname Phil to refer to the subject. I wondered if anyone had managed to rifle through my diary but I am fairly certain no one did; it was just an odd coincidence.

On Sunday 22 September just before the Team left Cranwell for the transit flight to Blackpool Airport ready for the Southport show, I took the Team's Executive Officer, Mark Zanker, to one side and explained the whole thing. He was remarkably calm about it – disappointingly so. I asked him to brief the rest of the pilots on the Monday morning so that they would have time to telephone wives and partners and invite them to College Hall for the recording. I told Mark that all the Red Arrows would be needed on stage for the recording and so he had to make sure that none of the pilots had made any other arrangements.

I then briefed JR, in private, for the last time!

'Mark Zanker will brief the pilots about what is going on,' I said to JR. 'Please be on time to the nearest second and fly over the flight line from the direction of Sleaford. You will see Michael Aspel out on the airfield with a camera crew recording his introductory piece to camera as the Reds arrive overhead. Please taxi slowly back to dispersal so that the camera crew and Michael can reposition on the flight line to film the hit with Ray Hanna. There will be a couple of helicopters parked next to your parking slot. Take your time getting out of your aircraft so that all the other Reds have time to gather round. We want all the Reds in the picture. When you get out of your aircraft, if look towards me you will see me standing alongside the camera crew with Michael and Ray Hanna. We will then come to you at the steps of your aircraft and you can tell Michael about your connections with Ray and what a good job he did in the early days of the Red Arrows. And that will be that.'

I knew I could rely on JR to do exactly as he had been briefed but I was beginning to feel very guilty about setting him up.

It all went as planned, to the nearest second. As the Reds dismounted from their aircraft there was a huge crowd of people from all parts of the station crowding round. JR got out of his aircraft and looked in my direction. A questioning look appeared on his face. He could see me but there was no sign of Michael Aspel nor, of course, Ray Hanna. Michael, who had been hiding behind one of the helicopters, walked the few yards to JR, clasping the famous Red Book.

'Hello John. Happy landings. For once in your life, your entire Team is one step ahead of their Leader. They all helped me to fly in to say,

Leader of the Red Arrows, Squadron Leader John Rands, OBE, This Is Your Life!'

JR looked slowly from Michael to the name on the book and then across at me. Then he said in a loud voice, clearly picked up by the microphones and transmitted in the programme:

'It wasn't meant to happen like this!'

I handed over to JR a suitcase containing a clean red flying suit and his toilet things and then he was whisked off to the Belton Woods Country Hotel a few miles away near Grantham. There were three hours before the recording was due to start and it was important that JR was kept incommunicado, and sober, during that time.

After making sure that everything was happening as planned in the College Hall Mess, the Producer asked me to go the Belton Woods Hotel, sit with JR and then escort him back to Cranwell to arrive just before 7pm ready to have a quick session with the make-up lady before making his ceremonial entrance. Apparently they always get a trusted friend to sit with the subject between the hit and the start of the recording, they call it baby-sitting! I was soon to learn why they had not asked me to arrange a baby-sitter.

JR and I returned to Cranwell in good time in the limousine hired by Thames TV and I asked the driver to hold short of the main entrance until the RAF Policemen on duty there gave me a pre-arranged signal that meant that the Chief of the Air Staff, flown in from London by helicopter, was inside College Hall and safely out of JR's sight. We then continued the drive up to the magnificent door leading into the College, where we were met by the Production Assistant who whisked JR off to the make-up room – actually the AOC and Commandant's private toilet. I was about to make my way behind the scenes to check up on the arrangements for the post-recording party when Mandy, the researcher rushed up to me.

'Tony, one of our guests hasn't turned up. He was going to be on the stage during the recording. You'll have to take his place.'

'Sorry, Mandy,' I said. 'I made it quite clear that I did not want to be on the stage.'

'Please, Tony,' pleaded Mandy. 'All the shots are lined up – we can't have a blank place, it would confuse the cameramen.'

Reluctantly I allowed myself to be led onto the platform and I sat down where Mandy indicated. Barely 30 seconds later the fanfare trumpeters of the Band of the RAF College struck up and the recording began.

It was only the following day, after I had time to read through the Thames' shooting script, that I realised my name had been included in the stage party right from the beginning. It was Thames' Television's way of thanking me.

For once I had been out-manoeuvred.

21

A Sad Russian Visit

WHILE I WAS IN THE THROES OF ORGANISING This Is Your Life, there was a sad visit to the Red Arrows at Cranwell in August 1996. The Leader of the Russian Knights aerobatic display team, Lieutenant Colonel Alexsander Vladimirovich Lichkun, and three other Russian pilots re-visited the Red Arrows by invitation of Air Chief Marshal Sir Michael Graydon, Chief of the Air Staff. This time they arrived by road having first flown more comfortably and quietly by British Airways Boeing 767 from Moscow to Heathrow.

Accompanying the Squadron Commander were: Colonel Vladimir Pavlovich Basov, the very first Leader of the Russian Knights and now a staff officer at the Russian Ministry of Defence in Moscow; Lieutenant Colonel Sergei Yureivich Ganichev, another of the original Russian Knights and now on the staff of the Aviation Display Centre; and Lieutenant Colonel Vladimir Aleksandrovich Kovalskiy, deputy Leader of the present Russian Knights.

'The purpose of our visit,' said Colonel Basov, 'apart from our wish to meet the Red Arrows again, is to learn about sponsorship, public relations and the operational planning that goes on behind the scenes, and to see for ourselves how the Red Arrows work in an operational environment. We readily admit that we can learn much from the world's premier aerobatic display team. Not how to fly,' he added with a mischievous twinkle in his eye, 'but how to sell ourselves to the public.'

In four years following the initial Russian Knights' visit to Scampton in 1991, the team had travelled widely and their fame had grown amongst the international aviation fraternity but little news about their activities was published in the West. The Knights had given displays in

America, Belgium, Canada, France, Germany, and Slovakia, as well as within the Russian Federation and the newly-independent former Soviet republics, but they had not re-visited the United Kingdom. Their most recent performances had been in December 1995 at Langkawi, Malaysia, where they once again met up with the Red Arrows. Colonel Basov was keen to tell me the Russian Knights' version of what happened on their way home because he believed the real facts had been hushed up to protect a senior officer. He and I sat outside the Red Arrows' crew room in a pleasant patio area, drinking coffee, while he narrated an horrendous story which he wanted me to publish.

After departing from Langkawi for the long trek back to their base at Kubinka, their first scheduled landing was to be at Cam Ranh Bay in Vietnam for refuelling. Unlike the way the Red Arrows do things, five of the Su-27s had been transiting in close company with their Il-76 transport aircraft. The Red Arrows never transit in formation with their Hercules support aircraft although occasionally, for PR purposes, they will make a flypast with their Hercules, as they did at Cape Town in 1995.

There was a very good reason why the Sukhois had to stay close to their support aircraft. The Su-27s had no navigational aids or radios on board that were compatible with worldwide standards and so they could not meet the international air traffic control requirements for flying in airways. These requirements are mandatory because the only way the ground controllers can guarantee safe separation between aircraft in the airways is when all aircraft can maintain their assigned course to a high degree of accuracy and when they have the appropriate equipment to maintain two-way radio contact with the controllers. However, embarrassing though it was, the Russians had become used to this and their standard practice when flying outside Russia was to remain close to the Ilyushin until, when they were within sight of their destination, they were able to proceed independently for landing.

For much of the flight from Malaysia the six aircraft flew at about 35,000 feet well above the weather. All the pilots were relaxed and looking forward to getting home in a few days. As they approached Cam Ranh Bay airfield, the pilots were alarmed to see that the clouds beneath them were getting thicker and the tops were getting higher. That deterioration had not been forecast. A few years earlier even that would not have been a problem because Cam Ranh Bay had been home for several squadrons of the Soviet Navy's TU-95 long-range bombers and reconnaissance aircraft and the airfield had been well equipped with navigational aids that both the Sukhois and Ilyushin could use. Since the break up of the Soviet Union, however, there was no urgent operational need to maintain the base in Vietnam. It had been allowed to fall into disrepair and almost all the radio navigational aids were out of commission.

The Ilyushin crew were in radio contact with the ground controllers at Cam Ranh Bay and they were told that the weather at the airfield was quite reasonable. The lowest cloud over the airfield was said to be about 1,000 metres and the horizontal visibility was fine. The Captain of the Ilyushin relayed the weather conditions to the Sukhois. Because there were high mountains quite close to their destination, it was agreed that the Sukhois would remain in close formation with the Ilyushin as they descended through the cloud until they came into good visual contact with the ground beneath. The Sukhois closed up, three on the starboard, including the two-seat Sukhoi 27UB, and two on the port side of the Ilyushin. Shortly after starting the descent from high level the formation went into thick layers of medium level cloud and it became very turbulent. The Sukhoi pilots had to work very hard to maintain position.

The Ilyushin captain had failed to tell the Russian Knights one crucial piece of information. There was no serviceable radar equipment at the airfield. This meant that the air traffic controllers had no idea where the aircraft were and had to rely on the Ilyushin's position reports. In fact, the only aid on the ground that was working was the middle marker radio beacon, part of the Instrument Landing System, which is only of any use when the aircraft is lined up with the runway on final approach to a landing. Had the Sukhoi pilots known this they might have decided against following the Ilyushin.

Colonel Basov told me that the Ilyushin captain positioned his aircraft overhead the airfield as accurately as he could and then initiated a tear drop descent pattern. This was rather like a pattern called a QGH that the RAF used to use 30 or 40 years ago. QGH was aviators' shorthand for a controlled descent through cloud. To carry out a QGH the ground controller would take frequent bearings on his radio direction finding equipment and tell the aircraft what headings to fly to home to the airfield. When the aircraft passed through the airfield's overhead, the bearings indicated on the direction finder would fluctuate rapidly as the aircraft passed through the equipment's cone of silence. The aircraft would then be instructed to descend on a known safe heading until it was down to half its original height plus two thousand feet. It would then turn inbound onto a reciprocal heading towards the airfield, descending to a specified minimum safe height at or above which the ground should become visible. If the ground was not visible at that minimum height, the approach would be aborted and the aircraft would climb away to try something else. The safety of a QGH was entirely reliant upon an accurate position overhead the airfield before the descent started. The problem for the Russians was that the ground controllers at Cam Ranh Bay had no direction finding equipment and the Iyushin captain had to estimate his position and start the procedure when he thought he was overhead, a sort of do-it-yourself QGH which was both illegal and foolhardy.

Having decided he was overhead the airfield, the captain of the Il-76 led the formation into a starboard turn and started to descend. Unfortunately, for reasons which never became clear to Colonel Basov, the formation was actually about 30 kilometres from the airfield's overhead when they started descending and the starboard turn put very high ground between the aircraft and the runway. During the latter stages of that fateful descent through the thick turbulent cloud, one after the other in quick succession, the two outermost aircraft on the starboard wing struck the ground and exploded on impact.

'The pilot of the third and last remaining Sukhoi on the starboard side, the one nearest the Il-76, was heard on the radio starting to say "Ejectirovat", the Russian command to eject, but he never got past the first syllable before he also crashed into the ground,' said Colonel Basov. 'Sadly, all four pilots on the starboard side, Colonel Boris Grigoriev, and Majors Aleksander Syrovoi, Nikolai Kordukov and Nikolai Gretchanov, were killed. At that point the Il-76 rolled out of the turn and initiated a maximum rate climb. I estimate that its starboard wing tip could have been no more than one or two metres from the ground.'

Try to imagine what it must have been like for the two Sukhoi pilots on the port side of the Ilyushin. They knew that three aircraft had just struck the ground, therefore they and the Ilyushin were perilously close to the ground. Suddenly the Ilyushin started to roll towards them and then went into an emergency climb. The Sukhoi pilots knew that if they did not push down on their control columns the Ilyushin would collide with them. On the other hand if they did push down, thereby making their aircraft descend, they would almost certainly hit the ground themselves. It was all very disorientating especially as visibility in the thick cloud was so poor that they could not even see the entire wing span of the Ilyushin.

Lichkun and Kovalskiy, the pilots of the two Su-27s in very close formation on the port wing, did what any professional pilots would do in that situation: they independently broke out of the formation in a steep left hand climbing turn and immediately reverted to flying on instruments. The two remaining Su-27 pilots needed every ounce of their skill to retain control of their aircraft and not become totally and fatally disorientated. Lesser pilots may well have collided with the transport aircraft, leading to the total destruction of every aircraft in the formation.

Fortunately Lichkun and Kovalskiy came out of the cloud almost immediately and saw open ground in front of them – and an airfield! Without knowing which airfield it was, and receiving no reply to their radio calls, they made a visual circuit of the airfield and landed, in a state of considerable shock, a few minutes later. It turned out to be a civil airport which used a different radio band which was why they had received no reply to their radio transmissions. As soon as they climbed out their aircraft they were promptly arrested by Vietnamese officials for landing without permission. They were held in custody, incommunicado, while the civil authorities sought instructions from their own Vietnamese military command. Communications being what they were between Vietnam and Russia, it was 36 hours before the Vietnamese were able to establish where the Sukhois had come from. The surviving pilots were then taken to Cam Ranh Bay by road.

The Ilyushin, having somehow found a safe area to descend below cloud, had landed safely at Cam Ranh Bay some considerable time after the other Sukhois had crashed. No doubt that crew was in an advanced state of shock. They knew three aircraft had crashed but they had no information about the other two and assumed they too must have crashed. It never, apparently, occurred to them that they might have landed safely at another airfield. The bodies of the dead pilots were not recovered for 14 days after the accident and it was several more days after that before the bodies were repatriated to Russia.

According to Colonel Basov, there was no official inquiry into the tragedy because the captain of the Ilyushin had been ordered to make the fatal descent through cloud against his better judgement by a high-ranking general travelling as passenger. Quite what prompted the General to give the fatal order has never been established but majors in the Russian Air Force, having been brought up the Soviet way, would not question the orders of a general. In the RAF, an air marshal would not question the actions of the captain of an aircraft in which he was a passenger – or at least I hope he would not.

'Since then the Russian Knights have not flown as a Team because we could not get any more aircraft to replace the crashed ones,' Colonel Basov told me sadly. 'Even if we get new aircraft, it will take a considerable time to train up new pilots to take their position in the Team but we are working at the problem.'

In the difficult economic situation which pertained in Russia in the years after the dissolution of the Soviet Union, the Russian Air Force had learned the lesson the RAF learned about Lightnings in the early 1960s – that a display team using operational high performance aircraft may provide a thrilling spectacle for the crowds but the operating costs are almost prohibitive.

'On many occasions in recent years within Russia, partly to save fuel but mainly to cut down on other costs, we have flown to a display location as passengers in a transport aircraft and then displayed in aircraft belonging to a locally-based squadron,' said Lichkun. 'That is very embarrassing for us and no other international aerobatic team has to operate like that.'

'The Il-76 aircraft is not ideal for the Russian Knights' purposes anyway,' added Colonel Basov. 'It is much too large and expensive to operate. Even on that first visit to Scampton there was room in the

Ilyushin for about 80 passengers not directly connected with the display, as well as all the ground servicing equipment and technical personnel that were required. However, we use it because it is one of the few transport aircraft our Air Force owns that has a comprehensive fit of navigational and radio equipment and its operating crews are by now thoroughly familiar with international operations. The Team hopes very much that the Russian Air Force will allocate resources for the purchase of modern navigation equipment that is compatible with western air traffic control systems. I'm doing what I can to persuade the High Command. Modern navigation aids fitted to the Sukhois, and perhaps to one of the smaller transport aircraft, would allow us to travel overseas in greater safety and at much lower cost. As with the Red Arrows, it is not always desirable to fly in close company with our transport aircraft. It is more economical and efficient to transit at the Sukhoi's optimum operating heights and speeds.'

Asked if the Russians would continue with the Russian Knights or form a team with smaller aircraft Colonel Basov said, 'The Russian Air Force may decide to start an aerobatic display team with training jets like the Red Arrows but that is not for me to comment on. I want the Russian Knights to continue with the Su-27 – it is a powerful aircraft and it gives exciting displays. There is a place for our team of Sukhois on the international display circuit.'

During their time with the Red Arrows, the two Russian Knights and Lieutenant Colonel Ganichev flew in the Hawk back seats on a number of transit sorties and on the Red Arrows' scheduled displays at Fowey, Stoneleigh, Elvington and Leicester. Colonel Basov had a long-standing medical problem which prevented him from flying. The pilots had learned sufficient English to cope with any emergency that might have cropped up whilst airborne but extensive ground briefings on Hawk operations, flying techniques, and the ejection seats and other safety equipment were conducted through an RAF interpreter before they were allowed to fly in a Hawk. Only when individual Red Arrows pilots were satisfied that the Russians were safe to fly in their back seat were they permitted to fly on display sorties and then only in the front five positions of the formation.

Social highlights of a busy six days included a civic reception at Fowey and an evening visit to a Lincoln Indian curry house. While the Red Arrows had a busy day operating out of Stansted Airport for displays at Eye and Chelmsford, the Russians and their interpreter went off for a day at Alton Towers where they were able to experience more high g manoeuvres! Their visit ended with an exchange of gifts and a few beers in the crew room after the Reds returned to base late that evening from Stansted.

The Russian visitors left Cranwell at dawn on 27 August for the journey back to Heathrow and the flight to Moscow and on to Kubinka, their home base, 60 km west of Moscow. Colonel Basov said on leaving, 'The way ahead for us is commercial sponsorship. You have given us some good ideas. It has been a great pleasure to visit the Red Arrows again. Now you must come back and visit us – soon.'

The Red Arrows are still waiting for their second visit to Russia.

22

Nine to Seven and Eyes Front!

SOMETIME LATE IN 1997 WHILE STARTING the work up for the new Season, Squadron Leader Simon Meade, the Team Leader, told us that it was his intention to introduce a totally 'crowd front' show for his final Season in 1999. This was so that the Red Arrows' show would once again conform to European directives. For some years the Red Arrows had benefited from a waiver which allowed them, and no other formation aerobatic team, to fly certain manoeuvres over and some directly towards the crowd. The British waiver had been accepted by all the countries the Team displayed in apart from France and the Netherlands. We knew that Simon had originally wanted to introduce the crowd front show for the 1998 Season but the long and tiring Far East tour at the end of 1997 had put paid to that idea. With no major overseas tour planned for the end of the 1998 Season, Simon felt confident that he would have sufficient time to produce a crowd front show for his final season. Being able to dispense with the waiver for his final year, he felt certain that the Team would once again be welcome to display in France and the Netherlands.

Almost from day one back in 1965, the Red Arrows had started their show by arriving directly overhead the crowd from behind. This so-called 'crowd rear' arrival was spectacular and it always surprised a large percentage of the crowd – those out of earshot of the public address system and those who had never seen the Red Arrows perform before. It also enabled the Team to demonstrate their claim to arrive on time, to the nearest couple of seconds. There are a few seaside locations where the Team commentator and the expectant crowds are down at sea level while the aircraft approach from inland over cliffs and are invisible until the instant they roar overhead. This invisibility extends to UHF radio waves which will not bend around cliff tops and so the commentator has to rely on an accurate watch to start his opening announcement over the public address system: 'Will your please welcome the Royal Air Force Aerobatic Team, the Red Arrows.' If all is well, and it usually is, the word 'arrows' will immediately be followed by what is affectionately known as the 'whoosh' – the unmistakeable roar of nine British Aerospace Hawk jets passing close overhead.

Apart from the traditional crowd rear arrival, there were several other manoeuvres where individual aircraft flew both over and towards the crowd and it was not just the Red Arrows doing it: most of the European display teams had similar manoeuvres. But all that changed following an appalling accident at the USAF Ramstein base in Germany on 28 August 1988 during a display by the Italian Air Force Team, *Frecce Tricolori*. Three aircraft collided with each other whilst performing the 'Pierced Heart', one of their more flamboyant manoeuvres which involved aircraft approaching each other from several different directions. The Red Arrows have never performed manoeuvres where more than two aircraft, or two groups of aircraft, are approaching each other on a potentially collision course. Some people may argue that the Red Arrows' 'Five-Four Split', where a group of five aircraft heads towards a group of four aircraft, violates this rule. Not so, because there is only one pilot leading each group and each knows whose responsibility it is to avoid the other. The remainder of the pilots are, of course, maintaining formation on their own group leader.

Three of the Frecce's pilots were amongst the 70 dead and around 400 injured at Ramstein. Sadly the vectors of the crashing aircraft were towards the crowd and that accounted for the large number of fatalities and injuries. The Red Arrows were performing at Leicester and Cowes on that fateful day instead of being scheduled to display at Ramstein although they had displayed there on 13 occasions between 1973 and 1987. The official Red Arrows end-of-season report for 1988 commented thus on the Ramstein accident:

'This accident immediately caused national and international reverberations about display safety and the future of formation and other display flying. It was of immediate concern to the Team since

Farnborough was only a week away and any proposals to forbid the over-flight of spectators would have required such a change to the display sequence as to preclude any further displays for the season. However, high level negotiations and a validation display in front of the Farnborough Safety Committee allowed the Team to display for that week and the remainder of the season within the United Kingdom without change to the sequence.'

More or less immediately after the accident the German Government banned all formation aerobatics, a ban that was still in force on the day I retired. It is difficult to argue with the decision in view of the high number of casualties in Germany. However, some idea of the popularity of air displays in Germany can be obtained from the fact that up until the Ramstein accident the Red Arrows had performed 170 displays in Germany, a number which still, 13 years on, far exceeds the number of Red Arrows displays in any other single overseas country. The last two occasions the Red Arrows were seen performing in Germany were at Cologne on 21 August 1988 and RAF Wildenrath the day after that. It would have been nice to have had British, American, and French formation teams flying over the Brandenburg Gate in Berlin when the Wall came down and the two halves of that beautiful city merged but it was not to be.

A further repercussion following the Ramstein accident was that some other European countries banned all over-flight of the crowd by display aircraft, whether singly or in formation. After much sucking of teeth in high places, the Red Arrows were authorised to continue flying certain over-the-crowd manoeuvres, provided the aircraft were in a stable formation or were diverging from each other. This decision was justified because of the trust the RAF placed in the skills of the Red Arrows pilots. However, the crowd rear arrival was changed so that the aircraft flew overhead at not below 1,000 feet above the ground. That change was no more than a sop to criticism from some quarters; the arrival was flown with all nine aircraft in a stable position relative to each other and there was no collision risk. Increasing the height by 500 feet made no difference whatsoever to the safety of the manoeuvre.

Another manoeuvre where aircraft fly directly towards the crowd is my all-time favourite, the Vixen Break; seven aircraft fly towards the crowd and then break upwards and outwards in what is perceived by many as the Team's most spectacular manoeuvre. The Vixen Break has always been considered safe because each aircraft diverges from all the others but, depending on wind conditions, some individual aircraft used to end up flying over the crowd at low level. There have always been a number of other occasions when some, or all, of the aircraft flew behind the crowd; for example, when the Synchro Pair retire crowd rear after many of their manoeuvres. They do so to gain adequate clearance from the other aircraft and so that the crowds' attention can be focussed by the Commentator on the main section performing crowd front. However, those crowd rear passes are usually flown at least 1,000 feet above the ground and are permissible because they are generally outside the main display area.

The RAF's unilateral decision to allow the Red Arrows to continue flying these particular manoeuvres did not find favour in some overseas countries. In particular the French and Dutch authorities thought the decision was arbitrary and discriminatory and they refused permission for the Red Arrows to continue performing in their airspace. This was particularly sad since the Red Arrows first ever public display had been flown in France.

The week beginning 2 March 1998 was a very traumatic week for the Team. It began with great expectations. The first nine-ship formation practice of the 1998 Season was expected to be flown sometime that week – weather permitting. On the Tuesday afternoon just as Simon Meade was about to start the pre-flight briefing for the final seven-aircraft sortie of the day, he was called by the Adjutant, Warrant Officer John Howard, to talk to the Commander-in-Chief on the telephone. That in itself was quite remarkable. It is very rare for the Boss to be summoned during or immediately before a briefing. Only operational matters relevant to the sortie about to be flown are allowed to interrupt briefings and even very senior officers understand that. The Adjutant had explained to the Commander-in-Chief's aide that a briefing was in progress but the ADC insisted that the Team Leader should come to the phone immediately.

Simon went downstairs to his office to take the call in private. It was not surprising, therefore, that during his absence there was much speculation about the reason for the high-ranking intervention. It just so happened that I was sitting in on that particular briefing with a group of corporate visitors from Breitling, the watch people. The presence of the visitors inhibited the rest of us from trying to guess out aloud the real reason for the interruption but it is fair to say that none of us would have got anywhere near the real reason. It was a good 20 minutes before Simon returned, smiling disarmingly. He continued with the briefing without saying anything to anyone about the telephone call. It was infuriating and Simon knew full well that we were all intensely interested to know what the Commander-in-Chief had wanted to say that was so important that it could not wait until after the sortie. But Simon, always the professional, was more concerned with the job in hand.

I was then off sick for two days and completely forgot about the incident. Late on the Thursday the Manager, Squadron Leader Mike Williams, telephoned me at home. He wanted to know if I would be fit enough to go to work on Friday because the Boss had something to tell me that could not be discussed on the phone. Although I was intrigued, I did not connect this summons with the Commander-in-Chief's call to Simon earlier in the week. I said that I would be there on the following day. I started work on Friday morning at my usual time, just after six-o-clock, and got on with dealing with the ordinary mail and the e-mail that had accumulated during my two-day absence. The time passed quickly as it always did at that time in the morning and by the time Simon arrived at his usual time, about 7.50, I had almost forgotten that I had been asked to come in especially so that he could talk to me. He came into my office and closed the door. That was unusual – my office door was rarely closed.

'The CinC told me on Tuesday that with immediate effect the team is to be reduced from nine to seven,' Simon announced, without any preamble.

I was flabbergasted! 'That's ridiculous,' I said.

'The reason he gave,' continued Simon, with the little smile that I knew so well hovering on his lips, 'is the shortage of Hawk airframes forecast for the next couple of years while the engineers get on with some major work involving the main spar of all the Hawks. It seems the

CinC has a difficulty with letting the Red Arrows keep 13 Hawks while the flying training school at Valley is struggling to keep their training throughput going.

'I told the CinC that we were about to fly our first nine ship practice on Wednesday,' continued Simon. 'Of course, he understands how psychologically important that is – especially for the FNGs. I asked him, in the interests of good morale if nothing else, to let me at least fly the first nine. He agreed – a bit reluctantly I think. I then asked if I could programme a nine-ship practice for Thursday as well – just in case something cropped up to spoil the Wednesday flight. He finally agreed to that as well.'

The Team flew their first nine-ship of the season on the Wednesday and another one the following day. Only after that did Simon tell his pilots of the decision to reduce the Team. Thus, whatever else came to pass, the three first-year pilots in the 1998 Team, Flight Lieutenants Andy Evans, Andy Lewis and Ian Smith, had at least flown twice in a nine-ship formation.

'The CinC told me that he thought it was likely that the seven aircraft Team would continue for up to five years and after that it might be possible to revert to nine.'

'I don't believe it,' I said. 'Once they reduce us to seven aircraft they will never allow us to go back to nine. There will always be a reason to keep us at seven.'

Simon seemed to think that someone at MoD might have already leaked the news to the media but he would not be drawn and I never did get to the bottom of it. Had someone told Simon to tell me that? Was it a veiled suggestion to me that I should leak the news to the press? Surely not – they knew me better than that! Simon merely said he wanted me to be ready with a suitable story in case the media got in touch with me, and they surely would when the local spotters saw the Team practising with seven aircraft again so soon after the first nine ship sorties.

I racked my brains. What story could I put out? The idea of reducing the world famous Red Arrows to a team of just seven aircraft was both humiliating and extremely bad PR for the RAF – and for UK plc. It would reduce the Red Arrows to a second-rate team in the eyes of professional aviators the world over. I thought it highly unlikely that British Aerospace would wish to continue their long association with the Team and that it was probable that there would be no more overseas tours sponsored by British Industry. As for the suggestion that the Team would be restored to nine aircraft a few years down stream – well no-one, but no-one, would believe that.

'If you want my opinion,' I said to Simon after a few seconds thought, 'if the RAF is really so desperately short of Hawk aircraft, I think the Team should be disbanded altogether. At least that way the Red Arrows can go out on a high note.'

'Give the matter some more thought,' said the Boss, rising to leave. 'I've got a lot to do.'

Having spent years working in military intelligence, I always assumed that all my telephone calls were monitored: paranoia maybe, but it was a habit I had got into. I frequently used to make joke comments in the middle of a telephone call to colleagues such as, 'I'll just say that again slowly for the tape.' So, when I spoke to John Turner, the Command Public Relations Officer, about half an hour after Simon had broken the news to me I did so in guarded terms. It immediately became obvious, however, that John knew what I was talking about and that he had already been involved in some sort of briefing at Command HQ. John's immediate advice, when I mentioned a possible leak at MoD, was that we should deny any knowledge of the matter – in other words I was to tell lies, something I have never done in all my time as a PRO. I told him I was not at all happy with that suggestion and he agreed to seek further advice.

The weather on that Friday morning was appalling. There were high winds, low cloud and torrential rain. Further north, at the RAF's flying training school at Linton-on-Ouse in North Yorkshire, there were even sleet and snow showers. The Red Arrows were scheduled to fly an Out-of-Season Practice at Linton but that had to be cancelled because of the inclement weather. This was very convenient and gave us all a little breathing space. Had the weather been suitable for the OSP, it would have been difficult to explain why we had cancelled what is an annual event for that station, much appreciated by staff and students alike. Another piece of good fortune was that, unusually, there were no scheduled visitors to the Team's HQ that day so we did not have to guard against someone accidentally letting the cat out of the bag.

The aircraft remained in the hangar and Simon was able to take time out to interview the three first year pilots individually and at some length. The proposal was for one of the new pilots to remain with the Team and become the Team Manager, thereby allowing the posting of the pilot who had been pre-selected for that post to be cancelled. I was not privy to the discussions but I assume the Leader was discussing with them which two of the three should leave if it came to that. It was hoped that two would be allowed to remain on the Squadron doing odd jobs and then become the new pilots for the 1999 Team – only two being needed for 1999 anyway. That plot would, of course, mean that the 20-plus applicants who had already been through part of the pre-selection procedure, would all be told they had not been selected.

The reduction from a nine to a seven aircraft team would have an important impact on a television company's plans. Walkabout Film and Television, a company based in the West Country, had earlier been given approval to make a fly-on-the-wall video over a 15-month period covering the entire selection process through to the first public display of 1999. I had worked with this company on Red Arrows' projects before and the two directors, David Fitzgerald and Mark Twittey, had become good friends of mine and the Team as a whole. I knew that they had committed a lot of money to their project and already had interviews in the can with quite a few of the pilots who had applied to join the 1999 Team. My problem was that I could not yet tell them that the Team was going to be reduced in size and that much of their material might be wasted.

In the meantime there were other problems that had to be dealt with. Michael Heath, who had recently set up the Red Arrows Merchandising Company, would soon discover that all his Diamond Nine logos and, therefore, lots of his highly popular merchandise, were out of date – but of course I was not allowed to tell him that. There was a problem for the Team Manager: he had completed work on the 1998 glossy brochure which included pictures and mini-biographies of the new pilots. The finished art work was already at the printers, indeed the first print run might already have been made. Finally, and probably the most difficult and time-consuming of all, the Team Leader would have to completely re-design the 1998 display routine on which he had been working for months and which was just about settled.

All things considered, the decision to reduce the Team could hardly have been made at a more difficult time and it appeared, not for the first time, that someone, somewhere, had it in for the Red Arrows. On Friday afternoon of that dark and wintry week, John Turner and I had another guarded conversation. John told me that the most senior civil servant in the Command Secretariat, the group of civil servants that advises the Commander-in-Chief, had decided that we PROs should not tell outright lies. That was very decent of him, I thought! The senior civil servant apparently recommended that, if questioned, I should say something on the lines of, 'Yes, I have heard the story about the Red Arrows reducing from nine to seven aircraft but I'm unable to confirm or deny it since decisions of that nature rest with Ministers.' To my mind that was a lengthy way of saying 'no comment' and passing the buck. I told John that I preferred not to make any reference to Ministers – they were the prerogative of the Ministry of Defence PROs not one at station level. Eventually it was agreed that, if asked about the reduction, I would say that I had heard the story and that I was waiting for further information from our HQ. John and I both knew that if reporters got wind of the story from any source, they would telephone both of us and the Ministry of Defence Press Office to check if we were all putting out the same line. It was all part of the PR game.

Some time on that same busy Friday afternoon a rumour started going around Cranwell which postulated that the whole story about the Red Arrows having to reduce to seven aircraft had been invented to test reactions to the idea within the RAF and amongst the general public. It was even suggested that 'they' actually wanted the story to be leaked to the media to achieve that very aim. A concurrent variant on this rumour said that the decision to reduce to seven had been taken by the full Air Force Board but the air marshals wanted the announcement to be made by the Minister for the Armed Forces, thereby absolving the Air Force Board of all blame! Intriguing thought. What gave rise to those rumours? No-one outside the Red Arrows was supposed even to know that the reduction was being planned. Simon Meade asked me to keep him informed of any media enquiries or other developments over the weekend.

In the meantime I suddenly remembered that I had made some arrangements that would have to be changed. Doug Nicolson, a staff photographer on the Dundee Courier, had been waiting for a photographic trip with the Red Arrows for about six months. He had flown on a couple of air-to-air photographic sorties in F4s from RAF Leuchars, just across the Tay estuary from Dundee, and had sent me some beautiful air-to-air and air-to-ground pictures of Tornados to press his case. I could see that he was an excellent photographer and, having survived a number of sorties in Tornados, he was not likely to be air sick flying in the back of a Red Arrow.

The photographs I distributed to the media and display organisers for pre-season publicity each year were usually taken in Cyprus during the Springhawk detachment and most of them had either a scorched earth background or featured the acres of orange groves just outside the Akrotiri base. We had the photographs taken in Cyprus each year because all nine display pilots were flying together, because the weather conditions were more reliable than in the English spring and therefore likely to produce nicer pictures, and because there was usually a bit of slack in the flying programme to give us the luxury of flying a tenth aircraft around the formation with a visiting professional photographer in the back seat. I had kept putting Doug off during the winter training season until I reckoned the 1998 Team would have started flying nine-ship formations. I wanted to make use of Doug to get a selection of pictures with a UK theme and Simon had readily agreed to lead the nine aircraft over some of the local landmarks and tourist spots. In late February I had telephoned Doug to invite him to fly with the Manager on Monday 9 March and I kept my fingers crossed for good weather. He had readily agreed and said he would drive south on the Sunday ready for a very early start on the Monday.

Although Doug did not know it, that plan had already had to change even before the nine-to-seven bombshell because at short notice Simon was now scheduled to be away from base on that day on other business and that meant the full formation could not fly. I did not want to put off Doug any longer but, because of the imminent reductions and with

Simon away for the day, I agreed with the Engineering Officer's request to utilise only two aircraft, with Doug flying in Red 10's back seat and Wing Commander Dick Johnston flying the second aircraft. That would at least have provided me with air-to-air shots of one red Hawk. However, when he heard of this plan, the Boss decided that it would be an unwarranted nuisance for the ground crew to prepare two aircraft to fly on what would otherwise be a non-flying day. The ground crew had a backlog of work that needed a maximum effort in the hangar so it was reluctantly decided that I would have to cancel Doug's visit. I rang him late on that Friday evening and suggested that he should postpone his trip because there was no longer any possibility of his getting any air-to-air photographs of the Red Arrows. Doug did not seem too put out and I promised that I would keep him at the top of the list of people waiting to fly with the Team and that it might still be possible to fit him in for a sortie before the end of March. Of course, what I did not tell him was that he might be the first photographer to get some pictures of the 'new' seven-aircraft team – that might be his exclusive and would no doubt be adequate recompense for him!

Rather to my surprise I had no calls over the weekend. I rang John Turner first thing on Monday morning and he, too, had had an uninterrupted weekend. Wing Commander Johnston, who was just back from the USA, and the CFS Commandant, who had just returned from a business visit to South Africa, were in conference with the Team Leader. The Team Manager called into my office to tell me that he had put on hold all the 1998 publicity material.

A whole week passed and although many rumours had started to circulate all around Cranwell, there was no official news. We were all a bit mystified that there had been no leaks to the media. I suspect that some of the pilots and ground crew thought that I was failing in my duties for not ensuring that the story had hit the headlines. Perhaps the MoD were disappointed by the lack of leaks? Or was I being too cynical?

The Team Leader did get approval to fly nine for a Red Arrows' Families' Day on Friday 13th. About 80 friends and relations watched an excellent rolling show. Also visiting on that day was a small group from the Classic FM radio station: Susannah Simons, Presenter of the weekly programme 'Masters of Their Art', her Red Arrows-mad 15-year old son

Sebastian, and Producer, Tim Lihoreau. They were recording interviews with the pilots for a one hour programme that I had suggested earlier in the year. I had told the researcher that Flight Lieutenant Andy Evans, Red 2 in the 1998 Team, was an accomplished pianist and bassoon player and had played in the Sussex County Youth Orchestra and I thought it might make a nice change of theme for their programme – after all the Red Arrows are indeed Masters of Their Art. I always wanted to get a photograph of Andy in his Hawk cockpit playing his bassoon 'over the side' – but he would never agree to pose for it. The programme was a great success when it was broadcast on Classic FM later in the year, twice, although in the event it concentrated on Simon Meade rather than Andy Evans. Well, that is the Boss' privilege, I suppose.

On Wednesday 18 March I had a long conversation with Tom Rounds, the RAF spokesman in Defence Press Office in London. He was preparing a brief for the Minister for the Armed Forces about the 'nine to seven' decision. Tom thought that the decision would be rubber-stamped by the Minister but he wanted my views on likely media reaction and how we should handle the inevitable media questions. I said that a form of words had to be found to indicate that the RAF needed the Hawks for pilot training and that we could not justify the use of 13 Hawks by the Red Arrows while the advanced flying training school at Valley was desperately short of aircraft for its daily training programme. It was up to MoD spokesmen to explain why we had got ourselves into that parlous state. I told Tom that whatever we PROs said, the aviation press at home and overseas would have a field day about the worlds' premier aerobatic team being reduced to second-class status. I said that our own local and regional media would certainly give a lot of coverage to the story and that might encourage the national media to follow up the story. National broadsheets would certainly report the news but probably concentrate on the shortage of training aircraft without dwelling too much on the Red Arrows' aspects. The attitude of the tabloids was less certain. I thought the red tops would make a big thing about the Red Arrows being reduced in status in the eyes of the world. The story could run for weeks – well into the display season. I think I worried him – and that was my honest intention!

The very next day, 19 March, Simon told me that the Minister had reprieved the nine for at least a year. I wondered if my advice offered to Tom Rounds had had something to do with that decision. Another edict from our own Command HQ, handed down at the same time as the reprieve, was that with immediate effect the Red Arrows must fly a crowd-front show and that seemed to me to be both vindictive and revengeful.

The decision to fly a crowd front show with immediate effect, and at such a late stage of the winter training, posed serious problems for the Team Leader. The winter training season was virtually over, the first nine-ship formations had been flown, and all that was needed was a few weeks in Cyprus to polish the routine. It was not a simple matter to delete those manoeuvres where aircraft flew over or towards the crowd. Every show routine is an intricate sequence of manoeuvres designed to flow smoothly from one to another in both time and space. If the Team could no longer arrive from crowd rear, it would have to arrive from crowd left or right and that would mean changing the sequence or timing of all the following manoeuvres. The second half of the show would need the most changes: all the Synchro Pair manoeuvres would need re-planning and re-timing and if the Vixen Break could not be flown, some other manoeuvre would have to replace it.

It other words, it would be necessary to design a new show from scratch and that, in turn, would mean reverting to practising with small groups of aircraft before gradually building up once again to nine-ship formations. The past three months of winter training were largely nugatory and it would be several weeks, well into Springhawk, before the Team flew a nine-ship again. Could all that be achieved in time for the Commander-in-Chief to award Public Display Authority in early May or would the start of the season have to be delayed?

There was no arguing with the crowd front order and on the day he received it Simon was sorely tempted to cancel that afternoon's Out-of-Season Practice at Kirton Lindsey, an Army base about 10 miles north of Scampton on a former RAF grass airfield. I persuaded him to fly at least part of the show because I knew there would be a large crowd of army families and local school children to watch what had become an annual pre-season free event. Simon agreed and while the Team were airborne Tom Rounds from the Defence Press Office telephoned me. He wanted to tell me himself the news that the Minister for the Armed Forces had been persuaded by the arguments I had put to Tom the previous day and that it was the Minister who had rescinded the order reducing the Team to seven aircraft. Success for PR! Tom had not heard about the crowd front decision but that was not really his concern. A couple of days later a copy of a minute that had been sent from the Minister's office to the Air Force Board in which it said that the Minister could not agree to the decision to reduce the Red Arrows from nine to seven and that he felt sure there was another solution to the problem of a shortage of aircraft at the flying school at Valley was widely circulated. The minute was unclassified but such documents were not normally circulated at station and squadron level for everyone to read and so I will not reproduce it here.

As I saw it, the two most likely media questions that I would have to answer would be: why have the Red Arrows now fallen into line with most of Europe after holding out for nine years, and, why had it been left almost to the end of the training season to implement these changes? It was only a matter of two or three days before official requests came in for displays in France and the Netherlands so the news had reached the international stage very quickly from one source or another. The locals around Cranwell and Scampton, however, did not notice the crowd front changes as quickly as they would have noticed a reduction to seven aircraft and that gave us a few days grace before I had to answer questions. Once again it was BBC Radio Lincolnshire and the Lincolnshire Echo that heard about the changes first, but neither organisation would tell me what their source was.

As a bit of light relief, I was asked by William Wright, a presenter with BBC Radio Lincolnshire, to help him with an April Fool's story he was preparing. Anything to deflect attention from the crowd front story, I thought, so I was happy to oblige. Accordingly, several times on the morning of 1 April the following news item was broadcast:

'NASA has bought up the airfield at RAF Scampton so that it can be used as an emergency landing strip for the Space Shuttle. A spokesman for NASA explained that the 9,000 foot runway was not long enough. The famous bulge in the A15 trunk road would be moved even closer to the village of Hackthorn to accommodate the extra runway length. There would be some inevitable noise nuisance because the Shuttle would be supersonic when it entered Lincolnshire airspace. Scampton was an ideal airfield because the airfield was now used only by the Red Arrows. Furthermore, if the shuttle crew got into trouble they could aim first for Lincoln Cathedral which was clearly visible from space and had been used during World War Two as a navigation aid by Lancaster crews returning from operations over Germany. Another spokesman speculated that it might be possible for the Red Arrows to formate on the shuttle for a photo opportunity as it came in to land.'

I think the Sunday Sport missed a great opportunity for one of their specials based on this story. Most people recognised this item for what it was but, nevertheless, a few gullible people called the radio station and me to ask for further details.

After that, it was back to the crowd front story. It was eventually decided by the MoD that we would not formally release the story because of the awkward questions it would raise. Instead the PROs were given a question and answer brief we could use should any reporters ask questions. The point about Q & A briefs is that you only answer the specific questions that are asked. I kept my copy close to hand because I knew it would be only a matter of time before someone leaked the story to the media. On 3 April I sent the following message to our Command HQ.

'I have just spoken to Tom Rounds in the Defence Press Office about an enquiry I had this morning from the Deputy News Editor of the Lincolnshire Echo. The Echo man was wondering why we have not been flying very much recently when we normally fly three times a day every day at this stage of the training season. As agreed with you earlier, I explained that the Red Arrows are changing their show to conform with EC regulations and that the Team leader and his pilots needed time to re-organise the routine and to eliminate crowd over-flights. Inevitably the News Editor asked why we are changing the show at this late stage. I referred him to the Defence Press Office for an answer to that!

'NB. The Lincs Echo has asked to send a reporter and photographer to Cranwell on Monday next (06 April) to cover the Team's departure for Springhawk. I have said they are welcome but we can expect more questions then.'

The reporter from the Lincolnshire Echo persevered. He telephoned the Defence Press Office, our Command PRO and me several times. Someone obviously did spill the beans – and it certainly was not me! The Lincolnshire Echo was first off the mark, as far as I am aware, and I answered their reporter's questions straight out of the Q & A briefing notes. They really went to town. The next day the single word headline across five columns was 'BANNED'. Under the headline was a large and superb colour picture of a Vixen Break and under that the story. There was also a World Exclusive tag. It does not happen very often that a regional newspaper can claim a world exclusive!

The Mail had the story next and it seemed to me to be based almost entirely on the Echo's piece. The Mail's headline was, 'Red Arrows lose strings from their bow in safety crackdown.' It continued:

'For more than 30 years the Red Arrows have enthralled crowds with their aerobatics. But a tightening of safety rules means that their most famous stunts will soon disappear from the skies forever. The daredevil pilots have been told that they will have to rewrite much of their programme to meet regulations. Some of their most famous manoeuvres involve them flying over the crowd at low level. Legislation prohibiting certain manoeuvres was introduced in many European countries 10 years ago, but the Red Arrows, regarded as the best in the world, were the only aerobatic team to have a special licence allowing them to caring out the daring stunts. A Ministry of Defence spokesman said: "There was a lot of ill will among other display teams that the Arrows were allowed to perform things that they weren't. All aerobatics are governed by the Civil Aviation Authority, and it was deemed that the RAF could not allow the Red Arrows this special privilege any longer.'

Although the Mail's story was essentially correct, especially the comment about the Red Arrows being the best in the world, there were certain statements in it that did not tell the whole story, possibly because the reporter did not ask the right questions of his source. No-one from the Mail spoke to me at all. The Red Arrows pilots cringe when they hear their manoeuvres described as stunts because the word 'stunt' has an implied suggestion of foolhardiness and the way the story had been written implied that the Red Arrows' displays had not been entirely safe in the recent past. That implication was something that I had been particularly keen to avoid. I was surprised at the statement attributed to the MoD spokesman: I have never heard of any of ill will amongst the other aerobatic teams because of the Red Arrows' waiver to fly certain manoeuvres over, or towards, the crowd.

After that I was inundated with requests for interviews from media outlets all over the country. The Team Leader and I gave both live and recorded interviews with radio stations as far away as Jersey and the Isle of Man. Television stations in the north and the Midlands carried the story and the local BBC television stations re-used gruesome footage from the *Frecce Tricolori*'s 1988 Ramstein accident.

It was particularly galling, certainly for the Team Leader. Introducing a crowd front show in his third and final year would have been his legacy to the Team. By forcing its introduction right at the end of the training season for his second year, it seemed more like compulsion than a legacy. All in all, this whole saga was a good example of how not to handle sensitive PR stories and I was professionally embarrassed that I had to be associated with it.

The Red Arrows flew off to Cyprus for Exercise Springhawk as scheduled on 6 April. However, any stories about the Red Arrows were now of interest to the national press so I was not altogether surprised when, on 9 April, I had another call from an official in the Defence Press Office. An informant, who was known to the Press Office and whom the official described as 'a disgruntled former MoD employee, we know his name but dare not pass it on to you', had allegedly sold a story to the Sun newspaper to the effect that the Chief of the Air Staff had stepped in to prevent the Red Arrows dedicating one of their 1998 manoeuvres to Princess Diana. I was able to tell the MoD spokesman that there was no truth in the story as far as I knew. The MoD man had already checked with the Chief of the Air Staff's office and they had denied the story as well. The official wondered if I could throw any light on the matter. I said there might be two possible reasons for the confusion.

Firstly, at Langkawi in Malaysia on 1 December 1997, nominated as World AIDS Day, the Team Manager in his public commentary during the Red Arrows display dedicated the red Synchro Heart manoeuvre to the memory of Diana, Princess of Wales, in recognition of the work she had done during her life for AIDS foundations around the world. I told the official that the heart manoeuvre was a routine part of the 1997 display and that nothing was altered specially for the event. That dedication had received considerable publicity in the Far East and possibly nearer home. Secondly, someone who had been in our briefing room earlier in the year may have seen the Delta Roll described as Diana Roll on the wall display where the pilots worked out the sequence of manoeuvres. I told the man at the Ministry that the name 'Diana' had been merely a tentative thought at a very early part of the training season as an alternative for what has always before been known as the Delta Roll. The pilots themselves had eventually dropped the idea because they thought it very tacky. There was a third possibility. It could have been a deliberate ploy on the part of the informant to try and sell to the Sun what would have undoubtedly been an eminently saleable story – had it been true.

The national media always like a political angle to any story about the armed services and the Red Arrows are not immune from that sort of treatment. Some years earlier, when Squadron Leader Miller was the Team Leader, there had been several spurious stories about the Tango Roll, a manoeuvre resembling the letter T. One national newspaper declared that the T was for Thatcher and that the manoeuvre was the pilots' tribute to the Prime Minister of the day – the implication, presumably, being that all officers, or at least all Red Arrows, are Conservatives. The next day another newspaper declared that it was a tribute to the Team Leader – Tim Miller. In fact the real reason was much less inventive: 'Tango' is the internationally recognised phonetic pronunciation of the letter T.

Halfway through April I was able to file the following story with the RAF News:

'The Team's Springhawk detachment is now about halfway through. Work on the new crowd front show has been progressing well in the excellent Cyprus weather – quite different from the appalling wintry conditions there have been at Cranwell. Instead of the traditional crowd rear arrival, the Red Arrows will now arrive from crowd left in Big Nine and change into a Diamond loop in front of the crowd. The Team has been practising a new version of the Vixen Break which starts from a point further away from the crowd. This should allow all aircraft to break hard to left and right to avoid them over-flying the crowd. In good weather the Team Leader will pull vertically upwards from the Vixen and then rejoin the others; when the cloud base is too low for that, he will break to the left after the other aircraft on the left have broken.

'The Heart manoeuvre, a real crowd favourite, has been retained for 1998. This year the Heart, formed by Reds 6 and 7, will be "speared" by Red 8 to add variety. One manoeuvre brought back into the show after an absence of several years is the one we call Delta. It is a triangular shape with one of the flat sides leading, formed by Reds 1 to 5 in line abreast. The manoeuvre is called Delta because the shape closely resembles the Greek letter of that name.'

After six weeks of concentrated rehearsals in sunny Cyprus, Air Chief Marshal Sir David Cousins, the Commander-in-Chief, was an audience of one at RAF Akrotiri on 13 May while Squadron Leader Simon Meade led his pilots through the 23-minute display.

'Essentially, I have to consider two things,' said Sir David just before the display. 'First, I must be entirely satisfied that the flying is safe – not just for the pilots but also for the public who will be watching. Then, I have to be satisfied that the display routine itself is up to the very high standard that the public has come to expect of the RAF Aerobatic Team. Only if I am satisfied on both counts will I award the Team's Public Display Authority.'

He was, and he did.

It turned out that the new display was not, as some feared it might have been, less exciting to watch. In fact the reverse turned out to be true. The Team now arrived from crowd left instead of crowd rear. On a clear day the aircraft could be seen running in a good minute before they eventually whooshed overhead, giving Red 10 plenty of time to drum up the excitement. The modified Vixen Break, starting a little bit further away from the crowd than in previous years, was just as exciting as it had always been. There was added excitement to the finale because, just as the seven aircraft in the main section broke upwards and outwards in front of the crowd, the Synchro Pair roared past at low level from opposite ends of the display line. During the year the Team had comments from a huge number of people, including many very senior officers and air display aficionados, saying how brilliant they thought the 1998 display was. Some people even opined that it was been the best display ever. It is certainly a credit to the Leader and his pilots that they were able to design, and then hone to perfection, an entirely new display in five or six short weeks.

The new crowd front show removed the obstacle that had prevented the Team appearing in France and the Netherlands. No sooner had word leaked out about the new show, which was long after the 1998 schedule had been published, than invitations arrived from both countries. It was not possible to fit in the Dutch request for 4 July because the Red Arrows were already scheduled to display at Koksijde in Belgium on that date. However, a deal was worked out by the two display organisers themselves whereby Leeuwarden in Holland was substituted for Koksijde. The Team's programme had a suitable gap on 13 and 14 July and so the French invitation to display at Evreux, just west of Paris, was accepted. It speaks volumes for the Team's international reputation that these invitations were forthcoming so quickly.

Unfortunately whilst taking off from Brize Norton for the transit to Evreux, Flight Lieutenant Dave Stobie, number 6 in a stream of 10 aircraft taking off, had a major bird strike just as his aircraft became airborne and whilst the undercarriage was travelling up. Dave made a split-second decision to put the aircraft back on the ground rather than eject. The aircraft came to rest on the edge of the runway after sliding spectacularly for about 1,000 metres on its belly. It is reported that Dave and his Circus back-seater were seen hugging each other after vacating their aircraft unaided. The Team re-grouped and flew on to Evreux later that same day but arrived too late for the first scheduled display. The following day, French National Day, the Red Arrows gave their 50th display in France, the first since the one at Toulouse on 29 September 1987. Dave's decision to put his aircraft back on the ground rather than ejecting, saved a valuable and irreplaceable aircraft from destruction and he was subsequently awarded a Green Endorsement. The Hawk was back in service with the Team a few weeks later.

23

Flypasts

RED ARROWS' DISPLAYS ARE NOT FREE. Display Organisers have to pay to have the Team at their show. The algorithm for working out the payment is complicated and the details need not concern us, which is just as well because I have never really understood them. The basic principle behind the charges is that the RAF Aerobatic Team is established to give about 100 displays each year and it is a legitimate charge against public funds for the Team to do just that at their home base. Of course there would be little point in putting on all the displays at Scampton or Cranwell and so any costs incurred in displaying away from base should be recovered from show organisers by one means or another.

This principle of show organisers paying for 'extra costs' was established as early as 1966. It is interesting to note that a huge amount of correspondence was generated in the autumn of 1966 when the Command accountants challenged the sum of £99 8s 0d submitted to them by the Red Arrows to cover the costs of hotel bills and other miscellaneous expenses necessarily incurred by the pilots and engineers in Italy accruing from displays in Turin and Pescara. Almost every end of season report contains some comment about the cost of displays and the out-of-pocket expenses incurred by the red-suiters.

In the 2000 Season the cost of a Red Arrows display had risen by inflation to about £6,000, including VAT. That sum is of minor import to the organisers of large, well-attended displays run for commercial gain. At an entrance fee of, say, £15 per head, the organiser needs only 400 extra punters passing through the turnstiles and he has paid for the Red Arrows. These days every organisation that provides a service for the show organiser wants a fee: policing off site, security on site, signposting of approach roads, providing refreshments for the visiting aircrew and support personnel, provision of toilets for the public, clearing up the mess afterwards, not to mention the cost of insurance premiums to cover third party risks. For the organisers of small shows, many of them raising money for local charities, £6,000 just to pay for the Red Arrows may well be more than they can afford. It is not surprising, therefore, that for this reason alone the number of small air shows at which the Red Arrows appear each year is reducing.

It goes without saying that the Red Arrows have to fly from base to the flying displays and back again but if the display location is more than about 80 miles from base, the Team has to land somewhere nearer to the display site to refuel. These transit flights give valuable opportunities for low level flypasts at small village events. The Red Arrows travel in a tidy group, but not necessarily in tight formation, whenever they are flying in sight of the ground so that anyone looking up and seeing them by chance will see a disciplined group of aircraft and not a gaggle. In aircrew parlance, a group of aircraft seen flying in a very loose formation usually brings forth sarcastic chants of 'same way, same day!' The Red Arrows do not want that charge levied at them.

Flypasts are an ideal PR tool because potentially millions of people can see the Red Arrows. The great advantage for those who request flypasts is that they are free. The big disadvantage is that they cannot, or should not, be advertised in advance as a confirmed attraction. Flypasts may be cancelled at the last minute for a whole variety of reasons. We cannot guarantee a flypast will take place until the morning of the event so organisers must be very careful how they advertise them. In particular we tell them that they should never describe a flypast as a display because we, and the many organisers who have transgressed this rule, know that hundreds of people who would not normally go to major air shows will drive long distances to see a Red Arrows' display but they will not do that for a simple flypast. Any organiser who breaks this rule and disappoints the punters is likely to get lots of complaints. That alone would not have worried me too much but, regretfully, many of the disappointed punters assume the failure to appear was the fault of the Red Arrows and then I have to start writing letters of apology.

Complaints and the need to apologise are counter-productive in PR terms.

Surprisingly, politics once got involved in the subject of flypasts. In the late 80s, before I was on the scene, the Team Leader was able to authorise flypasts himself without reference to any higher authority. As long as the proposed flypast could be achieved without deviating far from the planned transit route on the particular day requested, then he could go ahead because no additional expense to the RAF would be incurred. Story has it that one weekend the Red Arrows were transiting back to Scampton from a display in Scotland and en route, by request, they made a low level flypast over a golf course in the north west of England where an important competition was being played. The same day the Team Leader declined to fly past a miners' gala in the north east of England because to have done so would have required a large deviation from the planned route, resulting in perhaps 10 or 15 minutes being added to the flight time. Later someone complained officially that it was typical of the Red Arrows to bypass a miners' gala and choose instead to fly past a golf club. Although the complaint was not justified, ever since then flypast proposals have to be approved in advance by the RAF Participation Committee who are, presumably, deemed to be less politically partisan than the Red Arrows. What nonsense and what a lot of extra and unnecessary work that decision has caused.

During the display season there are more letters and other communications on the subject of flypasts than on almost any other topic and over the years, as more and more people learned about free flypasts, it become a major task dealing with them all. Early in 1998 the Team Leader, Simon Meade, had what seemed a great idea for reducing the amount of administration involved in organising flypast requests while at the same time exploiting the possibilities to the full. I drafted for Simon the following letter which was sent out to the Chief Executive of every County Council or equivalent body in the whole of the United Kingdom.

'Let me, please, introduce myself and then explain why I am writing this unsolicited letter to you. I am Squadron Leader Simon Meade and 1998 is my second year leading the Royal Air Force Aerobatic Team The Red Arrows. Each year we fly upwards of 80 displays at locations covering the length and breadth of the United Kingdom. For full displays we are tasked by an organisation known as the RAF Participation Committee; most large show organisers already know how to go about requesting displays, so I will not dwell on that aspect. However, a lot of people do not realise that when the Team is in transit between two locations we can often plan to carry out flypasts at smaller events such as village fetes, carnivals, and local and regional sporting events. In a typical year we already provide many such flypasts. Quite a few wily organisers have learned the knack of organising their events on dates when they know we will be passing close by. I believe that given advance information about such local events we could carry out even more flypasts, thereby allowing more people to see the Team in the air. I am hoping to enlist your aid in obtaining this information.

'First of all I must define "flypast" so that there can be no confusion with "display". In this context, the 9 or 10 Red Arrows' Hawks would make one straight flypast over the desired location at a height of about 1,000 feet above the ground, trailing white smoke for greater visual impact whenever possible. To reassure people who may be disturbed by low-flying operational aircraft in your area, it is worth pointing out that 10 Hawks flying over at moderate speed, 1,000 feet above the ground, make considerably less noise than a single front line high speed jet such as the Tornado or Harrier.

'Unlike full displays, there is no charge for flypasts but, because of that, there are certain limitations on which bids we may accept. To avoid increasing our fuel bill, the desired location for the flypast must be reasonably close to the route already planned as part of our annual display programme. I have to ensure that flypasts obey the official rules for low level flight, and that precludes any flypasts over, for example, noise sensitive areas. In fact, although for most of the time we routinely transit over the sea or open countryside, we do frequently have to pass close to villages and recreational areas that might be the venue for the sort of events I have mentioned. No guarantee can be given to event organisers in advance that the Red Arrows will turn up; for example, if a full display is cancelled, any associated flypast will also be cancelled. To avoid disappointing people, event organisers should, therefore, be careful not to state in any publicity material they may issue that the Red Arrows will definitely fly over and they should use the word flypast rather than display. On the day of the proposed flypast, the event organiser would be told whether the flypast was to take place and at the same time he would be given an accurate time and the direction from which the Team would approach.

'The 1998 Display Programme is still being put together but it is not too early to start looking out for events close to well-known Red Arrows' routes. The Team regularly travels from our base at Cranwell in Lincolnshire northwards towards Scotland, across the Midlands and East Anglia towards the west country and the south coast, and over the Pennines towards Wales, north west England and the Isle of Man. It is, therefore, relatively easy to plan our transit routes to pass close to most parts of the country.

'The first display in the UK this year is likely to be on 23 May, and the last one on 20 September. If the idea appeals to you, would you please ask one of your staff to keep a look out for events in your area between those dates where a Red Arrows' flypast might be welcomed by the organiser. You can then either pass the details to me or you may prefer to talk to the organiser and invite him or her to write to me.'

Almost all of the Chief Executives replied to the letter and most passed copies to other departments within their administrative areas, especially the tourist offices and PR people. The results were not what either Simon or I expected. We had intended to send a display list to all the areas that showed an interest. Instead, within days letters started flooding in with long lists of events in various counties, boroughs, towns, villages and hamlets and we had to wade through them all to see whether or not we would be able to make a flypast within our parameters. It was a nightmare but the exercise served to prove what a great attraction the Red Arrows are. In subsequent years, we targeted our letters once we had a firm display list to work with and that saved a lot of wasted effort and disappointment.

Surprisingly often we fly unexpectedly over important events but we only know about these serendipitous flypasts if someone writes in to tell us about them. Almost every year we hear of a wedding we have flown over, often as the happy couple are posing for photographs after the ceremony. In 1998 we flew over two weddings in North Wales in a single

30-minute sortie just as the happy couples were having their photographs taken. We have letters from both couples expressing their gratitude. I also had a very moving letter from a lady who told us that we flew over the cliffs at Sidmouth just as she was consigning her father's ashes to the deep.

'Although Dad was not in the RAF, he was a bugler in the Duke of Cornwall's Light Infantry,' wrote the lady, 'your flypast was like a tribute to him for all that he had done for his country in his lifetime and through the Second World War.'

We once flew over a Christening party just as '30 children and 40 adults were celebrating in the garden,' wrote the Father. 'We all love the Red Arrows and we were delighted by this unexpected flypast. You can do it again any time you like – but not too soon because I can't afford another Christening just yet!'

A few years back the Team flew over a funeral ceremony in the Peak District just as a keen Red Arrows' fan was being lowered into his grave. His widow wrote to thank the Red Arrows for that 'great honour' and wondered who had arranged it. The Red Arrows were on their way back to base from a public flying display and so it was just luck – or was it really an Act of God as the lady herself suggested?

The Lady Captain of a golf club in the Peak District wrote to thank us for the beautifully timed flypast over the 19th Hole just as she was being presented with a gift by the members at the end of her year of office. That, too, was pure good fortune although it is well known that Red Arrows' pilots are very keen on the game. It is not true, by the way, that a decent golf handicap is an essential pre-requisite for selection for the Team but, nevertheless, pilots with low handicaps do seem to do quite well at interview!

Some requests are a bit over the top. An event organiser in Blackpool thought it would be a good idea to have the Red Arrows flying down the Promenade from opposite ends of the beach at Midnight on the final night of the celebrations of the 50th anniversary of the post-war Blackpool Illuminations. He thought it would be good if the aircraft fired red, white and blue flares because he knew the coloured smoke would not show up very well at midnight. Another request for a night flypast came from a chap in Essex who wanted the Red Arrows to fly over his private

Millennium Party at Midnight on New Year's Eve. He seemed quite surprised when I said the pilots had better things to do at that time on that particular night!

In 1992 the Team broke one of their own rules. Normally they will not fly special formation shapes however important the occasion or whoever makes the request. The reason for this is that it takes time to practise a new shape and time costs money. You cannot just draw the shape on a briefing board and then go out and fly it. The RAF gave permission for the Team fly a figure 1 formation to mark the 25th anniversary of BBC Radio 1. In the Leader's back seat would be Noel Edmunds and he would be transmitting live on air as the Team passed over major towns and villages in the 50 minutes or so it would take to fly between London and Edinburgh. The idea was that people tuned into Radio One would nip outside and see the Red Arrows as they flew over.

The Team took off from Odiham at 0746 hrs and set course for central London. Unfortunately, shortly after taking off, the Team found themselves flying in brilliantly clear conditions but over a thick layer of fog. As they approached London the only thing visible was the top few hundred feet of Canary Wharf. The Team persevered northwards but found themselves flying over fog or low cloud most of the way to Scotland. Noel did his inserts into the radio programme but no-one saw the Red Arrows. The Team had intended to land at RAF Leuchars on the east coast but bad weather there forced them to divert to Prestwick on the other side of Scotland.

There was a bit of a do at Brixham in South Devon in August 1998. The Red Arrows made a flypast over the Leonard Cheshire Home at the request of one of the residents to celebrate the 50th anniversary of their foundation by Group Captain Lord Leonard Cheshire VC, one time CO of 617 Squadron after the Dams' Raid. The flypast was flown on a routine transit flight from Cranwell to St Mawgan. The staff and residents at the home were treated to a great spectacle in fine weather and, so we were told, raised their champagne glasses in salute as the Hawks flew past. Unfortunately, a couple of miles away across Torbay at Paignton, another group of people were also celebrating the same 50th Anniversary at a civic event. They had been told by someone that the

Red Arrows would be flying over their event and the local newspaper, in all innocence, had published the story and given the times and direction of flight. There were, apparently, thousands of people on Paignton beach watching at the appointed time but all they saw were the Red Arrows flying from left to right across the bay two miles out to sea. It looked to them as though the Red Arrows had missed their target and that is exactly the story that all the local newspapers printed. It all goes to prove that PR can so easily go wrong through no fault of the PRO!

In November 1998 four of the Red Arrows made a flypast for a 16 year old's funeral in Cranwell village. He had died suddenly and had been a great fan of the Reds, although we did not know it. Normally the Red Arrows cannot do anything public when they are out of season without getting special permission. However this request could be granted because the funeral cortege was timed to arrive at the church at the start of a normal training sortie when the Team were on their way to Scampton. Half an hour later, quite unknowingly, the four aircraft flew over another funeral in nearby Ruskington village on the way back to Cranwell. Both families were very grateful.

Another highly successful flypast was that of the still unfinished Millennium Dome at Greenwich on 26 June 1999. The Team needed special permission to fly at low level over central London but this was granted because the Dome was big news at that time. The flypast duly took place when the Red Arrows were en route to Biggin Hill, positioning for an air display. They flew at 1,000 feet above the ground at a speed of 400 mph. I publicised the route widely in advance – from the M25 junction at Swanley direct to the Dome – and millions of people must have seen us. The Team photographer, Colin Searle, got some excellent pictures from his vantage point in the back seat of Red 10 and his work was seen in newspapers, magazines and show brochures all over the world.

The Red Arrows were delighted and honoured to be tasked with another series of flypasts over Central London, this time for the Royal Military Tattoo 2000, which coincided with the 100th birthday celebrations for our Commandant-in-Chief, the Queen Mother. The Red Arrows took off from Cranwell each evening at 2052. There were two flypasts each evening, the first at 2110, the second one 5 minutes later. After passing over Horse Guards Parade from north to south, Andy Offer led the nine Hawks around a large teardrop pattern south of the Thames to pass over Horse Guards Parade again from south to north. The formation returned to Cranwell following the same route as they had used southbound. In a bid to forestall low flying and noise complaints, I publicised widely in advance through the Internet and all the local media covering towns and places on the low level routes, the exact route and times that the Team would be flying at low level. The aircraft landed back at Cranwell at 2132, almost at last light. On one night the Chief Constable of Lincolnshire, Richard Childs, formerly with the Metropolitan Police, flew with Red 2 so that he could have an elevated and unusual view of his old patch.

I received only two complaints. Both came from near Nuthamstead, Hertfordshire, one of the waypoints on both the southbound and northbound runs. The first came on the fourth night and was resolved when I telephoned the complainant. He wanted to know what was going on because his young children had been woken up several nights running. I told him, and explained that there would be two further disturbed nights. He was completely happy with that. The second complaint was a written one asking what we were doing at that time of night. I wrote to that man and sent him a pile of brochures and other gizzits and heard nothing more.

24

Frequently Asked Questions

As I GET TOWARDS THE END OF THIS BOOK I find that I have not got around to answering some of the frequently asked questions about the Team. In view of the popularity of the Red Arrows, it is not surprising, perhaps, that large numbers of people are fascinated by those little gems of knowledge that are usually known, deprecatingly, as trivia. I know of one person who had been accepted by BBC TV to appear on Mastermind with the Red Arrows as his specialist subject. That person was trying to extract from me every little fact and figure about the Team, but the BBC discontinued the programme before he could make his appearance. Here are the answers to just a few of the FAQs and some small items of trivia.

A lot of the most frequently asked questions relate to weather conditions and the different types of show the Team can fly to take account of the weather. As I mentioned earlier in the book, the Red Arrows have three variants of their show, the full, rolling and flat. People sometimes ask if the pilots fly lower when the weather is bad. The answer is a definite no! The base height of the display is the same irrespective of the weather conditions. However, when the weather is bad people on the ground sometimes get the impression that the aircraft are flying lower than normal. This is usually due to aural and optical illusions. Low cloud reflects the aircraft noise downwards and by adding to the noise coming directly to your ears can make the display seem noisier than usual. Similarly, a low cloud base acting as a backdrop to the display rather than the limitless blue sky gives the visual impression that the aircraft are lower than normal.

Sometimes the Team has to call off a display at the very last minute because the weather is worse than the minimum conditions required for a flat show. The Team Leader will always leave his decision to the last possible minute to avoid disappointing the spectators. Very occasionally, if the weather conditions are reported as being marginal, the Team Leader will decide to fly to the show and have a look for himself. This accounts for the odd occasion where the Team makes a single fly past and then disappears for good; a case in point was the Dartmouth display I mentioned earlier. The Team Commentator on the ground should make it clear over the public address system exactly what the Team is doing. I was often asked why the Red Arrows do not offer some sort of limited display in really poor weather instead of simply not turning up. A variant of that question is why two, three or four aircraft do not give a display when the weather is too bad for all nine. The answer to both questions is that the Team has devoted all winter to working up for a nine-aircraft display and that is the display they were authorised to perform in public when the Commander-in-Chief awarded Public Display Authority on Red Suit Day. Any variations from that routine would not only be illegal but could be dangerous due to lack of planning and practice. In any case, people expect to see all nine aircraft and would feel cheated if only a small number performed. If the weather is sufficiently poor to prevent even a flat show, individual Hawks would be able to do only straight flypasts and that would not be very interesting for the spectators.

In order to answer a question from a member of the media shortly before I retired, I had to do something that I had been meaning to do for a long time. I used the best information available to me to work out how many people have watched the Red Arrows since their first public display back in 1965. There is no completely reliable way of working out an exact figure because no-one kept those sorts of records. However, based on such records as there are, and by using a bit of judicious interpolation, I conservatively estimate that over 350 million people have seen the Team in action, either at one of the formal displays or at one of the hundreds of flypasts the Team has made. No-one has ever challenged my figure so I think you can accept it as the official answer.

There are all sorts of claims about the number of spectators who have watched the Red Arrows at various air shows. We have on record official estimates of 800,000 at Edwards Air Force Base, USA, on 14 May 1983, and 650,000 at both Lisbon, Portugal, on 13 June 1973, and at the start of the Tall Ships Race at Whitburn Bay, North East England, on 10 August 1991. Nowadays it is common to claim even larger figures. It was officially estimated that well over one million people watched the Red Arrows over the weekend of 24/26 May 1997 at each of the air shows at Southend and Mildenhall – but there were two displays at each location.

Islamabad, capital of Pakistan, literally ground to a halt on 24 November 1997 when the Red Arrows displayed over a city centre recreational area to honour the 50th anniversary of both the country and the Pakistan Air Force. Traffic was grid-locked for miles around; one police superintendent unofficially estimated that half a million people were crammed into the park and surrounding areas, including me, but there were countless thousands of others trapped in their vehicles.

So much for large crowds but what about the smallest crowd? Well, that is a bit embarrassing for the organiser, and the town concerned, so I will not reveal the exact location. It was a well-known seaside resort – it still is a well-known seaside resort but you know what I mean! To avoid the Hawks having to fly over the town centre, the organiser had arranged for the display to be centred on a beautiful and popular stretch of beach a few miles south of the town. Unfortunately, he forget to mention that in his publicity handouts. The day of the display was bitterly cold, wet and windy, not the sort of day when people would normally stand around on the beach except to watch the Red Arrows. However, when Red 10 arrived to set up for his commentary, to his surprise he found the beach virtually deserted. There was no sign of the organiser and certainly the expected Public Address system to relay the commentary was nowhere to be seen. The Commentator was quite sure that he was in the right place on the right day. The Red Arrows were already en route so as soon as two-way radio contact had been established he called the Team in to start the display on schedule. As the minutes ticked by a few beachcombers gathered around and one or two other folk, walking their dogs, stopped momentarily to see what was going on. The total number of spectators at the location was under 100 even at the end of the 22 minute display – but there were sizeable crowds in the town centre wondering why the Red Arrows were just specks on the horizon.

The 1995 Season, the Team's 31st, was the busiest ever in terms of displays flown – 150. It was also the longest season stretching as it did 10 months from the first display, at Akrotiri on 24 April 1995, to the final one, at Bangkok on 13 February 1996 on the way home from Australia and Singapore. The 1997 European Season produced the lowest number of displays, 64, since 1975 when there were only 56 displays because of a fuel crisis. The low number in 1997 was caused almost entirely by bad weather, not any diminution in interest. The first year the Team gave over 100 public displays was in 1973 when they performed 103 times. There were over 100 displays in every year from 1976 to 1985 inclusive.

The 1999 Team was composed entirely of pilots of single-seat aircraft – Jaguars and Harriers – the first year there had been no pilots from multi-seat aircraft on the Team. Squadron Leader Andy Offer, who led the Team in 2000 and 2001, was the youngest ever Team Leader – he was still only 33 when he took command in December 1999.

Can I have a trip with the Team? The Red Arrows get about 100 such requests each year asking to fly with either the Team on a display or in a single Red Arrows' Hawk. The letters are often ingenious, often very touching, and mostly written on behalf of someone else. The back seat of a Hawk during a Red Arrows' flying display is no place for an unqualified passenger. In any case, if we gave one person a ride, we would be inundated with requests from others.

Before flying in a fast jet aircraft all crew and passengers must pass a stringent RAF medical examination: there are no exceptions to this rule. The Hawk, like any other fast jet aeroplane, is potentially dangerous unless you have learned all the emergency drills and can carry them out instinctively with 100% accuracy. What is the point of sitting on a rocket-powered ejection seat if you do not know how to use it? All aircrew take out special life and accident insurance policies to cover military flying risks: civilian passengers would not have this and any existing policies they had would probably be invalid. On top of all that, if we gave a trip to one civilian we would have to do it for everyone else and there simply would not be enough sorties in the year. So please do not write in asking for a trip, however good you think your case might be. A couple of years ago we rejected an offer of £10,000 to a charity of our choice in exchange for a trip with the Red Arrows. Any such request offering donations has to be turned down because it would be seen by the media as a rich person buying a trip.

I was very peeved with a free-lance writer who had one of the strictly-rationed media trips with the Red Arrows. He wrote an excellent article which was printed in the Observer magazine in August 1999 and re-printed in many overseas newspapers and magazines. It was just the sort of publicity I wanted – right up until the final paragraph. After writing eloquently about the excitement he had had during the aerobatic manoeuvres he added, 'Readers craving the same sensation might like to know that the Red Arrows do offer flights to some civilian enthusiasts who write in. Would I recommend it? You bet.'

Wrong! We do not offer flights but that did not stop several hundred people writing to me asking for one. If the public cannot have a trip with the Team, how is it that media people can? There are three sorts of media trip: flights for celebrities; flights for specialist photographers; and flights for newspaper, radio and television reporters. Celebrities are usually invited by the MoD to fly with the Team because of the good PR that should accrue afterwards. In my time Jason Donovan, Noel Edmunds, Richard Branson, Nigel Mansell, Eddy Irvine and David Jason, amongst others, flew with us. Specialist photographers are often not known to the general public but both Lords Lichfield and Snowden have flown with us as have John Dibbs, Katsuhiko 'Kats' Takunaga, Chris Bennett and E J van Koningsveld, all of whom are well-known in the specialist aviation world for their superb photographs. Newspaper, radio and television reporters have to make out a good case for having a trip. How are they going to report it; where will their material be published or shown? All requests are carefully considered and we treat each case on its merits. However, whoever they are, the rules I explained earlier apply.

I was often asked how low the aircraft fly. There is no secret to this; the limits are laid down in the Team's Standard Operating Procedures. Manoeuvres in front of and parallel to the crowd can be flown down to

200 feet. The Synchro Pair are allowed down to 100 feet in straight and level flight in front of and parallel to the crowd line. Inverted flight by the Synchro pilots is not below 150 feet above the ground. The limits may not always have been strictly enforced in the early years but they are now!

Occasionally people ask me if the Red Arrows' flying is dangerous. I would have hoped no-one would ask that question because the answer seems obvious to me. If it were dangerous, the Team would not do it. There is, of course, an element of danger in any form of flying but the type of flying carried out by the Red Arrows is not inherently dangerous. The pilots have been selected for their above average flying skills and they are all highly proficient at formation flying before they get anywhere near selection for the Team. Some of the Synchro Pair's manoeuvres in the second half of the show may look dangerous but that is showmanship, the art of making a perfectly safe manoeuvre look exciting.

Now for some of the really trivial items for those who like that sort of thing.

One man in Austria sent us an e-mail asking us to settle an argument about whether the Red Arrows are American, French or English. In another e-mail, a 20 year old in Brazil asked if we would pay for him to come over and visit the Team. Then there was one from a bee-keeper in Lincolnshire who said that he enjoyed watching us but we would please keep our aircraft away from his bees. The most poignant e-mail came from Scampton village, on the very edge of the base: a blind man told us how much he enjoys sitting out in his garden listening to the Red Arrows practising overhead while his wife provides the commentary.

Within hours of a Red Arrows display in Amman, Jordan, in 1966, a British businessman received an order from a Jordanian company for 1 million Christmas cards featuring the Red Arrows. Surprising perhaps in a predominantly Muslim country.

The C-130 Hercules was first used as support aircraft for the Red Arrows in 1970. Before that the Argosy, often known as the whistling wheelbarrow, had been used.

The black and white cine film used by the Team to record displays in the early years was available only from the USA. In 1971 a lengthy postal strike in the USA eventually deprived the Team of any film and so most of the work-up period was flown without the benefit of film for debriefings. It was recommended that video replace film in future. Video was introduced in 1972 and has been used ever since. Digital video cameras and recorders have been in use since 2000.

1972 was the first year that a week's leave in August for the Team was introduced even though it meant cancelling a number of shows. A week's leave in August is now seen as an essential break and major display organisers plan around it.

The Team moved from Kemble to Scampton in the Spring of 1983 but mail addressed to the Red Arrows at Kemble is still, in 2001, being received by the Postmaster at Cirencester and faithfully forwarded. One letter reached my desk addressed simply 'Red Arrows Ellen One'. RAF Scampton's postcode is LN1.

For a while during the summer of 1983 the Red Arrows operated from RAF Barkston Heath near Grantham while their new accommodation at Scampton was being built. Not a lot of people know that.

The famous photograph of the Red Arrows flying in formation with Concorde over the QE2 was taken by Arthur Gibson in 1985. There is no point in writing to the Red Arrows asking where you can get a copy, although many people do. An original signed print is now worth a considerable sum of money. If I knew where a copy was to be had, I would not tell anyone!

The first time the Red Arrows deployed to Cyprus in the Spring was in 1980. The intention was then, and is now, to find good weather for the concentrated work up period. The first time the detachment was called Springhawk was in 1985 but the detachment was still arranged on an 'as required' basis. It was not until 1986 that Springhawk was officially recognised as a necessary annual training detachment.

Why do the Red Arrows fly the Hawk? The Red Arrows have always flown whichever aircraft is in service as the RAF's advanced jet training aircraft, currently that is the British Aerospace Hawk or, to be accurate, I should now write BAE SYSTEMS Hawk. From 1965 until 1979 the Red Arrows flew the Folland Gnat, the Hawk's predecessor. The idea of utilising front line operational aircraft for formation aerobatic display teams was dropped in the early 1960s on the grounds of cost; that was the main reason why a single RAF Aerobatic Team was established and all individual squadron aerobatic teams were disbanded. The 2,000[th] public display in the British Aerospace Hawk was flown on 11 May 1999 at Deblin in Poland.

Why do the pilots shout at each other on the radio? A lot of people use scanner receivers at air shows to listen in to what is going on. It is quite difficult talking normally when you are subjected to high g forces so there is a natural tendency to shout. However, when the pilots know that the Commentator is re-broadcasting the Team's radio chat over the public address system, the pilots sometimes exaggerate the shouting to make it sound more exciting. Actually, come to think of it, they shout at each other all the time! By the way, if you have scanning equipment that can transmit on the Red Arrows' radio frequencies, do not do it! Some idiots do. It is not only illegal, it is highly dangerous: at best you will distract the pilots; at worst you could blot out a vital transmission. In the same vein, if you are a private pilot and think it would be a jolly good wheeze to formate on the Red Arrows as they pass by in transit, or even during a display, think again. I find it incredible that some pilots still try to do that. All such instance are reported to the Civil Aviation Authority and the offenders are almost always traced by following them on radar to their destination.

Incidentally, if you decide to go in for Mastermind after reading this book, please do not write to me asking for help unless you enclose a cheque. For a start I am now retired and, in any case, I have it in mind to offer my services as the setter of specialist questions to the Discovery Channel who have recently resurrected the Mastermind programme.

25

Back Home

ONCE MY 64TH BIRTHDAY HAD PASSED in 1999, I started reminding the Team Leader and Wing Commander RAFAT that the time was approaching when they ought to start considering my replacement. Not that I anticipated they would have any difficulty in replacing me, I was not that indispensable, but I thought they should be made aware of the various options and have time to consider them. I could, of course, have been replaced by another Retired Officer and had I done nothing to prompt consideration of who my successor should be I imagine that an RO would have been appointed. I knew of a couple of officers, one still serving but about to become an RO and another already an RO, who were keen on taking over from me.

As I said right at the beginning of this book, ROs like me, approaching final retirement, were supposed to protect their appointments by ensuring that the job specifications were written, and if necessary re-written, in such a way that the posts could only be filled by retired officers. I had always been clear in my own mind that I would not get involved in such a restrictive practice. It may sound pompous and sanctimonious but throughout my long RAF career I had always believed that if job specifications were to be of any value they should be properly drawn up. The right and proper way of going about it was to decide what the job entailed, then write the specification to reflect the requirements and only then decide what manner of person would be best fitted for the job. That was something else that Clutcher Sutton had taught me back in 1962 when I was the Adjutant on his squadron.

I may be thought ungrateful, and I often felt rather ungrateful when considering other options, but I had gradually come around to the view that the best sort of person to be the Red Arrows' PRO in the new millennium, which of course really started on 1 January 2001 as we had been taught at school 50 years earlier, was someone who was professionally qualified in media work. Regularly I used to joke with Team members that my replacement should be young, pretty and female. The fact is that in my last couple of years or so the job changed out of all recognition and I, even I, found it difficult to accept the changes. Instead of simply getting on with issuing a news release telling the media what we wanted to tell them, now before writing the release or offering a facility to the media we first have to define the message that we are trying to put across. Is it a 'force for good' or is it 'aid to the community' or the 'RAF defending UK interests' or some other esoteric objective? Everything we Corporate Communication(s) Officers want to do has to be 'on message' and capable of slotting into a neat pigeon hole. If I want to invite my local media to come and meet the new pilots, as I did at the start of every new training season for 11 years, I am supposed to consider what the message is that I am endeavouring to put across. To my simple mind the message is that we are introducing the new pilots to the public – and the media certainly never need any further inducement to turn up.

In the middle of March 2000 I had a couple of telephone calls from reporters at the Mail on Sunday. An 'RAF source' had apparently told them that the Red Arrows were flying off to Cyprus the next day because they had invented a new corkscrew manoeuvre that was so dangerous that the pilots needed to practice it in secret in Cyprus. I was intrigued. Although there was absolutely no truth in the story the newspaper was entitled to follow up their information and I was interested to find out the basis for it. I thought at first that the manoeuvre in question was the Corkscrew which had been around for several years, but it soon became apparent from the reporter's description that the story referred to a new manoeuvre called, provisionally, Mirror Image Barrel Roll, in which the two Synchro aircraft start off from crowd right with Red 6 inverted close over the top of Red 7. The two aircraft then fly a synchronised slow barrel roll which means that Red 6 has negative g applied all the way round. Only experienced pilots can really appreciate the difficulty of flying such a manoeuvre and the pleasure that it can give to the pilots executing it. The tip-off to the Mail on Sunday could only have come from someone who had been watching the Red Arrows practise overhead Scampton but that someone did not know what he, or she, was talking about. I explained to the reporter that the Red Arrows go to Cyprus every year in Spring for final polishing of the new season's display routine and that there was nothing secret about that.

'All our manoeuvres require skilled pilots,' I said. 'There's nothing dangerous about the Mirror Image Barrel Roll, it just happens to be a brand new manoeuvre – one that your informant has presumably never seen before and doesn't understand.'

By this time it was common knowledge amongst the media and the general public, but not officially announced, that the Red Arrows would be returning to Scampton sooner rather than later. All that remained to be decided was the date. Off the record those within the Red Arrows knew that the move could not take place before the Spring of 2001 because the essential works services needed at Scampton could not be completed any earlier and there were other associated unit moves into and out of Cranwell and other nearby stations that were financially interdependent. From the Red Arrows' point of view there were only two periods in each year when a move was practicable: one was in the three-week end-of-season leave period in October and the other was in April when the Team was away on Springhawk. Trying to move during the display season would be very disruptive operationally and very awkward for the families. Trying to move when the winter training season was already underway would create huge problems for the engineers because that is the time when a lot of scheduled maintenance is carried out on the aircraft. Heavy ground servicing equipment and the bulk store of spare parts cannot be in two places at the same time and having to split resources between Cranwell and Scampton would be very expensive in terms of both manpower and time.

A few days after talking to the Mail on Sunday, I heard that the Minister for the Armed Forces, John Spellar, would be making an informal visit to the RAF College at Cranwell on 29 March. Such a visit was not all that unusual in itself; Ministers and other government officials regularly visit the College. What was a little unusual was that the Minister had decided to give a press conference at the end of his visit.

When a Minister decides to give a formal press conference, rather than an off-the-cuff Q and A session, it is usually because he has something to announce. Because the Red Arrows belong to the Central Flying School and not to the RAF College and since the Red Arrows were away in Cyprus on Springhawk, it was assumed that the Minister's visit was nothing to do with the Team. It had also been assumed in London, naively in my view, that the media would obediently confine their interest to the subject of the Minister's visit and not ask any questions about the Team. How wrong could the advisors be?

As soon as I heard the plans, I advised the Command Public Relations Officer, now renamed Head of External Communications, that whatever the Minister intended talking about during his visit to Cranwell, the media would have questions on only one subject. The Minister would need to be forewarned about this otherwise it could be very embarrassing for him. My colleagues agreed with my assessment and a friend in the Defence Press Office in London subsequently assured me that the Minister had been briefed accordingly. Someone then advised the Minister that if he really wished to come to Lincolnshire it would be better to move his press conference to Waddington. Presumably, the person who briefed the Minister thought that Waddington, a station in RAF Strike Command, was far removed from Cranwell when in fact it is less than 10 miles away – and even closer to Lincoln where most of the local media have offices and studios.

Rumour Control went into top gear when word reached the media that the Minister was going to Waddington and would be hosting a press conference. Without exception they all assumed that Mr Spellar would announce that the Red Arrows would be moving back to Scampton and for once the rumours were correct. We public relations officers were provided with an advance copy of the speech that the Minister intended delivering at the press conference – in fact, over three or four days leading up to the visit we were provided with several different versions of what the Minister would say, the last one having 'This is the FINAL, FINAL version!' scrawled across it in handwriting. The frequent changes to the text concerned the details of why Scampton was being reopened and the justification for that decision, not the fact that the station was being reopened. All PROs were warned that there was to be no discussion or speculation about the date of the Red Arrows' move and I made sure all the Red Arrows' personnel at home and in Cyprus were briefed accordingly. There was an embargo placed on the speech; it was not to be released until 1330 hrs on the day of the Minister's visit, that is to say 15 minutes after he had delivered his speech. I later learned that the media had also been issued with advance copies of the Minister's speech with a similar embargo placed on it.

BBC TV Leeds in their early news broadcasts on the morning of the press conference trailed the story but, wisely, used expressions such as 'the Minister is expected to announce.....' Nevertheless, their first morning local news bulletin at 6.25 am led on the story of the Reds' return using a package recorded the evening before outside RAF Scampton's main gate and which included library footage of the Red Arrows flying at Scampton. BBC Radio Lincolnshire was off the mark even earlier; they referred to the story in their half-hourly news broadcasts from 5am onwards. The radio reports included the words, 'If the Minister announces that the Red Arrows will move to anywhere other than Scampton it will be a very great surprise.'

I went to Waddington to help out the Station's Community Relations Officer by meeting and greeting the media – most of whom were, of course, well known to me. There was a very large crowd, including representatives from BBC Radio Lincolnshire, Lincs FM, the local independent radio station, the Lincolnshire Echo, the Sleaford Standard, Carlton Central TV from Nottingham, Yorkshire TV and BBC TV from Leeds, BBC TV from Nottingham, and various freelance reporters and photographers representing regional and national newspapers. There was also a staff reporter from the Daily Telegraph who was travelling with the Minister. Everyone wanted to be in on the act. I had not seen such a large crowd of photographers, cameramen and reporters since the Russian Knights arrived at Scampton in the dying days of the Soviet Union. We all congregated in the Station Operations Room from about 1300 hrs to await the Minister's arrival. The question most of the media asked me and the RAF Waddington hosts before the Minister arrived to make his statement was, 'Why has everyone come to Waddington instead of Cranwell or Scampton to hear about the future of the Red Arrows?' From the look on his face, the Waddington Station Commander was wondering the same thing.

Just after 1300hrs a large number of copies of the midday edition of the Lincolnshire Echo were delivered to the Operations Room and we all grabbed one. The Echo had devoted three full pages, including the entire front page, to welcome the news about Scampton and claim that it vindicated the Echo's long fight to save the station. The opening paragraph stated:

'Defence Minister John Spellar today confirmed that the Red Arrows are to return home to RAF Scampton. The announcement, just after 1pm today, marked a victory for the Lincolnshire Echo-led Save Our Scampton campaign which has fought for more than six years to return the display team to the historic base.'

As we awaited the Minister's arrival, the media representatives present were joking with each other about who had breached the MoD embargo and to what extent. In the event, I cannot see that any harm was done other than a dented principle. When he did stand up, the Minister read out a lengthy prepared statement which led on his short visit to Waddington. He talked about the value of AWACS, the airborne early warning aircraft based at Waddington, he made passing references to the Kosovo conflict, he made a complicated statement about the Defence Housing Executive which nobody appeared to understand and, finally, he made the announcement that the Red Arrows were to move back to Scampton. It was only when the Minister reached the Red Arrows' part of his speech that the TV cameramen switched on their cameras and the scribblies poised their pens. The media can be very disrespectful when it suits them; you would have thought they would at least make the pretence of taking an interest in the other parts of the speech! The Red Arrows' part of Mr Spellar's statement bore little resemblance to the 'final, final' script that we had been given in advance but it was, nevertheless, music to my ears.

'The Red Arrows have thrilled thousands of people across Britain and the world with their incredible flying skills,' said the Minister. 'The manoeuvres they do require tremendous skill, hours of practice, and total reliance on each other as a team that works as one in the air. More to the point, the Red Arrows pilots are not just display pilots. Each one is a highly trained fighter pilot and would be called on to go into battle if we needed them. Many already have battlefield experience. I know the RAF, and in particular the Red Arrows, has a special place in the affection of the local people at Scampton and I am pleased to announce that the Red Arrows will be returning to RAF Scampton on a permanent basis.'

After the formal statement the Minister spent the best part of 45 minutes giving a whole series of one-to-one interviews with each of the media organisations represented. When challenged by the BBC Radio Lincolnshire reporter about the 'u-turn' on Red Arrows' basing, Mr Spellar said: 'I do not want to make a political point; the previous administration did what they thought best in the run down from the Cold War and the ensuing defence cuts. We have done a full review of defence needs. We have brought aircraft back from Germany and we need bases for them. My announcement today is very good news for the RAF and very good news for Lincolnshire.' During at least two of the one-to-ones Mr Spellar, in answer to the inevitable question 'When will the Red Arrows actually move?', apparently replied, '…before the end of this year' and that response was then widely quoted in the local and regional media. It is not for me to conjecture whether this was a considered response or a slip of the tongue but it was not what the RAF or the Red Arrows wanted to hear. A move just before Christmas 2000, in the middle of the winter work-up period, was the last thing everyone wanted – except me.

Whilst Mr Spellar was giving his one-to-one interviews at one end of the briefing room, I was cornered at the other end of the room giving one-to-one interviews with all the media in turn except the Telegraph man. As a result I did not personally hear the Minister say that the move would take place before the end of the year and, in any case, I stuck to the brief I had been given which made it very clear that we were not to make any reference to a time scale for the move. I, therefore, found myself in a bit of a quandary when asked to comment on the Minister's pronouncement about the date of the move.

As far as I could ascertain, none of the media reported anything other than the Red Arrows and Scampton elements of the Mr Spellar's visit to Waddington. The phrase 'my announcement is very good news for the

RAF and very good news for Lincolnshire' was repeated frequently. Many vox pops were used on local radio and television and in the local, regional and some national newspapers and every single comment that I heard and saw was favourable. There was a half-hearted inquest afterwards about which media organisations had dared to break the embargo but the most important bit of news that came out of the press conference was the definite statement that the Red Arrows would be back at Scampton before the end of the year 2000.

Amongst the vox pops reported in the Echo was one from a councillor of the West Lindsey District Council who lives near Scampton. He stated:

'I am delighted that the Red Arrows are coming back here and the base will be functioning as it should. The whole area felt the blow of closure and this will give it the lift we've long been waiting for. I know that everyone has missed the Red Arrows.'

There was a brief and forlorn hope that the RAF might get away with saying that what the Minister really meant to say was 'before the end of this financial year' but that idea was soon dropped. There was a lot of frantic work in the following months. Once the Minister had announced publicly that the Red Arrows would return to Scampton before the end of the year, everything was geared up to making sure that it happened, however inconvenient it might be. I was asked if I would be willing to stay on past my 65th birthday in September long enough to cover the return. I readily agreed to stay on until the end of the year and, naturally, I got the job of organising the media facility for the Red Arrows' fly-in.

In the short term, RAF Scampton was being re-activated primarily as a home for the Red Arrows and to that end the station would remain under the Command and Control of the Station Commander at Cranwell. The airfield would also be used as a relief landing ground for any training aircraft that needed a runway to practice on. For day-to-day matters, Wing Commander David Bolsover, Wing Commander RAFAT, would be the Detachment Commander at Scampton. The Central Flying School HQ was to remain at Cranwell and so the Commandant would have to travel to Scampton when he needed to supervise the Red Arrows.

The plan was for the Team to fly out of Cranwell for the last time at midday on 21 December 2000. Since that was in the middle of the winter training period the Team Leader could not fly nine aircraft in formation and that was a pity; it would have been nice to have a ceremonial arrival of all nine aircraft together. As it was, there would be a maximum of seven aircraft taking off from Cranwell; they would reach Scampton at 1210 and carry out a normal training sortie before landing at 1245. The rest of the Red Arrows' aircraft would have already been moved out of Cranwell into 4 Hangar at Scampton to undergo normal winter maintenance. We intended to invite the local and regional media to attend at Scampton from 12 noon and the Station Commander agreed that we should invite quite a few local dignitaries and residents to the event.

As the date for the homecoming approached, I suggested that it might be a nice idea to ask the Minister for the Armed Forces if he would like to be present at the PR event. All PROs were under remit to keep their ears and eyes open for suitable 'good news' events for the Minister to attend – events that would keep the RAF, and the Minister, in the public eye for all the right reasons. I was delighted and not at all surprised to hear that John Spellar readily agreed to turn out, even so close to the Christmas holiday. There was then a minor protocol matter that I had to resolve. Her Majesty's Lord Lieutenant for Lincolnshire, Mrs Bridget Cracroft-Eley, lives in Hackthorn village, just off the A15 end of the Scampton main runway. Mrs Cracroft-Eley, and her family, have long been great friends of RAF Scampton and the Red Arrows and she rarely misses an opportunity to attend functions at the base. However, when the Lord Lieutenant attends an event in an official capacity she is representing the Queen and has to take precedence over everyone else present, whatever their rank and status. That would have caused a slight embarrassment because the RAF wanted the Minister to be the senior guest. No problem! I telephoned Bridget and she readily agreed to attend in her other capacity, that of local parish councillor.

In early December I went to Scampton to record an interview with the well-known broadcaster Laurie Taylor for a BBC Radio 4 programme called 'Thinking Aloud' – which title, for the purposes of the radio audience, could have been interpreted as 'Thinking Allowed'. When I was first contacted by the researcher I assumed that he wanted someone to talk about the Red Arrows and I asked if Laurie would rather interview the Team Leader. However, it was me they wanted! The 30-minute programme was devoted entirely to stories about the City of Lincoln and my 10-minute contribution was about Scampton, its history, and that black dog. We had intended doing the interview standing alongside Niggers' Grave but it was dark, windy and pouring with rain so instead we made the recording standing in an empty shell of an office in Station Headquarters that had once been the Station Commander's office and would soon be the Detachment Commander's office. I did, however, insist on driving Laurie, his producer and his researcher along the waterfront, pausing to get wet, cold and wind-swept at Niggers' Grave, before we went to work. I considered the interview needed that for authenticity.

The weather in the week beginning 18 December was appalling, starting with thick freezing fog which gradually gave way to very low cloud, mist and rain. No flying was possible on the first three days of the week and late on the Wednesday afternoon the decision was made to cancel the media event planned for the Thursday and as a result several weeks' work was wasted. It began to look as though the Red Arrows' aircraft would have to remain at Cranwell until the New Year and that would have been particularly inconvenient. However, the weather lifted just sufficiently during the Thursday afternoon for the Hawks to fly into Scampton almost unnoticed. The whole Squadron then went off home for Christmas and my second planned retirement date passed.

My successor should have started work on 8 January but in the event that was the date that the interviews took place for the candidates who had applied for my job. Surprisingly, there were only three applicants and one of those pulled out literally at the very last minute. The successful candidate had to give three month's notice to her current employer and so I was asked to stay in post until mid-March. I agreed, but less readily this time. To be strictly accurate I was not asked in advance; I heard about my latest extension when a personnel officer at Cranwell casually mentioned that he had heard that I was now staying on until March!

A few days after my successor had been offered the job, the Red Arrows flew off to RAF Akrotiri for a 25-day 'Winter Hawk' training session while those technicians who stayed behind at Scampton got on with the work of setting up the engineering services in 4 Hangar. I started arranging another civic event to mark the Red Arrows' return and that took place on 9 February, a week after the Red Arrows returned from Cyprus. This time the weather was kind and the event was very successful. However, in spite of my suggestion that we should renew the invitation for the Minister for the Armed Forces to attend, the RAF did not invite him. I was frustrated for this one last time and can only speculate on the reason for not inviting him. A good news event is only good news after it has happened. If there is the slightest possibility of a potentially good news story going wrong, then it is better not to have it at all. That seemed to be the thinking anyway. Another wasted opportunity!

How long will the Red Arrows continue to fly? How long will Scampton remain open? Those are questions that my successor will have to deal with. There used to be a joke in the 1960s that whenever the RAF spent a lot of money renovating one of its stations, that station would soon close; at the time Acklington and Chivenor, flying training schools at opposite ends of England, were just two examples that seemed to prove the rule. But times have changed. The fact that Scampton has been reopened and had a lot of money spent on it neither suggests it will soon close again nor guarantee that it will survive. The magnificent Scampton Officers' Mess had over £1 million spent on it just to renovate the roof after a great storm in the early 1990s flooded most of the upper floor. More large sums of money were spent on the Mess and the Station soon afterwards to fit it for a royal visit. The Officers' Mess is now sadly derelict through years of neglect and there are, as far as I know, no plans to reopen it. The Airmen's Mess, the former operations building where the Dam Busters' raid and many others were briefed, was condemned in the early 1990s when it was found to be overrun by cockroaches. There was no money left to decontaminate it and so that historic building is also lying empty. The problem with Scampton is that it is in an unfashionable part of the country and no-one wants to buy the estate. Had a suitable buyer come forward during the five years the Red Arrows were based at Cranwell, and great efforts were made to find one, I have little doubt that the base would have been sold off.

I now read stories in some newspapers that the RAF may soon have to close at least one more main airfield so that real estate can be sold off. Names being bandied around are Brize Norton in Oxfordshire, its near neighbour Lyneham, and St Mawgan in Cornwall. I no longer have inside information so I cannot tell if the stories are true, are wrong, or are merely spin, but I recognise the signs.

And so my story almost comes to its end. Every time I visited Wakefield during my years of exile I used to pass a particular house on Denby Dale Road, barely a mile from the M1 motorway, and wonder about the girl called Ruth who used to live there and who was at St James' School with me in the 1940s. Just after leaving Scampton for the last time I was interviewed at home in Lincolnshire by Yorkshire TV. They wanted to know about the book I was writing and an animated television series called 'Reds Away', based on the Red Arrows, that I have created for pre-school children. A few days after the television interview was transmitted, I received a letter from Ruth, the first contact we had had for more than 45 years. She had heard part of my television interview whilst doing the ironing in a back room and wondered if I was the same Tony Cunnane she had known as a child. It was another of those strange coincidences that have kept cropping up in my life. Ruth and I have since exchanged letters and e-mails and we have met several times. She told me on our first meeting that shortly before I joined the RAF I wrote to her and used the word 'emanate' in my letter. Ruth remembered nothing more about the content of the letter other than that word, but she remembered that because she had to look it up to see what it meant. I had to admit to Ruth that I did not recall writing the letter so I have no idea why I needed to use that word. It cannot have been a very interesting letter because she never replied to it! When we met in Lincoln, Ruth told me something else I did not know: apparently I was the heart throb of all the girls in the class at St James'. Why did not someone tell me that at the time? Ruth was not, I hasten to make clear, the girl who had advanced my education in the air raid shelter during the dark days of the war but she and I had a lengthy discussion trying to work out who that particular girl was. Although we narrowed the possibilities down to three or four and I can still see the girl in my mind's eye and remember exactly where she lived, that is another name I have forgotten – and that is perhaps just as well. I expect the lady to contact me when she reads this; since she is several years older than I, she must certainly recall the incident.

I thought it would be a wrench having to retire but it has been nothing of the sort. I moved out of Lincolnshire in Spring 2001 and came back to Wakefield, which I have always considered my 'home town'. I now find that my time is so fully occupied that I cannot imagine how I ever found time to go to work. Joy of joys, I am now entitled to a Senior Citizen's Metro Bus and Train Pass which allows me to travel anywhere within West Yorkshire for the princely sum of 20p. Wakefield has changed of course but the people are as friendly as ever and all my old haunts are still here. The Pennines are now visible on most days, not just two or three days a month and they no longer form a topic of conversation. The Admiral Duncan pub is still there but the fish and chip shop, the Co-op and both the 'little' and 'big' schools have disappeared. Bridge 58 of 99 is still there and, thanks to my Metro Pass, I have passed over the bridge more times in the last few months than I ever did as a child. QEGS is still there, naturally, and my old form room windows can still be seen from the main road. I have not yet asked to go inside but I will one day, for old times' sake. The school uniform is now worn differently; today there seems to be no cap so the boys cannot raise them when they greet ladies, and shirt tails are mostly worn outside the trousers. That would have resulted in a visit to the Head Master in my day had anyone had the temerity to do it!

The samovar presented by the Russian Knights.

Former Red Arrows team leaders. Taken in 1998.
Left to right, front: Dickie Duckett (Leader 1975-6), Richard Thomas (Leader 1985-7), Dickie Patounas (Red 5), Adrian Thurley (Leader 1991-3), Bill Loverseed (Leader 1971). Left to right back row: Andy Evans (Red 2), Russ Jones (Red 10), Andy Offer (Red 8), Gary Waterfall (Red 9), Dave Stobie (Red 6), Andy Cubin (Red 7), Andy Lewis (Red 3), Simon Meade (Red 1)

Student pilots at South Cerney in 1966
Back: Plt Off Chris Smallwood; front row left to right: Plt Off Calvert, Author, Plt Offs Donaldson, Kelly, Williams, Naylor, Aldridge, Gallanders and Johnson.

A young grumpy schoolboy, 1941.

Wings' Presentation by Air Vice-Marshal W D Disbrey, 3FTS Leeming, 3 March 1967.

Budding musician, 1951.

Proud owner, RAF Finningley, 1961.

Presented to HRH The Duke of Edinburgh at RAF Valley, 1968.

With my parents at Blackpool, 1946. (My sister Kathleen out of shot to the left).

Anson Crew at RAF Swanton Morley 1956. Left to right: ?, Joe Harris, Andy Davidson, Taff Davies, Author.

Author operating Shackleton radar, 18 Sqn somewhere over the Mediterranean, 1959.

The first Red Arrows display team, 1965.

Blue Peter presenter Katy Hill being interviewed with some of the 1999 Team for the BBC children's show with (left and right): Gary Waterfall, Andy Lewis, and front left to right, Jim Provost, Ian Smith, Simon Meade.

The official naming of the Virgin Trains locomotive "The Red Arrows" on York Station in 1997. Holding the plaque at back right is Team Leader Simon Meade and Virgin Trains' Chief Executive Brian Barrett.

The Red Arrows make a spectacular Vixen Break towards the Royal Enclosure at the opening of the Dubai 97 Air Show. Red 6 can be seen streaking across from right to left.

Passing Out Parade at Cranwell in July 1998. Only families and friends can see the flypast because those on parade are giving a General Salute to the Reviewing Officer, the Chief of the Air Staff, Air Chief Marshal Sir Richard Johns (who was a Cranwell flying instructor during the author's first tour at Cranwell in 1968).

The Red Arrows (top) leading the Russian Knights over the head of HM Queen Elizabeth the Queen Mother at Birkhall in the Balmoral Estate in September 1991.

The Red Arrows make a spectacular "bomb burst" arrival over the South African flag at the Air Force Base at Waterkloof, Johannesburg, in October 1995.

Enid (Reds 1 to 5) make a colourful Twizzle over Table Bay Capetown in October 1995 – with the superstructure of a large freight ship intruding into the safety zone.

EJ van Koningsveld shot of a Diamond Nine.

EJ's shot of a right hand break for landing. (Red 1 furthest away, Red 2 just breaking, and part of the wing of Red 3.)

Press Conference in the Rotunda of the 5-star Al Bustaan Hotel, Dubai. Note the model Hawk hanging in the Rotunda. Author looking very relaxed on the left controlling the event. [Author]

The author's very first digital photograph: a spectacular, but entirely fortuitous shot, of Gypo (Reds 6 to 9) practising early one morning in 1997 overhead Cranwell. [Author]

'This is Your Life', 1996 – Michael Aspel surprises team leader John Rands.

Air Vice-Marshal Mike Lyne at Cranwell where he was once Commandant, seated for the very first time in a Red Arrows' Hawk. He led the world's first ever jet formation aerobatic team, albeit an unofficial one, in July 1947.
Sadly he died a few days after this photograph was taken.

The cast and production team of "Darling Buds of May" in a break from filming at Yorkshire TV's HQ in Leeds in 1991. This was David Jason's thank you to the Team for his flight with them. Author third from the right in the back row.

A pensive Jason Donovan waiting for his flight with the Red Arrows.

A triumphant David Jason immediately after his flight.

Soviet Hats at Kiev in 1990. Team Leader Tim Miller (left) and Air Vice-Marshal Mike Pilkington (right). Our Soviet interpreter in the background.

A British Aerospace film crew making a documentary about the Soviet Tour during a pre-flight briefing at Borispol, with Soviet interpreters and KGB officers in the background. Team Leader Tim Miller (red suit centre) looking rather pensive.

Hawk cockpit.

Author about to board the Soviet Mi-8 for his trip to Chaika.

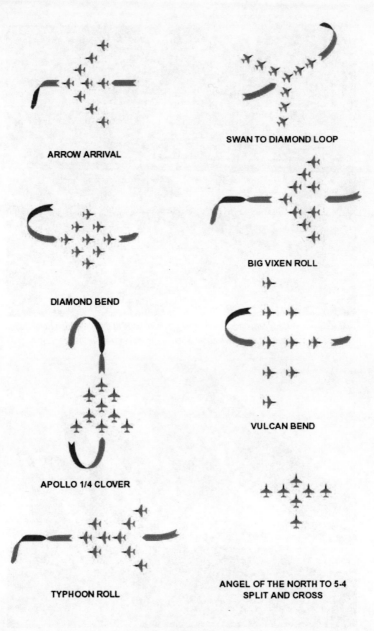

ARROW ARRIVAL

SWAN TO DIAMOND LOOP

DIAMOND BEND

BIG VIXEN ROLL

APOLLO 1/4 CLOVER

VULCAN BEND

TYPHOON ROLL

ANGEL OF THE NORTH TO 5-4
SPLIT AND CROSS

Red Arrows manoeuvres.

Half-scale model Hawk suspended in the roof of the Rotunda at the Al Bustaan Hotel Dubai in 1997. It was there again when the Team returned in 1999.

Tail markings. Note the letter Is which replace the figure 1s (see story, page 275.)

Also published by Woodfield...

The following titles are all available in high-quality softback format

RAF HUMOUR

Bawdy Ballads & Dirty Ditties of the RAF • A huge collection of the bawdy songs and rude recitations with which RAF personnel would entertain one-another in off-duty hours in WW2. Sure to amuse any RAF veteran. (uncensored – strictly adults only!) *"Not for the frail, the fraightfully posh or proper gels – but great fun for everyone else!"*   **£9.95**

Upside Down Nothing on the Clock • Dozens of jokes and anecdotes contributed by RAF personnel from AC2s to the top brass... one of our best sellers. *"Highly enjoyable."*   **£6.00**

Upside Down Again! • Our second great collection of RAF jokes, funny stories and anecdotes – a great gift for those with a high-flying sense of humour! *"Very funny indeed."*   **£6.00**

Was It Like This For You? • A feast of humorous reminiscences & cartoons depicting the more comical aspects of life in the RAF. *"Will bring back many happy memories. Highly recommended."*   **£6.00**

I Have Control • former RAF Parachute instructor **Edward Cartner** humorously recalls the many mishaps, blunders and faux-pas of his military career. *Superb writing; very amusing indeed.*   **£9.95**

Who is in Charge Here...? • Former RAF Parachute instructor **Edward Cartner** regales us with more inglorious moments from the latter part of his military career as a senior officer. *Superb writing; very amusing indeed.*   **£9.95**

MILITARY MEMOIRS & HISTORIES – THE POST-WAR PERIOD

A History of the King's Flight & The Queen's Flight • An illustrated history of the RAF's Royal illustrious squadron, responsible for the air transport of the Royal family from its inception in 1936 to its disbandment in 1995.   **£15.00**

Flying the Waves • **Richard Pike** describes his eventful second career as a commercial helicopter pilot, which involved coastguard Air/Sea Rescue operations in the Shetlands and North Sea.   **£9.95**

From Port T to RAF Gan • The history of the RAF's most deserted outpost is comprehensively and entertainingly charted by **Peter Doling**, a former RAF officer who served on Gan in the 1970s. Many photos, some in colour.   **£20.00**

Korea: We Lived They Died • Former soldier with Duke of Wellington's Regt **Alan Carter** reveals the appalling truth of front-line life for British troops in this now forgotten war. *Very funny in places too.*   **£9.95**

Meteor Eject! • Former 257 Sqn pilot [1950s] **Nick Carter** recalls the early days of RAF jets and his many adventures flying Meteors, including one very lucky escape via a Martin-Baker ejector seat...   **£9.95**

Pluck Under Fire • Eventful Korean War experiences of **John Pluck** with the Middlesex Regiment.   **£9.95**

Return to Gan • Michael Butler's light-hearted account of life at RAF Gan in 1960 and the founding of 'Radio Gan'. *Will delight those who also served at this remote RAF outpost in the Indian Ocean.*   **£12.00**

The Spice of Flight • Former RAF pilot **Richard Pike** delivers a fascinating account of flying Lightnings, Phantoms and later helicopters with 56, 43(F) & 19 Sqns in the RAF of the 1960s & 70s.   **£9.95**

Tread Lightly into Danger • Bomb-disposal expert **Anthony Charlwood**'s experiences in some of the world's most dangerous hotspots (Kuwait, Iraq, Lebanon, Somalia, etc) over the last 30 years.   **£9.95**

MILITARY MEMOIRS & HISTORIES – WORLD WAR 1 & 2

A Bird Over Berlin Former Lancaster pilot with 61 Sqn **Tony Bird DFC** tells a remarkable tale of survival against the odds during raids on the German capital & as a POW. *"An incredible-but-true sequence of events."*   **£9.95**

Algiers to Anzio with 72 & 111 Squadrons Former engineer officer **Greggs Farish**'s diary and photos are a superb historical record of RAF squadron life during Operation 'Husky' – the invasion of Sicily/Italy in 1943.   **£9.95**

An Erk's-Eye View of World War 2 • former 'instrument basher' **Ted Mawdsley** salutes the work of the RAF ground crews of WW2, who played a vital role in keeping the RAF's aircraft flying in often adverse conditions.   **£9.95**

An Illustrated History of RAF Waddington Former crewmember of the famous Battle of Britain flight Ray Leach has researched the wartime history of this important RAF base. Many photos. *"A superb achievement."*   **£20.00**

A Lighter Shade of Blue • A former Radar Operator **Reg O'Neil** recalls his WW2 service in Malta and Italy with 16004 AMES – a front-line mobile radar unit. *'Interesting, informative and amusing.'* **£9.95**

A Shilling's Worth of Promises • Delightfully funny memoirs of **Fred Hitchcock,** recalling his years as an RAF airman during the war and later amusing escapades in the UK and Egypt. *A very entertaining read.* **£9.95**

Beaufighters BOAC & Me • WW2 Beaufighter navigator **Sam Wright** served a full tour with 254 Sqn and was later seconded to BOAC on early postwar overseas routes. *'Captures the spirit of the mighty Beaufighter'* **£9.95**

Carried on the Wind • **Sean Feast** tells the fascinating story of Ted Manners, a 'special duties operator' with 101 Squadron, whose job was to 'spoof' enemy radar and intercept their surface-to-air radio messages in WW2. **£9.95**

Coastal Command Pilot • Former Hudson pilot **Ted Rayner**'s outstanding account of his unusual WW2 Coastal Command experiences, flying in the Arctic from bases in Iceland and Greenland. **£9.95**

Cyril Wild: The Tall Man Who Never Slept • **James Bradley**'s biography of a remarkable Japanese-speaking British Army officer who helped many POWs survive at Sonkurai Camp on the infamous Burma railway. **£9.95**

Desert War Diary • **John Walton's** diary and photos record the activities of the Hurricanes and personnel of 213 Squadron during WW2 in Cyprus and Egypt. *"Informative and entertaining."* **£9.95**

Espionage Behind the Wire • former POW **Howard Greville** tells the fascinating story of how he worked as a spy for British intelligence (MI6) from inside a German POW camp. **£9.95**

From Fiji to Balkan Skies • Spitfire/Mustang pilot **Dennis McCaig** recalls eventful WW2 operations over the Adriatic/Balkans with 249 Sqn in 43/44. *'A rip-roaring real-life adventure, splendidly written.'* **£9.95**

Get Some In! • The many wartime adventures of **Mervyn Base**, a WW2 RAF Bomb Disposal expert **£9.95**

Hunt Like a Tiger • **Tom Docherty** an illustrated history of 230 squadron – equipped during the war with Sunderland flying boats which were put to many uses in many theatres of war. A fascinating piece of RAF history. **£9.95**

Just a Survivor • Former Lancaster navigator **Phil Potts** tells his remarkable tale of survival against the odds in the air with 103 Sqn and later as a POW. *'An enlightening and well written account.'* **£9.95**

Memoirs of a 'Goldfish' • The eventful wartime memoirs of former 115 Sqn Wellington pilot **Jim Burtt-Smith**, now president of the Goldfish Club - exclusively for aviators who have force-landed into water. **£9.95**

Nobody Unprepared • The history of No 78 Sqn RAF is told in full for the first time by **Vernon Holland** in this absorbing account of the Whitley/Halifax squadron's World War 2 exploits. Full statistics and roll of honour. **£14.95**

No Brylcreem, No Medals • RAF MT driver **Jack Hambleton** 's splendid account of his wartime escapades in England, Shetlands & Middle East blends comic/tragic aspects of war in uniquely entertaining way. **£9.95**

Nobody's Hero • Former RAF Policeman **Bernard Hart-Hallam**'s extraordinary adventures with 2TAF Security Section on D-Day and beyond in France, Belgium & Germany. *"Unique and frequently surprising."* **£9.95**

Operation Pharos • **Ken Rosam** tells the story of the RAF's secret bomber base/staging post on the Cocos Keeling islands during WW2 and of many operations from there. *'A fascinating slice of RAF history.'* **£9.95**

Over Hell & High Water • WW2 navigator **Les Parsons** survived 31 ops on Lancasters with 622 Sqn, then went on to fly Liberators in Far East with 99 Sqn. *'An exceptional tale of 'double jeopardy'.* **£9.95**

Pacifist to Glider Pilot • The son of Plymouth Brethren parents, **Alec Waldron** renounced their pacifism and went on to pilot gliders with the Glider Pilot Regiment at both Sicily & Arnhem. *Excellent photos.* **£9.95**

Pathfinder Force Balkans • Pathfinder F/Engineer **Geoff Curtis** saw action over Germany & Italy before baling out over Hungary. He was a POW in Komarno, Stalags 17a & 17b. *'An amazing catalogue of adventures.'* **£9.95**

Per Ardua Pro Patria • Humour and tragedy are interwoven in these unassuming autobiographical observations of **Dennis Wiltshire**, a former Lancaster Flight Engineer who later worked for NASA. **£9.95**

Ploughs, Planes & Palliasses • Entertaining recollections of RAF pilot **Percy Carruthers**, who flew Baltimores in Egypt with 223 Squadron and was later a POW at Stalag Luft 1 & 6. **£9.95**

RAF/UXB The Story of RAF Bomb Disposal • Stories contributed by wartime RAF BD veterans that will surprise and educate the uninitiated. *"Amazing stories of very brave men."* **£9.95**

Railway to Runway • Wartime diary & letters of Halifax Observer **Leslie Harris** – killed in action with 76 Sqn in 1943 – poignantly capture the spirit of the wartime RAF in the words of a 20-year-old airman. **£9.95**

Seletar Crowning Glory • The history of the RAF base in Singapore from its earliest beginnings, through the golden era of the flying-boats, its capture in WW2 and on to its closure in the 1970s. **£15.00**

The RAF & Me • Former Stirling navigator **Gordon Frost** recalls ops with 570 Sqn from RAF Harwell, including 'Market-Garden' 'Varsity' and others. *'A salute to the mighty Stirling and its valiant crews.'*   **£9.95**

Training for Triumph • **Tom Docherty**'s very thorough account of the amazing achievement of RAF Training Command, who trained over 90,000 aircrew during World War 2. *'An impressively detailed book.'*   **£12.00**

To Strive and Not to Yield • An inspiring account of the involvement of No 626 Squadron RAF Bomber Command in the 'Battle of Berlin' (1943/44) and a salute to the men and women who served on the squadron.   **£14.95**

Un Grand Bordel • Geoffrey French relates air-gunner **Norman Lee**'s amazing real-life adventures with the French Maquis (Secret Army) after being shot down over Europe. *"Frequently funny and highly eventful."*   **£9.95**

UXB Vol 2 • More unusual and gripping tales of bomb disposal in WW2 and after.   **£9.95**

Wot! No Engines? • Alan Cooper tells the story of military gliders in general and the RAF glider pilots who served on Operation Varsity in 1945 in particular. A very large and impressive book with many photos.   **£18.00**

While Others Slept • Former Hampden navigator **Eric Woods** tells the story of Bomber Command's early years and how he completed a tour of duty with 144 Squadron. *'Full of valuable historical detail.'*   **£9.95**

WOMEN & WORLD WAR TWO

A WAAF at War • Former MT driver **Diana Lindo**'s charming evocation of life in the WAAF will bring back happy memories to all those who also served in World War 2. *"Nostalgic and good-natured."*   **£9.95**

Corduroy Days • Warm-hearted and amusing recollections of **Josephine Duggan-Rees**'s wartime years spent as a Land Girl on farms in the New Forest area. *"Funny, nostalgic and very well written."*   **£9.95**

Ernie • **Celia Savage**'s quest to discover the truth about the death of her father, an RAF Halifax navigator with 149 Sqn, who died in WW2 when she was just 6 years old. *"A real-life detective story."*   **£9.95**

In My Father's Footsteps • **Pat Bienkowski**'s moving account of her trip to Singapore & Thailand to visit the places where her father and uncle were both POW's during WW2.   **£9.95**

Lambs in Blue • **Rebecca Barnett's** revealing account of the wartime lives and loves of a group of WAAFs posted to the tropical paradise of Ceylon. *"A highly congenial WW2 chronicle."*   **£9.95**

Radar Days • Delightful evocation of life in the wartime WAAF by former Radar Operator **Gwen Arnold**, who served at Bawdsey Manor RDF Station, Suffolk. *"Amusing, charming and affectionate."*   **£9.95**

Searching in the Dark • The amusing wartime diary of **Peggy Butler** a WAAF radar operator 1942-1946 – written when she was just 19 yrs old and serving at Bawdsey RDF station in Suffolk   **£9.95**

Tales of a Bomber Command Waaf (and her horse) • very entertaining book composed mainly of wartime letters received and sent by **Sylvia Pickering**, who served as a Waaf at RAF Cottesmore and RAF Coningsby.   **£9.95**

More Tales of a Bomber Command Waaf (and her horse) • The second part of **Sylvia Pickering**'s war was spent at RAF Coningsby and HQ 5 Group (Bomber Command) at Morton Hall. Many more entertaining reminiscences.   **£9.95**

Why Did We Join? • In this entertaining book **Eileen Smith** recalls the camaraderie, excitement and heartbreak of working as a Waaf on an operational Bomber Command Station – RAF East Kirkby in Lincolnshire.   **£9.95**

MEMOIRS & HISTORIES – NON-MILITARY

A Beat Around the Bush • **Alastair Tompkins** recounts a variety of his extraordinary experiences– many of them very amusing indeed – as a Bush Policeman in British Colonial Kenya, 1952-62. Very entertaining.   **£9.95**

20th CenturyFarmers Boy • Sussex farmer **Nick Adames** looks back on a century of rural change and what it has meant to his own family and the county they have farmed in for 400 years.   **£9.95**

Call an Ambulance! • former ambulance driver **Alan Crosskill** recalls a number of light-hearted episodes from his eventful career in the 1960s/70s. *'Very amusing and entertaining'.*   **£9.95**

Harry – An Evacuee's Story • The misadventures of **Harry Collins** – a young lad evacuated from his home in Stockport UK to Manitoba, Canada in WW2. *'An educational description of the life of an evacuee'*   **£9.95**

Just Visiting • Charming and funny book by former Health Visitor **Molly Corbally**, who brilliantly depicts colourful characters and entertaining incidents from her long career.   **£9.95**

Occupation Nurse • **Peter & Mary Birchenall** pay tribute to the achievement of the group of untrained nurses who provided healthcare at Guernsey's only hospital during the German occupation of 1940-45.   **£9.95**

The JFK Assassination: Dispelling the Myths • Prepare to revise everything you thought you knew about the most famous assassination of the 20ᵗʰ Century. British historian **Mel Ayton** examines the many 'myths' that have grown up in the 40 years since JFK was murdered and debunks them all. You may be surprised at his conclusions.   **£9.95**

FICTION

A Trace of Calcium by **David Barnett** • A commuter comes to the aid of a young woman in trouble, becomes implicated in murder and must use all his resources to clear his name. (contains sex & violence)   **£9.95**

Double Time by **David Barnett** • A light-hearted time-travel fantasy in which a bookmaker tries to use a time machine to make his fortune and improve his love-life with hilarious consequences. (contains sex & violence)   **£9.95**

Dust & Fury by **David Barnett** • An epic family saga set in the Sultanate of Oman, featuring the lives and loves of an Omani family during the bitter war that led to the foundation of modern Oman. (contains sex & violence)   **£15.00**

The Brats • this very entertaining novel by **Tony Paul** is based on the true story of his grandfather, who as a boy along with several friends, stowed away on a ship bound for Canada. The youngsters' brutal mistreatment at the hands of the Captain and Mate of the ship caused a scandal that made headlines in Victorian times.   **£9.95**

The Cherkassy Incident by **Hunter Carlyle** Terrorists plot to steal nuclear missiles from a sunken Russian nuclear submarine; can an international team of security agents stop them? (contains sex & violence)   **£9.95**

BOOKS FEATURING THE SOUTH COAST & THE SOUTH DOWNS REGION

A Portrait of Slindon • **Josephine Duggan Rees** has written a charming history of this attractive and well-preserved West Sussex village, from its earliest beginnings to the present day, taking in the exploits of its many notable residents over the years. Very informative and entertaining. Illustrated with many photos, some in colour.   **£14.95**

Retribution • **Mike Jupp** has created an outrageous and very funny comedy/fantasy novel for adults and older children, featuring bizarre goings-on in a fictional quiet English seaside town that bears a striking resemblance to Mike's home town of Bognor Regis. Brilliantly illustrated. *One of the funniest books you will ever read.*   **£9.95**

Unknown to History and Fame • **Brenda Dixon**'s charming portrait of Victorian life in the West Sussex village of Walberton via the writings of Charles Ayling, a resident of the village, whose reports on local events were a popular feature in *The West Sussex Gazette* over many years during the Victorian era.   **£9.95**

A Little School on the Downs • **Mary Bowmaker** tells the amazing story of Harriet Finlay-Johnson, headmistress of a little village school in Sompting, West Sussex in the 1890s, whose ideas and classroom techniques began a revolution in education. She also scandalised society at the time by marrying a former pupil, 20 years her junior.   **£9.95**

The South Coast Beat Scene of the 1960s The South Coast may not have been as famous as Liverpool in the swinging sixties but it was nevertheless a hotbed of musical activity. Broadcaster **Mike Read** traces the complete history of the musicians, the fans and the venues from Brighton to Bognor in this large and lavishly-illustrated book.   **£24.95**

Boys & Other Animals • **Josephine Duggan Rees's** warm-hearted and delightfully funny account of a mother's many trials and tribulations bringing up a boisterous all-male family on a farm in rural Sussex during the 1950s-70s.   **£9.95**
